Free Land, Free Country

OTHER McFARLAND TITLES
BY JOHN HRASTAR

*Breaking the Appalachian Barrier: Maryland as the
Gateway to Ohio and the West, 1750–1850* (2018)

Liquid Natural Gas in the United States: A History (2014)

Free Land, Free Country
Setting Down Roots of Revolution in America, 1600–1790

JOHN HRASTAR

McFarland & Company, Inc., Publishers
Jefferson, North Carolina

This book has undergone peer review.

ISBN (print) 978-1-4766-8885-5
ISBN (ebook) 978-1-4766-4893-4

LIBRARY OF CONGRESS AND BRITISH LIBRARY
CATALOGUING DATA ARE AVAILABLE

Library of Congress Control Number 2022052517

© 2023 John Hrastar. All rights reserved

No part of this book may be reproduced or transmitted in any form or by any means, electronic or mechanical, including photocopying or recording, or by any information storage and retrieval system, without permission in writing from the publisher.

On the cover: *Top*, signing the Declaration of Independence, John Trumbull, artist, print (Library of Congress). *Bottom*, map of North America as the seat of war, 1776 (Library of Congress)

Printed in the United States of America

McFarland & Company, Inc., Publishers
Box 611, Jefferson, North Carolina 28640
www.mcfarlandpub.com

To Tim,
for his invaluable encouragement
and support

Acknowledgments

The process of researching and writing a book on history requires the help and patience of many others who contribute in various ways. First, of course, I thank my wife Fran for her support. She not only encouraged the project, but put up with time this took away from other projects. I also thank others who contributed directly and indirectly including McFarland editor Susan Kilby and my colleagues at the University of Maryland libraries who assisted in finding and providing the research material used to write the book.

However, special thanks go to three people without whose help this book would not have been possible. My brother Tim, a writer and lecturer of American history and culture, was one of the two major reviewers. My nephew Nathan Revor was the other. Their reviews and suggestions helped turn my input into a readable history book. I also thank David Deis, a cartographer who did the maps for my previous book, one of which is used here also.

Going from the historical research to a readable book took the help of all these family, friends and colleagues.

Contents

Acknowledgments vi

Preface 1

Introduction 3

Prologue: From the Conquest to the Colonies 13

CHAPTER ONE
Discovery and Claims 23

CHAPTER TWO
Land in English Colonial America: The Settlement 55

CHAPTER THREE
Populating the Land I: Colonial Expansion 86

CHAPTER FOUR
Populating the Land II: Immigration and Expansion 121

CHAPTER FIVE
War for Empire: Still More Land 155

CHAPTER SIX
End of Expansion: Rebellion and Break 185

Epilogue: Free Land in the Move West 229

Chapter Notes 243

Bibliography 265

Index 279

Preface

I have had the privilege of writing two previous books for McFarland. Both of these have been stories about a process or breaking through a barrier. This book is different; it is about an idea regarding one of the causes of the American Revolution.

The American Revolution has been very well documented by many distinguished historians. The stories are also very familiar to the general public: the Sugar Act, the Stamp Act, the Boston Tea Party, and others. It appears that there is nothing left to add, and that is basically true. However, sometimes a different perspective can give added insight to the existing stories. This book presents a different perspective on one of the causes of the Revolution.

The narrative for the Revolution usually centers on the struggles between the colonies and Parliament, usually about the various revenue acts after the end of the French and Indian War, and the issues about who had the right to govern the colonies—Parliament or the colonies. All these issues are certainly relevant and convey the story very well. They help explain why the colonists, who never felt prouder of being British than just after the French and Indian War, within 13 years declared their independence.

There is another aspect, another perspective, that went back more than 170 years that had a major impact on colonial thinking about independence; that aspect was free land. In the early years of the English colonization of North America it was determined that the best way to encourage colonization was to use an abundant resource that was available—land. Land was given away to those willing to come to America to increase the labor supply needed for successful colonies. This giving away, or selling land cheaply, continued for the entire colonial period. Considering the colonists were coming from England, where almost all the land was spoken for by the nobility, free land was considered a privilege—as it was. Over the decades, however, it came to be seen as a right rather than a privilege; one expected to be able to move west at will and occupy new land. So it is not surprising that when that right was taken away by the Quebec Act of 1774, what quickly followed was the First Continental Congress; the path to independence was opened. It is the thesis of this book that free land during the colonial period eventually led to independence, that is, a free country.

It is important to note that the perspective of the book is from the Europeans who received the free land and who settled here. It is not a book about Native Americans even as we acknowledge they were killed and displaced as these European colonists moved west, as they thought they had a right to do. Clearly the perspective of the Native Americans was different, and a book about these Native Americans would be an entirely different book. Most of the facts here have been covered in other histories. The idea here is to focus on the land issue to emphasize the importance that land, especially western land, had as one of the grievances that led to the Declaration of Independence. It was just as important as the other well-known issues, and was the final one, the straw that broke the camel's back.

Attempting any historical research is always a challenge because cultural norms, usage, spelling, and other ideas change with time, and one cannot be sure the terms mean the same in the present as they did in the past. I have chosen some simple, but I hope acceptable, ground rules. I have chosen to use spelling as it is in the original source. I am confident the reader will have no trouble with the spellings in context. Similarly, I have maintained the original spelling in all quotes so as to avoid the constant use of the Latin term *sic*. There are a few exceptions in which brackets are used to make the quote intelligible. Once again, the reader will have no difficulty in interpretation. For practical purposes I use the terminology of the time, present or past. For example, I use the accepted term "indigenous American" whenever possible, and use "colonist" or "settler" rather than "white man." However, it is not always possible to use modern terms because sometimes they would make no sense in the context of the past. For example, the settlers of the time used the appellation "Indian," if not the coarser term "savage," right from the beginning. The indigenous Americans themselves accepted the term and used it when describing themselves as Indians. The title "French and Indian War" is well accepted in historical works but would have no meaning as the "French and Indigenous American War." I trust the reader will understand the reasons for these ground rules.

Introduction

Free land in North America did eventually lead to an independent United States. Free land in North America, ignoring the indigenous American, was a gift of nature, but not one that was claimed easily. In fact, originally the land was not free; all of it was claimed by the Crown of England. So the steps from the original request for land grants, through the difficult settling process, and the movement of the frontier westward, were never easy, never inevitable, and certainly not the simple occupation of free land. These steps were the result of human endeavor, decisions, mistakes, and perseverance. Some of these decisions—mistakes, really—led to disastrous consequences for some peoples, including indigenous Americans and enslaved Africans. The desire to acquire and settle on land that appeared to be free was a strong motivation to come over in the first place and then to continue to move west. The colonists learned to take care of themselves, learned how to govern themselves, and finally outgrew their dependence on the mother country.

In 1893, University of Wisconsin professor Frederick Jackson Turner declared the end of the American frontier.[1] Conquering the frontier had led to individualism, democracy, and independence. In one sense Turner was correct, in that the free land of the frontier, starting with the Atlantic coast, which was a frontier for the Europeans, was a root cause of the eventual independence of these United States. His thesis, however, was incomplete in that he saw the resource, the land itself, as the source of individualism, democracy, and ultimate independence. It was the human agency, however, that worked all this through. It was the original and future settlers who sought the land, carved a settlement from it, fought the prior inhabitants for it, and eventually used it for good, with yeomen farming, or ill, with slave plantations. Through all this they learned they could govern themselves and then demanded to govern themselves.

But before that...

The English had lived in a closed society for 500 years before they started the colonization of North America. There was no free land, no land that anyone could buy. The king had claimed ownership of all the land since the Norman invasion, and he used it to buy the loyalty of his supporters. He awarded fiefs to his barons, who in turn owed him fealty for the use of the land; this was feudalism. The lords in turn erected manors on the land and allotted land on the manor to serfs who worked the land for the lord; this was manorialism. The serfs owned nothing, not even personal possessions; they owed everything to the lord of the manor. There was no such thing as land changing hands, no such thing as a market in lands. All the land was held by the nobility.

Things started to change in the sixteenth century with trading companies. These companies, chartered by the various crowns of Europe, found it profitable to exploit the resources of other lands, first by trade, and then, if necessary, by conquering the indigenous people to form colonies. In this mercantilist economy, trade was seen as a zero-sum endeavor; it was to be conducted exclusively with one's own colonies, because maintaining a positive balance of trade with another sovereign country was seen as difficult and impractical. Virginia was the first English colony, founded by the Virginia Company of London in 1607, a trading company. The first objective of the colony was to find someone nearby to trade with and then look for gold as the Spanish had done. Following Virginia, other English colonies were established in North America. All of them were established as commercial ventures by private companies to increase the wealth of the company, even those we see primarily as religious endeavors; none were established by the crown. English North America was claimed by discovery in the late fifteenth century by John Cabot under an exploration charter from Henry VII. It was assumed, therefore, that the crown controlled this land and could allow this free land to be used by companies to which it granted charters.

The Spanish had started their colonization of the west in the early sixteenth century, about a century prior to the English. They found a relatively large population of indigenous people in the lands they conquered in the west, ones they were able to subjugate with relative ease. The Spanish empire in Central and South America was directed by the Spanish Crown, unlike the English colonies, which were separate commercial enterprises. The *conquistadores*, crown representatives, were assigned large groups of the indigenous peoples to perform services for the crown, supposedly as vassals, but more like serfs. The agricultural and mineral wealth of the land was thus exploited through this hierarchical social structure. This system, in which few people controlled a great deal of land and had the services of the indigenous serfs, started as a government operation. However, over the centuries it evolved into a private, *hacienda* (estate) system in which the *hacendado* was the complete master of this large estate, much as a feudal lord in the manorial system. For centuries, land in New Spain was always controlled by large landowners. There was never any land that was free, that could be granted or sold to a small landowner. This history was different from the one experienced in English North America, which had no *conquistadores* or *hacendados*. This centralized control of land likely contributed to the fact that independence from Spain wasn't achieved by most of Spanish America until the 1820s, even though Spanish American colonies preceded English American colonies by a century.

The Virginia colony had a difficult first 15 years. Colonists came over singly or in small groups to work for the company. The death rate was high because of unpreparedness, disease, and conflicts with the Indians. It was during this time that the company switched from being a company looking for trade and gold and became an agricultural colony, mainly because of the discovery of tobacco as a cash crop. There was another factor, one they had in common with the Separatists of the Plymouth colony established in 1620, that increased the stress on the populations. In both cases the colonists were sponsored by, and worked for, the interests of the company that had financed the plantations. Everything was done communally, and done for the company first; there was no private land, and productivity suffered. In both cases this was recognized fairly early, and in both colonies, small plots of land were *given* to the colonists for their own use, their own private land. Productivity increased in both places, and lessons were learned about the importance of private land ownership.

Two important things happened that changed the course of events in these early years. In the second Virginia charter (1609), the king gave the Virginia Company the right to control land distribution rather than have it controlled by the crown, as it had been at first. The second was the establishment of the Virginia House of Burgesses, the first elected body in North America. Also, at this time the company finally realized that they had an abundance of land, and that it could be used as an inducement to encourage immigration to address the colony labor shortage. Fifty acres of free land was given out as a "headright" to anyone who could get themselves to Virginia. This offer was particularly attractive to indentured servants, men and women who had little prospects in England who agreed to a few years of indentured servitude in America, after which they could try to make it on their own on land available through the headright. Similarly, the General Court, the legislative body of the Massachusetts Bay colony, distributed land not to individuals but to townships, who in turn distributed it free to families. In the ensuing years the Puritans of Massachusetts Bay steadily expanded westward into the colony, and the Virginia settlers moved inland up the rivers using this free land.

Land became a central focus of both the colonial governments and the colonists. Whether it was the Virginia governor granting land through headrights or to royalist exiles during the English civil war, or the General Court in Massachusetts Bay granting more land for townships, it involved everyone. It took time and effort to apply for, grant, survey, patent, and settle the land. It was through the churning of the land that the colonies learned to govern themselves effectively. The government also learned to effectively distribute the land. It became second nature to assume one could go over the next hill, or farther up the river, to get better land. It entered the American psyche that land, settlement, and self-rule were inextricably tied together. The human agency, the collective effort, of working the land gave colonists in the new land confidence they could take care of themselves.

The population grew somewhat rapidly during the seventeenth century, mostly by emigration from England; by 1700 the colonial population was about 251,000. However, the end of the century saw a rapid increase in population, and it virtually exploded in the eighteenth century. It had grown by 81,000 by 1710 and was over 2.7 million by 1780. These immigrants now came from outside England itself: from the England-Scotland borderlands, the Ulster Plantation in northern Ireland, and from Germany. Land was now the explicit draw. These immigrants were fleeing rack-rents, violence on the border, plots too small to be productive, and poverty. The American provinces were eager to welcome them and give or sell them land. William Penn, for example, went to England, Holland, and Germany to entice Quakers and German Pietists to come to Pennsylvania for religious toleration and land. There were so many Germans in Pennsylvania that for a while Ben Franklin was worried that they would "Germanize" the Pennsylvanians. He later changed his mind and lauded the efficient German farms.[2]

Virginia was always the most populous colony, and the one most interested in expanding westward. Not many of these new immigrants came into Virginia directly, but many, like the Scots-Irish and Germans, came through Pennsylvania, moved west, and made a left turn at the mountains to head south toward Virginia on the Great Valley Road; many continued down to Carolina. These two ethnic groups were the first to populate the Shenandoah Valley, which Virginia encouraged to protect its western borders from the French and Indians.

There were winners and losers in this land rush, as one would expect. Clearly the biggest losers were the indigenous people, the original inhabitants, the Indians. They recognized the hegemony of one tribe over a land area for its own use, but did not recognize the existence of land ownership; the land was free to those who could use it. Thus, they were dealing with the colonists, who did claim land ownership, on uneven terms.

The colonists justified their land acquisition by the theories of John Locke who claimed the land belonged to anyone who could use it and work it. In their minds they did not see the Indians as using the land, so it was available to them. The Indians were gradually pushed back by both New Englanders and Virginians, sometimes peacefully with treaties, and sometimes by force.

Another group that had a special impact on this westward land movement were the squatters. The squatters were always ahead of the others on the frontier, just over the frontier. These were people who would risk fighting the Indians for the purpose of claiming what they saw as free land. Sometimes they would purposely enter the territory just to expel Indians. Most often these were Scots-Irish immigrants from Ulster or the England-Scotland borderlands, for whom fighting for land was a way of life. Squatters would often improve the land and would risk eviction if the land was legitimately granted or sold to someone else. However, over time their contributions to moving the frontier were recognized, and they would be given the right of preemption, the right to buy the land they had squatted on before it was sold to someone else. Squatters, therefore, could be both winners and losers.

The westward expansion continued through the mid-eighteenth century, when it reached a natural barrier, the Appalachian Mountains. The barrier was not impenetrable, and many traders and squatters made it beyond the mountains, but at first the settlers did not. The barrier was not only a physical barrier but a de facto, unofficial border between New France and the British colonies.

The French also had colonial aspirations for North America. They had started their explorations in Canada in parallel with the English in the early seventeenth century. However, their interest was primarily in the fur trade rather than settlement. Through various explorations they eventually claimed the Mississippi and Ohio river valleys. This included the rich Ohio Country, everything west of the mountains and below the Great Lakes including the Ohio Valley.

The colonization of New France was very different from the English colonization of North America. The project was run by the French Crown, not by individual companies with an entrepreneurial ethos, willing to take risks. The land was partitioned in *seigneuries*, which would include laborers, each run by a *seigneur* assigned the land. This was a vestige of an old feudal system and not very inviting to settlers. There was no incentive to leave France and come over for land, and nothing to push settlers to New France from France. Non-Catholics were not allowed to immigrate to New France. This kept out what would have been a vibrant French population of Huguenots. All these factors contributed to keeping the population low compared to that of English America. The low population would become a liability by the mid-eighteenth century. The claim for New France to the land was tenuous because they did little to occupy the land, which was generally seen as a requisite for ownership. The population of New France was centered mainly in Canadian cities such as Montreal and Quebec, and at the mouth of the Mississippi River; most of the territory was sparsely inhabited. Nevertheless, their land claim west of the mountains was meant to keep the English colonies boxed up on the coast.

Some provinces, such as Pennsylvania and Maryland, had fixed western borders. They looked to trade with the Indians in the Ohio Country, but had no designs on acquiring land beyond the mountains. Virginia, however, the most aggressive westward-moving colony, did have designs on the Ohio Country, which it justified based on its 1609 sea-to-sea charter. In 1748 investors from Virginia formed the Ohio Company of Virginia. They requested, and received, a grant from the crown for land in Ohio Country, specifically on the Ohio River near present-day Pittsburgh. The stated intention was for trade and settlement. This was a rather aggressive move to obtain land that was known to be claimed by New France. The insatiable desire for new land was stronger than ever, and they felt entitled to the land. Many others, however, realized that this reach for land beyond the mountains could lead to a conflict with France.

By 1750, tensions over land in America came to a boil between Great Britain and France. The English colonists were land obsessed, and were always looking west for more free land. The French were using their vast land claims west of the mountains, as mentioned above, primarily as a barrier to keep the English bottled up on the coast. They had heard about the Virginia Company claim on the Ohio Country and were determined to resist. There were some preliminary skirmishes, but the spark for war was lit when the governor of Virginia sent Major George Washington of the Virginia Regiment as an envoy to warn the French out of the Ohio Country, because it belonged to the Crown of England. A short time later, a fatal encounter between a small French force and Washington's small force is widely seen as the spark that led to the French and Indian War. It is not unfair to say that an aggressive overreach for land was a major contributor to initiating the war.

This war, between the French and their Indian allies and Great Britain and her colonial provincial allies, took place between 1754 and 1760. The wider world war between France and Great Britain, known as the Seven Years' War, took place between 1756 and 1763. Unlike many wars of the preceding two centuries, this was not a religious war, nor one fought to ensure the possession of a particular crown in Europe. It was a war for territory—for land. It was a war for empire to determine who would control

North America from the East Coast to the Mississippi, from Canada to Florida. The huge population advantage the British colonies held over New France was a major contributor to Great Britain winning this war and taking control of Eastern North America. The Treaty of Paris was signed in 1763.

Over the next eventful dozen years the population kept expanding, mostly from the Scots-Irish emigration from the England-Scotland borderlands and from the Ulster Plantation. From 1760 to 1780 the population increased by 1.2 million or 75 percent. The need for more land increased and the rush for more free land was greater than ever. Adding to the pressure now were the large land companies, speculators, seeking to claim large land grants in the west. Overcrowding the East Coast was not in the colonial plan; moving the frontier west was, because free land in the west was now embedded in the American psyche.[3]

The rational assumption was that now, with all this new land wrested from France, the status quo ante would apply. That meant the provinces could move west, with the provincial governments allotting the land through grants or sales. That was not to be the case; the war had changed the crown's view of the now-expanded American empire. First there was concern about the lawlessness on the border, the inability of the provinces to stem the flow of settlers beyond the provincial boundaries. Then there was a new concern about the relations with the Indians. There seemed to finally be a moral awakening, of the need to have a more humane and realistic view of Indian rights to their own land. The cost of the war had also become a major concern; the national debt had increased dramatically during the war. Finally, the crown thought it was time to deal with the recalcitrant colonies. Over the years both Great Britain and her North American colonies had benefited greatly from the economic ties between them, but during that time the colonies had learned to take care of themselves economically and to govern themselves very well. They had drifted farther from the influence of the mother country; they were becoming more independent. A combination of these factors contributed to changing the British policy from one of imperial neglect to one of imperial control. The crown would now take a more active part in controlling the North American empire.

This new assertion of control first manifested itself in a proclamation on land. The Proclamation of 1763 decreed that settlement beyond the mountains was prohibited, and anyone already settled there was to return. The land west of the mountains was to be reserved for the Indians. The Proclamation was intended to be a temporary expedient until the government could devise a more permanent solution to the Indian and border problems. It was a serious blow to anyone who held land, or wanted to acquire land, in that area. It hit land companies hard, especially speculators from Virginia. Some of their holdings were now worthless. It was worse than that; it was seen by the colonies as abrogating their right to grant or sell their land as they had been doing for over 150 years. They saw their right to land as violated.

The following decade was a tumultuous one, both in the east and in the west. The colonists fiercely resisted a series of revenue acts, including the Sugar Act, the Stamp Act, and the Tea Act, imposed by Britain to provide income to pay for the war debts. During this time of increased imperial pressure, the colonists became *less* dependent on Britain rather than more, as was the goal. They argued that their rights as British citizens were being violated. In the west the frontier was still in a state of flux, with some settlers challenging the Indians for land and the Indians retaliating. One major war, Pontiac's Rebellion, took place, with an even larger one threatened, but averted. Crown officials negotiated treaties, including Fort Stanwix, Hard Labor, and Lochaber, with new boundaries for the Indian lands. Some land cessions were made by the Indians, and some previously prohibited land beyond the mountains appeared to have been made available to the land companies. Despite these Indian land cessions west of the mountains, the British government never rescinded the Proclamation of 1763. It remained in place until the Revolution.

The year 1774 was arguably the most critical year leading up to the war. It was the year the land conflicts in the west came together with the taxing issues of the east, and joined to form the critical mixture of interests that tipped the balance toward independence. The Boston Tea Party, a protest against the Tea Act, took place in December 1773; there would be repercussions. In February 1774, a new land policy was announced, a major blow that impacted the interest of those seeking land in the west. It revoked all provincial authority to dispose of their own lands and any lands in the west. The royal governor was to have the land laid out by a surveyor in 100- to 1000-acre segments, and it was to be sold at auction, with a minimum price, to the highest bidder. This was how the crown planned to control the land as the Indians ceded it in the west. Royal control of all western land was to be absolute. This appeared to be the worst outcome ... until it got worse a few months later.

In March, Parliament passed the first of a series of Coercive Acts, called the Intolerable Acts by the colonists, designed to bring the colonists to heel. It was the Boston Port Act, which closed the port of Boston to commerce. This was devastating to the inhabitants because Boston did most of its commerce by sea. The last of the five Intolerable Acts was the Quebec Act, passed in June; it was the straw that broke the camel's back.

Up to this time there still hadn't been an answer to lawlessness at the border, and the British did not intend to keep an armed force in the west indefinitely. The idea of the Quebec Act was to provide some civil government to control the border, and be responsible for allocating the land. The solution was the creation of the Province of Quebec, or rather the expansion of the Quebec province that was established at the time of the Proclamation of 1763. Originally it was a sliver of land around the St. Lawrence River that contained most of the Catholic population of Canada. The boundary of the new province went up the St. Lawrence, down through the lakes, down the western border of Pennsylvania, to the Ohio River, then to the Mississippi River and back north to Canada, a huge swath of territory. This included the Ohio Country. The province was placed behind the original colonies and blocked most of them from the west. Catholics were to have some measure of home rule in Quebec, but the royal governor had the final say, and he reported to London. Quebec would control its own borders and land. It was hoped that the animosity between Protestant colonists and the Catholic regime in Quebec would discourage any movement across the border from the eastern provinces.[4]

The Quebec Act enraged all the colonies, not just the ones interested in western land. It led Thomas Jefferson to write "A Summary View of the Rights of British Americans," a paper that claimed that the king had no right to grant *any* lands in America, that those lands belonged to the colonists who came and settled them in the first place. It was almost a preamble to the Declaration of Independence. As Thomas Curtis in "Riches, Real Estate, and Resistance: How Land Speculation, Debt, and Trade Monopolies Led to the American Revolution" observed, the land policy of 1774 and the Quebec Act brought together the interest groups of the northern merchants, planters, states with western claims, and pioneers when they hadn't been together before. By 1774 England had created an American opposition solidly opposed to her domination. This was directly a result of her land policy.[5] The first English colonists arrived in British North America just after the end of the feudal age in England. They left a country in which all the land was tied up in great estates owned and controlled by the nobility. There was no such thing as private land ownership by the vast majority of the population so there was little concept of what it meant to own one's own land. That changed within a couple of decades of their arrival here, when colonizing companies realized that the labor shortage they faced could be offset by giving away the one resource they had in abundance to induce settlers to come—land. Free land now became the draw. In just a few generations free land came to be seen not just as a privilege, but a right. It completely flipped the concept of a few large landowners to ownership by many small farmers. As more people became involved in land ownership, more people became involved in governing, which was part of the ownership process; they learned how to govern themselves, and then demanded to govern themselves. In the following chapters we will see how the concept of free land in British North America eventually led to self-government in a free country.[6]

Very few revolutions in governing succeed; most fail. Even the ones that succeed in establishing a new government do not often remain stable and endure. The American Revolution against Great Britain did succeed, although its existence was precarious for a number of years. There were a number of complex issues that came together: cultural, religious, economic, land, tax, slavery, right to govern, and others that resulted in a successful revolution. No single issue can be considered the one most successful. The case put forward in the following pages is that free land was one critical factor. However, even in the act that is considered the tipping point, the Quebec Act, there are multiple factors that contributed to making it the tipping point. There was the blocking of the western land to the eastern provinces, the loss of control of the Indian trade, and the fact that there was now a province in Protestant British America that was a hated Catholic haven. Thus, the Quebec Act, which is considered herein to be primarily an act to control land, was laced with cultural, religious, and economic factors. So, although land was a key issue in the 170 years leading up to the Quebec Act and rebellion, even it was not simple and comprised cultural, religious, and economic issues.

> The history of America's land is the history of the country itself. America grew into its defining institutions even as it grew into its land. The land inspired American independence; it spawned American democracy; it undergirded America's rise to world power. Land symbolized opportunity to generations of Americans, starting with the colonists who never had the chance of owning property in Europe; the vast continent gleamed in their eyes and its frontier drew them west.[7]

Prologue: From the Conquest to the Colonies

An interesting story provides some insight into the feudal system of thirteenth-century England. "To this Richard[, the] Baron of Kendall gave the Manor of Kentmere in the time of King John (about the year 1206). He slew a wild boar, which did great mischief in the ajoining [sic] mountains, and thereupon took for his arms in field or a Sanglier or boar sable armed and tusked gules, which his posterity have born ever since."

This Richard was Richard De Gylpyn, an early ancestor of the Lewis family of Maryland; the account comes from the Lewis family genealogy. It is not clear if this courageous feat was accomplished by axe, by lance, on foot, on horseback, whether he did it alone or with the help of others. It is clear, though, that Richard was a nobleman, part of the warrior class. He was fulfilling his part of the feudal contract, which was protection of the weaker members of the manor or village; in this case probably the peasants of the De Gylpyn manor. He was rewarded by the Baron of Kendall with a manor and the adjoining land, which was the primary means of rewarding those who provided service in the late Middle Ages England. Using land as a reward and as an instrument of control in England, had really only started about 140 years previously at the Norman Conquest of 1066. After the Conquest, William (1028–1087) claimed he, as king, owned *all* the land in England; this was a novel claim even then.[1]

The Conquest

The Anglo-Saxon England that William conquered was lightly populated, with two million people or less, and a lot of empty land. There was no one central English government, but multiple kingdoms and numerous local lords protecting the villages and manors. Land was controlled by an Assembly of the People, the Witen or Witenagemot. The king could give away land to individuals, but only with the consent of the Witen. A lot of the land was held by freemen, ones with no overlord, and farmed by the freeman. This person could sell his land and move where he wished. He could also choose his suzerain for the protection he needed. There was also a servile class, serfs, bound to the lord of the manor, who were not free. Even though it resembled feudalism with lords, freemen, and a servile class, the concept of community-owned land and freedom of movement distinguished it from the more rigid feudal systems of the continent. The Anglo Saxon English were relatively independent.[2]

In 1066 William changed all that. He seized all the land, deposed thousands of the Anglo-Saxon nobility, and claimed personal ownership of all the land of England. He divided the land into baronies and allocated them to his nobles as a reward for their support in the Conquest; he created a rigid feudal system. He held about a fifth of the land himself, allowed the church about a quarter, and let about half be held by his followers. "Less than one hundred and eighty persons are found holding estates whose annual value is more than £100 a year. Moreover, about half the land held by lay tenure from the King after the Conquest had been granted to only ten men."[3] He used the land to maintain control, provide knights and soldiers for his army, and extract loyalty; the independence of Anglo-Saxon England was over. This small group was expanded, and by the time of the Domesday Book in 1086, the tenants-in-chief, those who held land directly of the king, would number around 1,400. Most of these were from Normandy; very few were wealthy Anglo-Saxons who had supported William from the outset. The subtenants, those who held land of the tenants-in-chief, would number about 7,900. The subtenants would owe service to the tenants-in-chief over them. Some of these were former Anglo-Saxons who had lost land to William.[4]

With this stroke William created a nobility that controlled England for centuries. The king needed the support of this nobility to maintain his control. To ensure that support he had to provide for their needs. It was not practical for him to feed and clothe them directly, so he used land tenure, property rights to land, so they could support themselves. He allocated land in the form of a fief, a tenure of land subject to feudal obligations, to the barons below him. They in turn allocated some of their land to tenant lords below them, the vassals. Each vassal pledged loyalty and service, military service or some other service, to his superior lord, up to the king at the top. The fief was conditional; it could be withdrawn if the service was not performed. They did not own the land; all were tenants, even though the lords were freeholders, owners, with respect to their own land. "No absolute ownership of land was possible, except by the King."[5] Thus all the land was spoken for and held by various lords in the hierarchy. This was the essence of the feudal system, a personal, "man-to-man" system of service to the person above and loyalty to the persons below. William had imported a rigid feudal system from the continent to consolidate his control over England. It served well for a few hundred years to provide control and security for those involved, and everyone was involved.[6]

The Manorial System

The feudal system served a political and military need but could not put food on the table. The economic engine of the Middle Ages was the manor. The manor was the lord's residence, an estate, the center of the farming community that provided food for lord and peasant alike. It was a self-sufficient economic unit that had arable land for farming, and common pasture land for livestock. A forest on the manor proper, or nearby, provided fruits, wood, and game. This manorial economy was not part of the feudal system, but existed alongside it; manorialism and feudalism were analogous but separate systems.[7]

The lord, the owner of the manor, or manors, was the link between the feudal system and the manorial system. Everyone below him on the manor was associated with the manorial system, not the feudal system. He was the mesne, or intermediate, lord if he was below the tenant-in-chief; he owned the demesne land on the manor. The manor land was divided into three categories: the demesne land, the lord's land, which was usually the best arable land; the land of the freeman; and the land allotted to the servile class, the serfs or villeins, as they were known in England. The freeholder owned the land he held on the manor, but he paid rent to the lord. He was free to alienate, or sell, the land. The villeins were not free; they held land at "the will of the lord" and were bound to that land, and bound to perform services for the lord. If they tried to leave the manor they could be hunted down and returned by force. However, they were not chattel slaves; they did have a few rights, mostly by custom, but everything they had belonged to the lord, including any personal property. The service they paid the lord for the privilege of working their villein land was service on the lord's demesne land, perhaps two or three days per week. The lord presided over the manor, or manors if he held more than one, including meting out justice over the villeins on the manor in the lord's court. Thus, everyone in the manorial system had his place and was rigidly located in the system. Although the manors were independent of a central government, they were controlled by a powerful lord who in turn was imbedded in the rigid feudal system introduced by William. William introduced "feudalism and its furnishing—an aristocracy which offered nothing in return for its privileges, an oppressed and impoverished peasantry forced to work without reward."[8]

The manorial system predated the feudal system and would outlast it. It originated in the Roman Empire in the first and second centuries of the Common Era (CE), although it is likely it would have existed at any time or place where some farmers needed the protection of a strong lord or chief. The Roman wealthy had moved to villas outside the city at the same time large agricultural farms, *latifundia*, were established outside the city. As the latifundia displaced small- and medium-sized farms these farmers moved to the city, which had few jobs to employ them. To stop this immigration, the city legislators enacted laws to tie these farmers to the land of the latifundia; the latifundia would be required to hire the farmers whose land they had taken. These farmers became known as *coloni*, supposedly legally free tenants. However, they were not truly free; they were "small tenants of low social standing who cultivated the land directly, formally free but lacking one of the fundamental requisites of the condition of full freedom: the ability to abandon their workplace and move elsewhere."[9] As the Empire collapsed, these latifundia became islands in a sea of chaos headed by a local lord who provided protection for the resident farmers, the coloni. Besides the coloni forced to work them, free farmers who needed protection would seek to be attached to the latifundium cum manor, thus giving up their freedom for the security of the manor. They would then become tenants on the manor of the lord; the chief of the latifundium. It is easy to see how these coloni would become the serfs or villeins of the Middle Ages.

The Villein

The life of the villein was both stable and unstable in different degrees. He held his land "at the will of the lord," which meant he could be removed at any time. However, if he kept out of trouble the land would be his for his life and would pass down to his son; villeinage was a bondage that was heritable. There was an economic incentive for the lord also, since "the soil without the labor to till it was of little value."[10] There was uncertainty in another sense, day-to-day uncertainty. Every day the villein awoke without knowing what the lord would have him do that day.[11]

Farming the manor required cooperation. The fields of the manor were divided into long strips for the villein, the freeholder, and the lord's demesne. The strips were not contiguous, so one villein's land would be scattered over a large area separated by the land of others. The primitive plows, pulled by as many as eight oxen, were unwieldy and could not turn easily, so it was easier to plow in a long strip, and then turn around and plow on another, probably, noncontiguous strip. The oxen teams, which they all shared, were composed of animals contributed by many villeins. This separation of the land in strips had an advantage in that at least some of the land would be good, arable land, so one would not get stuck with all poor land. They used a three-field system, meaning two were under crops each year and one was left fallow. All these attributes of the farming system required a good deal of cooperation among the peasants. They had to decide together when to plant and when to reap. It was a very ordered age and custom was strong. The manorial system was static. Generation after generation the villein remained in bondage and provided service to the lord; he did what he could on his allotted land. The villein clearly owed much to the lord and used customary gift giving to stay in his graces.[12]

> On certain days, the tenant brings the lord's steward perhaps a few small silver coins or, more often, sheaves of corn harvested on his fields, chickens from his farmyard, cakes of wax from his beehives or from the swarms of the neighbouring forest. At other times, he works on the arable or the meadows of the demesne. Or else we find him carting casks of wine or sacks of corn on behalf of the master to distant residences. His is the labour which repairs the walls or moats of the castle. If the master has guests the peasant strips his own bed to provide the necessary extra bed-clothes. When the hunting season comes round, he feeds the pack. If war breaks out he does duty as foot-soldier or orderly, under the leadership of the reeve of the village.[13]

The Black Death and the Villein

In 1000 C.E. the population of England was approximately two million, but it was starting to increase. By the mid–fourteenth century the population had increased to about five million. The increased population meant labor was plentiful to work the manor lands. However, things began to change in the fourteenth century. The major impact was the Black Death, which descended on England in 1348 and started a century-long population decline. This plague reduced the population by a third to a half, and it continued to fall until the mid–fifteenth century when it reached about two million. This had a profound effect on the manor and its workers. As many villeins died, their land became vacant and unproductive. "The scarcity of hands produced by the terrible mortality made it difficult for villeins to perform the services due for their lands."[14] The lords could not find replacements, and surviving villeins felt emboldened to leave their manor to look for a better deal elsewhere, either at other manors or in the village. The surviving villeins gained leverage because labor was scarce and the lord needed labor for the manor. In some cases, the villeins were given more favorable terms for their tenant lands, and sometimes they took over the lands of deceased villeins. In this way, some villeins built up considerable holdings. Although legislation, the Statute of Labourers (1351), was tried to force the villeins back to work, it failed. "After 1450, therefore, it became very rare to find a manor still cultivated by the compulsory labor of villains [villeins]."[15]

Up to this time the villein had held his land "by will of the lord" and in theory could be evicted at any time. He was a tenant according to the "custom of the manor."

> To hold in villainage meant to hold according to the custom of the manor: and title to land so held had been established by the testimony of men that knew this custom. But by reason of the greater fluidity of the rural population that grew up in the last half of the fourteenth century and the disorder of those troublous times, such testimony ceased to be adequate. It now became usual, therefore, to do what at an earlier date had rarely occurred: to appeal for evidence of title and of services due by reason of it to the roll of the manorial court. A copy of the entry on the court roll became the title to customary land, and the name being adapted to the fact, the tenant was said to hold "per copiam rotuli curiae," or by copy.[16]

The villein now had a "copyhold" tenure, a written title to his land on the manor; a stronger form of land tenure than was provided by the previous custom of the manor. The villein could now have a piece of paper that gave him the right to be on that land, a copyhold—an enforceable title. He had more rights as a copyholder, although still not the same as a freeholder who owned his land. The central government, relatively weak compared to feudal institutions, had little to say up to this time, but now the Crown (Henry VI) stepped in to bolster the security of this tenure. "From 1439 onwards a stream of equitable jurisdiction flows out from the Chancery to secure the title of the very class which has hitherto had no legal title at all. Tenure in villeinage becomes copyhold.... A copyholder is a tenant by copy of Court Roll according to the custom of the manor, and this custom is primarily what regulates his rights and obligations."[17]

The Black Death and the Lords' Enclosures

The lords also reacted to the after-effects of the Black Death. Having lost coercive power, and without the labor to farm the demesne land, they started to break it up and lease it out for money rent to freeman farmers, who hired laborers to farm the land. The manor now contained copyholds and leaseholds, which are almost equivalent, although both are still tenant lands. As the manorial barter economy fades, it is gradually replaced by a money economy. Gradually the lords commuted the villein service requirement, and land was rented for money instead. Efficiency becomes more important than the relationships between lord and tenant.[18]

Wool had been an important commodity for centuries in England, with the ubiquity of sheep on all manors and wasteland. More recently it was becoming important in international trade as well. For this reason, it became apparent to the lord that the open fields could be more productive if they are enclosed by hedges and fences and used for sheep pasture. After the Black Death, when land was vacated by death and abandonment, many lords seized the property of their tenants and enclosed this land for pasture. Lands that weren't abandoned were often seized by eviction. At first enclosure was done gradually, by some peasants combining their land into enclosed areas. However, in the fifteenth and sixteenth century the lords find it advantageous to enclose first the common lands, making them unavailable to the peasants who used them for grazing, and then they enclosed the leased demesne lands. They start to force out copyholders, who find their land rights not as solid as they had thought, by raising rents. Pasturing required less labor than tillage, so many people were forced off the land, adding to an increasing landless laboring class. Smaller farms were bought out, and the larger landholders engrossed many smaller holdings into much larger farms worked by laboring farmworkers. Not a lot of land was involved in this first enclosure movement; "in the century and a half before 1607 something over half a million acres of cultivated land were taken out of the hands of the tillers of the soil, and inclosed [sic] for sheep pasture,"[19] but significant numbers of people were displaced, some 30,000 to 50,000 in twenty-four counties. "The movement was so extensive as in parts of England to cause serious suffering and disturbance."[20] Many moved to the cities and towns and became laborers, specialist workers, and craftsmen; some moved back to the manors to become subtenants on the land they once held. The depopulation caused by the Black Death destroyed many villages and caused the collapse of the manorial system; in the fifteenth century villeinage had disappeared.[21] This agrarian revolution, which was caused by enclosures, and by the collapse of the manorial system, contributed to a large class of unemployed laborers who, early in the seventeenth century, looked for opportunities being offered in the New World. Land in England was now held by fewer and fewer landowners.

The Rise and the Decline of the Yeoman

However, despite the increased power of the upper class of landowners, some villeins and freeholders who had managed to hold on became the seed of a new middle class. They needed some help to accomplish this.

About 10 percent of the villages in the south midlands disappeared in the fifteenth and early sixteenth centuries. In many cases, enclosure was the immediate cause. After the accession of Henry VII, the Crown sought to check these depopulations. The most effective policy was judicial: eviction enclosures could proceed only because of the insecurity of customary tenure. Granting the tenants enforceable title forestalled enclosure. This change converted villein tenure into peasant proprietorship and created the English yeoman. Thus, in most of the midlands, the sixteenth and seventeenth centuries saw the consolidation—not the collapse—of the English peasantry.[22]

The enforceable title was the copyhold tenure in its various forms. Although the lord still owned the manor land, under the ultimate ownership of the king, the villein, who had become a copyholder now, had proprietary rights to the land he was working. "This converted villeins into peasant proprietors."[23] Along with leaseholders, and freeholders, the copyholders became landholders which were known as yeoman farmers.[24] Again, though, this class came under increasing pressure from the landowning class. "The early seventeenth century marked the high point of yeoman property rights. These rights, however, were not absolute and were not sufficient to preserve the yeoman social structure. Large landowners continued to resist royal efforts to protect peasants ... the vesting of power in a parliament controlled by large landowners laid the basis for the final destruction of the English peasantry in the late seventeenth and eighteenth centuries."[25]

It was later in the seventeenth century that things started to change again. Large landowners started to buy out peasant property.

> Manorial lords bought small freeholds and heritable copyholds, and ran out (i.e., did not renew) beneficial leases and copyholds for life ... most farmers lost their land between 1650 and 1800...By the end of the eighteenth century only 10 per cent of England belonged to owner-occupying farmers, so the decline from 1688 was precipitous.... Yeoman agriculture was eliminated as large estates embarked on a long term policy of land acquisition towards the end of the seventeenth century. The aim of the policy was to increase farm size for efficiency reasons.... Farm amalgamation was driven by the desire to realize the profits of large scale.[26]

This was the end of the yeoman's revolution and the beginning of the landlord's revolution. The land of the yeoman, copyholds, leaseholds, and freeholds was bought by the landed families, and so the number of owners of English land shrank. The great estates that were accumulated were "let at will to substantial farmers. The result was the three-tiered system of wealthy landowners, large-scale tenant farmers, and landless labourers that epitomized English rural society in the nineteenth century."[27] The large farms were let to tenants who worked them with wage labor.[28]

Farm efficiency, and profits from large scale farms, were two reasons for this land buyout, but there were others. It was about this time that the wool industry became important in England, and that changed the incentive for land use. Now that there was a constant and increasing demand for wool, it became the interest of the landowners to raise sheep rather than to grow corn, especially as tillage was becoming less profitable because of labor costs due to the Black Death. Instead, cloth became the main industry; by the end of the seventeenth century, wool accounted for two-thirds of exports.[29] Another reason for the expansion of the great estates was, that after the civil war and restoration, land ownership rather than royal favor was the source of political power and social prestige. The wealthy landowners were willing to pay more for land than it was worth. The yeoman could therefore make more by selling than by farming. This land consolidation by the wealthy continued through the eighteenth century. A second round of enclosures occurred in the eighteenth century, driven by acts of Parliament, in which a greater amount of land was enclosed.[30]

Land Legacy of the Conquest

When William conquered England, claimed all the land as his own, and then parceled it out to his supporters, he established an aristocracy and land tenure system that would persist for centuries. The servile class under that aristocracy, the ones who would farm the land, were at first bound to the land by force and by custom; they had no options to change their status. They were servile tenants of the lords of the manors. The Black Death of the fourteenth century caused a population drop of a third to a half, and changed everything. The serfs, or villeins, gained a freedom of movement they never had previously. They achieved a more secure title, copyhold, to the land they held by tenure on the manor, and except for the tenancy were free to farm the land as they wished. They paid money rent, but no longer services, to the lord of the manor; they became the virtually free yeoman farmers of the sixteenth and seventeenth centuries. When they lost coercive power over the villeins, the lords also took steps to improve their position. By taking over vacated tenancies, evicting some tenants, and buying out others, they started to enclose land to use for pasture rather than for farming; this displaced many peasants. Some returned as subtenants, or laborers on land they once farmed, and some emigrated. The yeoman's success crested in the sixteenth and seventeenth century. Following that, the wealthy landowners started buying back and enclosing more land, so that by the end of the eighteenth century most farmers were farming on tenant lands again. By the 1780s perhaps 90 percent of the land in some counties was occupied by tenant farmers, and by the end of the eighteenth century only 10 percent of the land belonged to owner-occupying farmers. "Thus, enclosure before the eighteenth century did lead to rising inequality and emigration."[31] The rise in inequality and landless laborers, caused by the enclosure movement and the agrarian revolution of the sixteenth century, led to the emigration to America of many in the early seventeenth century.

This process of accumulation of land by wealthy landowners continued into 1881 "where only 360 people owned one-quarter of the land in all of England and Wales, and 350 landowners had possessed two-thirds of Scotland in 1873," and is still evident in the English land holdings today.[32] In one of the great democracies of the world, Kevin Cahill, in *Who Owns Britain*, documents that of the UK's 60 million acres of land, most of the 59 million person population lives on 4.4 million acres; 12 to 15 million acres are mountain, forest, moorland, roadways, and industrial land; and 40 million acres of productive countryside are owned by only 189,000 families. These aristocrats, baronets, and landed gentry are descendants of the wealthy landowners noted above. They can trace their heritage back to the manorial lords of previous centuries and ultimately to the barons who received land from William the Conqueror. To this day most of the land is owned by a few. The aristocracy established by William the Conqueror has left a legacy after almost 1,000 years.[33]

The thread that runs through those centuries is the tight hold on land ownership by the aristocracy established by William I in the eleventh century. Throughout most of that time the farmers who provided the food for the people farmed as tenants on land owned by an aristocrat; very few actually owned their own land. In the sixteenth century England claimed vast stretches of North America by virtue of discovery. In the early seventeenth century colonization would start in earnest and continue through most of the eighteenth century. Would the history and custom of land tenure of the mother country be duplicated in the New World? Would everyone again end up as tenants on land owned by others?

CHAPTER ONE

Discovery and Claims

Once upon a time, more than five hundred years ago, Europeans began a grand, long-term campaign to extract material and other advantages from underpopulated or underdefended territories by establishing permanent settlements around the world.[1]

In his 1584 *Discourse of Western Planting*, Richard Hakluyt, a fierce promoter of English colonization in the New World, listed as one of the reasons for this colonization "that this enterprise will be for the manifold employment of numbers of idle men, and for breeding of many sufficient and for utterance of the great quantity of the commodities of our realm." He then goes on to list many of these commodities these presently idle men would work on, such as "felling of timber for masts of ships ... burning of the fires of pine trees to make pitch, rosin, tar, and soap ashes." He goes on hopefully to suggest also finding gold, silver, copper, lead, and iron. Hakluyt (1552–1616), an English geographer and writer, had a great deal of influence in Elizabeth's court. He was writing near the end of the age of discovery and exploration, and near the beginning of the age of colonization. He was trying to convince Queen Elizabeth (1558–1603) of the importance of establishing colonies in the New World, trying to supply a *push* to new adventures. Spain had already been well established in that enterprise, but England lagged behind. It was a time of rapid change.[2]

The rebirth of intellectual curiosity in the Renaissance led almost naturally to an increasing curiosity of western Europeans about the world around them; they wanted to see and explore distant lands. This was spurred by a coincident decrease in the safety of the Silk Road. The Silk Road, literally a path through Central Asia connecting Asia and the west, had been used for centuries as a trading route between east and west. It became increasingly unsafe with the decrease of Roman power in the east and the rise of Arab powers in the near east. The Mongols revived it in the thirteenth and fourteenth centuries, which is when Marco Polo traveled east. When that empire was breaking up at the end of the fourteenth century, it again became unsafe to use a land route across central Asia. Coincident with their new-found curiosity, westerners started to look for better routes to maintain trade with Asia. This search for new routes took place mostly from the mid–fifteenth to the mid–sixteenth centuries, the Age of Discovery, and was led first by the Portuguese. Familiar names such as Prince Henry the Navigator, Bartholomew Diaz, and, even after Columbus, Vasco de Gama, found their way around Africa and eventually to the Far East. Their intent was to find a better way to the east for trade. The explorations, however, had unintended consequences.[3]

About halfway into the Age of Discovery, Spain joined the search for a better route through the well-known explorations of the Genoese explorer Christopher Columbus. After his 1492 discovery of the "Indies," in the form of a small Caribbean island, he made three more voyages over the next 10 years. On the second voyage in 1493 he established the first permanent Spanish settlement of the New World, Isabela, on the island of Hispaniola. It was not until his third and fourth voyages that he found the mainland of South and Central America; he never did make it to North America.[4]

The early discoveries forced a change in the thinking that heretofore had guided the motivation and destinations of these voyages. When he landed, Columbus did not find the sophisticated cultures of the Far East which could provide the spices and silk they sought; instead, he found a Caribbean culture, different when compared to the highly developed Spanish culture. If there was to be trade, it would be different from that which they had expected. Clearly, they had to rethink their exploration and trade objectives. One of their objectives, as it always was for their Far East destinations, was gold. They found evidence of gold on the islands, and recoverable gold on Hispaniola. They had found their new objective.[5]

Preoccupied with the One Hundred Years War with France and the internal dynastic struggle of the War of the Roses, England had little time for exploration when it started in the mid–fifteenth century. However, later in the sixteenth century Henry VII (1457–1509) became concerned about missing out on the potential riches of the New World recently uncovered by Columbus. So, when another Genoese mariner, Giovanni Caboto (John Cabot), sought a permit to explore western lands, it was readily granted. He was empowered to "discover and find whatsoever isles, countries, regions or provinces of heathens and infidels, in whatsoever part of the world they be, which before this time were unknown to all Christians." The permit was granted to Cabot and his sons by Henry in 1496, but they didn't sail until May 1497 in the *Matthew*. They landed in June on or near Newfoundland, Cape Breton or Labrador, and claimed the land for England. Unlike the Spanish, the English did not immediately follow up on the North American discovery. Later in the century there were sporadic attempts to settle the mainland, but permanent settlement of North America did not happen until early in the seventeenth century.[6]

New Spain

The aim of the Spaniards in their conquest of the New World was threefold.

> First of all, they sought to extend the realm of the crown. This was the primary motive assigned for the initial voyage of Columbus.... Next in importance, and closely associated with it, was the zeal for bringing pagan nations to a knowledge of the Christian faith. The third motive which prompted the Spanish occupation of the New World was the acquisition of wealth. These three aims directed the Spaniards in their settlement of the New World and the establishment of what eventually became the characteristic system of land tenure in Spanish America.[7]

During his first voyage of discovery to the West Indies (1492), Columbus landed first on the island in the Bahamas he named San Salvador, but he touched many other islands in the area, including Cuba and the island he named La Isla Española (Hispaniola). Over the course of his four voyages, he discovered many other Caribbean islands, including Jamaica, Puerto Rico and islands in the Lesser Antilles. However, his touchstone was always Hispaniola, which he visited on each voyage. On returning from his first voyage, he now had other ideas about conquest and colonization. He noted in his journal to Ferdinand and Isabella that on Hispaniola, and the other islands in the area, the islanders needed only a government "to command them to do what you wish." He went on to describe the inhabitants of Hispaniola as "naked with no experience of arms and very timid ... they are suitable to take orders and be made to work, sow and do anything else that may be needed." He now had the model for future colonization: control over the land and an indigenous population that could be made to work for the colonizer.[8] His second journey, in 1493, was more ambitious, comprising 17 ships and hundreds of would-be *pobladores* (settlers).

He found the settlement he had established on the first voyage, La Navidad on Hispaniola, had been destroyed, presumably by the Indians, so he established another colony on the north shore of Hispaniola; Isabela, which was the first permanent one. As a colony this wasn't successful, and Columbus returned to Spain in 1496 with several hundred disheartened colonists; he left his brother in charge on Hispaniola. The Columbus brothers were fine navigators but poor colonial administrators. Columbus had promised his men salaries but did not follow up to pay them. As a result, when he returned on this third voyage in 1498, he found the settlers in revolt; they opposed his brother Bartholomew's command in Hispaniola. In order to achieve stability and salvage settlement on this fertile island, he sanctioned a system whereby groups of Indians were distributed to specific settlers to work the lands and the mines for these settlers. This system, *repartimiento*, or distribution, became popular with the settlers on Hispaniola, and later on the other Caribbean islands, because it provided a stable source of Indian labor, and gave the settlers a great deal of independence and prestige.[9]

Repartimiento was not new. It had been "employed earlier in the conquest of the Balearic and Canary Islands and in the reconquest of southern Spain from the Moors." Each colonist was assigned an Indian chieftain and his followers to work the fields or the mines for the colonist. In turn the colonist was to treat them justly and to instruct his charges in Christian doctrine, and the ways of civilization. *Repartimiento* is a harsh word when applied to human beings. "Distributing" them invokes ideas of slavery, which in many cases did happen de facto. Once it was introduced in the West Indies, "*repartimiento*, by reason of the severity of the service demanded, had practically depopulated the islands within a few decades. It had, however, effectually brought the islands under Spanish authority, had given the invaders possession of the soil, and had provided them with labor whereby they could live without performing manual work, which the inherited notions of the Castilians rendered distasteful." However, Queen Isabella was always concerned about the welfare of the Indians and feared their mistreatment. Thus, perhaps in order to mollify her concern, the term was changed to *encomienda*, which means entrust. Thus, the Indians were "entrusted" to the care of the colonists instead of "distributed." However, the terms *encomienda* and *repartimiento* came to be used interchangeably.[10]

For a surprisingly long time after Columbus, Spanish colonization was contained in the Caribbean to islands like Hispaniola (1496), Puerto Rico (1508), Jamaica (1509), and Cuba (1511). "The Caribbean Sea served as the funnel through which the Spanish power entered the New World."[11] From these outposts they could explore the region and expand the empire. As late as 1516, little or nothing was officially known of the Yucatan and mainland Mexico. These islands were colonized, *repartimiento* was established, and the preparations were made for the move to the mainland in 1519.[12]

In April 1519, Hernan Cortes was stationed on San Juan de Ulua, a small island off the eastern coast of Mexico. He and his men, based in Cuba under Governor Diego Velazquez, had just cruised off the coast of

Yucatan when, on April 22, he took 200 of his 530 men and headed to the mainland. When he reached the mainland, he was well received by the Totanic Indians, a local group under the Aztec Montezuma. In an appropriate ceremony he took possession of the land, and that which was yet to be explored, in the name of Charles I (1500–1558), King of Spain. These were his orders from Velazquez: "in all the islands that are discovered you shall leap on shore in the presence of your scribe and many witnesses, and in the name of their Highnesses take and assume possession of them with all possible solemnity." The orders from Velazquez were for "trade and exploration," not for conquest or settlement. However, Cortes had other ideas; he intended to poblar, settle, or populate the land.[13]

Velazquez had intended to set himself up on the mainland and govern it himself. But, by a series of maneuvers, Cortes was able to defy his superior, and secure his own authority from the king. He and his expeditionary force then constituted themselves as a community, and on June 28, 1519, incorporated the town of Villa Rica de Vera Cruz, the first Spanish community on the Mexican mainland. On August 8, Cortes and some 300 of his men started toward the interior. "As they moved inland, they ... picked up a host of Mesoamerican allies who were chafing under the dominion of the Mexica."[14] They encountered the sophisticated Aztec civilization and proceeded to overwhelm these Mesoamerican people, aided by their Indian allies, superior weapons, armor, horses, and their aura of almost godlike aliens. They captured Montezuma, and after more than two years captured the capital of Tenochtitlan. The claim he initially made of possession was now a fact. "Mexico had become, in fact as well as theory, a possession of the Crown of Castile, and in due course was to be transferred into Spain's first American viceroyalty, the viceroyalty of New Spain."[15] "But once the lineaments of a great American landmass were revealed, and Cortes went on to overthrow the empire of the Aztecs, it was clear that Spain's empire of the Indies had come to stay.... Here were vast sedentary populations, which could be brought under Spanish control with relative ease. Dominion over land brought with it dominion over people, and ... dominion over resources on an unimagined scale."[16]

Besides the search for gold, the civilization and conversion of the native population would be part of the mission. The native population was not only seen as an object of conversion to Christianity, but as a labor force for public and private works, not technically slaves but vassals of the crown. Vassalage was to be a throwback to the feudal structure of the European past.[17]

The Spanish decided to stay, settle, and exploit. "Spain had the advantage of not only sponsoring the discovery but on stumbling on the parts of America that would bring the quickest profits." Other *conquistadores*,

Pizarro, for example, also came looking for riches and found them, in Peru. This *pull* of riches in the New World had replaced the *pull* of trade with the Far East. By the middle of the sixteenth century Spain had control over much of South America and the North American Southwest and West, extending from Florida to Alaska. The extraction of gold and silver, and conversion of the pagan Indians, became the major objectives of the occupation.[18]

This attraction of riches, however, would make the settlement of New Spain different from that of what would become the North American colonies. It is true that the willingness to settle for a modest lifestyle would suffice for many immigrants. "'This is a good land for those who want to be virtuous, hard-working and well-respected,' wrote a settler in Mexico in 1586.... But the presence in Spanish-occupied lands of precious metals and a docile labor force served to perpetuate ... conceptions of wealth in terms of booty and lordship." Consequently, "at least the first-generation Spanish settlers, would set much less value on land as a commodity in itself than the settlers of seventeenth century English America. It was vassals, rather than land, that they wanted." Thus, the conquistadores first subjugated the densely populated indigenous areas, the regions that gave the best hope of lordship over vassals and a better chance for riches. "The recognition that labor was essential to extract income from colonies was one major reason (the wealth of the areas settled was another) why the Spanish, the first Europeans to organize colonies in the Americas, chose to focus their efforts on the more densely-populated and richer areas we know as Mexico and Peru."[19]

Conquest and exploitation were not a long-term strategy, however. Cortes had experience with that in the Caribbean, and he knew more had to be done to solidify control over the land. His philosophy was "without settlement there is no good conquest, and if the land is not conquered, the people will not be converted. Therefore, the maxim of the conqueror must be to settle."[20] To encourage settlement and to reward the conquistadores who helped conquer the Indians of the mainland, he established *encomienda*, the direct descendant of the *repartimiento* of the islands.

Encomienda was an area of land inhabited by Indians outside the town, which was granted to an elite citizen, conquistador, or official. It was granted in order to tie the person to the town and the land, to encourage settlement rather than the search for gold. "The concept of *encomienda* was an elusive one—not an actual grant of land but a license to dredge benefits in the form of tribute and labor from the land and its inhabitants."[21] The crown retained ownership of the land by virtue of conquest, so there was no incentive to seek land, *per se*, in New Spain. Instead, "the young gentlemen hidalgos who followed Cortes to seek their fortune in

New Spain did so knowing that, in strict legal terms, all they could own was the produce of the earth and the labor of the Indians—a reality encapsulated in the aphorism they coined, *sin indios non hay Indias* ('without Indians, there's no Indies') meaning that without their ownership of the people, the rich land was worthless."[22]

In theory, the Indian labor was to be time-limited and wages were to be paid; in practice, this was often ignored. Control of the Indians was more important than the land they occupied. In essence, the indigenous population was divided up to support the conquerors' settlements. The *repartimiento* and *encomienda* system established in New Spain was an obvious throwback to the feudal system of Europe a century earlier. In a sense, it was worse; the vassals in the feudal system were basically freemen who owed certain obligations to a lord but were otherwise free. These indigenous people were analogous to the serfs or villeins, of the feudal era rather than vassals; they were not free.[23]

"He [Cortes] assigned *encomiendas* to 300 of his men—about 40 percent of the survivors of the army that captured Tenochtitlan, and about 6 percent of the total European population of the Indies at that time." Later Pizarro did the same with the Peruvian Indians. The *encomienda* system became common all over New Spain and Peru. "By the 1540s there were some 600 *encomenderos* [the holder of an *encomienda*] in the viceroyalty of New Spain and 500 in Peru. This suggests that a New World feudal aristocracy was already in the making." The crown knew about the brutality of the *encomienda* and fought it, partly by requiring the encomenderos to live in town rather than on the feudal *encomienda* estate. The *encomiendas* were to revert to the crown on death of the owner, and not automatically to the family. "Above all, the *encomienda* remained what it had always been—a grant of Indians, not of land. When the land was abandoned by the Indians, it reverted to the crown, and not to the encomenderos to whom the Indians had been assigned." Despite these constraints many encomenderos were able to purchase large tracts of land and keep them in the family for agriculture. "However, there remained strict limitations on land ownership in Spain's American possessions. The possession was conditional on its occupation or use ... the subsoil remained the inalienable possession of the crown."[24]

The *encomienda* system was essentially a government operation intended to reward the conquistadores who had conquered Indians of the New World. The crown assigned the Indians and the land; the Indians were to pay tribute to the encomenderos. Tribute, that which was due from a conquered people to the conqueror, could be in the form of gold or agricultural products, but was often in the form of labor. The first encomenderos, however, saw this "as provision for unlimited personal opportunism." They abused the Indians, "they overtaxed and overworked them. They jailed them, killed them, beat them, and set dogs on them." The crown strongly disapproved of the mistreatment of the Indians, but at first could do little because of their distance from Spain. Many of these encomenderos saw themselves as lords over an estate.[25] According to a report from a royal agent in Mexico "in some regions the villagers consider the lords and encomenderos of the villages as their kings, and they know no other sovereign."[26]

Cortes and the conquistadores had established expansive control over large parts of New Spain and were rewarded with *encomienda*. "He [Cortes] received the title of marquis and the grant of substantial lands with 23,000 Indian vassals for his services." This control, however, was seen as a lack of control by the crown. The crown could not assure the humane treatment of the Indians on the *encomienda*, nor could they preclude the encomenderos from acting as independent lords of the estates, like feudal masters. There was need of "a second conquest—that of the conquerors by the crown." A series of steps were taken to reestablish control by the crown.[27]

The first step was the establishment of the *Audiciencia*, or high court, in 1530. This was to provide juridical oversight by the crown over New Spain. Next, in 1535, they established the Viceroyalty of New Spain. The viceroy was to oversee the crown's interest in New Spain and report to the crown, not to any local official. Then they established the *corregimiento de Indios*, an institution for the administration of the traditional Indian population.[28] This institution was to oversee the Indians who were not commended to private control. It was also to cover any new conquered Indians, and ones escheated to the crown from the encomenderos. These *corregidores* (correctors, magistrates[29]), officials of the crown, reported to the viceroys and were therefore under crown control. As the corregimiento gained in power, the private encomenderos lost power through the loss of their Indians. In 1542 the crown promulgated the "New Laws" of the Indies. This was an attempt to end the *encomienda* system. It terminated the *encomienda* on the death of the longest-lived encomenderos, outlawed slavery, released the enslaved, and prohibited new *encomienda*s. In 1549 the crown went further, ordering that encomenderos could no longer require personal services from the Indians; they could only collect tribute. The tribute was to be paid to the royal treasury; the treasury in turn would pay the encomenderos as pensioners.[30]

These steps were the beginning of the end of the *encomienda* system. However, it was not the end of control by the encomenderos. Through the decline of the *encomienda* system, they were able to acquire the land itself, not Indian control, and turn it into private estates. They transformed a government-controlled land system into a private, capitalistic *hacienda* system. The encomenderos were transformed into *hacendados*.

As the *encomienda* system declined, so, coincidentally, did the Indian population. The crown blamed the cruelties of the *encomienda* system for the population decrease. In New Spain, one estimate has it decrease from about 25 million in 1519 to slightly over one million in 1605.[31] Faced with the loss of juridical control over the Indians on the *encomienda*, and the decreasing Indian population, the encomenderos turned to land acquisition to maintain their status and fortunes.[32] Some encomenderos managed to acquire personal land on the *encomienda* over which they presided, even during the height of the *encomienda* system early in the century; they used the privilege of political authority. "It has been said that although *encomienda* did not itself allow for property ownership it facilitated property acquisition."[33] Lockhart, in *Evolution of the Great Estate in the Spanish Indies,* notes that, during this period the encomenderos did own private land and some of it on their own *encomiendas*.[34] Gibson, in *Spain in America,* also argues that "only as the lands became unoccupied through depopulation did the Spaniards become interested in acquiring them."[35] This is because during *encomienda*, land ownership was unnecessary; they controlled the Indian labor. However, as Lockhart previously noted, they acquired it anyway. "Land had not previously been given away in large quantities, because it had little real value except for those who had access to the labor necessary to work it, and the demand for it was therefore small outside the immediate vicinity of the Spanish towns. It was only in the 1550s, with the abolition of the encomenderos' labor monopoly and the increased availability of Indian labor through the labor *repartimiento*, that there grew up a significant demand for land."[36]

The decline in Indian population coincided with an abundance of land becoming available, and also an influx of new Spanish colonists needing land. Some land was bought from the Indians using fraudulent means. Another source of land ownership came from the land grant or *merced* (favor) in which the king, through the viceroy, would grant land as a favor to his supporters. The petitioner would request land, on which he was already living, from the viceroy. The land could be for stock raising (cattle, goats) or agriculture.[37]

From the mid–sixteenth century, the nature of land tenure in New Spain began to change. In the early days of the Conquest, the crown would grant rewards to the conquistadores for their service in conquering the land. This was in the form of jurisdiction over Indians on land the Indians were already working, *encomienda*. This jurisdiction would allow tribute to be collected from the Indians and also personal services in the form of labor. The tribute and labor would allow the encomenderos to enrich themselves. It was very much a feudal state in which the encomenderos were the lords of the estate and the Indians the serfs, although euphemistically called vassals by the crown. The *encomienda* system was a government operation; the crown claimed ownership of all the land. However, the encomenderos were on the way to becoming an independent aristocracy by virtue of the control they exercised over the Indians and the land of the *encomienda*. When the crown reasserted jurisdiction over the Indians, and the Indian population decreased, the encomenderos lost control of the *encomienda*, although they had started to acquire land independent of the *encomienda*. The pattern had been set; control of the land in New Spain was to remain in the hands of a privileged few. This class would continue its control through the *hacienda* (estate) system.

> For Spaniards land became the symbol of wealth that *encomienda* had formerly been, and by and large this meant a new colonial aristocracy not related to the earlier conquistadores and *encomenderos*. By the seventeenth century the Spanish demand for land had caught up with depopulation, and Spaniards made efforts to free lands from their remaining native occupants, both in legal and illegal ways.... The great haciendas of Spanish America came into being through land grant, purchase, usurpation, accretion, merger, and economic competition. Lands originally granted in small amounts were bought up by colonial speculators and often sold and resold a number of times before taking final form as segments of huge estates.... Haciendas repeatedly incorporated and absorbed native towns, and hacienda society emerged in the familiar form as a stratification of white owners and native laborers.[38]

As the hacienda movement expanded from the mid–sixteenth century and the *encomienda* system declined, there was a tendency to say the former was a direct result or extension of the latter. Both Keith, in *Hacienda and Corregimiento in Spanish America,* and Lockhart make the case that the connection was not quite that close, but acknowledge the similarities; clearly the same people were in control.

The encomenderos' families were able to become proprietors of lands within the jurisdiction of the *encomienda* towns. They did this either by a grant (*merced*) or purchase. This way they could set up a hacienda within the *encomienda*. The cloak of the *encomienda* would be used to set up a hacienda.[39]

Although concentrating on the production of the Indian labor on the *encomienda*, the encomenderos would frequently take possession of land on or near the *encomienda*, usually with a formal land grant from the town or governor He would raise livestock and crops for himself and for sale, on these so-called estancias.[40] Whether it was devoted to livestock or crops, the word "estancia" was commonly used in this period.[41] It was from the estancia that the hacienda evolved.[42]

Chapter One. Discovery and Claims

The similarities between the *encomienda* and hacienda are multiple. The type of men who ran both the *encomienda* and hacienda were all upper class, cut from the same cloth, used to ruling the countryside and city. These estates passed down through their families.

The encomenderos and hacendado came from the same social strata; they both felt themselves to be an aristocracy. The staffs of the two institutions were almost identical, the work done at the lowest level was done by Indians in both cases, and so, although not a direct descendant of the *encomienda*, the hacienda certainly provided a continuity of functions.[43] The workers from the villages, who worked the estancias, and then the haciendas, came first through *encomienda* obligations, then *repartimiento*, and finally individually. The estancias were part of the estates of the encomenderos.[44] The transition in the ownership of land in New Spain from *encomienda* through estancia and to hacienda was a transition from a non-capitalist semi-governmental system to the private, land-owning capitalist system. The encomenderos did not own *encomienda* land, but had only the labor of the Indians to produce wealth. The hacendados now had their wealth tied up in the land they *owned*. It was a transformation from a feudal aristocracy, where the crown owned the land and the encomenderos were the masters of the estates, to an aristocracy of wealth where the hacendados privately owned the land and controlled the employed labor.

> Haciendas employed the inhabitants of Indian towns as *peones* and controlled all their activities. The wealthiest and most powerful persons in the colony—viceroys, high-ranking officials, prosperous merchants, ecclesiastics—became *hacendados*.... Haciendas repeatedly incorporated and absorbed native towns, and hacienda society emerged in the familiar form as a stratification of white owners and native laborers. The *peones* formed the proletariat of every hacienda. The *hacendado* was its absolute master, euphemized in the term *patrón*. The *hacendado's* house was a magnificent dwelling.... To the *peones* of the hacienda the *patrón* was an apotheosis of authority, immediate in a way that the viceroy and king never were. His ostentatious possessions—his horses and carriages, his elaborate attire, his silver and finery—were visible symbols of wealth. Disobedience to his will brought severe and exemplary punishment. A prudent servility was essential.... Thus the hacienda fitted the universal character of Spanish America.[45]

The New Spain, and then Mexican, land tenure system, although not called such, was essentially equivalent to the English feudal system of the eleventh through the fifteenth centuries. The control of the land and laborers was by the encomenderos and hacendados; the Indians and peons were equivalent to the serfs and villeins. This system lasted five centuries, starting at the Conquest and going to at least the Mexican Revolution

(1910–1920). The system conferred ownership of much of the land to large non-indigenous American landholders. It had the effect of concentrating economic and political control in the hands of an elite and precluded widespread ownership of land. This helped to retard the economic and political development of Mexico. "On the eve of the Mexican Revolution, the figures from the 1910 census suggest that only 2.4 percent of household heads in rural Mexico owned land. The number is astoundingly low.... The evidence obviously conforms well with the idea that in societies that began with extreme inequality, such as Mexico, institutions evolved so as to greatly advantage the elite in access to economic opportunities, and thus they contributed to the persistence of that extreme inequality."[46]

Thus, the Spaniards as the first colonizers in the western hemisphere were unable to preclude the transfer of an essentially feudal system from the old world to the new. At the Conquest they could not resist exploiting a relatively large, passive Indian labor force, and settled in to exploit that labor force for gain, for both the crown and the conquistadores. There were some concerns, mostly by the queen, about the treatment of the Indians, but little was done to ameliorate their condition. The crown was concerned about the apparent ability of the encomenderos to convert themselves into an independent aristocracy, but the concern was based largely on loss of control by the crown rather than concern about the Indians. The system evolved from *encomienda* to *corregimiento* to *hacienda*. Changes were made to the new *repartimiento* labor system, giving the Indians a little more freedom, but it still required their labor for the Spanish masters.

The Spaniards brought with them to America the vision of a noble lifestyle. It included an estate, a mansion, servants, livestock, crops. This was the vision for successful Spaniards in the new world.[47]

This vision persisted for centuries and kept the land of Mexico in the hands of the elite into the twentieth century.

English America—The Prelude

The prelude to English America occurred in a turbulent sixteenth-century England. It was a time of rapid transition from a feudal state to a modern capitalist state that was on the verge of claiming an empire around the world.

Wool had been a ubiquitous presence in England for centuries because sheep thrived there. Trade had started in wool as early as the twelfth century, but accelerated in the sixteenth century to become a major factor in the economy. The trade in wool led to the formation of trading companies, and eventually joint stock companies, whose purpose was to promote and protect the new industry. The agrarian revolution of the same century enhanced this trade. As landowners enclosed their property to pasture sheep for wool, they became graziers and cloth merchants, joined the previous wool and cloth merchants, and helped make the English one of the world's premier trading nations.

This wouldn't have been possible without the direct and indirect support of the crown. Throughout the century the Tudors, from Henry VII (1457–1509) through Henry VIII (1491–1547) and Elizabeth I (1533–1603), all supported a strong shipping industry and a strong navy, because England is an island nation. However, except for Henry VII's support of John Cabot's voyage to Newfoundland just prior to the turn of the sixteenth century, they were late to the idea of claims on North America. Elizabeth did grant patents to two adventurers, Sir Humphrey Gilbert and Sir Walter Raleigh, to plant colonies on North America, but except for a small colony on Newfoundland they were unsuccessful. Spain and France made some tentative moves on the east coast of the mainland but fortunately for the English did not stay.

England is a small island nation, and one would expect that it would have to depend on trade to prosper, because it would be unlikely to command all the needed resources for that prosperity on the small island landmass. By the end of the century, it had not only mastered the business of trade, but began to prosper and have an outsized influence on world trade. It was ready to move into new trading areas.

When England did finally make a move to plant a colony in Virginia, just after the turn of the seventeenth century, it was not a crown move as it had been for Spain, but the effort of a joint stock company in pursuit of more trading opportunities.

Wool, Trade, and Joint Stock Companies

The story begins with sheep. "By the middle of the sixteenth century, there were 11 million sheep throughout England, outnumbering humans by around four to one. They grazed everywhere—on the tiny tracts of land rented by peasant farmers as well as on the great estates of noblemen, bishops, and abbots. Their ubiquity was attributable to one factor: the age-old importance of wool to the English economy."[48]

Raising sheep for wool goes back well before the sixteenth century to feudal England, where sheep were raised on the manors and common land; the peasants from the manors and villages produced woolen fiber in their cottages. "As early as the twelfth century, raw English wool was exported to the Low Countries, then the epicenter of Europe's clothmaking industry, and textile makers there considered it to be the finest in Europe."[49]

The earliest guilds of wool-weavers can be traced to the mid–twelfth century under Henry II (1133–1189). In mid-century there were several guilds in several English towns. The guild members would band together to promote and protect the trade in their craft, in this case wool production and a monopoly of wool trade.[50]

The wool industry started with these weaver's guilds in several of the larger towns. There were other guilds also, goldsmiths, and butchers, for example. The voluntary banding together of these craftsmen was considered revolutionary at the time, considering it was still in the midst of a strong feudal system. It was under Henry II that the guilds gained the sanction of the government. Later, in the fourteenth century, it became government policy to bring the guild system countrywide to bind the craftsmen together in organized bodies. This, of course, turned private associations into organs of the state and made government control of the industry possible. The wool cloth industry in England at this time was a local, not an export industry.

Regarding cloth, England was still a poor country at the time. Although English cloth was important for the manufacturing centers abroad, it was in the hands of the Hanse of London and Teutonic Hanse. There was no cloth for export from England; most her own finer varieties were satisfied by the Low Countries.[51]

In order to improve the prospects for cloth manufacturing at home, the government prohibited the export of wool and the import of cloth during the thirteenth and fourteenth centuries. Finally, in the fourteenth century, Edward III (1312–1377) allowed for the immigration of foreign cloth makers so the English weavers and dyers could learn the trade. Data show that about 20 years after the foreign craftsmen came to England, there were large quantities of cloth exported from the country. The weavers' guild was at first weakened by the immigration of the foreign craftsmen but recovered and again gained control of the trade in London. By the fifteenth century the cloth manufacturing industry became more specialized and split into recognized parts of the trade. It also created a class of merchants and dealers in the finished article. There was now a distinct class of dealers and traders, as distinguished from the makers of cloth. These dealers in cloth also dealt in other commodities, so they became a distinct merchant class.[52]

As the English cloth manufacturing industry grew, it changed the face of English trade and commercial activity. England had been exporting wool and importing cloth, but now turned it around to export cloth. Finally, under Elizabeth, the export of wool is banned. At this time the Society of Merchant Adventurers, an early trading company, is associated with cloth exports and gives England her commercial supremacy in that commodity.[53]

Chapter One. Discovery and Claims

The Merchant Adventurers were chartered in 1407 by Henry IV (1367–1413).[54] It was the first of the many trading companies, often called adventurers, which dealt in many commodities. The name in the title, adventurers, indicated that they were never tied to one industry or one commodity, but were open to all trading locations and commodities, more like a chartered company than a guild.[55] In a 1601 history of the Society the secretary wrote that "it consisteth of a great number of wealthy and well experimented merchants, dwelling in diverse great cities, maritime towns and other parts of the realm, to wit: London, York, Norwich, Exeter, Ipswich, Newcastle, Hull, etc. These men, linked and bound themselves together in company for the exercise of merchandise and seafare, trading in cloth, kersie and all other, as well English as foreign commodities vendible abroad."[56]

The wool trade which had been operating in England for hundreds of years, first on the manors, then within guilds in England, now had become a full-fledged industry generating a separate merchant class to trade English cloth for other European goods. The competition with the cloth industry of the continent was intense, but they managed to compete. Henry VII saw the Merchant Adventurers as an aid in nationalizing English commerce; he gave it his full support, and in 1505 gave it a new charter.[57] Later, under Elizabeth, the Flemish cloth industry was destroyed and the English cloth industry rose to prominence in the sixteenth and seventeenth centuries. The English trading supremacy had been born.[58]

Now it became more profitable to raise sheep rather than grow corn.[59] The growth of the wool industry in the fourteenth and fifteenth centuries led to the agrarian revolution of the sixteenth. The landowners who had enclosed the land for sheep became graziers and ultimately clothiers. They grew the sheep for the wool on their land, employed local people to turn it into cloth, and sold this to the drapers or dealers in London.[60] These London drapers and dealers then sold it to the merchants who did the overseas trading.

The Merchant Adventurers Company was regulated by the crown, with each member trading on his own account, with his own money, according to the rules established. In other words, they were independent businessmen risking their own money to further trade interests. The money made by these wealthy merchants often came as the result of their enclosure of the manor lands to raise sheep. As Tawney discusses in *The Agrarian Problem in the Sixteenth Century*, this was a time of increasing inequality, when landowners who enclosed the land for the sheep and wool industry became wealthy and influential, whereas the serfs who previously worked the land in feudal times became landless and formed a poor labor class, often unemployed. This latter problem would later be a factor in the *push* for colonies in America.[61]

The early trading companies, such as the Merchant Adventurers, were given royal charters which allowed them to trade as monopolies in certain areas; for the Merchant Adventurers, it was Northern Europe. This worked well where conditions were stable, i.e., between England and the Low Countries. It did not work well for other adventures, for example, trading with more distant lands such as the Far East. It was too risky for traders using all of their own money. The joint stock company evolved from the trading company to provide more capital for these riskier ventures and to limit the liability of each stockholder; it is the forerunner of the modern corporation.[62] In a joint stock company, capital was sought from a wide range of investors, most having nothing to do with the adventure at hand. They were passive investors who bought a certain number of shares, which was the limit of their liability. They would share in any profit of the company, but any losses would be limited to the capital they invested.

"Trade among English merchants continued to flourish from the mid–fifteenth century to the early sixteenth century." As it flourished, private trading companies became more commonplace.[63] The crown saw an opportunity to cover its increasing expenses and established royal charters for the companies to assure it received part of the profits.

One of the first joint stock companies in England was the Muscovy Company, established in 1553 by a group of merchants to promote trade with Russia.[64] Trade with the Low Countries and France, just across the Channel and North Sea, had been going on for centuries and was low risk. Clearly Anglo-Russian trade would require a much greater distance and much more risk. Thus, a joint stock company was established with a limited liability for individual traders, the risks, and potential profits, being spread across all the shareholders.

Another trading company that planned to push the trading boundary even farther was the East India Company. The potential for profit was high if trade with the Far East could be revived, but the risk was also high. The company was therefore formed as a joint stock company and was chartered by Elizabeth in 1600. The joint stock company model was gaining interest for investors who had earned their wealth from the English wool industry and long-distance trade, and desired to invest further in trade.

Joint stock companies were now well established for the purpose of opening trade with distant regions. They formed a cooperative arrangement with the crown in which both benefited from any profits that were generated. "The trading companies chartered in the period between 1550 and 1640 represented a technique whereby national government, at little or no cost to the exchequer, could act to promote the expansion of English commerce. In fact, so successful was the strategy that by the 1580s it was only trade with France, Scotland and Ireland that was not in the hands of a company."[65]

It would be a joint stock company that would first settle in North America in the early seventeenth century for the purpose of enhancing trade.

Sixteenth-Century North America

Just prior to and during the sixteenth century, there would be three major English attempts to claim land in North America. Also, during the sixteenth century the Spanish and French would make desultory explorations of North America.

Cabot's Claim on Newfoundland

Henry VII, the first Tudor king of England, can be seen as a transitional monarch connecting the end of the feudal era with early modern England. Early in his reign enclosures had gained momentum and tenants were being displaced and evicted. The crown under Henry, concerned about depopulation, took judicial steps to stem the evictions; it granted tenants enforceable title, copyhold. Enforceable copyhold converted villein tenure into peasant proprietorship, and helped create the yeoman farmer. As discussed in the Prologue, this was the beginning of the century that saw the rise of the yeoman farmer and the end of villeinage.

"The reign of Henry VII was a time of transitions and beginnings in English History. Particularly was it a time of economic beginnings. Henry favored the new commercial class, and repressed the old nobility. The interests of a strong central government went hand in hand with those of industry and commerce."[66] Henry was interested in fostering trade to add revenue and build up the industries of the country. He increased and regulated the income of the crown, and rendered its expenditures subject to control.[67] Trade increased early in the sixteenth century, which added to the coffers of the king as well as to a general prosperity. As a consequence of his support for trade, he supported navigation and the production of shipping for the business of trade. For the business of defense, he established a navy office, which later became the Admiralty. The navy, which was non-existent in 1485, started under Henry VII, and was strengthened by his son Henry VIII and later by Elizabeth.[68]

For all his interest in trade, in shipbuilding, and in enriching himself and his country, Henry seemed hesitant about new adventures, until "1493 when Columbus returned from his famous voyage. 'All men at the court of Henry VII,' says Sebastian Cabot, 'affirmed it to be a thing more divine than human to sail by the West to the East.' [John] Cabot approached the

King with a Petition for discovering new lands." Henry was finally convinced to do something.[69] By some accounts he was reluctant to support Cabot's voyage and agreed back him only if Henry could receive part of the profits and bear none of the cost.[70] Others would say, "Henry was willing to support anyone who might add to England's wealth by opening up new trade routes."[71] Both could be true, considering Henry's desire to enrich himself. The explorer, Cabot, took the initiative, not Henry. This would become a familiar pattern much later when other explorers and joint stock companies applied for charters to expand trade in other parts of the world. The petitioners would ask for financial support and royal charters which would provide legitimacy and royal backing.

Columbus was completing his second voyage, about to return home in June, when Henry granted letters of patent, on March 5, 1496, to John Cabot to explore in his name. Cabot and his sons, at their own cost, were to "discover and investigate whatsoever islands, countries, regions or provinces of heathens and infidels, in whatsoever part of the world placed, which before this time were unknown to all Christians." Then they "may conquer, occupy and possess as our vassals and governors lieutenants and deputies therein, acquiring for us [Henry] the dominion, title and jurisdiction of the same towns, castles, cities, islands and mainlands so discovered";[72] Note that Cabot was to be a vassal of the king, and the king was to own all the land discovered, "the dominion, title and jurisdiction." Any land that Cabot claimed was to be held of the king. This was in the spirit of William I, who claimed all the land of England at the Norman Conquest. Henry was also to get 20 percent of any profit.

Cabot and his sons departed May 2, 1497, and arrived, probably at Cape Bonavista, Newfoundland, although the exact location is unclear, on June 24. They arrived back in England on August 6. This was a very fast turnaround, but time enough to make the first English claim for land in North America. There was great rejoicing and a claim that "the king has claimed a great part of Asia without a stroke of the sword."[73]

The agreements between Columbus, and Isabella and Ferdinand, and between Cabot and Henry VII were remarkably similar. In both cases the new land was to be the possession of the crown, not the discoverer. Columbus would be viceroy over any land he found, and Cabot would "conquer, occupy and possess" the land as a vassal of Henry. Both sovereigns assumed a feudal hierarchy in which there would be vassals holding the land for the king. The Spanish designated the Indians as vassals, although we know they were more accurately described as serfs or villeins. Columbus and Cabot each would receive part of any profits from the land but no control over the land itself; they would own nothing. In Cabot's case, he would take all the financial risk of the voyage himself.

Chapter One. Discovery and Claims 41

The claim of dominion over all the conquered land by the crown is reminiscent of the claim of William I at the Conquest of 1066. William was able to make good on his claim through a feudal system in which he held tight control over his vassals by controlling which land they held as fiefs. He kept both his friends and enemies close on the relatively small island of England. The rigid feudal system of William's England was unable to be duplicated in the New World, primarily because of the distances involved. However, as we have seen in New Spain, a de facto nobility did develop. The encomenderos were given control, through an *encomienda*, over the indigenous people and the land they had been working before the Spanish Conquest. This put the encomenderos in a perfect position to establish their own estates, estancias, by buying land on their own *encomienda*. Over the century the *encomienda* evolved first, followed by the hacienda system; the pattern had been set. The encomenderos, and later the hacendados, strove to acquire private land as a means of wealth rather than only as government overseers of Indians. They were successful and acquired great estates. The encomenderos and hacendados were seen, correctly, by the workers as lords of the estates, to whom they owed deference. The system had become as rigidly hierarchical as had been the feudal system of William's England, and remained that way for centuries after the Spanish Conquest.

There would be a different outcome in North America.

Cabot made at least one more voyage in 1498, presumably for trade around Newfoundland, although by one account he traveled as far south as Cape Fear. Little is known of that voyage, and Cabot disappeared from history in 1499 or 1500. Surprisingly, neither Cabot nor the king took what seemed to be the next logical step, which would have been to colonize the area. The king seemed to lose interest and Cabot was gone. What did happen, though, is that a vigorous fishing industry started almost immediately, beginning with the English, who were quickly followed by Portuguese and French fisherman and traders. Cod fishing became an important industry, and fleets of ships would use Newfoundland as a place to stop, and perhaps dry their fish, before returning to Europe. They had no real interest in major land settlements although it was reported that there were 40 or 50 houses in Newfoundland in 1522, most likely fishing settlements.[74]

Spanish and French Explorations

The English did little or nothing over the next several decades to colonize North America, the land claimed by Cabot for England. "There was something ephemeral about all the efforts at exploration which followed immediately the success of Cabot.... The thought of colonization does not seem to have entered the calculations of anyone."⁷⁵ The robust fishing industry around Newfoundland was the most profitable enterprise. There were several voyages by others, Portuguese, Spanish, French, the latter two especially, that explored eastern North America and could have claimed land and settled prior to the first successful English settlement in 1607 at Jamestown.

Juan Ponce de Leon was part of Columbus's second voyage and later, in 1513, explored the Caribbean with his own party; he eventually became governor of Puerto Rico. He went on to land on the mainland, around St. Augustine, and named and sailed around Florida. He was given permission to colonize Florida but died in 1521 from an Indian arrow wound he had received there. A Spanish follow up to Ponce de Leon in Florida would have provided them with a foothold on the east coast mainland, but that was never pursued except in isolated settlements such as St. Augustine. After a number of bloody expeditions, including de Soto's, the Spanish finally did claim Florida, but made no significant colonization attempts except for St. Augustine.⁷⁶

Hernando de Soto was an explorer of Central America. He partnered with Francisco Pizarro in the early 1530s. He gained wealth as a conquistador with Pizarro but broke with him and returned to Spain in 1536. In 1538 He started an expedition to North America with 700 men. In 1539 he landed near Tampa and moved north looking for treasure. They went through the present-day regions of Georgia, the Carolinas, Tennessee, and then down to Alabama. The party was continually harassed by Indians, and lost most of what they did find, which included pearls, but not gold. They made their way west to Mississippi, Arkansas, and finally Louisiana. The expedition was decimated by Indians, and de Soto caught a fever, died and was buried in the Mississippi River. This expedition had one purpose: the search for gold, not land. Perhaps expecting North America to be like Mesoamerica and South America, with easy access to gold and an Indian population that was either sedentary or easily conquered, they were disabused of both concepts. Given the disastrous results of the expedition, the Spanish Crown probably saw no reason to pursue a difficult path to conquest and colonization, considering how relatively easy it had been in their earlier conquests in the south.⁷⁷ This was the last attempt by the Spanish to exploit the east coast above Florida. Although Ponce de Leon claimed Florida, neither he nor de Soto were interested in ownership and settlement as were Columbus, Cortes, and the later English settlers. The Spanish interest in North America remained in the southwest and west in North America.

Francis I (1494–1547) of France was 20 years old when he gained the throne. He was ambitious and was seen by Costain, writing in *The White and the Gold: The French Regime in Canada,* as being in a self-described competition with two other contemporaries, Henry VIII of England and Charles V (1500–1558) of Spain. The French, as with the English and Spanish, had done little regarding North America after Cabot's claim of the continent for England. Francis finally acted in 1523 choosing Tuscan Giovanni da Verrazzano to claim some of North America for France, not coincidentally, with the fanfare caused by the Cortes conquest of Tenochtitlan. Verrazzano sailed in 1524, reached the present Cape Fear, North Carolina, and then moved north along the coast, visiting New York Bay, Narragansett, and then traveled toward Newfoundland before returning to France. This was by far the most thorough examination of the North American coast yet, and should have provided France with an ideal opportunity to claim and colonize it, "and if the new King had been a ruler of determination and singleness of purpose the result would have been an earlier move to acquire this great new country."[78] At the time Francis became involved in a conflict with Charles V and was taken captive. This certainly would have constrained his ability to do anything about colonization. However, later events would show Francis would probably not have acted on colonization at that time anyway. Francis was eventually released from captivity, and about 10 years later had another chance to look toward North America.[79]

This time, in 1534, King Francis chose Jacques Cartier to lead the expedition to North America. The commission to Cartier hasn't been found but the king did issue an order in March of that year, "to discover certain islands and lands where it is said that a great quantity of gold, and other precious things are to be found." A second objective was also suggested: the route to Asia. These objectives say nothing about colonization.[80] Cartier's route took him directly to the Newfoundland area, *not* toward the lower latitude east coast which Verrazzano had explored and described to the king in terms which would have made it a very good land for colonization.[81] With the objective of "gold and other precious things" this route also belies the objective of colonization, but instead reveals an objective to search for riches, and for Asia. Cartier made three voyages to the area, discovering the St. Lawrence River and getting as far as present-day Montreal, but of course did not find a way to Asia. Early in the following century Samuel de Champlain did establish a colony in what became Canada, but the objective was primarily to extract the riches of the area in the form of fur, beaver pelt. Eventually France claimed vast territories in North America but never did follow up on extensive colonization. The population of all her territories was always a small fraction of what would become the English colonies of the east coast. This served her ill during her competition with the English for control of North America in the mid–eighteenth century.

Gilbert and Raleigh Claims

Through extraordinary good fortune the English claim on coastal North America, by way of Cabot's claim on Newfoundland, held up through most of the sixteenth century. Other major powers such as Spain and France had opportunities to claim and settle that land, but for various reasons chose not to. The opportunity for colonization of North America came back to England under Elizabeth I. "Fearing war with Catholic Spain and coveting Spanish wealth from Central and South America, Elizabeth saw the American coast as a potential haven for privateers such as Sir Francis Drake."[82]

Sir Humphrey Gilbert, a friend of Elizabeth before she was queen, was always interested in North America and a passage to the Indies. He worked for years in Ireland and was interested in exploiting land, which led to his interest in claiming land in America. He put together a plan and presented it to the queen, who granted him letters patent to discover and occupy in the next six years from June 11, 1578, "remote, heathen and barbarous lands, countreys [sic] not actually possessed of any Christian prince or people." He had exclusive rights within 600 miles of his claim. He could hold and convey land there in fee-simple, but would hold it in homage to the queen and was to pay her one-fifth of any gold or silver found.[83]

Gilbert started his first journey in 1578 to the east coast of North America, an area that Verrazzano had first sighted. For various reasons, including lack of organization, his first expedition failed and he returned home. His patent was running out, so he tried again in 1583. "The mishaps to his 1578 venture had the negative effect of turning him away from southeastern North America to New England and Newfoundland."[84] Perhaps his move to the north, to Newfoundland, was to more familiar territory, the center of a robust fishing industry started at the time of Cabot's first claim on Newfoundland. They landed in northern Newfoundland but then found their way down to the harbor at St. Johns. Edward Hayes, one of the expedition members, remembers there were 36 sails in the harbor, which at times during the summer months could reach 100 sails. These fishermen from various countries were at first skeptical of the newcomers, but were satisfied when Gilbert showed them his commission.

> His commission: by virtue whereof he took possession in the same harbour of St. Johns, and 200 leagues every way, invested the Queen's Majesty with the title and dignity thereof, had delivered unto him, after the custom of the English, a rod, and a turf of the same soil, entering possession also for him, his heirs and assigns for ever [sic]; and signified unto all men, that from that time forward, they should take the same land as territory appertaining to the Queen of England, and himself authorized under her majesty to possess and

enjoy it, and to ordain laws for the government thereof, agreeable so near as conveniently might be, unto the laws of England, under which all people coming thither hereafter, either to inhabit, or by way of traffic, should be subjected and governed.[85]

The principal legal justification for claiming the land, although not explicitly stated here, was the Roman principle of *res nullius*, "whereby unoccupied land remained the property of mankind, until being put to use."[86] Similar terms besides *res nullius*, things without owners, such as *terra nullius*, land without owners, and *vacuum domicilium*, devoid of inhabitants, were used.[87] All these were used as self-justification for going into lands that were supposedly empty. The Spanish also accepted the principle of *res nullius*, but didn't think it applied to their conquests in the Caribbean because of the Alexandrine bulls of 1493–94 (Pope Alexander VI), which divided the western hemisphere between Spain and Portugal at a line 370 leagues west of the Cape Verde Islands. They believed it gave them the land outright.[88] "But the land that was claimed still had to be physically occupied.... Technically in both Spanish and British America, the land was vested in the crown once its sovereignty had been proclaimed. It was then for the crown to arrange for its allocation, in order to attach settlers to the soil."[89] Gilbert did not follow up on this part of his patent.

Gilbert was to settle the land ("haue [have], hold, occupy and enjoy"). To encourage settlement, Gilbert was given "ful power to dispose thereof, and of euery [every] part thereof in fee simple or otherwise, according to the laws of England" as long as these settlers paid a fifth of the gold they found and paid homage to the queen. Fee simple ownership allowed the owner to do what he pleased with the land, use it how he pleased, and dispose of it how he pleased. It carries none of the obligation of service or rent to a higher lord, as many fiefs required in feudal times. This patent to allow Gilbert to dispose of the land as he saw fit in fee-simple was a more liberal grant than that of Henry VII to Cabot. Gilbert was to pay homage to the queen but did not have the burden of vassalage, as did Cabot. Clearly England was beyond the feudal era, and the queen was more interested in planting a colony on land claimed by England than acquiring vassals. Ultimately, as sovereign, the queen claimed possession of all the land, as she claimed all the land in England. This land was now part of England.[90]

Gilbert himself did not plan to stay and settle, and neither did the fishermen who were using Newfoundland to dress and dry their fish before returning to their home countries. Gilbert took advantage of their situation and his authorization to dispose of the land by granting parcels of land in St. Johns and nearby to these fishermen in fee-farm tenure.

Fee-farm is "a species of tenure, where land is held of another in perpetuity at a yearly rent without fealty, homage, or other services." In other words, Gilbert would rent the land to the fishermen so they could dress and dry their fish on land they had exclusive right to under the rental agreement. Previously they had done this without a fee, but they seemed to welcome this anyway, because now they were guaranteed access to land, whereas before they were often shut out by other fishermen who had arrived earlier. It is unclear if this was enforceable, because neither Gilbert nor the fishermen planned to stay and colonize. Gilbert died on the voyage home when his ship capsized in a storm.[91]

Newfoundland was the oldest continuous English colony in North America. It was the first in which land had been granted to a person, Gilbert. Later it was considered by Lord Baltimore for settlement when he was granted land in North America; he abandoned it for land in a more agreeable climate along the mid–Atlantic coast. Thus, weather might be a clue as to why Newfoundland was not a "breakout" colony, one that thrived, grew, and eventually spread to other parts of America.

Sir Walter Raleigh (Ralegh) was a half-brother of Sir Humphrey Gilbert and had the same zeal for adventure in America. Gilbert's death prompted Raleigh to have Gilbert's patent reissued to him, but excluding Newfoundland. The charter issued by Elizabeth on March 25, 1584, is almost identical with the one issued to Gilbert, including the aspect of claiming lands and holding them in fee simple. The exclusion of Newfoundland, and the intent to settle in the southeast coast, in "Virginia," meshed with the exhortations of Richard Hakluyt in the *Discourse of Western Planting*. Hakluyt was pushing English colonization on the mainland of North America.[92]

The story of Sir Walter Raleigh and the "Lost Colony" is a familiar one to many people; it played out over the next several years in several voyages. In the first attempt to explore the North American southeast coast, in April 1584, he sent out two small ships with about 75 soldiers and sailors aboard. They landed at or near the Outer Banks in present-day North Carolina, and made friendly contact with the Indians. There is no record of settlements on this voyage. Staying only a short time, the ships left in August with two prominent Indians: Wanchese, a Roanoke, and Manteo, a Croatoan, who both returned willingly to England so they could learn of the English "otherworldly spirit or power." They learned English and were presented at court amid the fanfare of the positive results reported on the voyage. This is the time Hakluyt pushed his *Discourse* to the queen.[93]

Raleigh now had the support of both the crown and Parliament. He was knighted in January 1585, and "he assumed a title, Lord and Governor of Virginia that revealed a new name for the Queen's colony." In

Chapter One. Discovery and Claims   47

April 1585 he sent out seven ships with about 600 colonists, all men, but including about half soldiers and others who were tradesmen such as carpenters, smiths, cooks, and at least one minister. They reached the Outer Banks about 80 miles from Roanoke Island in June, where they lost a ship carrying supplies, thus jeopardizing the expedition. They explored the area in July, including the mainland, but were dependent on the Indians for food and guidance. Some of the Indians were friendly, but others were wary and unfriendly with the invaders. This was exemplified by the behavior of Wanchese and Manteo, who were included in the mission. Wanchese fled back to his native people and warned them the English could not be trusted. Manteo remained with the English, concentrating on his English skills. Sir Richard Grenville, leader of the expedition and cousin of Raleigh, returned to England later that summer, leaving 108 men behind under Ralph Lane. They were expecting a relief mission, but it did not come. In June of 1586 disaster struck again in the form of a June hurricane, and a relief ship was lost; Lane and his men returned to England. Grenville returned to Roanoke in July with six ships and 200 colonists. They remained only a few weeks, and for some unknown reason, perhaps trouble with the Indians, returned to England. Grenville left 15 soldiers at Roanoke with provisions for a year. Up to this time all of Raleigh's efforts at colonization ended in one sort of disaster or another. But the worst was yet to come.[94]

He made one last attempt. On May 8, 1587, he sent a colonizing expedition, led by the artist Thomas White, to settle on the Chesapeake Bay, rather than Roanoke Island, because the Indians were friendlier. They arrived on July 22 but first stopped at Roanoke to check on the 15 soldiers left there the previous year. They did not find them alive, but "we found the bones of one of those fifteen, which the Savages had slain long before." Continuing the bizarre series of events, the colonists were not allowed to reboard the ships by the captain so they could move to the Chesapeake Bay site, so they remained on Roanoke Island. The origin of the dispute between White and the ship captain, Simon Fernandes, is murky, but the result was that the colonists remained on Roanoke, contrary to the directions of Raleigh. White returned with Fernandes, leaving on August 27, to brief Raleigh on the events. Events were moving rapidly across the Atlantic also, including hostilities with Spain and the Spanish Armada. Just months before the famous battle, Raleigh tried to send a two-ship relief mission, which was unable to get through because of an encounter with French naval forces, and was sent back to England. White himself was not able to mount a relief mission until 1590. He landed on Roanoke on August 18, but found the camp was abandoned. "The Lost Colonists, as they came to be known, were never found."[95]

Turn of the Seventeenth Century

More than 100 years after John Cabot had claimed North America for England, in the form of Newfoundland, the island nation still did not have a thriving, robust colony on the mainland. A number of factors contributed to that, including a pair of monarchs, Henry VII and Henry VIII, who showed little interest in expanding the empire, or felt an inability to do so considering the strength of their European neighbors, especially Spain. Elizabeth, on the other hand, saw an opportunity to use an outpost on the mainland as a way to harass Spanish ships and settlements by using the navy that her grandfather and father had built. She supported privateering by English ships as, for example, those of Sir Francis Drake. She must have been frustrated when all the efforts of Gilbert and Raleigh came to naught, except for the small claims Gilbert made on Newfoundland. One could hardly harass the Spanish American empire from Newfoundland. "Further attempts at New World settlement in Elizabethan England were heavy proscribed because of the costs and needs associated with the Anglo-Spanish War of 1585 to 1604."[96]

As the sixteenth century closed, England faced a number of challenges that needed to be addressed. These included the economy, trade, the war with Spain and the outsize impact of Spain on overseas territories, the reluctance of an indebted crown to take state action in colonization, and a concern about the legitimacy of claiming land overseas.

Economically the country was pressed by two factors: a population with labor surpluses and a shortage of resources.

> At the beginning of the 17th century, England and Wales contained more than four million people. The population had nearly doubled over the previous century and continued to grow for another 50 years.... Population increase created severe social and economic problems, not the least of which was a long-term price inflation. English society was predominately rural, with as much as 85 percent of its people living on the land.... Only London could be ranked with the great continental cities. Its growth had outstripped even the doubling of the general population. By the beginning of the 17th century, it contained more than a quarter of a million people ... most of them poor migrants who flocked to the capital in search of work or charity.[97]

The agrarian revolution of the sixteenth century, especially the enclosure movement that privatized much English land and caused the eviction of many of the lower classes, had an impact. "The number of Midland farmers cut adrift now increased as the enclosures ... continued.... The half-century after 1590 was a time of profound, unprecedented, and often frightening social ferment for the people of England. During these years nearly every member of the lower orders in the countryside and in the towns knew deprivation and genuinely feared insecurity...."[98] Many of those evicted from the rural areas fled to the cities, especially London, trying to find work as laborers. Population had also increased and wages were falling. "Enclosure, the growth of wage labor, and declining wages led to what officials considered an alarming epidemic of vagrancy."[99] These were conditions that Richard Hakluyt presented to Elizabeth a few years prior as reasons for colonizing America, to rid England of this increasing, unemployed, vagrant class of laborers.

Population pressures were not the only challenges the country was facing. Raw materials for the navy and shipbuilding industry the Tudors had built were becoming scarce. The growing population and increased agriculture meant that more resources were needed. The forests were being denuded as wood was used for fuel and housing construction. In the crucial shipbuilding industry, it was for masts, pitch, tar, and resin. Potash was used for the manufacture of woolens, an important industry at the time. The clear answer to these needs was to look to the colonies to supply these industries with the commodities they needed.[100] Nevertheless, Elizabeth had sponsored two unsuccessful attempts at colonization in America and did not seem inclined to take another step in that direction.

Social turmoil alone was not in itself thought to be a reason to attempt another project for an overseas empire; it did not tell the whole story. Because of enclosure and the agrarian revolution, inequality was increasing, with a prosperous merchant class at the top. Trade was flourishing, having increased with trading companies established earlier in the century. Trade was the major economic engine of England by the start of the seventeenth century. "London was the centre of government, of overseas trade and finance, and of fashion, taste, and culture. It was ruled by a merchant oligarchy, whose wealth increased tremendously over the course of the century as international trade expanded."[101]

At the time this merchant oligarchy saw no good reason to change, no reason to expand trade into new areas. "For their part, merchants remained reasonably satisfied even up to the closing decades of Elizabeth's reign, that they had sufficient access to the commodities of Asia, Africa, and America either through established European trading networks or through raids on Spanish shipping."[102]

This began to change late in the sixteenth century when members of Queen Elizabeth's government began to warn of the dangers from Spain that the Spanish had gained by their New World conquests. At first this did not sway the merchants, who still eschewed new, potentially costly, overseas adventures. By the early seventeenth century, when privateering decreased, partly because of the end of the war with Spain, and overseas trading networks were disrupted, also because of the war, they started to change their collective minds. These merchants then started an expansion in trading companies and trade that took them to the Levant, Africa, Russia, and India. One of these companies was the English East India Company chartered by Elizabeth in 1600. Another company that would result would be the one charged with settling a plantation in Virginia.[103]

Despite this expansion in trade, the monarchy was still reluctant to insert the crown into a possible risky colonial adventure.

> Elizabeth and the early Stuarts had few imperial aspirations, did little to help overseas adventurers and trading companies beyond the formal issuing of a colonial charter, and were hesitant to get involved even when such involvement appeared to be necessary and justified. Because of its laissez-faire approach to commercial matters, because activities in the New World before 1640 could yield little economic dividend and political power, and because the impoverished crown was unwilling to become involved in risky, speculative trading ventures, the monarchy deliberately refused to take responsibility for colonial affairs and relegated the mercantile "sea empire" to private commercial interests.[104]

According to Appleby, in *War, Politics, and Colonization, 1558–1625*, the cause of the lack of movement during the 100 years after Cabot "was the structural weakness in English enterprise which repeatedly influenced its character and conduct during this period. Ultimately this weakness stemmed from the lack of sustained support for overseas expansion. As a result, the burden of colonial and commercial development was left in the hands of private adventurers whose concern for immediate gain was detrimental to the long-term planning needed to promote colonization."[105] The crown, especially in the latter half of the sixteenth century under Elizabeth, was more interested in privateering than in colonization. Despite entreaties from persons such as Gilbert, Raleigh, Hakluyt, and others, and a few letters of patent, there was no royal effort to claim foreign land in America. Privateering, however, was a lucrative business and it became an interest of many merchants in the trading class. "The lure of profit attracted interest from a broad range of English society. Merchants and shipowners dominated the business, but sections of the gentry and nobility were also involved.... Behind such prominent promoters were hundreds of small investors such as butchers, innkeepers, shipwrights, and farmers" all eager for profits from the war with Spain.[106] Privateering, a business of the public and private sector, also was a boon to the shipbuilding industry. This partnership brought the merchants and the crown closer, and essentially made the private sector a major part of English foreign policy. With the decline of trade in cloth markets in the latter half of the century, the merchants were looking to open new markets, especially with the new ships that were available. Since Elizabeth no longer had an interest in foreign adventures, the merchant traders now took the lead to search for new markets.

At the end of the century the Dutch were waging a war of independence from Spain. In a bid to gain an advantage over Spain they sent trading ships to the Spice Islands. After a spectacularly successful Dutch trading voyage in July 1599, the English merchants took notice and revived their interest in the Far East. About 60 of them met within the following two months.

> Before long, more than one hundred investors had pledged around £30,000 in support of the proposed East India venture. Even though the English economy was in the doldrums, this was the largest sum ever invested in a single English expedition, and it showed not only the enthusiasm for the venture but also the sheer quantity of liquid capital available for high-risk investment, which largely came from the spoils of war. More than a quarter of the capital came from merchants who had made their fortune from privateering, when profits soared as high as £200,000 per year.[107]

They still needed letters of patent from the queen. She signed them, and in 1600 the East India Company was in business.

India was not the only place of interest for the East India Company. They took interest in George Waymouth (Weymouth), a young adventurer who had an interest in America. He got an audience with the new King, James I (1566–1625), but did not receive his support for an expedition. He then petitioned the East India Company for sponsorship of an expedition to look for the Northwest Passage. Surprisingly they listened to him, but they drove a hard bargain, promising to pay only if he was successful. He wasn't. The company considered backing him again but declined. The persistent Waymouth, however, found other investors and sailed for an expedition to America in March 1605. He and his crew met with the Abenaki people of Maine, apparently in a friendly manner, when he made a planned, but inexplicable, move to capture and kidnap five of the Indians to take them back to England. Once back in England, the Indians were treated well and were guests in the homes of Fernando Gorges and Sir John Popham, both ardent advocates of colonization in America. This interaction with the Indians may have solidified Popham's interest in colonization. It coincided with his fear of "the scourge of poverty and idleness in England" at the time. Perhaps a new colony could ameliorate this problem. "Popham had the funds to support his mission. He pledged the fantastic sum of five hundred pounds per year for a period of five years to the American venture, the largest commitment in England by a single individual to such an enterprise at that time." He conferred with other merchants, and he developed a proposal, hoping this would also be a profit-making venture. The proposal was presented to James I, who accepted it in 1606 and issued the First Charter of Virginia.[108]

As a result of the war with Spain in the 1580s and 1590s, England gained vast experience in the Atlantic, including the West Indies and the American coast. She was in a better position at that time to undertake colonization than at any time in the previous 50 years. Yet Elizabeth demurred in committing royal treasure or prestige to any such effort. The merchants though, many of whom had grown wealthy during the war, were still interested in expanding the trade empire. "Even before the war was over the privateering interest in London was transforming itself into a small but powerful group in favor of overseas trade and colonial settlement." These private adventurers, lacking any state support, were interested in opening new trade venues. Any colonization that came with the new territory would be secondary to the trade; they were interested in quick profits rather than long-term settlement. This priority would have a negative impact, especially in Virginia, the home of the first venture.[109] Francis Bacon observed this around 1620 when he said in his essay on plantations that "planting of countries is like planting of Woods; for you must make account to lose almost twenty years' profit, and expect your recompense in the end: for the principal thing that hath been the destruction of most plantations, has been the base and hasty drawing of profit in the first years. It is true, speedy profit is not to be neglected, as far as may stand with the good of the plantation, but no farther."[110] He acknowledged the need for profit; they were trading companies. But he suggested that long-term settlement had to be more important than short-term profit. The Virginia venture was to suffer from this focus on short-term profits at the expense of long-term settlement.

Another concern of the crown was the legitimacy of claiming land in distant places. All the patents and charters recognized land that had been claimed by other countries; there was always a phrase that prohibited occupation if the land was held by another "Christian Prince." In this regard they recognized the territory of New Spain, for example, and would not claim any part of it. But what if it was not held by another Christian prince? What if it appeared empty? In this case they appealed to Roman law, for by such "natural and canon law, unoccupied and uncultivated territories (*res nullius*) become the possession of the first person to discover them and put them to productive use, usually through cultivation."[111] Although it "appeared empty" what was one to make of the native population, the Indians, who did inhabit the land? "Unlike the Spanish, the English were … predominantly concerned with securing rights not over people but over lands."[112] If a docile labor force was available that would be fine, but if it was not, the Indians could be moved aside. "The English were always more interested in the possession and exploitation of land than the subjugation and conversion of native people." The early justification for taking possession was that dominion over the earth was achieved by settlement and cultivation, and the Indians, in their view, did not meet those criteria, hence the "land's vacancy was frequently used as the chief rationale for establishing lawful possession (*dominium*)."[113]

Another model they used to convince themselves of the propriety of their move to colonize America was that of the colonization of Ireland. Under Elizabeth there were serious efforts in the latter half of the sixteenth century to colonize Ireland. At first, they had two concerns. One was to establish legal title to the land, and the second was how the indigenous population would be removed. They concluded quickly that they had the right to the land by right of conquest. Secondly, they satisfied themselves that the Irish were pagans, and subsequently that they were barbarians. Thus, their long-term purpose was to convert the pagans to Christianity, and that "the Irish should be made subservient to the colonizing English so that through subjection they could come to appreciate civility."[114] "Many of the conclusions at which they were arriving about the Irish had already been reached by the Spaniards with respect to the Indians.... It can be established that many of the English associated with colonization were familiar with Spanish thinking, and it is quite probable that their attitudes and actions were influenced by Spanish precedents.... Less hesitantly and despite their hatred of the Spaniards, other Englishmen occasionally cited Spanish actions to justify their own extreme measures in Ireland."[115] No real effort was made to reform the Irish, "they were dismissed as a 'wicked and faythles peopoll' and put to the sword." The same justification was repeated in the treatment of the Indians in the New World. "It was argued that the Indians were an unsettled people who did not make proper use of their land and could thus be justly deprived of it by the more enterprising English."[116]

Later in the century John Locke (1632–1704) would spend a great deal of effort justifying the English possession of land in the New World. One of his claims was that it was the mingling of labor with the land that gives a person possession of that land; labor produces property.[117] He acknowledged some Indian rights and thought there was enough land for all, but his emphasis on English labor justifying property ownership won the day. His essays, *Two Treatises of Government*, were well received and were used to *ex post facto* justify the English land grab of North America, but they came several decades after settlement had occurred. The early justification was, and continued to be, *res nullius*.

Aside from an early lack of interest by the crown, some of the later attempts at colonization in the sixteenth century were plagued by poor organization, bad decisions, hostile natives, and even unforeseen circumstances such as war and hurricanes. For a multitude of reasons, England was about a century behind Spain in exploiting the New World. By the opening of the seventeenth century a group of traders and investors, profiting from the war with Spain, were interested in expanding trade into areas not yet exploited. It started with the East India Company in 1600, but then a group was interested in trade in North America, an area that previously had hosted a colony which had failed, but now seemed ripe for a new attempt. James I was still reluctant for the crown to be involved, but did charter a large area, known as Virginia, on the east coast of North America, to one company.

CHAPTER TWO

Land in English Colonial America: The Settlement

In the sixteenth century the stable, but stagnant, feudal age was over and nation states were moving toward more interaction with each other. There was more contact with distant nations and more need for economic growth. "One idea in particular, formulated for the first time in Europe around 1600, was to allow the continent to gain a position of spectacular global dominance: the medieval acceptance of human economic life as cyclical and stable was rejected in favor of the idea of continuing economic growth based on exploitation. This was to prove the generator of European wealth, built on relentless imperial and industrial expansion."[1] As feudalism was waning and the nation states were rising in the sixteenth century, there was a need for leaders of these states to project power. This was done through military power, with great armies which had to be financed. Taxes were raised, but there was a limit to what the population could bear, and going beyond the limit could lead to rebellion. New income was needed to increase the wealth of a nation so as to maintain a strong military presence in the world. Countries with large and strong navies saw the obvious answer.

"The solution to this dilemma was simple, argued Thomas Mun, director of the London East India Company: 'The ordinary means therefore to increase our wealth and treasure is by Forraign Trade, wherin wee must ever observe this rule; to sell more to strangers yearly than wee consume of theirs in value.' In other words, only a trade surplus could guarantee that taxes and tariffs would enrich the state."[2] This was the theory of mercantilism: sell more than you buy because trade was a zero-sum game, so you *had* to sell more than you bought to gain wealth. This was one of the reasons for the flourishing trading companies, usually organized as joint stock companies. Trading with other sovereign countries that were operating on the same positive balance of trade principle was not easy. It would be much better to be able to control the other end of the trade pipeline.

If a trading company could establish a colony in a distant land, it could have exclusive trading rights with that colony. This was the intent of the East India Company chartered by Elizabeth in 1600 for trade with the Far East. In this mercantile system the company trade with the colony was to be exclusive to England, and the trade balance for England was always to be positive; this they saw as the way to build national wealth. Raw materials were to be extracted from the colony, and goods manufactured in England were to be exported to the colony.[3] The first English colonization of America started as a trading venture by a joint stock company in 1607, a commercial trading company venture. This was to set a pattern for the next century and a quarter as the English colonies were established on the east coast of North America. "Not one of the thirteen original colonies was settled by the Crown. As a result, all of their governments originally were either corporate or proprietary in nature."[4] A trading company, organized as a joint stock company, was interested in trading in order to make money for the stockholders; however, it was not always interested in the projects needed for long-term occupation.

James I and the Virginia Company

Interest in planting in America had been around for decades, even before Richard Hakluyt's *Discourse of Western Planting* was presented to Elizabeth, and since the expeditions of Gilbert and Raleigh. The 19-year war with Spain (1585–1604) precluded any attempts in planting during the war, and concerns about Spain's intentions for North America even after the war caused hesitation. After the peace settlement of 1604 the time had come for another attempt to establish a trading company colony in North America. There were differing opinions on whether the plantation should be done by private parties, independent of the crown, or whether it was better done by a public-private partnership. The latter was proposed because conversion of the heathen was still considered an important objective. Although debated in Parliament, the idea of a public colonization effort did not materialize; it would be left to a private company to establish the colony in North America.[5]

George Waymouth's 1605 voyage to America rekindled interest in those previously interested in colonization, especially Sir John Popham and Sir Ferdinando Gorges, two who had hosted the Indians returned to England by Waymouth. Popham and Gorges were a prominent part of a group formed to petition the king for a charter to plant a colony in Virginia. Most of the group were experienced at sea and had engaged in the fight against Spain. "The first draft for the proposed first Virginia charter, annexed to the petition for the same, was probably drawn by Sir John Popham."[6] The individuals who had signed the petition were the ones named by James I in the charter he issued.

The Stuart James succeeded the Tudor Elizabeth on her death in 1603; he became James I of England; he was already king of Scotland as James VI. Although the crown was in debt, he had a number of potential investors interested in establishing a plantation in Virginia, so he accepted the proposed charter for Virginia.[7] In 1606 he chartered a joint stock company called the Virginia Company. The charter was divided between two companies, sometimes called the Virginia Company of London or London Company, and the Virginia Company of Plymouth or Plymouth Company. The London Company was called the first colony and the Plymouth Company was called the second colony. The first colony was to stretch from 34 degrees latitude to 41 degrees latitude or roughly from the present-day North Carolina to Long Island. The second colony was to start at 38 degrees latitude and go up to forty-five degrees latitude, roughly from Chesapeake Bay to Maine. The area of overlap between these companies could be used by either company as long as any settlements were not within 100 miles of one another. The grant for each was 50 miles north and south along the coast from the plantation, and was to extend 100 miles inland.[8]

> About 2,000,000 square miles of land were claimed by the crown, of which only 20,000 square miles were granted (and upon conditions) to both colonies. The whole of this Virginia, including the said very limited grants to the two colonies, was placed under the management of one and the same Royal Council of Virginia; "all of whom were appointed by the King; and to be increased, altered or changed at the King's pleasure and this Council nominated the councellors of the colonies," who were to govern according to such laws, ordinances, and instructions as should be given by the king.[9]

As Brown notes in *The First Republic in America*, "the document was a royal charter containing 'not one ray of popular rights,' although it granted sundry privileges to the companies. They could search for mines; coin money; invite and carry over adventurers; repel intruders. Duties payable by certain persons for trading to the colonies were to the use of the colonies for twenty-one years, then to the king."[10] They could keep any gold or silver found, except for one-fifth, which was to go to the crown. In other words, the companies would have a lot of power as to how they exploited the land in Virginia.

After describing the rights and privileges, and defining governing councils, in both England and the colonies, near the end the charter addressed land tenure. The land was to be held of the king, who was the ultimate owner.

> And finally, we do for Us our Heirs, and Successors, GRANT and agree, to and with the said Sir Thomas Gates, Sir George Somers, Richard Hackluit, Edward-Maria Wingfield and all others of the said first colony, that We, our Heirs and Successors, upon petition in that Behalf to be made, shall, by Letters Patent under the Great Seal of England, GIVE and GRANT, unto such Persons, their Heirs and Assigns, as the Council of that Colony, as is aforesaid, To BE HOLDEN Of Us, our heirs and Successors, as of our Manor at East-Greenwich, in the County of Kent, in free and common Socage only, and not in Capite.[11]

"The 'Manor at East-Greenwich' refers to the residence of King James I at the royal palace of Greenwich and was used as a descriptive term in many grants to indicate that the land in America was also considered a part of the demesne of the King. The land was not 'in fee simple' with absolute ownership ... but it was granted 'in free and common socage' with the holder a tenant of the King with obligations of fealty and of payment of a quitrent."[12] Socage was a form of land tenure "in which the tenant lived on his lord's land and in return rendered to the lord a certain agricultural service or money rent."[13] Thus the Virginia Company held the land of the king and was to return one-fifth of any gold or silver found and one-fifteenth of any copper. Although there was a great deal of freedom for the company regarding land use, the king retained the right of ownership of all the land in North America, as had been the history in England since the Norman Conquest. "The underlying theory of English land law was that the King was the ultimate and paramount owner of all the soil in the *terra regis* and that all other individuals held their lands from him, either directly [in capite], or indirectly through a chain of tenurial relationships. When the King made direct grants of lands lying outside the physical boundaries of the realm of England, as in Ireland or America, the land was treated as belonging constructively to one of the existing royal manors [East-Greenwich] or other properties."[14] In that regard this patent was different from those issued by Elizabeth in the sixteenth century to Gilbert and Raleigh. "The first royal grants of vacant lands in the New World were made during the critical period when the Stuarts were struggling to re-establish the waning feudal powers of the Crown. It was but natural that patents were in feudal form, the land to be held in free and common socage."[15] James I, an advocate of royal absolutism, therefore required the land to be held of the king through the Manor at East-Greenwich in free and common socage. The king retained the rights of government of this land through a council which he established for this purpose. Elizabeth, on the other hand, was not as concerned about royal prerogatives, especially with her friends. In her patents to Gilbert and Raleigh "the Crown conferred proprietorship of land with the right to grant it out in fee simple at will."[16] They included governmental rights also, i.e., jurisdiction, so did not require crown oversight. They were non-tenurial grants with homage required but not socage. Thus, regarding land tenure, James was reverting to earlier royal prerogatives in claiming the land.

"Although the charter emphasizes the government of the plantation, the Virginia Company was purely a commercial enterprise conducted by a private concern."[17] It is important to recognize the role the merchants played in the founding, especially the management style they brought from the merchant community.[18] The adventure to America, although in pursuit of both national interest and commercial interests, would be started as a commercial enterprise. The first settlement by the Virginia Company of London was to be a small colony on the James River in southern Virginia named Jamestown.

First Settlement Steps—Virginia

The patterns of settlement and governance in the New World would be predicated on what the merchants knew of the Old World in England. "In their ignorance European statesmen of the seventeenth and eighteenth centuries visualized the agrarian conditions of young and distant colonies in terms of old established and densely populated communities, drafted their regulations accordingly, and expected their enforcement."[19]

This vision would cause trouble for the Virginia colony in the first decade of settlement.

Although feudalism was dying, there was still not a culture of private land ownership in England. There was still an expectation that the aristocracy could set the rules and have willing tenants on land that they owned, and that they could expect landless laborers willing to accept the strict rules of the joint stock companies as they sought to establish trading posts in foreign lands. Thus, the Virginia Company would attempt a trading post in Virginia that was focused on a quick profit and had little regard for the welfare of the colonists, who would be given little to no control of their own circumstances. This can only be explained by the fact that they saw the New World through the eyes of the old.

The plantation at Jamestown was an experiment in a commercial venture. The Virginia Company of London landed 104 settlers, all men and boys, in Jamestown in May 1607 to establish this plantation. "It would be difficult to imagine a set of men less fitted to build a colony and found a nation than were those who settled at Jamestown in 1607. Among them were but twelve laborers, a few carpenters, a blacksmith, a mason, a barber, and a tailor, while more than fifty were 'gentlemen,' that is, men without an occupation, idle, shiftless men who had joined the enterprise without realizing that years of labor were essential to success."[20] The makeup of this contingent may have been because this was considered an experiment. It was an experiment in part to engage in trade if possible, and to see if there was a route to the South Sea and the Indies. Clearly it was meant only as a first step in a commercial trading venture; one cannot establish a permanent trading colony with an all-male settlement. The large number of gentlemen compared to skilled craftsmen is puzzling, especially since many were unfamiliar with the wilderness and contributed little or nothing to the building of the plantation.

> The settlers were given some very explicit instructions in a letter of guidance, in which the first indication of the real motive of the undertaking is found. The orders laid down were to "make choice" of the river "which bendeth most toward the North-West, for that way you shall soonest find the other sea," while the choice of a healthy location, wise intercourse with the natives, and the fortification and preparation of a single settlement were emphasized. The chief objects, however, were to plant in a place which should be fitted "to receive the trade of all the countries about," to discover minerals, and to find the passage to the western sea.[21]

A river that "bendeth most toward the Northwest" was their best guess for a route to the South Sea, and the chief objects of trade and mineral discoveries were clearly primary objectives. It was also clear in this guidance that the company was to come first. "It were necessary that all your carpenters and other such like workmen about building do first build your store house and those other rooms of publick and necessary use before any house be set up for any private persons, yet let them all work together first for the company and then for private men."[22]

Jamestown was the first English colony in North America to survive and grow, although it barely survived the first three years. The colonists were plagued by many problems, including disease, lack of supplies, bad weather, unfamiliarity with coping with the wilderness, and lack of willingness for industrious labor by many of the early gentlemen settlers. They had problems of Indian hostility, although many of those were of their own making because of how they mistreated them. Also, "among the factors that contributed to the lack of zeal among the settlers was the absence of private ownership of land."[23]

Jamestown was started as a trading post by a joint stock company that supplied all the capital for the adventure; the crown did not contribute financing. The crown, however, was intensely involved in both the government and decisions on land use. "Under this charter the company did not receive full ownership rights in the land.... The 1606 Virginia charter was strictly a royal charter, the government, as well as land distribution, was subject directly to royal control."[24] This was true even though the company had economic control over the colony and over the land. Under the first Virginia charter, land was assigned by the king to those approved by the council.[25] "From the scant records that survive, it is evident that promises of land were made to individuals who were willing to hazard the dangers of the new country." The land, however, did not belong to that person; instead, it was the property of the company, held of the king's manor at East Greenwich.[26] Under the first charter, land was not granted to individuals; it was held by the company and not subdivided to individuals.[27]

> The absence of private property is the most striking feature, perhaps, of this colony. Under the charter the soil of Virginia was given by the crown to the Virginia Company and held by the company at its own disposal. Houses were built upon the soil, and garden-plots were assigned to colonists, but there was nothing of permanence in the possession so given, and private property in land was thus absent. The labor of the colonists was pledged to the company for a term of years, being at the disposal of the company's governor in return for maintenance and future dividends.[28]

"In the absence of private title to land in the early years of the Virginia colony, the company relied upon a corporate form of management with the pooling of community effort to clear the land, construct buildings, develop agriculture, and engage in trade with the Indians.... Most of the settlers were more in a position of contract laborers performing services for the company."[29]

The occupation of houses owned by the company, on company land, the company holding the land on the king's demesne, and the company holding land in socage to the king, all suggest a parallel with an estate or manor of feudal England. James I had absolutist ambitions, so his land grant to the company was a reminder of feudal grants. Of course, the planters occupying the houses at Jamestown were not serfs but investors of the company. And the socage was free and common, which meant nothing was due the king except a fraction of any gold or silver found and a quit-rent. So, the analogy remains superficial. Nevertheless, private land ownership did not exist in early Virginia; people were living in houses that did not belong to them, and on land over which they had no rights. The early settlement resembled the Old World rather than the New World which held so much promise because of the vast expanses of land.

In retrospect, it is hard to understand how the company could expect to sustain this model of dependent tenants on company land producing goods for the mother country when the only hope of payoff was a future unknown dividend. This is especially true when that tenant could see free land very close by. The model was anachronistic and evoked more the recently passed feudal model than the now emerging market economy. In any case, by 1609 that model was to be updated with a new charter.

New Charter

The colony, experimental trading post would be a more accurate description, got off to a bad start. They were optimistic about quick riches and were ill prepared, not planting a crop the first summer. Disease had reduced the original 105 persons to less than 50 through summer. They would not have survived without the multiple infusions of supplies and new settlers in the following three years. The second supply, in late 1608, comprised 70 settlers, including some workman "sent over to produce glass, pitch, soap ashes, and other items profitable in England."[30] This was the company's attempt to produce items for profitable trade, the motivation behind the endeavor. "The winter of 1609–10 has been described through the years as the 'starving time,' seemingly, an accurate description. It saw the population shrink from 500 to about sixty as a result of disease, sickness, Indian arrows, and malnutrition."[31]

By 1609 it was clear that the company approach to establishing a trading post for quick profit was not working. Apparently both the crown and the company agreed that something different had to be tried. The company requested a new charter, and the second charter of Virginia was issued in 1609. There was a clear recognition that land was now the driving factor. Instead of a trading colony within a 100-mile square on the coast, the new charter gave title to "'all that space and circuit of land' lying 200 miles north and 200 miles south of Point Comfort from sea coast 'up into the land, throughout from sea to sea, west, and northwest' plus islands within 100 miles of the coast."[32] This was not the 10,000 square miles of the original grant, but over a million square miles. They were also seeking to expand the business venture, so there were about 650 names listed in this second charter.[33]

The charter did take away some rights, however; for example, martial law was now allowed, and the colony was under harsh, almost military rule, from 1611 to 1618. However, there were significant changes in the governance and land distribution authorities. Regarding governance, the power was shifted, "and the major change in control was the transfer of authority over the colony from the crown to the company with the powers of government in the hands of the treasurer and Council."[34] Some land was distributed in large blocks around 1616, but the most significant distribution was to follow the 1618 reforms; the granting of headrights, free land, of 50 acres to individual persons. Land distribution in Virginia will be covered in the next chapter.

The new charter had positive long-term effects, but the colony still struggled in the early 1610s. The settlers managed to send some useful products back to England, such as cedar, timber, pitch, tar, and sassafras, but only in small quantities. There was no breakthrough crop as yet. They were still in the communal mode, with a common storehouse, settler investors, and the planters, still working solely for the company. In 1614 the seven-year term for the original settlers expired. Some went back to England, but others stayed. They received plots of land from the governor and became tenant farmers of the company; in 1615 there were 81 of them. "By 1616 approximately 2,000 people had arrived under the company's auspices, but the population had declined to 351," mostly due to disease and Indian wars.[35]

Later in the decade the colony started to make some progress. Economically it was because of the introduction of tobacco as a cash crop. Tobacco farming was started by John Rolfe around 1611 and started to become profitable fairly quickly. An experimental shipment was made to England in 1613 and was successful. By 1616, 1,250 pounds were shipped, and by 1617 anywhere from 10,000 to 20,000 pounds were shipped.[36] This quickly eclipsed any of the crops they initially tried to produce for export back to England. Agricultural development now seemed like a real possibility, at least for tobacco.

The situation now started to stabilize and martial law was relaxed. In 1614, or perhaps slightly earlier, Governor Thomas Dale took a step that would lead to long term consequences. Perhaps to bolster the company's poor image, he took the step "of allotting 'to every man in the Colony ..., three English acres of cleere corne ground, which every man is to manure and tend, being in the nature of farmers.'... This greatly advanced individual responsibility and was a big step toward the evolution of private property."[37] They were relieved of some company duties also, and just had to pay a yearly levy of two barrels of corn. It wasn't much, but *it was the first private property grant in America* in a colony that was to become the first English colony to eventually prosper.

The intention of the reorganization of the company after the 1609 charter was to end the joint ownership of land and distribute land dividends to the shareholders, adventurers and planters, after seven years, in 1616. This would mean that the company investors, the adventurers who stayed in England, and the planters who move to Virginia, would actually own land in America. Of course, it would still be in socage tenure to the king of his manor in East Greenwich.

It was in 1616 that things started to turn around for the company and the colony.

Land Use in Jamestown and in New Spain

Superficially, land possession in New Spain and in Jamestown was similar in that all of it was held by the respective crowns, a throwback to feudal tenures. The way the land was settled, however, differed greatly in each case. The Spanish Crown allotted large groups of the conquered Indians, and their attendant lands, to *encomiendas*, headed by encomenderos responsible for the welfare and Christian conversion of the Indians, and for the extraction of wealth from the land. These encomenderos used the tribute and labor from the Indians to enrich themselves and acquire land for themselves, estates (*estancias*), often on their own *encomienda*. The *encomienda* system evolved into the hacienda system, and thus a relatively small group of Spanish gentry and nobility gained control over most of the land in New Spain for 500 years after the Spanish Conquest.

The evolution of landholding in English America would take a different path. In this case a private joint stock company, the Virginia Company, would be chartered by the crown and would be responsible for the development of the plantation in America. The company would be in it for gain, mostly for possible trade and the extraction of resources, which would benefit the English economy as well as the company. The company held the land tight and used the planters who emigrated from England, for the company, as contract laborers on company land. This model worked for a while, but then evolved into a system in which people could eventually own their own land. This evolution set the tone for the following English colonies. Land became an inducement to come to America, and ownership was eventually seen as a right. When this right was put into jeopardy later, the bonds with the mother country were seen as more of a hindrance than a help.

Colonial Land Tenures

Many historians categorize Virginia as a corporate colony because the charter was issued to a joint stock company. Harris, however, in *Origin of the Land Tenure System in the United States*, categorizes it as a royal colony because of the strong crown control in the early years up to the second charter in 1609. As rigid as this system was, it began to change relatively quickly, within three years, even before the establishment of the other colonies. This had an impact on the establishment and history of the other original colonies. The company was given authority in governance and land granting rights from 1609 until its dissolution in 1624. From 1624 until the American Revolution, Virginia was under strict royal control, not company control.

Virginia was the first of the North American colonies to take root and eventually thrive under royal control. The other colonies that followed through the seventeenth and early eighteenth centuries can be

Chapter Two. Land in English Colonial America 65

classified under different categories of governmental control and land tenure systems.

"From the standpoint of governmental or political control over the immediate development of the land tenure system, the thirteen original colonies may be conveniently divided into three classes... (a) royal, (b) proprietary, and (c) corporate."[38] Using these political governing classifications, at the time of the Revolution: Virginia, New York, New Hampshire, New Jersey, North Carolina, South Carolina, and Georgia were royal colonies; Pennsylvania, Maryland, and Delaware were proprietary colonies; and Massachusetts, Rhode Island, and Connecticut were corporate colonies. Sometimes corporate colonies are referred to as charter colonies, but this is confusing because all the colonies had charters. Ownership of land and government control, however, did not always reside in the same hands. In only eight of the 13 colonies were both the government and land ownership control in the same hands. In Virginia and New York, both the government and land control were in royal hands. In the colonies of Pennsylvania, Maryland, and Delaware, both the government and land ownership were in the hands of the proprietors. And in the corporate colonies of Massachusetts, Connecticut, and Rhode Island, the government and land control were in the hands of the people to whom the charters were issued. In the other five colonies (New Hampshire, New Jersey, North Carolina, South Carolina, Georgia), called composite colonies, the government control was royal and the land control was proprietary.[39] In fact, *none* of the original 13 colonies were settled by the crown, all were established by private companies or individuals, even though the crown maintained governmental control in most of them.

The English crown was interested in reaping the benefits of colonies in America, but never interested enough to take responsibility for establishing them. The crown and the business community both saw the advantages of a colonial empire: maintaining a base in North America to counterbalance the Spanish influence in the south; grabbing a chance to control resources that were depleted at home, such as material for the shipping industry; exploiting a resource for minerals; off-loading some of the surplus population from London; and gaining a trading post. Over the century and a quarter of establishing colonies, this abrogation of royal initiative and reliance on private corporations for settlement resulted in a patchwork of different approaches to settlement. There was no strategic plan, no long-term plan to settlement, that would assure that the objectives desired in the American experiment would be met. The charters for settlement went to private trading companies such as the Virginia Company of London, to friends of the king such as proprietors George Calvert (Lord Baltimore), and William Penn, and to corporations established to settle dissenters such as the Puritans in New England, just to name a few.

This diversity assured that there would be a variety of methods for how the land granted would be distributed and used. Some would be held closely by the crown at first, such as in Virginia, but then later would be distributed to Virginia Company stockholders. The New England land, held by a corporation, would be distributed in the form of townships. The owners of the proprietary colonies tried to set up manors resembling the feudal manors of previous centuries, but also sold the land. All this was going on at the same time, over 3,000 miles from the home country, and with the realization by the settlers that there was more land, almost limitless, farther west. These factors all mixed to create a mindset in the first settlers of the importance of land. Creative methods for working the land developed, all the way from the communal arrangements originally used in Virginia and New England, to the other extreme of squatters in Pennsylvania who assumed they were entitled to any land they could settle without paying for it.

The story of the use and importance of the land is an interesting one. The approach to acquiring and using land, along with the development of self-government, led to the radical concept in the late eighteenth century that the colonies had outgrown the need for the link with Great Britain. A few examples can show the variety of methods used to grant and distribute land in English America, and how the perception of land changed as the settlers got accustomed to the New World.

Massachusetts

The second company set up under the first charter of Virginia was the Virginia Company of Plymouth, or Plymouth Company. Whereas the sister London Company was a merchant trading group, as exemplified by the trading post they attempted to establish at Jamestown, this western England group were more gentry and nobility, and were interested in settlements rather than trade. They attempted a settlement at Sagadahoc on the Kennebec River in what is now Maine in 1607, at the same time as the Jamestown post was being established. This colony survived only about a year, and following its failure the Plymouth Company went dormant for several years. It was revived in 1619 by Ferdinando Gorges when he and his colleagues formed the Council for New England to supersede the Plymouth Company and settle New England. Acknowledging they were the same parties named previously as members of the second colony of Virginia, they petitioned the king for land in the northern part of the English claim on America, all of which was called Virginia at that time. They requested land between 40 and 45 degrees north latitude (roughly present-day New York to Maine) and said they would name it New England. The king responded favorably in the Charter of New England: 1620, and granted more land to the Council than they had requested; from 40 to 48 degrees latitude and from "sea-to-sea." The Council for New England gave out much of the land to council members in fiefs and manors; they intended the land to be developed "as a monolithic, aristocratic, Anglican province."[40] Ironically, it worked out to be totally different from their expectations.[41]

In the early seventeenth century, decades after the Protestant Reformation and Henry VIII's establishment of the Church of England, England was once again in religious turmoil. The Gunpowder Plot, in which a Catholic cabal tried to blow up James I and Parliament, was one unsuccessful attempt to overthrow the government and re-instate a Catholic monarch. Other dissenters came from within the Church of England; two in particular are notable. The Separatists, known later as the Pilgrims in America, were anxious to separate themselves from what they saw as the corrupt Church of England. They were persecuted, and for a time fled to Holland. They were not satisfied living abroad, and many finally decided to move to America to be able to practice their faith there. Similarly, the Puritans, not interested in separating, but interested in purifying the Church of England, were also moved to send some of their members to America, again for religious freedom issues.

The story of the Separatists' journey to this country provides an interesting connection between the Virginia colony and the Plymouth colony. Living in exile in Holland for 10 years, but fearing the loss of their cultural identity, they decided in 1618 to "live as a distinct body by themselves under the general government of Virginia."[42] They were encouraged by some to go further north to New England, but the Council for New England had not yet been chartered, so they could not receive a charter from that Council.

They applied for, and received, a charter from the Virginia Company of London in 1619 for a particular plantation in the Virginia colony, a colony within a colony. They never took up this first patent for reasons unknown. However, they applied again in 1620, and a patent was issued in the name of John Peirce on February 2, 1620. Coincidentally, on the very same day, in the very next paragraph of the company records, the company issued an important rule regarding self-government of these particular plantations. This rule allowed the leaders of such plantations to establish their *own* government until one could be officially set up for them, provided it did not violate any of the laws of England. This was to become the basis and justification for the future Mayflower Compact which later defined self-government in the Plymouth colony. This Peirce patent allowed them to set up anywhere south of the 41-degree north latitude limit of the Virginia Company of London. They chose the northern part of the colony, the mouth of the Hudson River, which was just within the northern limit. This put them far enough away from the more conforming members of the church in the south, and close to the fur and fishing industry in the north, which they expected to exploit.[43]

They got a late start, on September 6, 1620, and after a rough fall voyage that took them off course, made it to Cape Cod on November 9, 1620. They knew they were at 42 degrees north latitude, *north* of the limit of the Virginia Company of London patent, but it was too risky for them weather-wise to move to the Hudson River, so they decided to stay. However, before they left the ship, on November 11, they drafted and signed the Mayflower Compact, "[to] Covenant and Combine ourselves together into a Civil Body Politic, for our better ordering ... to enact, constitute and frame such just and equal laws, Ordinances, Acts, Constitutions and Offices." Although not within the Virginia Company patent it appears that the self-governing rule for particular plantations recorded in the company records was the motivation for this civil compact; they needed something to cover the civil order of the plantation. Later, in 1621, the colony did receive a patent from the Council for New England, which provided 100 acres of land to be given to the corporation for every person who moved to the settlement and stayed three years. They also had the authority to set up their own local government. Plymouth never received a royal patent and, until 1691, when they were united with Massachusetts Bay, "it was never incorporated legally into a body politic, but remained a voluntary municipal association.... Plymouth settlers maintained almost complete control, however, over their land system and government to the Revolution."[44]

The second English settlement in North America, like its southern cousin, also set some precedents that were not obvious at the time. The Mayflower Compact was the first instance in this country of a body agreeing to a set of rules for self-government and then abiding by those rules. Thus, it is related to the Virginia colony's establishment of the Virginia House of Burgesses in Jamestown in 1619, which established the first elected body in this country. These acts, along with the allocation of the first private lands in Virginia, and the 100-acre land grants in Plymouth, were the first hints at what might be possible in these new lands thousands of miles from the homeland.

These Separatists were unable to self-finance their move to Virginia, so they entered into an agreement with a merchant group headed by a London ironmonger named Thomas Weston. Naturally this merchant enterprise was interested in a profit, so the pilgrims had to accept some undesirable terms. The investors were dubious that the settlers, 3,000 miles away, would work company land for company profit if those settlers owned their own land and houses; they feared the company would get short-changed. Thus, they required that everything be owned by the company, and that the profits be shared between those in America and the company in England. "Only by insisting that all accumulated wealth was to be 'common wealth,' or placed in a common pool, could the investors feel reassured that the colonists would be working to benefit everyone, including themselves."[45] Weston was a loan shark, and fiddled the books so that no matter how much the settlers sent back, they were always in debt. They felt they were being taxed by their investors at a 50 percent rate.

Working for the company with no private property was exactly how the colony at Jamestown had started about 15 years previously, and it was no more successful. It was not the tax problem that caused the most concern, but the communal sharing that harmed morale. That fit with what Plato had said, that "the taking away of property ... was found to breed much confusion and discontent and retard employment.... For the young men that were most able and fit for labour and service, did repine that they should spend time and strength to work for other men's wives and children without any recompense ... this was thought injustice."[46] The response to this was the same as the eventual response in Jamestown; the company allotted private land to each family.

> So they began to think how they might raise as much corn as they could, and obtain a better crop than they had done, that they might not still thus languish in misery. At length, after much debate of things, the governor (with the advice of the chiefest among them) gave way that they should set corn every man for his own particular, and in that regard trust to themselves;... And so assigned to every family a parcel of land, according to the proportion of their number, for that end, only for the present use ... and ranged all boys and youth under some family. This had very good success, for it made all hands very industrious, so as much more corn was planted than otherwise would have been by any means the governor or any other could use, and saved him a great deal of trouble, and gave far better content. The women now went willingly into the field, and took their little ones with them to set corn: which before would allege weakness and inability; whom to have compelled would have been thought great tyranny and oppression.[47]

The decision to grant individual allotments was made in 1623. "The next year an acre of land near the town was granted to every person"[48] Following that, eight of the planters on behalf of the settlers bought land from the Council and made it available to the settlers. The land was divided more generously than in 1624, when each man received one acre. Now good land was divided among heads of families and all able men. Each received 20 acres of land, five acres on the banks of a stream and four acres in depth.[49]

So once again, as in Jamestown, the lesson was learned that people will not work for a company, 3,000 miles away, in a communal manner, unless they could benefit personally from the fruits of their own labor. The environment undoubtedly helped. They could see almost endless land to the west, uninhabited or sparsely inhabited. They were not in England, where the choice might be to labor for someone else on either a farm or in a shop in the city. The thought might well have been, "I see all this land, with my industry and ability I should be able to own a small portion of it."

So now the land ownership precedent had been established in the first two English colonies in North America, Virginia, and Plymouth. It would be perpetuated in the next one, Massachusetts Bay, albeit in a slightly different manner.

The Puritans were of the Church of England but believed that it needed to be reformed from the last remnants of "popery," Catholicism. They rejected the separation from the church that the Separatists or Pilgrims espoused, but sought reform within the church. In that sense they rebelled against the church hierarchy and were persecuted for it. By the mid–1620s many wanted to leave England to achieve distance from that country and practice their pure form of Anglicanism.

In 1622 a merchant group with a strong Puritan bent decided to set up a fishing colony on the coast of New England. They obtained a fishing license from the Council for New England and set up their fishing operations at Cape Ann in present-day Massachusetts. The founders of the company, the Dorchester Company, John White and Arthur Lake, were Puritan clergymen from Dorchester and saw this colony as a refuge for Puritans as well as a fishing company. The company struggled for a few years, but finally failed in 1626 because of poor fishing prospects and a poor agricultural environment. White kept his faith in the effort and supported a few dozen men at Cape Ann. He still hoped the colony would become a refuge for non–Separatist dissenters. Later these men were urged to move to a location with better prospects, one which would later become known as Salem. Another joint stock company was formed after the failure of the Dorchester Company; this company was called the New England Company for a Plantation in Massachusetts-Bay. The company received a patent from the Council of New England in 1628 for land between the Charles and Merrimack rivers. Salem is on the coast between these river boundaries. Though ostensibly a merchant company, it was still seen as a refuge for Puritans; the leadership of the company was still strongly dominated by Puritans. "Fourteen of the adventurers signed the strongly puritanical instructions given to John Endecott before he sailed out to govern the new colony in June 1628."[50] Endecott was a prominent Puritan and one of the grantees of the New England Company; he is credited as a co-founder of Salem. This was a small colony and not yet the beginning of the major Puritan exodus from England.[51]

Events started to move more quickly. "To guarantee the Company's land grant, John White, the barrister, drafted a petition for a royal charter confirming the grant of the Council for New England."[52] Through the Charter of Massachusetts Bay: 1629, the New England Company was changed into the Governor and Company of Massachusetts Bay in New England, known as the Massachusetts Bay Company. This charter by the crown was surprising for a couple of reasons. First, the Council for New England had the intent to grant land in the feudal mode, that is, fiefs and manors, so granting land to a predominantly Puritan company was unusual. Second, the Church of England hierarchy opposed the Puritan theological positions, and those advisers would be expected to advise the crown against any grant to this company. So, it is surprising that the charter got through. As Bridenbaugh says, John White accomplished this "by using his very influential connections." There were many well-placed Puritans in the government and business communities.[53]

The charter was approved on March 4, 1629, and signed by the king on March 18. In between, on March 10, Charles I (1600–1649) had dissolved Parliament; this was to enable him to act as the absolute monarch he saw himself. This latter act gave the Puritans considerable cause for concern. They felt they were losing any protection they might have had from Parliament. "Consequently, a small party of leading Puritans met at Cambridge in August of this year and adopted the 'Cambridge Agreement,' to migrate to Massachusetts, on condition that the charter and seat of government be transferred thither. To this the Massachusetts Bay Company agreed, and John Winthrop, a gentleman of wealth and education … was chosen governor."[54] This location stipulation was unusual. Most of the time the charters for these companies specified where the parent company was to be located, and where it was to meet, which was always in England. Location in England, often London, meant the crown and Parliament could look over the shoulder of the company and exert influence on a regular basis. Either by accident or design, this charter did not specify the company location. The company, now dominated by Puritan businessmen, took advantage of this, located the business in Massachusetts, and took the charter with them when they went.[55]

John Winthrop led a contingent to Massachusetts Bay the following year, in 1630. "The formidable flotilla, the largest single shipment of emigrants ever to have left England, consisted of eleven vessels carrying approximately 700 passengers. Six other vessels followed in the weeks thereafter, bringing the total within the single year to approximately 1,000 migrants, most of whom landed at the ramshackle fishing village of Salem."[56] The Great Migration had begun. In the next 10 years more than 20,000 Puritans had sailed into the area of Massachusetts Bay from England.[57]

The land grant policy for Massachusetts Bay was started early, on March 5, 1629, when a committee met to consider how to divide the land. This was only a day after the charter was approved, and well before Winthrop traveled to Massachusetts Bay. The first grants were to be similar to those at Jamestown. Each adventurer (investor) who held £50 of stock would receive 200 acres. Headrights of 50 acres were awarded to any adventurer who went or transported another person. These grants were made by the company representative in America before Winthrop and the charter arrived the following year. After that, all grants were made by the General Court.[58]

Grants were made to private persons as well as to groups for plantations. The first grant to a private person was to John Winthrop for 600 acres in 1630, the only one that year. The following year there were six grants averaging 148 acres. Other grants were made to people important to the community, for example to Mr. Eaton, a teacher, on the condition "he continue his employment with us for life." There were much larger grants to individuals, some of thousands of acres, but these private grants were not what defined the Massachusetts Bay Company nor New England as a whole. These larger grants were not numerous and many were never occupied. The characteristic of the land granting process in New England was the way land was granted through townships.[59] "But by far the greater part of the land disposed of was granted to communities of settlers, who were sometimes members of some existing community, sometimes men who had never lived in the country, grouped from various causes. The formation and development of these communities constitute one of the most important chapters in the history of the political and social institutions of New England."[60]

In contrast to the immigrants to the Chesapeake colonies of Virginia and Maryland, who were mostly young and single, the immigrants to Massachusetts Bay were middle-class families, and more than that, often friends and neighbors from the home country; they wanted to stay together. "They soon embarked on the formation of new, permanent communities based on the principle of voluntary association.... Settlement would be a corporate enterprise as groups of colonists voluntarily gathered to establish towns." In 1629, before the major influx of immigrants who started with Winthrop, the company had set up a headright system of allotting land. Once the first large group of settlers came in 1630, they quickly realized that this headright system would not work if they wanted to maintain a community; it was inconsistent with community. Given individual headrights, the colonists might well spread themselves across the land, much as they had in Virginia, and preclude an integrated community. It is not clear when the transition took place, but "by the mid-1630s, the General Court was regularly granting land not to individuals by headrights, but to towns as corporate entities as a way of ensuring the New Englanders would settle together and stay together in geographically coherent communities." It is not surprising that these towns often resembled the towns they had left in England.[61]

Their intention was to find the middle ground between the rigid communalism of the early Plymouth colony and the unrestrained individualism of the later Virginia settlements, so they devised a process to provide both individual freedom and an integrated community. The process can be considered in four phases. First, a group would petition the General Court for land for a town. Then colony officials would turn to a group of prominent colonists to oversee the process of surveying the land and laying out roads. This would include public land and land for churches. If the petition was approved the town was laid out, and if this plan was approved the grant was made.

Second, the inhabitants arrived and did their own allocation of the land among the neighbors. There was a concern that everyone had an adequate amount of land, so they weighed community and individual needs. There was also a recognition of social status so a hierarchy was observed in this allocation. The large expanse of land in New England made this allocation relatively generous compared to the land available in England. One of the dividers, Edward Johnson, who divided Woburn's land, noted "the poorest had six or seven acres of Medow, and twenty five of Upland or thereabouts." This process spawned 23 towns in the 1630s and more later.

The third phase was when newcomers attempted to join the community. They had to be upright, God-fearing Christians who worshiped as the Puritans did. Although they had sought religious liberty in their move to New England, the Puritans were not very tolerant of others, even other Christians. The fourth phase was when latecomers came to the community and were denied access either because land was no longer available or for some other reason. These settlers moved on to found new towns of their own, where they could control the land distribution.[62]

The Massachusetts Bay colony established a land distribution system that, while respecting a hierarchy, was very equitably established, such that the land wealth gap was low compared to that of England. "When they turned to the division of land within their communities, the colonists made no attempt to reproduce the complex English tenurial system and instead adopted a nearly universal system of freehold ownership ... freeholders owned their land outright." Land was almost limitless, but labor was scarce, the opposite of the situation in England. This pushed the wages of labor up, including that of artisans. Nevertheless, these artisans and craftsmen concluded economic security lay primarily in acquisition of land, so they sought land also. By providing free land, the colony assured that few New Englanders would live in poverty. "In seventeenth-century New England, land ownership among adult white males was virtually universal.... In addition to owning a house and land, they generally possessed enough livestock, farm equipment, and household goods to provide a comfortable existence.... Most adult males owned land—freehold property—that guaranteed their economic security and personal independence."[63] This was in stark contrast to the stratified society of England.

There were other aspects of the land system that were also unique to New England. One was the restriction of alienability of the land. They were concerned that some people would enter the community that did not share their beliefs and thus disrupt the community, so they had some restrictions on alienability, that is, to whom they would allow you to sell your land. It worked like a neighborhood covenant, so to speak, although this restriction was eventually eliminated. Another feature was the absence of a quitrent, or land tax, paid to an absentee owner. The lack of a quitrent meant the person held the land in fee simple absolute tenure. Quitrents were common in America, but a reasonable restraint on alienation was acceptable instead, more so than a quitrent paid to an absentee landlord.[64] It was in most essentials very similar to present fee simple absolute tenures. The history of the town of Dedham, Massachusetts, described by Kenneth Lockridge in *A New England Town, the First Hundred Years,* is perhaps typical of the New England town experience. He was talking about the small agricultural surpluses distributed among three or four crops.

> Yet this simple subsistence economy was also an economy of abundance, for there was an incomparable abundance of land. To be sure, soil was often poor ... a man's grant might be distant from his home ... land that would take years of backbreaking labor to clear. Yet there was land. Privately owned land cost shillings an acre instead of pounds an acre as in England.... A man who lived in the town [Dedham] for any twenty-five year span between 1636 and 1686 received between fifty and 500 acres from the town. This was by no means a farmstead beyond the wildest dreams of a successful English yeoman, but it meant security for the whole society of the village since it made every man a potential yeoman, a status enjoyed by only a fortunate minority of the English rural populace.[65]

Another difference between England and New England land law was the New England rejection of primogeniture. Primogeniture in England was the system in which the eldest son inherited all the real estate of his deceased father; all second and later sons received nothing, they were on their own. This mindset reflected a mentality of scarcity. There was only so much land, and to maintain family status and power, it had to be passed on intact and not subdivided from generation to generation. "In New England the law provided for the division of the whole estate among all the children of the deceased." This included daughters as well as sons. It was the plenitude of land that provided this opportunity for the second generation. This law, though not its intended consequence, had a democratizing effect also. Generation after generation would have equal rights in land. Although there was a hierarchy in government and in the church, there would be no aristocracy based on land, no landed nobility. So even in the first generation of New England there were signs that the society would be different from the homeland, and that difference was based on land availability.[66]

One example of the absence of primogeniture is in the family of Arthur Scovell and his descendants. Scovell was born in County Dorset in England 1635–40, and immigrated to Boston around 1660. He owned no land in Boston, but did own some after he had moved to Middleton, Connecticut. He made a will in 1678 before his children were of age. This was unusual, but it was possibly done to provide for his children after his wife had died and before he married a second time. In his will he follows New England custom to leave his estate to *all* of his children, including his daughter. "Out of consideration of that natural affection and love which I have and bear unto my well-beloved children, Arthur, James, John, and Elizabeth Scovel.... I do give, grant, and confirm unto them all my rights, interest and propriety in my land and housing in Middleton ... to have and to hold from the day of my death forever, they to have it by equal proportions as many shall be then living."[67]

Connecticut and Rhode Island

The other two of the three corporate colonies, besides Massachusetts Bay, were Connecticut and Rhode Island. Both of these colonies were included in land that was originally part of the first charter of Virginia and later of the Council for New England. These two were similar to Massachusetts Bay in that the people were from the same areas, and the same religious background.

Connecticut was peopled mostly by migrants from Massachusetts Bay. A charter was granted to the corporation under the name Governor and Company of the English Colony of Connecticut in New-England, in America, in 1662. It was granted in free and common socage under the manor of East Greenwich.[68]

All of the settlers of Rhode Island were religious dissenters, even from the Puritan theology of Massachusetts Bay. They left Massachusetts Bay because they disliked Puritan rule. Originally, they did not have a royal grant, but settled as squatters and claimed self-government. "The church and state were always completely separated in Rhode Island. Religious liberty to the settlers meant complete liberty of conscience with no coercion from a civil authority." So, in America, where some had come to practice their Puritan religion exclusively, others were pushing boundaries even further by allowing freedom of *all* religions. Eventually Rhode Island did receive a corporate charter. In 1663 the charter was issued to the "Governor and Company of the English Colony of Rhode-Island and the Providence Plantations, in New England, in America." Again, it was held in free and common socage under the manor of East Greenwich. "The corporation held the land in trust for the use and benefit of the freemen of the colony."[69]

All three of these New England colonies were self-governing, and all used the same land distribution as described for Massachusetts Bay.

In the early to mid–seventeenth century one can already see the first signs of differences between America and England. From self-government with the Virginia House of Burgesses in 1619, and Massachusetts Bay in 1630, to the first expression of total religious freedom in Rhode Island in the 1660s; the separation was beginning to widen. These all depended on the colonists getting control of their own land.

Maryland, Pennsylvania, and Delaware— The Proprietary Colonies

As if to demonstrate the lack of a strategic plan for the settlement of North America, very soon after the corporate grant to the Massachusetts Bay colony, the crown issued a grant for a proprietary colony to Cecil Calvert (1605–1675), the second Lord Baltimore; the grant was issued on June 20, 1632, by Charles I. George Calvert (1579–1632), the first Lord Baltimore, had requested the grant on August 19, 1629, just days before the Cambridge Agreement of the Massachusetts Bay Company.

The grant was an extraordinary one, totally different from the Virginia and Massachusetts grants. In this grant to a single proprietor, the proprietor was to have almost monarchical powers. It would be a private domain, where the proprietor would have rights similar to a feudal lord. It was all spelled out in the charter. He would have the authority to make laws, to govern, to award titles, and to set up feudal manors. "In the corporate colonies … the colonists had complete control. In the proprietary colonies … the settlers were in a distinctly secondary position, being subject

Chapter Two. Land in English Colonial America

at every turn to the proprietary forms of holding land."[70] This would imply almost unlimited control by the proprietor, in contrast to the corporate colony of Massachusetts, which had colonial self-government. However, there was a section of the charter which stated that the proprietor was to make laws "with the Advice, Assent, and Approbation of the Free-Men of the same Province, or the greater Part of them, or of their Delegates or Deputies, whom We will shall [sic] be called together for the framing of Laws, when, and as often as Need shall require." In other words, there was to be a popular assembly involved in the process. So even in a supposedly feudal province, there was to be a process for some self-government, another widening crack in the separation from the mother country.[71]

Despite the radical difference between the charters of the proprietary colonies and the corporate colonies, the objective for their establishment was the same: to increase the wealth of the proprietor or corporation. Calvert had a secondary objective also. He wanted to establish a colony that would be a refuge for co-religionist Catholics, although he never envisioned a "Catholic colony"; his religious objectives were not as intense as those of the Puritans in New England. He also very much wanted to populate the colony in the feudal manner, consistent with his prerogatives in the Maryland Charter. His promotional literature clearly indicates that he envisioned not only houses and fields after the European pattern, but a similar social order as well, which, even though already decaying at home, would be based specifically on the English manor with landlords and their tenants. In his "Conditions of Plantation" he promised to anyone who undertook to transport five laborers at a cost of £20 each a manor of 2,000 acres, with all the rights and privileges "usually belonging to Mannours in England."[72] He wasn't successful in promoting the feudal manor to populate the colony to maximize revenues, since not many were interested in coming to establish a manor. "By 1642 only sixteen private manors had been surveyed with a total of 31,000 acres, an average extent of less than 2,000 acres each." These few manors did serve a purpose; they provided a haven for the predominantly young male immigrants, mostly indentured servants, who could live in the manor community instead of separate, isolated huts. However, the age of the feudal manor was passing in England, and it never caught on here, mostly because of the abundance of land that beckoned for anyone willing to work.[73]

Besides offering the terms for a manor, he offered headrights to those who brought in less than five laborers. "For taking into the province any number of persons less than five the adventurer was to receive a grant of one hundred acres for each one between the ages of sixteen and sixty, and fifty acres for every child under the age of sixteen. The annual rent in every case was to be ten pounds of good wheat for every fifty acres."[74] This was much more attractive to the individual settler. Calvert also made it simple to get the land. First, after establishing a headright a warrant was issued, then a survey laid out the land, and finally a patent was issued "conveying the title in fee simple subject to an annual quitrent."[75]

"Instead of manorial lords and faithful tenants, the single family freehold prevailed. These family plantations of 250 acres or less that dotted the tidewater soon outnumbered the large grants manyfold and gave evidence of the aversion early settlers had for tenant status when they could acquire land in their own right, if not entirely free, then at least relatively cheaply."[76] Maryland immigrants could acquire land from the proprietor, Cecil Calvert, who wanted to populate the province so he could increase his income through quitrents. Many came as freeman and held their own land. Many, though, came as indentured servants, as they did in Virginia. (More on indentured servants later.) After their indentured servitude, many of them would move on to become land holders themselves. Maryland, like Virginia, quickly gravitated to a tobacco economy. Tobacco was easily grown and transported on the coastal part of Maryland, although not so easily inland. Many rivers in Virginia, up to the falls, reached deep into the colony. This gave tobacco farmers easy access to the sea for exporting tobacco. Maryland had no such river access, so tobacco production remained near the coast. For this reason, the growing population remained near the coast for most of the seventeenth century. Tobacco production required intensive labor, so Maryland, as Virginia, used a lot of indentured servants. Later this production would be taken over by slaves. It would take other migration patterns in the eighteenth century before the agricultural potential of the inland parts of Maryland would be exploited.

William Penn (1644–1718) became a Quaker after college, and was imprisoned more than once for his non-conformist beliefs when he dissented from Church of England dogma. He came from a well-to-do family and was a friend of Charles II (1630–1685) as was his father; he inherited his father's estate in 1670. Previously his father had lent money to Charles to the extent of £16,000. When it was time to claim the debt owed to him, Penn decided to make sure it was in a tangible asset, *and* thought he could use it to further his Quaker orthodoxy. So instead of claiming it in sterling, he requested, and was granted, land in America. Like Lord Baltimore he was granted land as a proprietary province with all the rights that went with that. Although 50 years after the Baltimore grant, the Penn charter was very similar to the Baltimore charter. The charter for the province of Pennsylvania was granted to Penn in March 1681. The king himself named the colony adding "Penn" before the proposed name of "Sylvania."[77]

Penn's intentions were the same as previous colonial founders; he

Chapter Two. Land in English Colonial America 79

wanted to make money, his fortune was flagging at the time, and he wanted to establish a religious refuge, this time for Quakers. His approach, however, was very different from that of his predecessors, especially in land distribution. He had the authority to establish manors, and he did establish some, but that was a minor consideration. His choice was to sell land, not grant it in headrights as Calvert had done in Maryland, nor pass out small plots through established townships as was done in New England, but sell it outright in large blocks if possible.

> Throughout the Quaker colonies, land was distributed in a manner very different from that of Massachusetts and Virginia. In Pennsylvania and Delaware, William Penn's land policy was meant to serve two purposes. The first was to provide a source of capital for the founding of his colony—even a "holy experiment" needed a material base. The second purpose was to create a rural society of independent farming families without great extremes of wealth or poverty. Despite many difficulties and defeats along the way, Penn succeeded remarkably in that design.[78]

Penn was very adept at selling his land, using an advertising campaign to sell it not only in England, but also in Ireland, Scotland, Wales, and Holland. Friends of his in Holland translated these ads and passed them to others in Holland and Germany; his previous travels to the continent had made him known there. Getting the message to Germans would prove to be important in later decades when German migration to America started in earnest. Of course, he was particularly interested in getting Quakers to migrate because they were being persecuted for their beliefs in England. There was a particular group of Quakers, known as the First Purchasers, which was very interested in purchasing Pennsylvania land; many of the First Purchasers were affluent Quakers in London and Bristol. "Between July and October 1681, Penn sold 320,000 acres to 259 purchasers. By August 1682, when Penn himself sailed for America, he had sold another 300,000 acres to another 250 buyers. Altogether, the business records ... provide itemized information about 589 persons who bought 715,000 acres of Pennsylvania land from Penn between July 1681 and March 1685."[79]

Penn preferred to sell the land in large blocks so he offered 5,000 acres for £100, hoping the affluent would bring over renters or indentured servants to help the population. Anyone transporting an indentured servant was allowed a headright of 50 acres per servant for transporting them, and the servant would receive 50 acres after his indentured servitude was complete. He also wanted the poorer to middling sort to come, so he offered smaller parcels of 500 acres at £10 and 250 acres at £5, and even tracts as small as 125 acres. Anyone unable or unwilling to buy could lease or rent land from the proprietor for a penny an acre. "Most holdings in

Pennsylvania were between 100 and 500 acres. The average was about 250 acres—twice as large as town grants to individual families in Massachusetts, but less than half the average size of land patents in Virginia during the seventeenth century."[80]

The generous, and surprisingly equitable terms, plus the number interested in coming to a religiously tolerant province caused the population to surge. In less than 10 years the population exceeded the growth rate of even Massachusetts, which had a very strong growth rate its first 10 years. In 1690 the Pennsylvania population was almost half that of Maryland, which had been founded 50 years prior.[81]

The Pennsylvania experience with land was entirely different even from the Maryland experience, a similar proprietary province. It differed also from the New England and Virginia experiences. It was a new model for how the founder could make money on land granted from the king. Of course, Penn was interested in trade with England, so he was interested in the migration of many tradesmen, farmers, and artisans to help this trade, but the most important part of his land policy was the sale of land.

A Swedish trading company set up a colony in what is now Delaware in 1626, where they engaged in farming to support their fur trading. A Dutch army forced them out in 1655, and the land became part of New Netherland. "'The Three Lower Counties' ... as they were sometimes called remained part of New Netherland and New York until 1682 when the Duke of York conveyed them to William Penn." Delaware was now a proprietary colony under William Penn and the land grants were similar to the Pennsylvania pattern. These counties remained in Pennsylvania until Penn granted them a separate charter in 1701; a brief charter concerned with government and freedom of conscience.[82]

New York and the Five Composite Colonies

The other six colonies had variations of land tenure that were similar to the ones described above but were unique in some way that pushed each province even further away from the European model of control by the crown.

The early history of New York was complicated by many claims. Although the land was originally claimed by England in the first Virginia charter, it was not settled by the English at the time, but was claimed by the Dutch by virtue of Henry Hudson's explorations around 1607 and 1608. Again, it was a trading company that claimed land for a trading post in 1614, with no intention of granting land to private parties. Trading in New Netherland, however, was not profitable, so in 1629 a Charter of Privileges was enacted to encourage private individuals to establish settlements along the Hudson and Delaware rivers. They now wanted settlements, and made it easier for them to be established. Any person who could gather 50 persons 15 years old or older who would settle within four years was allowed a grant. They allowed the upper-class patroons to pick their lands along the Hudson or Delaware rivers. These were held in absolute ownership, and furthermore, they could govern their own property. These were often very large estates and had servants to cultivate them. The ownership was fee simple.[83]

Later these grants were watered down in size and limited to smaller areas, especially along the riverfronts. Of course, these large grants were not the only lands that were established in New Netherland. Smaller grants were made to new types of landholders known as "masters" or "colonists." These included grants of 200 acres, much smaller than that allowed the patroons. To encourage settlement, free passage was granted to those who came "between decks." So, besides the large patroonships, many small Dutch villages and towns were established in New Netherland. "The famous Dutch villages or townships developed from the influx of independent freeholders. It was upon these small units of local government and the persistent demands of the freeholders that a popular government was established. The desire for political freedom in New Netherlands was intense." Once again, availability of land and the need for local government engendered a desire for political freedom. These desires were only to grow in the following decades.[84]

New Netherland was surrendered to the English in 1664, the year Charles II granted the land to his brother James, Duke of York (1633–1701). The Dutch retook New York in 1673, but the English regained it in 1674, at which time Charles II reissued the charter to his brother. When James, Duke of York became king in 1685, the colony automatically became a royal colony. The English continued to grant land for manors, such as those to Livingston, Pelham, and Cortlandt, and there had been other English settlers while the Dutch had control.

New York had chartered large estates such as patroonships and English manors, and numerous farms. These two types of grants (patroonship and manor) supported each other. This encouraged a feudal aristocracy in that area, which marked the colony for a long time. However, these large estates did not dominate provincial New York because there were strong, numerous groups of freeholders.[85]

The Dutch in New Netherland established freedoms and liberties which helped to secure a strong agricultural community. In the 1629 charter they offered easy tenures and self-government. In 1640 they extended the right of freeholders to independent settlement. In 1641 a committee of 12 was formed to give the director advice; this was the first time freemen participated in government. These were all steps toward self-government.[86]

This was the environment in which the Duke of York found himself when he assumed ownership of the land. Though it became a royal colony when he became king, its history as a proprietary English colony when he was Duke of York gave it a legacy of self-government and numerous small freeholders.

The remaining five colonies were a composite, that is, they had at times a difference between the government function and the land distribution function.

The Council for New England granted land in 1622 to Sir Ferdinando Gorges and Captain John Mason in present-day Maine and New Hampshire. This land was never settled, and in 1629 Gorges and Mason decided to divide this territory. Mason received what is now New Hampshire. His rights were confirmed by the Council for New England just before it was dissolved in 1635. He hoped to set up a fief with himself as proprietor, but he did not reckon with the independent streak of the New Englanders; it didn't work. Prior to this, several small grants had been made to settlers by the Plymouth Company. Many of the settlements were religiously diverse, so there were many independent settlements without governments. New Hampshire is another good example where men learned to govern themselves. At first it had many independent, diverse settlements. Lacking direction from the proprietors, the colonists formed their own governments. These were all annexed to Massachusetts between 1641 and 1643. Because of the religious diversity and independent nature of the settlements, Massachusetts wisely allowed them a great deal of freedom in self-government. In 1677 a judge ruled it was no longer part of Massachusetts, and it became a royal colony.[87]

As in New York and Delaware, in New Jersey, occupation by the English was complicated by the fact that Swedes and Dutch had some previous claims and settlements on the land, even though the land was included in part of the claim of the original Virginia charter. These areas also included some dissenters from New England who had come down to settle. New Jersey was part of the grant from Charles II to his brother James, Duke of York, in March of 1664. James wasted no time, and in June conveyed the land to Lord John Berkeley and Sir George Carteret. The settlements in place were scattered, and the proprietors encouraged more settlement in their newly acquired territory, using headrights as one inducement. "The land tenure provisions were numerous and extensive, and were issued chiefly to interest new settlers in coming to New Jersey rather than to protect the settlers already there." After many changes in proprietors, New Jersey was reunited as a royal province in 1702; "the proprietors, however, retained their rights in the soil and continued to make grants to settlers."[88]

The grant for Carolina had been land that was previously granted to Raleigh in the various Virginia charters, but it hadn't been previously settled. In 1663 Charles II granted the land as a proprietary colony to eight proprietors. The charter was very similar to the one given to Lord Baltimore over 30 years previously. It gave powers to create manors and new tenures. It also granted the power to govern, as it had to Baltimore. The proprietors set out a plan for how the colony would be governed and the land granted. They seemed to be of two minds, or else changed their position after they started down one road. At first, they set up a democratic government with a strong elected assembly. However, within a few years they changed their minds and reversed direction. They had become wary of establishing a "numerous democracy," so they shifted to an aristocratic scheme of government outlined in the Fundamental Constitutions.[89]

The Fundamental Constitutions were written in 1669 by the well-known philosopher John Locke to provide the form of government and society for the Carolina colony. However, "the main purposes of the Fundamental Constitutions were to protect Proprietary interest and to avoid the creation of a democracy."[90] Both the land holding and the government were meant to revert to feudalistic concepts. It was almost as if they were trying to use the land in the New World to recreate feudal England before 1660 when the Statute of Tenures Act was passed. The Statute of Tenures Act "outlawed the last important vestiges of the feudal land system ... did away with major aspects of basic feudal tenures, except copyhold estates."[91] The Carolina proprietors tried to revert to the feudal system as it was prior to when the Statute of Tenures Act was passed. They would have titles, large manors, small freeholders, and even serfs. The judiciary and executive were to be formed under a highly aristocratic government in the hands of the proprietors and nobles.[92]

It didn't work. It became clear quite early that going back to feudal tenures was not going to work in a new colony, as it had not worked in previous ones (e.g., Maryland). The freemen rejected the Fundamental Constitutions as the proprietors tried to maintain them. The colonists and proprietors battled for half a century, but the Fundamental Constitutions were dead by the early 1690s. Small farmers banded with the wealthy to object to them. They envisioned the proprietors gaining full control for their own financial gain, and free land would not be available to any others. They would then become serfs.[93] This coalition thus contributed of the death of the Fundamental Constitutions.

Once again, the attempt to set up a feudal system in the New World failed. It worked partially in New York and in Maryland when some manors were established, but the measures were not as extreme as in Carolina, and the former eventually reverted to freer patterns of land ownership. Similarly, even though Penn's province was granted later (1681) and was a proprietary province, he never pushed for the extreme measures proposed in Carolina. His establishment of a few manors was as far as he went. He established a general assembly early, sold land, advertised widely to encourage settlement, especially by fellow Quakers, and in general opened the province to everyone.

Carolina was split into North and South Carolina in 1712, and a few years later first South Carolina and then North Carolina became royal provinces. The crown bought out seven of the eight original proprietors.[94]

Clearly, many living in England viewed the land in the New World through the eyes of persons used to the hierarchical English system of land ownership by a few, with a scattering of small freeholders and many tenants. Without seeing the New World land, they could not comprehend the impression the vast, apparently free, land made on those who were there.

Georgia was the last of the English colonies to be established in America. Twenty trustees under James Oglethorpe were granted funding from Parliament and a corporate charter from the king in 1732 for a period of 21 years. This was one of the original nonprofits. It was established to provide relief for the poor and debt-ridden in London; this was the opposite of a proprietary colony in that none of the trustees was to receive a profit. Because it was meant for poor relief, the limit on land holding was set at 500 acres. The corporation took a paternalistic approach. The poor were thought to be unable to govern themselves, so no general assembly was established. Rum was forbidden because it could cause idleness and drunkenness. It worked well enough for a while, even though some migrants from South Carolina chafed at the land limitations. The colony became a royal colony in 1752, just before the 21-year grant was to expire.[95]

The five composite colonies, New Jersey, North Carolina, South Carolina, Georgia, and New Hampshire, plus New York, all started as proprietary colonies and reverted to become royal colonies; all the proprietors of these colonies lost control to the crown prior to the Revolution. Significantly, the crown did not maintain support for the proprietors. Moreover, it tried numerous attempts to weaken proprietary control and assume more crown control despite the charters. This was clearly noticeable by the colonists and contributed to the push for free and certain tenures, i.e., more control of their own land.[96] In other words, the colonials could see the crown attempting to take back governance and land distribution in the seventeenth and eighteenth centuries almost as soon as it was given. In the decades that followed, land acquisition and ownership accelerated and land was seen as almost free, so the attempt by the crown to regain control was resented. This would come to a head in the late eighteenth century with the crown's attempt to restrict the expansion of land ownership. Eventually, this led to a break between the colonists and the mother country.

Chapter Three

Populating the Land I: Colonial Expansion

The most difficult step was always the first one in which the person or family decided to leave England and settle in America. Once the early settlers got to Virginia or New England and overcame the first shocks of resettlement, they saw things differently from the way they had seen them back home. The abundance of land impressed both the settlers themselves and the trading companies who allotted the land. It wasn't obvious at first, because the settlers had to build shelter, grow food, and protect themselves against the indigenous people, the Indians. The companies had to search for trade opportunities and look for profit in minerals, and possibly continue to search for the holy grail of a route to the Indies. Once the basic needs were met, it became obvious to both settler and company that the land itself was their greatest asset.

The population growth of the English North American colonies was slow at first, and uneven, but strong after that. Virginia grew very slowly at first for many of the reasons discussed in the previous chapter. The colony had only about 3,000 people in 1630, which was 23 years after the first settlement. One reason was the high mortality rates, especially in the 1620s with a mortality rate at 45 percent. Massachusetts had approximately 1,900 people in 1630, most probably from the Endecott-led Puritan settlement at Salem in 1628. The next great jump was the Puritan Great Migration, which saw upwards of 20,000 coming to New England between 1630 and 1640. Sir William Berkeley (1605–1677) came to Virginia as governor in 1642 and immediately had an impact that boosted immigration. "[He] began a campaign to draw some of England's elite to Virginia.... Many of the future leaders that Virginia provided to the United States ... were descendants of these aristocratic immigrants." Virginia immigration surged in the 1640s, so that by 1650 the population was up to about 17,000. It wasn't only the elite who came. About three quarters came as indentured servants, so there was a wealth gap that opened and remained open in Virginia beyond the Civil War.[1]

For the first half century, or until the middle of the seventeenth century, percentages obviously have little significance as indicating normal growth, because they were violently affected by every shipload of colonists that arrived. From 1660 to the close of the century, as the population began to assume greater proportions and to extend over larger areas of territory, the percentages of increase, both in individual colonies and in the aggregate for all colonies, tend to become more uniform, and thus to reflect the influences of natural increase as compared with artificial increase by additions from Europe.[2]

The rate of increase slowed after 1650 but remained at very high levels. The rate of increase of the population from decade to decade from 1650 to 1760 was over 30 percent per decade except once, when it dropped to about 29 percent.[3]

As Malthus observed, "in the United States of America, where the means of subsistence have been more ample, the manners of the people more pure, and consequently the checks to early marriages fewer, than in any of the modern states of Europe, the population has been found to double itself in twenty-five years."[4] As implied above, the natural increase became more important by the end of the seventeenth century, but that didn't mean the immigration waves had slowed. Significant waves occurred in the late seventeenth century with the Quaker influx to Pennsylvania, and throughout the eighteenth century with the influx of Germans and the Scots-Irish right up to the Revolution.

Our focus is not so much on the population *per se*, but on the interaction of the people with the land—the impact of the people on the land, and the impact of the land on the people. These can't be separated. There were push-pull factors both ways, factors that would increase the population and increase the land required and desired.

There were many motivations for establishing plantations in North America. They varied from the desire to provide a new source of materials becoming scarce in England, such as wood for the masts of ships, and raw materials such as iron ore; a destination to ship some of the increasing population, much of which was unemployed; and a buffer to shield English interests from Spanish depredations. None of these was strong enough in itself for the crown to risk its resources, low at the time, to finance an expedition 3,000 miles away and keep it supplied for years until it could become self-sustaining and eventually return wealth to the crown. However, as we have seen, the increasingly robust and wealthy merchant community saw an opportunity to make money for their stockholders by establishing trading posts or plantations to bolster their position in the new mercantilist economy. After the slow start of the Virginia Company, many groups and individuals became interested in establishing plantations, and all were interested in making a profit. Even the Puritans who had a strong religious motivation to emigrate, started out as a fishing colony in Cape Ann in Massachusetts.

The problem was that hacking through the wilderness to establish a trading post or plantation was very labor intensive and, as the Virginia Company found out, it was difficult to attract settlers who were willing to bear the hardship of the trip, and be content to be tenants on company lands for some vague promise of a dividend in land years away. To make any profit, the company had to populate the land. There had to be some critical, if unknown, mass necessary so the resources of the new land could be exploited and return a profit. It took several years before they realized that the land itself was the incentive that could be used to attract the settlers. Once that notion took hold, land became the prime motivation for attracting existing settlers to stay and expand their footprint, and for new ones to come.

Land as an Inducement: Virginia's Land and Settlers

Virginia was the first colony, preceding Plymouth colony by 13 years and Massachusetts Bay by 23 years. Nevertheless, it had a rough beginning with poor population growth and high mortality rates. It wasn't until the reforms of 1618 that things started to turn around, and even after that the times were difficult. High mortality rates and maladministration finally contributed to the king's revocation of the company charter, and the reversion to royal control in 1624. However, the reforms of 1618 did have an effect, and Virginia started to grow and expand the territory under settlement.

The early Virginians always had an expansive view of the territory that was called Virginia. This was the result of the charter of 1609 that granted land from sea to sea from the east coast to the west and northwest. At that time the northwest part of that claim included all of Ohio and part of Pennsylvania. (Later there would be boundary conflicts between Pennsylvania and Virginia because of this charter.) This mindset meant that Virginia, more than any other colony, was always looking to expand westward. Many of the colonies, such as Pennsylvania and Maryland, had defined western boundaries, so even though their borders touched the frontier, they knew, and accepted the fact, that they had extensive but limited land with colonial boundaries. Of course, that didn't stop the traders from moving over the mountains to ply their trade. New Englanders eventually moved west also, but it was a much more controlled process, akin to the town building process they had established in New England.

1616—The Pivotal Year

As important as was the transfer of the government authority from the crown to the company in the 1609 charter, the more significant impact was in regard to granting land. In the first charter the king had granted the company land in Virginia, but he then assigned the settlers to the land. This was obviously a constraint on the company. In the second charter however, it was charged "that the said Treasurer, and Company ... shall from time to Time, under their common seal, DISTRIBUTE, convey, assign, and set over such particular Portions of Lands, Tenements, and Hereditaments, by these Presents formerly granted unto such our loving Subjects."[5] The lands, tenements, and hereditaments were those specified in the first charter to be held by the company as of the Manor of East Greenwich.[6] In other words, the company now had control over the land and could distribute it as it saw fit. "The tenure rights that the company held in the land were the same as in the first charter, except that the company had the full power to grant lands directly to the settlers. This power was of tremendous importance in the establishment of agricultural communities."[7]

> A significant shift was made in the second charter. Under the first Virginia charter, the king had final power in granting land to settlers, for he reserved the right to approve land grants recommended by the council. Under the second charter and all subsequent charters, the settlement agency was given the power to make grants of land. Withdrawal by the Crown from control over who would receive grants in the land in America was a marked step forward in expediting settlement and in the development of free tenures in America.[8]

These moves toward self-government and the freedom to grant land seemed to energize the company. Early in 1609 they issued a broadside

> calling upon all work-people, male and female, who wished to go to Virginia ... and "they will be entered as Adventurers in the present voyage to Virginia, where they will have houses to live in, vegetable gardens and orchards, and also food and clothing at the expense of the Company, and besides this, a share of all the products and the profits that may result from their labor, each in proportion, and they will also secure a share in the division of the land for themselves and their heirs forever more." "And all who would give [one hundred Philips] before the last of March will be admitted as Members of the Virginia Company and receive a proportionate share of the profits, altho they do not go in person on this voyage."[9]

This was a call for tenants to occupy company land and a promise that they would share in company profits as well as receive some personal land in the future. They were now opening the company to groups outside the original investors. The final charter wasn't signed until June, but right after this broadside, on February 28, 1609, they published a promotional tract titled *Nova Britannia* to encourage investment and settlement in Virginia. This tract was more explicit, equating the rights of adventurers and planters and a promise to donate the land to them after seven years.

> Wee call those Planters that goe in their persons to dwell there: And those Adventurers that adventure their money and go not in person, and both doe make the members of one Colonie. We do account twelve pounds ten shillings to be a single share adventured. Every ordinary man or woman, if they goe and dwell there, and every child above tenne yeares that shall be carried thither to remaine shall be allowed for each of their persons a single share, as if they had adventured twelve pounds ten shillings in money ... if any goe to be planters will lay downe money to the Treasurer, it shall be also registered and their shares inlarged accordingly be it for more or lesse. All charges of settling and maintaining the Plantation ... shall be borne in a joint stock of the adventurers for seven yeares ... till the end of seven yeares: at which time wee purpose (God willing) to make a division ... of all the lands granted unto us by his Majestie, to every of the Colonie, according to each mans severall adventure ... which wee doubt not will be for every share of twelve pound tenne shillings, five hundred acres at least.[10]

Now instead of investing in the company and expecting the company to send and support tenant workers who would provide the anticipated products expected to make a profit for the investors, the company was saying, invest in the company either as an adventurer, investing money only, or as a planter, going to Virginia, and after seven years we will divide up all the land given to us by the king, and allot it to the investors based on their share value.

The company was still a joint stock company, but now under the name of Treasurer and Company of Adventurers and Planters of the City of London for the First Colony in Virginia. ("The connection between the London and Plymouth companies ceased, and the colony in southern Virginia became a separate body."[11] For convenience hereafter, this company will still be referred to as the Virginia Company of London or London Company or Virginia Company.) The company was still to be run as a commune, with the company supplying the plantation and running a company store for the settlers. They were not permitted to trade on their own, but only with the company storehouse. This joint stock company was to continue for seven years, to 1616. At the end of the period, land suitable for cultivation was to be divided, with at least 100 acres to be given for each share of stock. Optimistic predictions suggested that each share would be worth 500 acres.[12] Both the date and the amount of land were overly optimistic; neither held. However, it was the start of change that would prove crucial later. The first two charters for Virginia were different. In the first, James I, an absolutist, was determined to keep the company and the colony under royal control. The second charter in 1609 represented an opening up of control. It was the beginning of more local control, and therefore a step toward what would become the "genesis of the United States." Land could now be given to individuals by the company without the need for royal permission. It also left much of the governing of the colony up to the company. At the same time, it guaranteed all the liberties and privileges of free Englishmen to the colonists. The clamor for these rights was again sounded just before the War for Independence.[13]

The intention of the reorganization of the company after the 1609 charter was to end the joint ownership of land and distribute land dividends to the shareholders, adventurers and planters, after seven years, in 1616. This would mean that the company investors, the adventurers who stayed in England, and the planters who moved to Virginia, would actually *own* land in America. Of course, it would still be in socage tenure to the king of his Manor in East Greenwich. However, there was a catch. In 1616, after the seven years were up, the company did not have the funds "to defray the administrative costs for the land division."[14] In a *Brief Declaration of the present state of things in Virginia,* the company explained it was expensive to send the ships and surveyors, so to accomplish the division they required each adventurer to pay an *additional* 12 pounds and 10 shillings to enable this division to take place. Each adventurer who did this would receive "a further Divident of land in proportion." This was not a share in the company, but an offer to sell land without investing in the company more than he already had.[15] More surprising was the last paragraph, in which they opened the offer to non-company members. "It is resolved and granted by the Company, that all new–Adventurers, subscribing and performing the conditions before mentioned, for twelve pounds tenne shillings, or more, shall partake in proportion as freely in this present dividend, and in any other privileges and freedome in Virginia, as if with the Old Adventurers they had been partakers from the beginning."[16] In other words, even if you were not an original investor of the company, you could now pay 12 pounds and 10 shillings and receive the same amount of land as an original investor; you bought the land. This was the first offer of a "treasury right," a sale of land directly for money. The ability to purchase land in Virginia by treasury right lasted until the crown took over the colony in 1624, but reappeared later in the century. There was now a means of purchasing land without becoming an investor in the company.

Distributing Virginia Land

There were now at least four ways in which land was distributed in Virginia by the governor and council. The first way was the purchase of a bill of adventure; a dividend in return for investment in founding the colony. "Few details were given either in the charter or 'Instructions' of 1606 about distribution of land. Provisions did state that grants of land in the colony would be made in the name of the king to persons whom the local Council 'nominate and assign'; but no details were given of the method of land distribution. From the scant records that survive, it is evident that promises of land were made to individuals who were willing to hazard the dangers of the new country."[17] One of these apparently was Henry Dawkes. The earliest surviving copy of a bill of adventure is to Dawkes.

> Whereas Henry Dawkes now bound on the intended voyage to Virginia hath paid in ready money, Sr. Thomas Smith Kt. Treasurer for Virginia the some of twelve pounds tenn shillings for his Adventure in the Voyage to Virginia.
> It is agreed that for the same the said Henry Dawkes his heires, Executors, Admrs, and assignes shall have rateably according to his Adventures his full pte. Of all such lands tenemts. And hereditamts. as shall from time to time bee there planted and inhabited, And of all such Mines and Minneralls of Gould, Silver and other metals or Treasures, pearles, pretious stones or any kinds of Wares or Merchandize, commodities or pfitts. Whatsoever, which shall be obtained or gotten in the said Voyage, According to the portion of money by him imployed to that Use. In as large and ample manner as any other Adventurer therein shall receave for the like some.
> Written this fowerteenth of July one thousand six hundred and Eight.
> Richard Atkinson
> [Clerk of the Virginia Company][18]

Henry Dawkes bought both a share in the company as an adventurer, and went to Virginia as a planter. This bill of adventure was issued in 1608, still under the original charter, so Dawkes was named by the king after probably being nominated by the company. Since this was under the original charter, when there was no private ownership of land, this investment by Dawkes assigned him some company land in Virginia with the promise of any dividends in land, or other goods, the company might pay in the future. This bill of adventure, basically a stock certificate, was probably written out and in all likelihood was the same format used for all the bills of adventure issued under the original charter. Later, when these became more common, the form was printed leaving blanks to be filled in for the names, dates, and amounts. "Of those who paid their subscriptions and took there for bills of adventure, it may be stated, as approximately correct, that about one third came to Virginia themselves and settled on their lands; about one third sent over their agents, or finally their heirs, to occupy theirs; while the remaining third sold their shares to others, who generally settled on the lands. These classes were the landed gentry, and they brought, or sent, over another class as servants."[19] After the *Brief Declaration* of April 1616, some adventurers came forward to claim their land. The one that appears to be the earliest of the surviving records, *the first individual land grant title created in Virginia*, was to Simon Codrington in March 1616. "A Bill of Adventure of 12£ 10s granted to Mr. Simon Codrington, being one share of land in Virginia."[20]

A second way of distributing land in Virginia was by selling it to "private plantations." This will be covered in the following section.

A third form of land distribution in Virginia was for meritorious service. This would include land granted to ministers of the church, officers of the State, physicians, and others. Other contributors, such as Captain Newport, the one who led the successful expedition to Virginia in 1607, received 36 shares, and Governor Sir Thomas Dale was allowed 700 pounds sterling in land. They were always concerned about Indian attacks on the frontier, so land was awarded to those who would agree to put up and maintain forts on the frontier. Among these was a 600-acre grant to Captain Abraham Wood for maintaining Fort Henry on the Appomattox. The shortage of labor also meant that tenants or servants were highly prized, as well as the religious or administrators. Each servant or tenant who had come previous to the return of Governor Sir Thomas Dale, in 1616, would be allowed 100 acres at the expiration of his term of service and an additional 100 acres if he erected a house on this land within three years.[21]

The fourth method of distributing land in Virginia, and the most important, was through the use of headrights. This was the result of the reforms of 1618 discussed below.

Private Plantations

It was around 1616 that the company, with its lack of commercial success and its treasury depleted, finally realized that land was its greatest resource and decided to use that resource to "expand the population of the colony and to enhance agricultural production."[22] They encouraged private organizations to settle on the company's patent. These were called "particular plantations" or "private plantations," and were granted by treasury right, direct sale. This was the second form of land distribution in Virginia.

There were people, separate from the company, who wanted to get in on the action, but not invest in the company. They were able to put up large sums of money. Although they didn't invest in the company, they received large tracts of land that they could settle on as they saw fit. Many of these also maintained their own civil jurisdictions.[23] This allotment of land by the company was an attempt to boost the treasury and encourage more settlement in Virginia. Many of the company investors at the time were losing patience with the lack of success and thought they could do better than the company had done. They were eager to try their hand at this new private plantation opportunity outside of the company properties at Jamestown. The company expected these private adventurers would transport themselves, families, and servants to develop their properties, and would therefore expand the population making Virginia a much more prosperous commonwealth.[24]

These particular or private plantations were "to be farmed for their own benefit separate and apart from the projects of the common joint-stock. They were developed under special patents from the company conveying to the patentees large contiguous areas of land with the privilege of farming the grant as a private plantation.... A patent was then secured from the company granting them a large area of land lying in one place, the size of which depended upon the number of shares held jointly by them in the company's stock."[25] These patentees were to fund, staff, and supply their private grants. They were also given some governmental powers over their particular plantation. These plantations were not subordinate, but co-ordinate, entities; thus, they were largely independent of the company, although many of the grants were to company adventurers now acting on their own. These settlements spread east and west along the James and outward along its creeks.[26]

There were three different groups of people that generally formed these plantations. Many individual company adventurers or investors could not afford to do much on their own, so they grouped to form associations to pool their resources for a private plantation. A second type of group formed when a company adventurer associated himself with an outside investor to secure a grant from the company for a private plantation. Finally, a third kind of group came about when a new adventurer, one not previously associated with the company, formed a group for a private plantation. These groups did not invest in the company; in fact, many were impatient with the company and wanted to do their own settlement, but essentially bought the land from the company by treasury right.[27] These plantations were often called Hundreds for reasons that are unclear.

These private plantations were originally based on the number of shares of stock purchased. For example, the Berkeley Hundred received 4,500 acres for the 45 shares purchased, at 100 acres per share. The five men who acquired the shares were "expected to build a town, including churches and schools, and to transport people to Virginia to settle on the plantation." They often started small but increased in size through various means. Captain Martin had invested money in the company early. In 1616 the company granted him a tract for 10 shares on the James River. "He was

Chapter Three. Populating the Land I

'...to enjoy his lands in as lardge and ample manner, to all intents and purposes, as any lord of any manours in England dothe holde his ground.'" He later invested more money in Martin's Hundred, £95 in 1618, £70 in 1620, and an additional two shares in 1622. These were small amounts compared to the claim that "Martin's Hundred contained about 800,000 acres at one time." The Martin Hundred had been expanded by other means. Others, for example, had taken out patents and added them to the Martin Hundred; Sir John Wolstenholme did it with his 20,000-acre patent. His acreage was also extended by headright grants (discussed below) for persons he brought to Virginia.[28]

The first of the private plantations was Smith's Hundred, led by Sir Thomas Smith, treasurer of the Virginia Company. It also was on the James River; later, its name was changed to the Southampton Hundred. In 1618 this group decided to send over 35 persons, but later sent over more, by some accounts "at least three hundred persons, and expended in its improvement six thousand pounds sterling." In 1625 it was already listed as containing 100,000 acres. These numbers, like those of the Martin Hundred, are very large compared to population estimates. For example, a census of 1625 listed 1,218 living persons in Virginia total, so the 100,000 acres of the Southampton Hundred must have been mostly uninhabited land at the time. Land was becoming abundant but the population still lagged; it was only 3,000 in 1630 and 7,500 in 1640. This would expose a labor problem which had to be solved.[29]

In the four years after 1619, 44 grants were made and six were claimed to have been made prior to this time, although not all were settled. The companies establishing these particular plantations were set up similar to the London Company, granting 100 acres of land for each share of stock, with an equal amount when the first grant was settled.[30]

These plantations were large and scattered. "The patentees were free to choose the site of their plantations.... No plantation, however, was to be placed within five miles of any of the four boroughs [of the company], nor within ten miles of any other plantation." This encouraged scattering beyond the company boroughs, especially along the rivers. They "resembled ... the feudal manor, in that they were private estates scattered at various intervals along the James River and possessed a certain amount of economic and political independence which set them apart from the rest of the colony." This encouraged very lucrative tobacco production, among other things, by the wealthy who invested in these plantations.[31]

> A large percentage of the colonists sent to Virginia in the years after 1618 went to those plantations, and some of the financial difficulties of the company may be partly attributed to the fact that so large a portion of the investments made

by adventurers in the colony during these years was diverted from the projects of the company itself to the support of their own private interests.... The population of the colony was increased from about 400 in April of 1618 to around 1,000 by the following spring, and this growth was largely due to the arrival of settlers sent by private adventurers.[32]

The crown had delegated the right to assign Virginia land to the London Company, and therefore lost control of land grants even though all Virginia land was still held of the crown as of the Manor of East Greenwich. Now a similar thing was happening to the company. Land was sold by treasury right to the owners of the private plantations, who were acting independently of the company to enrich themselves. They were self-governing, some even having representation in the new legislature. The Tidewater was gradually filling up with entrepreneurs who felt little obligation to the mother country. In other words, in the Virginia land system, "a land grant was never accepted as a grace of royalty ... the Virginia planter was a member of a community which once had been a corporation and as such had inherited a 'right' to a 'dividend' of land."[33] These planters in Virginia now felt entitled to land independent of the king. They were moving farther away from royal control.

These two changes, more local governing autonomy, and direct control by company officials on land distribution, as early as they were in the colonial process, started the fraying of control by the crown over colonies that were already 3,000 miles away at the end of a long line of communication. Despite the practice and semblance of control, the separation of the colonists from the crown had started and would continue to widen.

1618 Reforms

The private plantation land grants after 1616 were an ad hoc attempt to fill the depleted coffers of the company treasury, but they still hadn't divided the lands as they had promised in the 1609 reorganization, and in that sense were still disorganized, still struggling. In 1618 the company embarked on a more serious reorganization and issued a number of documents on how they would reform the political and economic life of the colony. "The program was prompted by a desire to make the Virginia enterprise a financial success, to increase the population, and to make the Colony attractive as well as to give the colonists more of a sense of participation."[34] One of these documents had an important political consequence. It provided for an elected assembly in the colony, the first elected body in the New World. This assembly met for the first time in 1619. The more significant document though, one that had an immediate impact on the economic life of the colony, was a set of decisions on how they would divide the land, a division which was originally planned for 1616. These were included in a directive to the new governor as *Instructions to Governor Yeardley, 1618*. George Yeardley was scheduled to take over as governor in 1619. These instructions were meant to determine how the land was to be divided, since land was now seen as the greatest asset in attracting settlers to Virginia. These instructions also defined a fourth way land was to be distributed, that is by headright.[35]

The *Instructions* first defined the four cities or boroughs that would comprise the company land. These were Jamestown, Charles City, Henrico, and Kecoughtan (Kiccotan, Kiccowtan), thereafter known as Elizabeth City. In each of these, 3,000 acres were reserved for the company to be farmed for the joint-stock company by tenants who would eventually receive half the profits of their labors. This was an attempt to consolidate and limit the extent of company land so they could allot more for private plantations. They then took care of the early planters, the ones who had come between 1607 and 1616; the ones who had endured the hardships of the early colony. They allotted land to all the adventurers and planters who had come up to the end of Sir Thomas Dale's departure in 1616. This land was allotted to these "ancient planters" in two ways. If they had come at their own expense and stayed three years, they were to be awarded 100 acres for their personal adventure to Virginia and 100 acres for every share (12 pounds 10 shillings) they held. If you had come at company expense, you would be awarded 100 acres for your personal adventure after your term of service to the company (seven years). If you came after Sir Thomas Dale's departure the rules were slightly different. If you paid your own way and stayed three years, you would be allotted 50 acres. It did not require you to be a member of the company, but only that you pay your own way. It was an *ex post facto* way of awarding what would later become known as a headright. Later in the *Instructions* it would be promised for the future also. If instead, your way was paid by the company, you would become a tenant on the company land for seven years with no promise of land after that term. Table 3–1 (shown on next page) summarizes this land distribution.[36]

The leaders of the company encouraged the private plantation adventurers with similar grants of land because they thought that it would help more quickly build the colony's population and hasten the day when Virginia would become a prosperous colony. They encouraged these private plantation adventurers by offering to give 50 acres for every person they would transport to Virginia if that person would stay three years. The private plantation would pay for the transport and receive the services of the immigrant. This was another example of a headright grant.[37]

Company Lands	Lands for Arrivals Between 1607–1616	Lands for Arrivals After 1616
• Four cities established • Jamestown • Charles City • Henrico • Kecoughtan • 3,000 acres in each city farmed by company tenants • Eventually tenants would receive half the profits of their labors	• Came at their own expense and stayed three years • 100 acres for their personal adventure • 100 acres for every share they held • Came at company expense • 100 acres for personal adventure after seven-year term	• Paid your own way and stayed three years • Fifty acres • Company paid your way • Become a tenant for seven years with no promise of land

Table 3–1. Land Distribution per the *Instructions to Governor Yeardley, 1618*

Having taken care of the "ancient planters" who had arrived before 1616, and the immigrants who had arrived between 1616 and 1618, the *Instructions* now addressed the present shareholders. The *Instructions* went on to grant land "in Virginia to such adventurers as have heretofore brought their money here to the Treasury for their several shares being of Twelve Pound ten shillings the share be of one hundred acre the share upon the first Division and of as many more upon a Second Division when the land of the first division shall be sufficiently peopled."[38] This was the land that was promised to be divided for the shareholders in 1616 but was only now being distributed. Then a bonus was provided to shareholders, one intended to increase the population. They officially added a headright provision for the future. "And for every person which they shall transport thither within seven years after midsummer day one thousand six hundred and eighteen, if he continue there three years or die in the mean time after he is shipped it be fifty acres on the first division and fifty more upon a second division."[39]

Every shareholder who transported an immigrant, free or bound by indenture, would receive a grant of 50 acres if that person stayed for at least three years. The grant would belong to the shareholder who paid for the transport, not the immigrant. This would become an attractive method of importing labor to work the land owned by the shareholder. This privilege was then granted to persons who were *not* shareholders, that is, persons outside the company. *Anyone* who immigrated and paid his own way, or paid for someone else to immigrate, was provided 50 acres per head.[40] This provision was included at the end of the *Instructions to Governor Yeardley*, which included the following paragraph.

> That for all persons ... which during the next seven years after Midsummer day, 1618, shall go into Virginia with the intent there to inhabit if they continue there three years or dye after they are shipped, there shall be a Grant made of fifty acres for every person upon a first division and as many more upon a second division (the first being peopled) which grants to be made respectively to such persons and their Heirs at whose charges the said persons going to inhabit in Virginia shall be transported with reservation of Twelve pence yearly Rent for every fifty acres to be answered to the said Treasurer and company, and their Successors for ever after the first Seven Years of every such grant.[41]

This allotment of land for every "head" brought in to Virginia was called a "headright." It essentially opened Virginia for the settlement business. If you could manage the transportation fee for yourself and your four-person family, you would be eligible to receive 200 acres of free land in Virginia. Furthermore, you wouldn't have to pay the 12 pence (one shilling) per 50 acres rent until seven years after your arrival, giving you enough time to get settled. The land belonged to the person paying for the transportation, so if you had the means, you could acquire land by paying for the transportation of an unemployed young man, with few prospects in London, to become an indentured servant in Virginia for seven years. You got the land, and he got a chance, after his indenture, to establish himself, perhaps with some land of his own. This headright provision would be extended beyond the seven years, which was stated in the *Instructions*.

The London Company had found a way to use its most valuable asset, land, to increase the population and move toward a successful agricultural colony. It would eventually thrive, but the troubles were not over. Population growth was still slow, and a disastrous Indian war in 1622 led to the death of hundreds. Finally, in 1624 the king dissolved the struggling company and made Virginia a royal colony. Although the colony was now under direct crown control with a governor appointed by the king, many of the land policies, such as headrights, continued, and immigrants continued to move to Virginia to take up land in one way or another.

> The head right was in operation in 1618, growing more and more important each successive year until it became the principal basis for title.... The law allowing this was eminently wise in the beginning. No more powerful influence could have been set in motion for increasing the volume of population in Virginia. The extant of land to be obtained by compliance with other conditions and even by the purchase of shares was necessarily small in comparison with the area which would be acquired by this means.[42]

The number of private plantations, mostly along the James River, grew, and headrights were used both to increase the numbers within these plantations and anywhere in Virginia the headright owner chose to settle, because he had the right to choose the location. The headright system was a major factor in increasing the population even though it suffered many abuses; it could be gamed. For example, a sea captain would come to the colony, and besides bringing over legitimate colonists using headright privileges, he would claim a headright for each member of his crew, most of whom would not stay, but return with the ship. The captain would then sell these headrights, since they could be bought and sold as any stock certificate. Despite abuses the headright system was an important factor in addressing the most critical need for the colony, the shortage of labor.[43]

There were not enough people to farm the land, especially in the first decades when tobacco, a very labor-intensive crop, was a valuable export. The company started to address this early, not always ethically, by bringing in indentured servants to work the company land as well as the land claimed by the private plantations.

Indentured Servitude

Indentured servitude was common in England at the time. A servant, usually a young male, would sign an indenture contract with a farmer and agree to work for a period of time, usually a year. He would receive his food, housing and clothing in exchange for his labor. After that time, he would either re-sign, move to another employer, or go out on his own. This era in England was still a time of coping with the changes of the agricultural revolution, when enclosure of land led to the consolidation of land into large estates, reducing the need for many farm workers. These people became landless and unemployed, and flooded the cities looking for work.[44] "With England's population growing steadily through the first half of the century (from 4.1 million to 5.3 million in those fifty years) real wages declining, periodic depressions disrupting key industries, and political upheavals unsettling development plans of all kinds, tens of thousands of unskilled laborers and insecure tradesmen and craftsmen face unemployment and its consequences."[45] As was noted previously, this high rate of unemployment was one reason that Richard Hakluyt proposed to colonize North America, to drain this excess population to the colony. This excess labor force in England coincided with the critical shortage of labor in Virginia. "At first the Virginia Company of London paid to transport servants across the Atlantic, but with the institution of the headright system in 1618, the company enticed planters and merchants to incur the cost with the promise of land.... The Virginia Company of London always had more land than labor to work it."[46] Once this door was open there was a rush to bring in indentured servants. Recruiters scoured the port cities, advertised in taverns and hiring fairs, and promised enticements such as the prospect of owning one's own land when the bondage was completed. Many were from a middling background and possessed some craft skill. Others, however, were "utterly destitute vagrants picked up by recruiting agents at 'beggars' fairs." And "week after week, month after month, children, male and female, were snatched from the streets of London for shipment and sale 'for a slave' in Virginia."[47] "Sandys [head of the company in Virginia] doubtless envisioned the transportation of these children, taken from the streets of London and sent without their consent, as a favor both to them and to those they served: he would rescue the boys from vice and idleness and at the same time reward the servant starved planters, who were to make Virginia prosper."[48]

The conditions of an indentured servant were more difficult in Virginia than they were in England. The terms were longer, four to seven years, compared to one year in England. This was necessary to cover the high cost of transportation. The conditions were also harsher. Instead of working on relatively settled farmland in England, they were clearing land in the hot, swampy Tidewater. They faced diseases unknown in England, and as a result the mortality rate was high. Tobacco was a labor-intensive crop grown in a hot and humid environment. However, "the records show that enough of them survived to make up almost the whole labor force and also the vast majority of the population of Virginia by 1625."[49]

"Yet however miserable their existence, however brutalized they may have been in service, most of the immigrants carried with them a sense of independence derived from the knowledge that their bondage was voluntary, contracted, limited in time, and they could look forward to an independent future and possibly a stake in the land."[50] The coincidence of the poor prospects in England coupled with the prospect of land in Virginia contributed to a large indentured servant immigration. The numbers were huge. "Approximately one hundred thousand Britons, the great majority English, are known to have migrated to the tobacco coast [Virginia and Maryland] in the seventeenth century. At least 70 percent of them and probably 85 percent came as indentured servants.... Middlesex County, between the Potomac and the Rappahannock rivers, a contemporary wrote, was a 'sea of servants'—45 percent of that county's entire population were servants in 1668."[51] Other estimates were also high. One analysis suggests that between 1623 to 1637 indentured servants made up 75 percent of the immigrants to Virginia. Another estimate is that 75 percent of the 50,000 immigrants to the Chesapeake Bay colonies between 1630 and 1680 were indentured servants.[52]

The indentured servants of course could not come on their own. It was the landholders, both local and absentee, who saw the opportunity to profit from tobacco that drove the market for servants. Morgan, *The First American Boom*, points out that Jamestown at his time was a boom town. The fortunes sought were not in gold or silver but in tobacco. If a man could get a few servants, he could make more in one year than he was likely to make in England in several. If he could get a large number, he could amass a large fortune. "Despite the fact that bound servants had to be fed, clothed, and housed, Virginians could not get enough of them. Everybody wanted servants. Even tenants who had been unable to pay their own passage to the colony wanted servants."[53] Fertile land in Virginia was cheap, so even a person of moderate means could have a plantation, but it would do him no good without the labor to clear the land and cultivate it. There were some laborers in Virginia at the time, but the wages were high; because of the shortage, indentured servants were much more economical.[54]

Although the vast majority of immigrants to the Chesapeake colonies during the seventeenth century were indentured servants, not all were. There were some middling families who could get headright grants and were able to pay their own way. If a family of four could pay their own way, they could receive headright grants, free land, totaling 200 acres. There was also the attraction of Virginia to the second sons of the gentry and nobility who could not inherit in England, because primogeniture guaranteed the right of the father's estate to the eldest son. During the term of Governor Sir William Berkeley, the civil war in England made it very uncomfortable for many wealthy royalists, cavaliers, in England. Berkeley encouraged them to come to Virginia, where he would provide them asylum. He made it easy for them to acquire land, and with their wealth they were able to set up large plantations. It was these families that would rule Virginia for the next century.[55]

Virginians Move West

After a slow start because of poor planning, disease, trouble with the native population, and maladministration, the Virginia population started to grow rapidly from the 1620s. The form of land grant known as the headright and the social system of indentured servitude fed off each other to increase both the population and the land under cultivation. The population of Virginia, about 3,000 in 1620, doubled to over 7,500 in 1640, doubled again to 17,000 in 1650, and doubled again to 33,000 in 1660.[56] Despite the high mortality rate, especially of the immigrant indentured servants, the total immigration and the increasing natural growth meant the colony could reliably take care of itself. The most important crop was still tobacco, but it did diversify into other crops. Finally, the population density was improving. There was less wilderness and more cultivated plantations.

Indentured servitude grew as the headright system grew. At first it was only the well-off individual who could afford to bring them in, but they brought in many to work their lands. These were not the gentlemen of England, but the new rich who had made their money, sometimes in questionable circumstances, in Virginia. "While tidewater Virginia was still a frontier it passed into the hands of a small, self-serving immigrant elite. In 1625 half the colonists were servants and half the servants were owned by ten men.... These men bought and sold their servants without regard to English law."[57] These were the core of an elite that started to become more common.

However, as more servants poured in to work the land of the private plantations (of the 811 servants who in 1619 were introduced into Virginia, 660 were destined for private estates[58]) and the land of smaller owners, the demographics started to change. Tobacco was a tough master and required large numbers of people from England to produce it. All available space was taken on the fleets coming over with the indentured servants for that purpose. The list of headrights shows 1,500 to 2,000 came annually to the Chesapeake region.[59] This migration would have an impact. After a few years the term of bondage for the servants was completed, and those servants would become free men. The indentured servants were usually young and the length of service was not long. This meant that eventually the freedmen would outnumber those still in service. Wertenbaker, in *The Planters of Colonial Virginia*, goes on to estimate that if there were 1750 headrights per year on average, and 1500 of these included servants, and assuming 20 percent died during their term of service and 5 percent served for life, then on average 1125 would remain to become freedmen. He estimated that there would have been about 6,000 in service at any one time; this is the number Sir William Berkeley claimed to be the case in 1671. These numbers are high and aren't supported by the actual population estimates, but the concept is basically correct; the freedmen eventually outnumbered the servants.[60]

So, what happened to these freedmen? They had no legal or racial barrier to joining the property class that owned small farms. Upon completion of their indenture the servant was provided with an agreed-upon amount of food and clothing, and perhaps some tools before he set off on his own. He was young and adventurous enough, in that he chose to emigrate from his home in England, so he was well prepared to take the next step. In the first 50 years in Virginia there was no real competition from slaves; labor was scarce so wages were high. He could thus work as a laborer for someone until he saved enough for his own farm, or be a tenant for another, again until he saved enough for his own farm. Land was still cheap at the time. "It would have been folly for the tobacco planter to expend his labor on another man's property, perhaps erecting barns and fences and otherwise improving it, when he could for so small an outlay secure land of his own."[61] "Nearly all immigrants expected access to the land colonial promoters promised. Told repeatedly that America was empty and that land was waiting to be farmed, they wanted their share.... Propertied men expected to hold and cultivate land more quickly than servants, but land hunger gripped everyone.... Land meant everything to the immigrants.... It was the bedrock of their prosperity.... Land hunger consumed immigrants, who realized without it they could neither marry nor begin households."[62] The Virginia Company's premise that a poor Englishman, who might not even own a cottage in England, would be happy with a day laborer's wage and a house in Virginia, proved unsustainable once people realized the cheap land that was available in Virginia. As the number of servants became freedmen, they sought land for their own farms. They were necessarily small, consistent with the lack of resources the newly freed had. The freedman could not always easily purchase a farm of his own. In some cases, he had to become a laborer or a tenant on someone else's farm. Those who did have larger holdings sometimes had to divide them into smaller sections and sell them because they couldn't get the labor to farm the larger holdings; the laborers wanted their own land. Others bought smaller holdings, to consolidate them. The population had been divided into two: the wealthy landowner, and the laborers who worked for them.[63]

Despite the start of the divide between the wealthy and those who served, early seventeenth-century Virginia was the land of opportunity. Whether one came as an indentured servant or as a freeman, it was possible to gain property and establish oneself as a person of consideration.[64] Early on, in 1626 for example, there were numerous small proprietors. "Of the holdings listed no less than 25 were for 50 acres or less, 73 for 100 and most others for less than 300 acres. The total number of proprietors listed is 224 and the total acreage 34,472, giving an average for each plantation of 154 acres."[65] This is a small plantation compared to what would come later, and for which Virginia would be characterized as a land of great plantations. Large estates were still limited by the shortage of labor.

This proliferation of landholders follows from the high percentage of the population that came over as indentured servants, eventually became freedmen, and went on to acquire land. Wertenbaker estimates that perhaps 30 to 40 percent of the landholders that came during and prior to 1635 came over as indentured servants.[66] Some of these former servants, now landholders, rose quickly in the Virginia society of the time. "Of the forty-four Burgesses who sat in the Assembly of 1629, no less than seven ... were listed as servants in the muster of 1624 ... in the Assembly of 1652, of the thirty-five members, eight or nine appear on the patent rolls as headrights brought over by others."[67] In Maryland, the other Chesapeake colony, the mortality rate was high, as it was in Virginia, but those that survived had a good chance of becoming a landowner, although it might take a while. "Fortunately wages were high, as the price of tobacco rose during the 1650s, so many servants, perhaps as many as half of those attaining their freedom, did acquire their own farms in time.... In one respect the 1650s was a golden period for servants, there being no elite other than the proprietor and a few gentry. Never again were social classes to be so fluid."[68]

At first the small planter, either by himself or with the help of a servant or two, cultivated his own land. With tobacco doing well he was able to keep up with the larger planter. However, as the population increased, land in the Tidewater became scarcer, and expansion started into the Piedmont. The piedmont region, at a higher elevation and beyond the fall line of the rivers, was actually a better climate for one's health and for general farming, but not as good for tobacco. The tobacco casks were heavy and in the coastal region they would roll them to the river where they would be loaded onto ships. One couldn't do that in the Piedmont region. With the influx of servants and growing population, land was becoming harder to find. Although at first, the freed servant stayed in the colony, it became harder to do so as land became scarce. "During the late seventeenth century a scattering of former servants moved into the piedmont and settled as squatters on the land. They were quickly pushed aside by the grandees of the tidewater, who acquired title to the best soil through their access to power. The men who sat in the Council and controlled the granting of lands in the colony awarded a large part of the piedmont to their own families."[69] This was the beginning of change in Virginia, settlers moving west and elite families starting to exert control.

Circumstances changed in Virginia at mid-century because of the upheavals in England at that time. Immediately after the restoration of Charles II to the throne in 1660, Parliament reenacted the Navigation Act originally enacted in 1651. The idea was to make the empire a closely knit unit between England and the colonies, and present a trade barrier to the rest of the world. The Navigation Act was the vehicle to enforce this barrier. Trade that had been going on between the American colonies with other countries would now be limited. Tobacco, the most lucrative Virginia crop, was on the embargoed list. It was now required that all Virginia tobacco go through England first. Eventually this caused a dramatic drop in the price of tobacco and severely altered the Virginia economy.

The lower prices made it difficult if not impossible for the small planter to compete.[70]

Servants kept coming for a while, but there was no work, so many ended up in dire poverty. It was no longer an advantage to be a servant in Virginia compared to being one in England because one could not work and save to buy land. "Another problem was that by this time all the best land had been claimed. Thus, 25 percent of all servants failed to become landowners, and only 6 percent actually became successful planters owning their own labor force."[71] Few indentured servants who came after 1660 succeeded in establishing themselves in Virginia. For example, in 1672 there were 672 listed as headrights, but later only eleven could be identified as landowners. "Of 1,116 names examined in the years from 1671 to 1674 inclusive, only 26 are positively those of persons listed as landowners in 1704."[72]

From Indentured Servitude to Slavery

As the price of tobacco dropped, the smaller planters could not compete, and many lost their farms to the larger planters. The latter still had the expense of labor for the labor-intensive tobacco crop. Indentured servants were expensive to import and keep, and their terms expired in a few years. It was much better to have an endless supply of labor that was inexpensive to keep without any end to the terms. Thus, came slavery. Although slavery came early to the colony, in 1619, it did not flourish during the relatively equal boom years in the first half of the century. In 1624 there were only 22 listed slaves; in 1649, with a white population of 15,000, there were only 300 slaves. They started to increase rapidly in 1670 in Governor Berkeley's term, growing to about 3,000 in 1680 when there were about 15,000 indentured servants. "By 1715 the ratio of free to unfree labor was almost exactly reversed, with 23,000 slaves in the province and 1,000 being imported annually."[73]

By the end of the seventeenth century there were fewer servants coming in, both because the conditions in England had improved the prospects for the young male there, and because slavery had taken root in Virginia. A slave's term was never ending, so the plantation owner never had to worry about importing and outfitting more, and costly, servants. The land granted as headrights for the importation of servants decreased as the number of servants decreased. However, there was still a need for land and for revenue. In 1624, when the company was dissolved by the king, the selling of land by treasury right was suspended; only headrights were used. Because they still wanted to use land for revenue and the use of headrights had dropped, in 1699 Virginia restarted selling land using treasury rights, but in a slightly different manner than they had used them when all the private plantations were sold early in the century. There was now a fixed price of five shillings for 50 acres.[74]

At the turn of the eighteenth century, Virginia took on the image for which it was known later in popular culture: large plantations owned by a wealthy few, and populated by thousands of slaves. The men who had managed to acquire land through headrights, or through treasury rights early in the century, or during the elite rule of Governor Berkeley, were able to consolidate and convert the land into large plantations. They bought out the smaller planters who could no longer compete.

The larger plantations needed laborers. In the seventeenth century these were mostly white indentured servants. At the turn of the century the increased labor needs came from black slaves. They were cheaper than indentured servants, and this fact put an end to indentured servitude. All the large plantation owners had a goodly number of slaves around them. This had a disastrous impact on the independent yeoman. The classes had now divided into the wealthy planters and their slaves, with the middle-class yeoman caught trying to eke out a living between these two.[75]

The Virginia culture reverted to the time in feudal England when the nobility owned all the land, and the villeins worked these lands for the lords of the manors. Only now it was even worse. The villeins had some rights and, although politically powerless, there were norms that protected them; they also had some limited freedoms. The slaves, on the other hand, were bound for life, had no protection, and were treated very harshly. They were considered property, owned by the plantation master. The villeins were never "owned."

It is ironic that the availability of free land, through the headright, or cheap land through the treasury right, would lead to an American aristocracy, that of the slaveholder. This wouldn't have surprised the Russian historian V.O. Kliuchevsky who predicted, correctly, that free land in Russia and Eastern Europe would lead to serfdom. He saw that free land would draw off the workers to land of their own. To preclude this, the landowners "bound the workers to the land through the institution of serfdom."[76] We saw this previously when free land in New Spain led to an aristocracy of landowners with their *encomienda* and haciendas, an aristocracy that lasted for centuries. The American historian Frederick Jackson Turner took the opposite view that free land on the frontier eventually led to democracy. His work was done after the end of slavery, and he treats slavery as an incident in the broader subject of the frontier. Kliuchevsky and Turner were both right and both wrong, as was to be shown in subsequent American history.

The aristocracy of the slave-holding elite was America's only aristocracy. It was spread and justified mostly by elites from England who were used to hierarchical social structures, easily claimed land in America, and could not resist the economic benefit of the free labor slavery provided. It was a blot on American history for over 200 years, and a brutal sore over 150 of those years—1700–1865. It was, however, ultimately conquered because of resistance to the attempt to move the system to the west. Although free land contributed to its rise, there were other factors that increased its likelihood. As Fischer and Kelly point out in *Bound Away: Virginia and the Westward Movement*, "in short, free land operated in one way in some regions and in quite another elsewhere." They postulate a social switching mechanism, and that "this switch in the hands of those who controlled access to the land, regulated the flow of migration, and established a framework of laws that defined the status of labor and land in a new environment.... In the northern parts of the United States, a system of small freeholds was introduced as a cultural artifact. In Virginia large land grants were common in the Berkeley era. The switch was thrown one way in the northern colonies and another way in the South."[77] So, controlling access to land was a key factor in whether or not the previously open land became free or slave-holding areas.

Virginia had the largest population of any colony, except for the decade from 1630 to 1640 when there was a massive Puritan migration to Massachusetts Bay. Even late in the seventeenth century as indentured servitude was being replaced by slavery, the population continued to increase, only not all of them remained in Virginia. Virginia was unique among the colonies in that many moved more than once. In Massachusetts many families moved once when they were young and then stayed put. Part of this can be explained by the destination of indentured servants, which was predominantly toward Virginia. These servants had less in common among themselves and did not have the religious attachment that those in Massachusetts had to each other, so there was less holding them in place. Also, Church of England Virginia was more tolerant of others compared to Puritan Massachusetts.

The poor moved more than the rich. When servant terms were up, they found it difficult to remain in the same county, although they did tend to stay in the same colony, at least at first. "Former servants gravitated to areas of inferior land that had been left behind by the great gentry.... Others moved toward the fringe of settlement, preferring to take their chances with the Indians rather than challenge Sir William Berkeley's cavalier elite."[78] The servant, after his term expired, was no longer able to establish his own farm, and the poor planter sold his holdings and moved to look for better opportunities.[79]

Chapter Three. Populating the Land I

Wertenbaker quotes Edward Randolph in his 1696 letter to the Board of Trade criticizing the Council for allowing the rich planters to patent large tracts of desirable land, which caused the migration of poor families away from the region.

> The chief and only reason is the Inhabitants and Planters have been and at this time are discouraged and hindered from planting tobacco in that colony, and servants are not so willing to go there as formerly, because members of the Council and others, who make an interest in the Government, have from time to time procured grants of very large Tracts of land, so that there has not for many years been any waste land to be taken up by those who bring with them servants, or by such Servants, who have served their time faithfully with their Masters, but it is taken up and ingrossed beforehand, whereby they are forced to hyer and pay a yearly rent for some of those Lands, or go to the utmost bounds of the Colony for Land, exposed to danger and often times proves the Occasion of Warr with the Indians.[80]

These Virginia migrants started moving west. They knew by the 1609 charter that the west was virtually unlimited to them. However, in the late seventeenth century the frontier still had to contend with Indian problems. Because of the Indian threat in the seventeenth century, land across the Blue Ridge, in the Shenandoah Valley, was settled later by other immigrants. So, at this time, as they moved out of the colony some would move to Maryland or Delaware, especially the eastern shore, or Pennsylvania, and some to the northern part of Carolina. "As a result, Maryland became a more diverse society, with more room for people of middling estate. Virginia in the late seventeenth century became more closed and homogenous"; it became the large planter's society. This migration of Virginians into and out of Virginia continued for many decades, into the nineteenth century. "The westward movement carried about a million people out of Virginia." It was by far the largest expansion of any province, partially enabled by the unlimited land they saw in the west.[81] "Virginia's great migration was drawn by one great magnetic attraction: land. Thomas Hardman despaired of ever being more than a tenant in Virginia and moved to Tennessee in hope of getting a farm of his own. Newlyweds James and Elizabeth McClure went to Texas because they could not find good land in Virginia.... Reference to western lands were often cast in paradisical terms.... John Filson extolled Kentucky as 'the most extraordinary country that the sun enlightens with its celestial beams.'"[82] Many of these people were former servants and laborers, some of them in rags. Most, however, were of middling circumstance, and some had even been prosperous. The attraction was still more land. "Harry Toulmin wrote of Virginia, 'Here persons who have but four or five hundred acres and a large family think it is time to begin to make a provision for them by going to

Washington County, Nelson, or Kentucky in order to exchange their five hundred acres for five thousand.'"[83]

Thinking of a move to Kentucky, which was then part of Virginia, was perfectly natural because the 1609 charter stated that Virginia went from "sea-to-sea." Virginians had been accustomed to believing they could always move west and remain in Virginia, and there would always be plenty of free or cheap land available.

Populating the Later Colonies

Virginia was, except for a short time in the 1630s, always the largest province and, early in the republic, the largest state with regard to population. The people that moved through the province were also the earliest ones to move west. However, Virginia was not the only province to grow in the seventeenth century. Even after the Great Migration of the Puritans in the 1630s, the New England population grew very rapidly, from about 27,000 in 1650 to approximately 106,000 by 1700.[84] There was also growth in the other colonies founded from mid-century until 1700, mostly from natural population growth but also from English immigration. There would be surges in the eighteenth century also from other parts of Great Britain and Europe. The attraction in all these cases would be land. The resident colonials saw the land just beyond their present location and considered it an outlet when it was time to move for a variety of reasons. There was an additional attraction for those across the Atlantic suffering for their beliefs; good land and the chance to practice their religion as they saw fit.

New England

In the Atlantic seaboard colonies, there seemed to be two extreme types of rural settlement, "the compact agricultural village and the isolated farmstead. Seventeenth century New England exemplifying the former type, was described by Edmund Burke as 'mosaic of little village republics.' Virginia and the other planter colonies of the South exemplified almost equally well the dispersed variety."[85] The middle colonies were somewhere between these extremes.

Virginians moved a lot. As we saw previously, "Virginians, rich and poor alike, seemed happiest when putting a large space between themselves and their neighbors."[86] There were few towns; tobacco planters didn't need them. The plantations grew along the rivers, which enabled them to ship tobacco directly from the plantation. As the servants achieved release from their contracts, they had no particular reason to stay near the

Chapter Three. Populating the Land I

original plantation, and so moved to the best land they could find. New Englanders, on the other hand, were different. As we saw, they had originally considered distributing land by headrights, but rejected that in favor of assigning land to groups to form villages, within which the families formed close-knit religious communities. After all, this is why they came in the first place, to strengthen their religious beliefs. "In seventeenth-century New England land was neither a source of income for the colonies nor an object of speculation by individuals. It was held in trust for bona fide settlers who planned to use it as a livelihood and was granted to them in such amounts as their immediate and prospective needs indicated. In the granting of land to groups rather than individuals the colonizing companies had in mind the stimulating of compact settlement."[87]

Despite the large increase in population in the latter half of the century there was not much movement, at least at first. An important reason for this lack of mobility was the large size of the early New England grants. One grant, Dedham, was so large it encompassed the land of almost a dozen modern Massachusetts towns. This meant that a town granted in a large area had room to grow for the second generation and beyond.[88]

However, the increasing population eventually did lead to movement for new land, but it was still an orderly process. The General Court would establish new towns as needed. At first the coastal towns would just be extended inland, but in 1635 the first inland town, Concord, was established. This was a break in the frontier line; now they were moving farther into the wilderness. In 1633 the Plymouth colony established a trading post on the Connecticut River. Soon a group from Massachusetts Bay moved to a nearby spot on the Connecticut River. "After 1640 the Connecticut settlers formed smaller villages with great rapidity. Hartford people moved across the river, and lived where formerly they had had only fields.... While new towns had been springing up along the rivers and coast of Connecticut, expansion had been going on rapidly in Massachusetts in much the same manner.... The crowding of the coast towns also tended to push back the frontier."[89] While much of this expansion was due to population increase, not all of it was. Some were displeased with the colony administration and wanted to move further away, and there were church quarrels that prompted people to leave a community and start another one. "Wethersfield, which had contributed settlers to Stratford, saw an exodus of about twenty families because of a church quarrel."[90]

New England expansion was not so much a purposeful migration in any one direction but more of an overflow of the original communities. It was clear though that the search for good land was a cause for emigration. New Englanders didn't move as often as Virginians but they did move at least once before they settled in their final properties. "To get land, immigrants left older towns and moved more often and over longer distances than they had in England. New England immigrants typically moved once, but between one-third and two-fifths stayed put. Young men moved most often."[91] Sometimes they found the land too small for their agricultural needs, or there was not enough arable land. In Gloucester, for example, "out of eighty-two persons named as proprietors of the soil between 1633 and 1650, two thirds ultimately migrated to new towns to try their luck under more favorable conditions."[92] "Before 1660, then, five of the present New England states had towns planted within their limits, and the two most populous ones, Connecticut and Massachusetts, had sent bands of pioneers up and down the coast, and far inland, to begin new settlements in the wilderness. But expansion did not cease at the Borders of New England; in 1640 the first English settlement was made on Long Island, at Gravesend, by immigrants from Massachusetts."[93] It wasn't only Long Island which attracted New England migrants. Around 1661 the new governor of East Jersey, Philip Carteret, sent a delegation to Connecticut to offer land with some liberal terms; East Jersey was still trying to attract settlers. Thirty families from Connecticut sailed down and established themselves in what is now Newark. "True to their traditions, the church in Newark was a Connecticut church moved in its entirety,—pastor, deacons, records, and major part of the congregation."[94] These Connecticut pioneers later established the College of New Jersey, now known as Princeton.

This collective experience of free land parceled out by the General Court in townships was clearly new to these colonists, but they got accustomed to it very easily. There was a lot of movement in England at the time because of the upheaval caused by enclosures, and the beginnings of a market economy, but the movers in England could not expect land at the end of the move; it had been spoken for and occupied. But if there was dissatisfaction for any reason, the New England migrant could look to move on. "The incoming English settlers who arrived from time to time seem to have settled in the older towns.... But the pioneer was most frequently the son of a pioneer, his wife the daughter of another, and together they began a new home where land was cheap and plenty, and the money went farther than it did on the coast."[95]

We met Arthur Scovell in the previous chapter, an immigrant from England who made a will equally dividing his estate among his children. We don't know how his children eventually got their land, but Arthur Junior evidently did well for himself. He was born in 1663-4 and apparently lived and died in Lyme or Old Lyme, Connecticut. In 1688 he was assessed a tax for one person, one horse, and £25,000. "At this time there were seventy householders taxed, in a territory of twelve miles or more. Their homes were in the southwest corner and along the shore of the [Long

Island] Sound, and probably along the Connecticut River. The sources of their wealth were the forests, the farms, the fisheries. Game was abundant. Fish and lumber may have been exported."[96]

As the population grew both naturally and from immigration, became more diverse in religion, and separated in distance, the government fell behind in extending land rights to newcomers.

> This resulted in an increasing number of citizens who were without land of whose holdings and rights were definitely restricted. These landless citizens, eventually a majority, having no sentimental bonds with the town's historic past, formed a discontented group to whom the idea of founding a new home beyond the establishments had great appeal. Many times it was a group migration that took place, but it was not unusual for a single family to strike out alone ... there came to be an increasing number of isolated farm dwellings. Some of these were established by "squatters" or "cottagers," ...the land-hungry class ... who, with or without permission from the proprietors, occupied small tracts of the undivided land.[97]

Clearly this idea of free land had taken hold in New England also. A squatter is one who squats on or occupies the land without any proof or pretense of ownership. The claim was usually "I need it, I can make it productive, it's unused, and therefore it is mine." The most available land was always on the frontier. So, the squatter, who moved to the frontier for the land, was always risking the dangers of the frontier including Indian attack, separation from the help of neighbors, and lack of access to needed supplies.

In the early eighteenth century, as New Englanders expanded in every direction, and congregations started to split, many having moved to the frontier, the orderly assignment of land to townships by the General Court broke down. The colonies "introduced the new practice of selling and granting land in large blocks to wealthy or prominent citizens or to cities. These in turn sold it for a profit to individuals eager to pioneer."[98] This was the start of land speculation in New England. Some wealth had been accumulated by those on the coast by then, and it needed to be invested. "Such speculations in land became an increasingly significant and important feature of the process of expansion."[99] This land speculation quickly filled up the desirable areas near existing towns. "The pressure for new lands must very evidently lead to emigration outside the boundaries of the colony, and the frontier must be pushed out into the wilderness to the north and west in order to furnish homes to those who wished to establish themselves of farms of their own, but were too poor to pay for higher-priced lands lying about the older towns."[100] The expansion of the towns in New England, originally controlled by the government and meant to be free for settlers, now more resembled the more chaotic approach of distributing land in Virginia. The value of cheap land was clearly recognized by all, especially young families who knew that they could always move a little farther out to get the land to start a farm, despite the risks involved. They also knew, that had they still been in England, there was no "farther out" where land was available.

Maryland and Pennsylvania

As we saw the plan to settle Maryland with large manors as they had existed previously in England had failed; few were established. However, Cecil Calvert was still interested in populating the colony so as to increase quitrents and family wealth. He gave away headrights as long as the persons receiving them would bring in indentured servants with them.

> The land system in Maryland during the life of the second Lord Baltimore was very closely connected with the enterprise of importing white servants into that colony. Land was parceled out to the adventurers directly in proportion to the number of servants brought with them from England.... Rewards, stations, and lands were offered in return for transporting people to Maryland.... Baltimore's scheme of settlement was one devised to secure as much revenue as possible from the new colony. Everything was done to settle the plantation as rapidly as possible, and as a means to this end, he resorted to the practice of importing servants on a large scale, a custom already familiar in Virginia.... There was no such thing as direct purchase of land from the proprietor. Each settler who came into the province received one hundred acres of land, but if he wished more he could obtain it only by importing servants.[101]

This emphasis on increasing population by bringing in servants meant that a large portion of the immigrants were servants; "70 percent of the colonists who came to Maryland between 1634 and 1681 arrived as indentured servants." Many free immigrants arrived in Maryland between 1646 and 1652, and between 1658 and 1667, but many of these came from Virginia, and were servants who had completed their terms of indenture. The 70 percent therefore may be an underestimate of the immigration from England. Menard, in *Economy and Society in Early Colonial Maryland*, estimates that perhaps 85 percent of the immigrants to the Chesapeake in those periods may have been servants.[102]

The law in Maryland gave 50 acres of land to each indentured servant when he had served his time. The land books in Maryland show the names of "over 21,000 immigrants, almost all indentured servants, for whose importation a headright was claimed." Although not all the land was good, and often "the servant assigned his right away as soon as he had proved it," the fact is that vast amounts of free land had been carved out of the proprietor's land. As in Virginia, many of these former servants obtained land of their own and became yeoman farmers.[103]

Although Lord Baltimore intended the land should be given away to those who brought in servants, he did not follow up to assure that would happen. Later speculators got involved and started abusing the headright system. "As a result of these abuses, the headright system was abolished by Calvert in 1683."[104] The old system of giving away land to persons who brought in servants was abolished at that time also, and a new one adopted in which land would be purchased by payment of a definite amount of money. This was also about the time the natural population increase would start to eclipse the increase due to immigration alone.[105]

Despite all the land given to settlers who brought in servants, and the land given to indentured servants who had finished their terms, the population remained mostly confined to the Atlantic coast, the Tidewater. This was because Maryland, like Virginia, was a tobacco economy, and tobacco could only be profitably grown near the coast or within easy access to the coast. Virginia had many rivers that allowed plantations along these rivers to gain easy access to the sea for tobacco, and later, easy access inland for the growing population. Maryland did not have this access further inland, so for all of the seventeenth and into the eighteenth century, the fertile land of central Maryland, the Piedmont region, was not exploited.

In Pennsylvania Penn continued to sell land to the First Purchasers, all Quakers, but he also used other means to increase the population. "He ... offered to lease lands to settlers at one penny per acre. Finally, to attract indentured servants, any master importing servants would be allowed fifty acres per servant as compensation for transporting them; and the servant himself, when his term had expired would be granted fifty acres of land."[106] This was unusual, although similar to Maryland, in that indentured servants in other colonies, for example, Virginia, did not automatically receive land of their own at the completion of their indenture. Again, to help the colony grow with the type of settler he wished to have, in July 1681 he issued a document on Conditions and Concessions. "On his part, Penn agreed to clear the Indian title on 500,000 acres of land, then to lay out a principal city wherein each purchaser would receive ten acres of land for each five hundred purchased. For those settling in groups, two hundred would be set aside for a village in each tract of 10,000 acres. The several towns and villages would be connected by highways, the right of way being donated by the Proprietor. Each man's land would be located with access to a navigable stream and to a village."[107] By donating highways, he was going even farther than the planned towns of New England. The sales to First Purchasers continued, less rapidly after 1690, to around 1700, when he had disposed of approximately 800,000 acres in addition to about 165,000 to a half dozen speculators, including the Free Society of Traders (20,000 acres), and the Frankfort Company (25,000 acres).[108]

Penn's first settlements were on the Delaware River then occupied by the Lenni Lenape, "Original People." Penn had a good reputation with the Indians and insisted on paying them for the land. He also forbade anyone from dealing directly with the Indians so he could preclude fraudulent purchases. He did have one blind spot, however. "His policy rested on the unstated assumption that the natives would inevitably transfer ownership of the land to the colonists. Penn offered the first purchasers some of the finest Lenape land, including choice river frontage, much of which had been cleared by the natives for use as summer base camps.... [However], land could not be occupied until all Indian claims had been answered. Penn followed through on this promise, spending some £1,200 on payments to Indians by 1685." Despite his generally good intentions, there were still some disputes about the land arising from the different views on land as property. The colonists viewed land in terms of exclusive ownership and saw undeveloped land as waste, whereas the Lenape saw land as embedded in the social fabric of the community. The Lenape made their peace with Penn's settlers but were forced westward as the colony expanded.[109] "By1690 over 8,800 English, Welsh, Scottish, Irish, German, and French Huguenot settlers inhabited the Delaware Valley, along with the remaining Swedes, Finns, and Dutch. Penn and his agents were tremendously successful in recruiting new colonists. By the turn of the century, 21,000 colonists inhabited Pennsylvania ... notable was the dispersion of the population.... The cheapness and ready availability of land allowed entrepreneurial colonists to establish themselves with relative ease and to accumulate land to pass on to descendants."[110] Pennsylvania population and land sales grew rapidly in the late seventeenth century, mostly through the immigration of Quakers from England. However, it surged again in the first third of the next century, which we will see in the next chapter.

The Lewis Family

In the Prologue we learned that the Baron of Kendall gave a manor to Richard DeGlypyn for performing a heroic deed. This Richard DeGylpyn was an ancestor of the Lewis family of present-day Maryland. If he hadn't been before, DeGylpyn was now part of the landed nobility; his family held the land for generations. The original Kentmere Manor was in Cumbria in the north, near the Scottish border. So the DeGlypyn line started out as borderlanders before the family moved south to Oxfordshire. Thomas Gilpin of the sixteenth generation of DeGylpyns (Gilpin) fought as a major for Parliament in the battle of Worcester in 1651, the last battle of the English civil war. He was from Warborough, Oxfordshire. He was a friend of William Penn, and following the war, he became a Quaker; a dramatic lifestyle change from warrior to pacifist. This was a time of intense persecution of the Quakers in England, and he must have felt that pressure. He died in England in 1682 or 1683, but his son Joseph, also a Quaker, was born in 1663 and immigrated to Chester County in southeast Pennsylvania in 1695-96. His wife's uncle gave her 100 acres of land and Joseph bought 425 more acres for 40 pounds; the family was apparently well off. Being one of the early Quaker settlers, he might have been a First Purchaser. Lewis Walker, another Lewis ancestor, was born in Merioneth Wales, moved to Pennsylvania and died in Radnor, Pennsylvania. We don't have any more information on Walker. He was also most likely a Quaker since many came from the prosperous Merioneth, and Radnor, Pennsylvania, was most likely named after Radnor Wales, also a Quaker stronghold.[111]

Peter Cook was born in Cheshire, England in 1674, married in 1695, and died at sea in 1713 while he was on his way to Pennsylvania. His Quaker widow Elinore, with six children, presented her certificate from Frandly Meeting, England to Providence Meeting in Chester County, Pennsylvania in 1714. The commissioners allotted her 100 acres of land, likely a gift to the widow. She resided in Chester until at least 1726, but the next generation of six children soon scattered. John stayed in Chester; Peter moved to York County; Thomas, Isaac, and Mary moved to the Carolinas; and Elinor married and moved to Delaware. So, the second generation of the Peter Cook family already found it necessary to move to other parts of British America, most likely for cheaper land.[112]

These families, Quakers from England and Wales, were among the first to settle in Pennsylvania from the Lewis family, some possibly invited directly by Penn. The next waves of immigrants to Pennsylvania would be large numbers of Germans and Scots-Irish who would arrive in the eighteenth century prior to the Revolution. They would also include members of the Lewis family. This will be covered in the next chapter.

The Need for People, the Need for Land

The provinces of Virginia, New England, Maryland, and Pennsylvania all were interested in increasing their population to increase the wealth of the colony. All used land to do so, either giving it away through headrights or selling it cheaply. The other provinces all did something similar. East Jersey offered land to New Englanders on liberal terms, and Carolina land was considered by New Englanders and Barbadians. So those seeking land were not only from England, but from other English colonies. Similarly, land was being offered by other colonies. Land was both the goal and the inducement.[113]

Engermann and Sokoloff, in *Once Upon a Time in the Americas*, postulate that the interaction between people and land in the Americas was a direct result of the scarcity of labor in the North American colonies. Once the Europeans started their quest for territory early in the sixteenth century, they had to decide how they were going to exploit it. Even if it were just for the extraction of materials, they would need some type of presence in that territory, a trading post at least, for the base of operations. They would also need the means to do the extraction. In other words, they would have to set up a process to take advantage of the territory for the enrichment of the home country. This meant a lot of people would be involved; they needed labor.

The Spanish focused on Mexico and Peru because they were densely populated and they knew labor was essential to extract resources. Obviously, the wealth of these areas was another reason.[114] In one sense it was luck that the Spanish made their early discoveries and colonies in the south, an area that had a relatively large, high-density native population. They were easily able to conquer these populations and establish the *encomienda* system with the native population working for the Spanish encomenderos. The *encomiendas* were very large, but the number of Spanish overseers was relatively small. Thus, they had an instant aristocracy with the native workers at the bottom. There was no need to import workers from Spain, and in fact "the Crown began early in the sixteenth century to regulate and restrict the flow of European migrants to its colonies in the Americas … there is no doubt that Spanish policies limited, rather than encouraged, the migration of Europeans to the New World."[115] This instant aristocracy was easy to propagate because the encomenderos, and later the hacendados, had control of the system. "Where labor was relatively abundant … elites had less reason to share privileges as a means of attracting more labor, and likely were less constrained in their ability to shape institutions to advantage them."[116] This guaranteed a very unequal land distribution system, with large estates in the hands of a few, which was propagated for centuries, even into the twentieth century.

When the English, and later the French, started to establish their colonies they faced an entirely different environment. In the eastern edge of North America, the first settlers faced an area which was heavily forested and contained a relatively low-density population of indigenous people. The variety of tribes practiced heterogeneous lifestyles from agriculture, to hunting and gathering, to a combination of both. There was not a uniform, indigenous agricultural society that could be subsumed by the migrating Europeans.

There was no strategic plan by the English Crown to settle North America. All the colonies were founded by entrepreneurs hoping to make a profit, and in addition, in some places to find religious freedom. Each colony had to make its own way into the forest, and its own policy on how to deal with the natives. Most of the English colonies lacked a large native population that could be used to grow and extract resources, so they had to rely on European labor.[117] In other words, the primary difference between Spanish America and English America was in how they achieved the labor force in order to exploit the territory they each claimed.

We saw how difficult it was for the Virginia Company to start a colony at Jamestown from scratch with only a few hardy settlers in the early years. There were not that many interested in going there even though there were a lot of rootless people in England because of the enclosure movement. The colony almost failed, and took over 10 years to become established and grow. The company finally realized that their greatest asset was the almost limitless amount of land they were given in the grant. They knew they had to have a labor force, had to increase the population, to increase the prosperity of the colony, so they used that asset to induce settlement. Virginia didn't really start to grow until the company started to pay dividends in lands, and more importantly, started the headright system. A headright was the promise of free land. If you could afford to bring yourself and family over you were entitled to 50 acres of land for each member of your family. That was expensive for most families, but planters who could afford it would bring over indentured servants, and receive a 50-acre headright for each servant, who would then be assigned to work that land. Indentured servants were used, in one form or another, in most of the colonies, and some have estimated that 75 percent of arrivals from Europe came as indentured servants.[118] The headright system was the vehicle used to import needed labor into Virginia and other colonies. In New England the labor was brought in with the migration of large family groups.

The increase in population led to an increase in the need for more land. When an indentured servant became free at the end of his obligated service time of four to seven years, he would not return to England, but instead seek his own land, usually farther out on the frontier where land was cheaper. This virtuous cycle helped increase the population, and therefore the labor force needed to assure a prosperous colony, which in turn increased the need for more land. Thus, in the seventeenth century the land in these coastal colonies was filling up with farmers, merchants, and craftsmen, which allowed them to become self-sufficient and carry on a vigorous trade with the mother country and others. Furthermore, this land was owned by the people taking it up; they were not tenants or farm laborers, as was the case in England.

This method of supplying a labor force by inducing Europeans to come for free land had another effect. The Spanish found a readily available labor force and imposed a ruling structure and ruling class to achieve their exploitation of the new colonies. This eventually led to a rigid aristocracy that lasted for centuries. It was different in the English coastal colonies. There was diversity from colony to colony. Free land in Virginia was distributed differently from the free land in New England. There was diversity in the populations also, from the young, male indentured servants in Virginia and Maryland, to the family structures of New England. They came singly to Virginia; they came in large groups to New England; but they all, individually, had to figure out how to settle, how to plant, and how to deal with the indigenous people. This led to the need for common action, which in turn led to elected Assemblies, starting with Virginia in 1619. Although still under the English Crown and Parliament, the local colonies had self-government. This labor force, unlike the Spanish labor force, learned how to govern itself.

The free land and later cheap land, used in English North America as an inducement to foster settlement and build a labor force, became an integral part of what it meant to be an English colonist. It wasn't long before access to free or cheap land came to be seen as a right.

Chapter Four

Populating the Land II: Immigration and Expansion

All the English North American colonies had been founded in the seventeenth century except Georgia, which was founded in the early eighteenth century. All had expanded in population, both by natural growth and by immigration from England. In some of the middle colonies such as New York, New Jersey, and Delaware, others, such as Swedes and Dutch, who preceded the English, were absorbed into the English colonies. As pointed out previously, the growth was rapid. In many colonies, such as Virginia and Maryland, indentured servants made up the vast majority of immigrants who came to work the land for others and hoped to get their own land eventually. In New England the major immigrant populations were families rather than single indentured servants. These families had large numbers of children, so New England's growth was more natural than immigrant.

All the colonies had been established as commercial ventures and all had the goal of increasing the fortunes of one party or another. Some had additional motivations, such as the Puritans and Quakers, who wanted to practice their religion without oversight or coercion. Land was distributed by the colonizing company, although the distribution methods differed widely from province to province. In New England the land was distributed to groups of colonists to enable them to set up towns that would enhance their religious communities. In Virginia land was distributed by headrights to encourage a labor force that would make the colony more prosperous. In these colonies land was abundant but labor was scarce.

The population of the colonies continued to rise in the eighteenth century, from about 270,000 in 1700 to about 2.8 million in 1780.[1] Natural growth remained high, but now new waves of immigrants came, and not just from England (and Wales), but foreigners. The term "foreigners" needs clarification. In 1707 Scotland joined the Kingdom of England and Wales to form the Kingdom of Great Britain, so the Scots, previously foreigners, were now part of Great Britain. There was significant migration to

British America from northern England, Scotland, especially the borderlands between England and Scotland, and the Ulster settlement in northern Ireland. The Ulster settlement in northern Ireland had been populated by many immigrants from Scotland, northern England, and their borderlands, as well as Irish. The term Scots-Irish will be used to collectively refer to all these groups. The other large immigration block came from Germany.[2]

There were both *push* and *pull* factors that stimulated these migrations. The push factors included religious persecution and economic hardship. These were similar to the reasons the original Puritans and Quakers came to Massachusetts and Pennsylvania, or the unemployed young men and women came to Virginia as indentured servants. The pull factors were also the same, the opportunity to start a new life and, perhaps more importantly, the opportunity to gain some land of one's own. At the end of the seventeenth century most of the colonists were clustered on the coast. Some had moved inland, as we saw previously, but the western parts were still mostly empty. By the mid-eighteenth century all that had changed. The expanding families of the original settlers and the newcomers had pushed west and filled up the colonial lands to the boundaries. It was primarily the Germans and Scots-Irish who pushed against these boundaries. By 1750 British-Americans were covetously eying the land across the Appalachian Mountains; some had already bled over them to claim land that New France had claimed a century earlier. By 1750, war between Great Britain and France in North America was all but inevitable, and it would be about the claims on land. The French would claim, correctly, to the Indians that they, the French, were willing to work with the Indians, but the British were only interested in getting their land.

Migrations from Europe

Migration from Europe had been going on for the better part of the seventeenth century, as discussed in previous chapters. Most of it though, had been from England. However, for various reasons, it now picked up from other areas of the newly formed Great Britain and from other parts of Europe, specifically from present-day Germany, although there was not yet a defined country called Germany. There were push and pull factors that explain these migrations.

Germans

The Germans and Swiss from what is now southwest Germany constituted the largest non-English immigrant group to come to America in the eighteenth and nineteenth centuries. Starting in the late seventeenth century and continuing into the eighteenth century, they came over in three somewhat distinct waves.

The earliest were clearly impacted directly by the proselytizing efforts of Penn himself. We know he sent recruiters, including himself, to Holland and Germany. In Germany he found Mennonites, a sect similar to Quakers and persecuted similarly. He found a ready acceptance by this and other pietist religious groups, ones that sought a direct relationship with God without the need for clergy. The predominant reason for the first phase of German immigration, 1683–1709, was religious persecution, including utopian religious experiments. Radical pietist groups fled central Europe for asylum in Pennsylvania.[3] With push factors like these there was not much need for a pull factor except the open arms of William Penn. This group was said to be small, but Penn was very successful in attracting others also, perhaps the more prosperous Quakers of England, because by 1700 there were about 20,000 inhabitants of Pennsylvania.[4]

Central Europe was the scene of numerous wars in the seventeenth and early eighteenth centuries, including the Thirty Years War (1618–1648), the War of the Grand Alliance (1689–1697), and the War of the Spanish Succession (1701–1714). These ravaged the area of what is now southwest Germany, specifically the area called the Palatinate. These depredations gave rise, in 1709, to one of the more bizarre tales of migration to America, the second German wave, and land was at the center of it. "[T]he primary impetus for the migration was a sensational book filled with descriptions of the riches and ease of life in Britain's Carolina colony." The book had been written in 1707 "at the behest of the Carolina proprietors…. The message proved almost irresistible especially to the rural poor. In a matter of weeks thousands of immigrants from dozens of principalities began streaming down the Rhine." This mass, unorganized migration of perhaps 30,000 expected to be transported to America and given free land. Their existing environment must have indeed been bleak for so many to try to leave. They moved to Great Britain, where, in brief, some were absorbed by Britain, some were returned home, and approximately 3,000 were shipped, at crown expense, to New York, not Carolina, although a few did reach Carolina.

The new governor of New York, Robert Hunter, was leaving Britain for New York and "he proposed bringing the Germans with him. He wanted to settle them in the pine forests of New York where they would make tar and pitch for the British navy and serve as a buffer between the British and French along the New York frontier. Once the Germans had repaid the cost of transportation and maintenance, the government would grant them each forty acres of land … after delays over 3,000 Germans set sail for New York in April 1710." The idea of making tar and pitch for the navy was as old as the original idea for colonizing the New World, going back 120 years, when it had been proposed by Richard Hakluyt to employ idle Englishmen. The idea for using immigrants as buffers between peoples would be used for other immigrants in the future. These new immigrants rebelled against the tar and pitch production idea because they wanted to be farmers, so they never received the 40 acres and were forced to make it on their own. "They ignored colonial land laws, attempting to purchase land directly from the Mohawks and squatting on property claimed by Dutch and English colonists." Although 50 families eventually moved to Pennsylvania, most remained and established a large German contingent in upstate New York. Once again, the attraction of supposedly free land set many people in motion on difficult journeys.[5]

The third wave of German immigration in the eighteenth century was the largest and longest-lasting. This one lasted from at least 1717 to the Revolution with thousands involved. Why did some 85,000 or more migrate from southwestern Germany and Switzerland in this period? In brief, there were some strong push factors as well as some relatively strong pull factors, most of which had to do with land.[6] The Thirty Years War, and others, devastated southwest Germany. It destroyed much of the demographic, political and social fabric of society, causing people to flee the region or succumb to war or plague.[7]

The population was devastated and only started to return to their homes near the end of the century. The rulers encouraged immigration, so thousands of French Huguenots, Swiss, and Flemish flooded the area on the abandoned lands of the seventeenth century.[8] These same rulers maintained tight control over their serfs, who were not allowed to emigrate without paying a high fee for manumission. They believed that people were the wealth of the nation and the more the better.

During this period of recovery from the devastation, land was available. Partible inheritance flourished and couples had an incentive to marry early and have more children so there would be plenty of land when they came of age. A partible inheritance is one in which the land passed down in a family is equally divided among the next generation siblings. This eventually became a problem.

The population did increase, which caused the opposite problem; there were now too many people for the land rather than too few. In many areas where partible inheritance was still the rule, many families were trying to live on smaller and smaller portions of land as the land became subdivided through the generations. The population soared because of natural increase and immigration. The climate and soil allowed new methods of agriculture, but their traditional inheritance customs multiplied the people per acre, and the plots became too small to farm.

The demographic policies of the area's rulers then exacerbated the problem. The governments reacted by banning immigration, forbidding marriage for those under 25, and forbidding the division of land into "too small parts."[9] The land parcels got smaller as land was handed down to family members, making it more difficult to make a living on the land. At the same time, the government was interfering with the villages and customs. For these reasons many peasants chose to look elsewhere for opportunities.[10] The push factors on families provided a very strong motivation to move to areas where they could practice their farming. One estimate has about 900,000 leaving Germany around this time. Most of them moved east to Hungary or Russia; land was available and they were welcomed; the journey was short and all over land. A small percentage decided to brave the trip to British America; this was an arduous and expensive journey. First, they had to move down the Rhine, and then to Britain. After the disastrous experience with the Palatines in 1709, the British no longer offered any help in resettlement. So from there, refugees took the long sea journey to British America, almost exclusively to Pennsylvania through Philadelphia. Once they arrived, they had to find land, usually on the frontier where they might have to contend with an Indian threat. With all these disadvantages, why move west instead of east?[11]

There were factors that would pull some to the west, to America, despite the expense and trouble. The lure of America was that enormous amounts of land seemed to be available, and one could acquire large holdings, 300 acres or more for reasonable prices. Then there was the freedom that America offered, freedom from the military and economic policies of the homeland.[12] Some of the families who did manage to acquire one of these "plantations" wrote glowing reports back to their old neighbors. This had the effect of promoting the new land in Pennsylvania and was a major factor in further emigration. One example is from Johann Christopher Sauer (Sower). He talks about the difficult journey to Holland, then Britain, and then to Pennsylvania through Philadelphia. He then gets to his observations on the land.

> Because one may hold here as much property as one wishes, also pay for it when one desires, everybody hurries to take up some property. One may choose where one pleases. The farther one goes, the better it is. This continent, as may be seen on the map, is almost as large as the other three continents together and has south of New England, say Spain, Virginia, Ne-gro-land, Pennsylvania; north of New England, New Holland, the borders of York, New France, unto the region lying beyond us, which cannot be inhabited on account of the cold. The farther the Germans and English cultivate this country, the farther the Indians retreat.[13]

Similarly, Durs Thommen writing home extolled his abundance. "I took a place with 350 Juchert (about 435 acres), two houses and barns, and have, believe it or not, 6 horses, 2 colts, 15 cattle, and about 35 sacks of oats, 46 sacks of wheat, 25 sacks of rye, and 23 sacks of corn. For all this land I have to pay no more than 7 shilling, or about 7 times 5 Swiss batzen, for tithes, quitrents, and other dues. In this country there are abundant liberties in just about all matters."[14] The Germans tended to come as family groups, and most were farmers and therefore needed land. The land in southeast Pennsylvania, near Philadelphia, filled up quickly, so the later one came in the migration, the farther out to the frontier one had to move. Not all families had the money to pay their own way. After one of these poorer families arrived, they were given a short time to find a friend or relative who would pay their debt. If they found no one, the family would be indentured until they "redeemed" their debt. These were Redemptioners, and one estimate is they comprised about one-half of the German immigrants to Philadelphia.[15]

The Germans came from many parts of old Germany and often were not as homogenous as they may have seemed to outsiders. However, there were cultural ties that led them to cluster together. Most were farmers and the quest for land was one of these ties. "The near universal quest for land determined the ways in which Germans made a living, participated in the market, and provided for the next generation ... land was the source of individual income and wealth, and they measured success in terms of land ownership.... The German settlers in rural colonial America ... had an agricultural mind-set according to which they invested in land for themselves and their children."[16] This obsession for land and the high rates of immigration, especially in mid-century, meant that these farmers could not stay near Philadelphia; they had to move farther to the frontier to acquire the land they needed. First, it was the close in counties of Berk and Lancaster, and then farther out until they reached the Appalachian Mountains. The mountains put a temporary halt to the westward movement of the Germans in Pennsylvania; there was no incentive at that time to cross the mountains. Not only would it be a difficult journey, but the land on the other side was claimed by the French; a war for that land would be fought just after mid-century. The natural move was to take a left turn and go south, paralleling the mountains and using the natural roads in the mountain valleys. This is exactly what happened, but it was also facilitated by the actions of the Virginia lieutenant governor at the time.

As we have seen in previous chapters, Virginians always had an aggressive stance when it came to claiming land in the west. Their motivation was the 1609 charter which granted land "sea-to-sea" so they assumed all the land in the west was theirs. The lieutenant governor's actions made it clear that he intended to maintain Virginia's claim to the western lands in the face of what he saw as increasing threats.

In the first quarter of the eighteenth century, spurred by the War of the League of Augsburg in 1697 and the opening of the War of Spanish Succession five years later, the British had to reevaluate their imperial policy. France was working on a continental empire on the other side of the mountains, the northern and southern Indians resumed attacks because they were losing land, and African slavery came to dominate even in the Piedmont. Their assumption, that all the wasteland beyond the Blue Ridge from "sea-to-sea" was theirs, was being threatened. They had to do something to assure this western land would remain with Virginia.

Now they were looking for settlers to inhabit the backcountry to provide a western defense. "In 1701 great tracts, from ten to thirty thousand acres ... were offered to companies who would bring in settlers, with the stipulation being that within two years there should be one able-bodied and well-armed man ready for defense for every five hundred acres, with a fort built in villages near the center of the tract. In 1705 fifty acres were offered free to any person who would settle in the up-country. Such offers brought no results ... for the Shenandoah was as yet unknown and unexplored."[17] At the turn of the eighteenth century, Virginia had stopped headrights and was selling land directly through treasury rights. One could patent land for five shillings per 50 acres and then go through the process of acquiring the land. This worked fine for the person of small to moderate means, but it was not the only way land was distributed in Virginia as Virginians moved west. The rules were different for the wealthy in Virginia; they always had been. Virginia belonged to the well-connected. The social elite drew together and ensured they controlled the land, and that it was kept within this social circle. Larger and larger quantities of land helped draw this group together, and helped them provide economic and political control of the colony.[18] The wealth and wealthy increased in Virginia during the English civil war (1642–1651), which coincided with the term of Governor Sir William Berkeley. He encouraged many royalists to come to Virginia where they would receive land or have access to invest their wealth in land. This elite always had access to land. "The Virginia gentry dominated the Council even more than it controlled the House of Burgesses. Though the governor was appointed by the king in London and given instructions to direct royal interests in the colony, land policy ended up being designed to increase the wealth of Virginia elite and governors accommodated themselves to the 'First Families of Virginia.' (FFVs)."[19]

While this revaluation of imperial policy was going on, Governor Alexander Spotswood, mindful of British interests, saw no reason that the new policy couldn't help the prosperity of the landowning class.[20] In other words he saw no reason that the elite could not profit from the need to secure these lands even as the empire benefited. He followed up when he obtained warrants for 40,000 acres for himself.[21] He wasn't the only one. The Virginia tobacco and slavery society we know so well took hold during the 1720s when the legislature, dominated by planters, gave out massive amounts of land in the Piedmont to others of their class.[22] As was discussed previously, the early years of the eighteenth century were the years indentured servitude declined and slavery became the primary labor force in Virginia.

Large plantations with slave labor became common in the Piedmont; however, they were not the answer to defending the backcountry of the Shenandoah Valley west of the Blue Ridge. There was concern that if slaves were introduced into the Valley, because they were on the frontier, they would either melt away into the backcountry or worse, collude with the French, who Virginians saw as the threat in the Shenandoah Valley. Although Spotswood was responsible for expansion into the Piedmont, it was his successor, William Gooch, who sponsored predominately non–English settlement in the Shenandoah Valley.[23] Lieutenant Governor Gooch originally endorsed the elite grants in the Piedmont, but later thought differently when considering the wasteland (non-incorporated counties), the Shenandoah Valley beyond the Blue Ridge. He wanted a large number of white farmers, specifically white Protestants, who would settle and defend this backcountry, because as he saw it, "foreign Protestants made excellent buffers."[24]

Fortuitously he came across just a group, the Germans, that themselves were looking for land and, over only two years, 1730–1732, Governor Gooch granted 385,000 acres in the Shenandoah Valley to non–English settlers. These were not the usual Virginia elite. These were the foreign Protestants whom he thought made excellent buffers for this border region.[25] He was looking for population density, so he required the density of one family for every 1,000 acres granted.[26] As a start on these grants on June 17, 1730, the Council granted John Van Meter 10,000 acres, Isaac Van Meter 10,000 acres, and Jacob Stover 10,000 acres in the Shenandoah Valley, and 12,000 acres to William Beverly in Spotsylvania County. (In following years Beverly was to be granted thousands of acres.) Van Meter was originally from Holland but more recently from New York. The condition was that he had to settle it within two years. If he got 20 other families, he would receive an additional 20,000 acres. Van Meter sold the land to Jost Hite (Joost Heyd), a Pennsylvania German activist. Hite was unhappy about how the Germans were being treated in Pennsylvania. He felt the pacifist Quaker government was not protecting the Germans from Indian attack, so he went looking for favorable conditions in Virginia. The generous grants kept coming. In October of that year Alexander Ross and Morgan Bryan, Quakers from Pennsylvania were granted 100,000 acres. Later, in 1731, Hite, along with a partner, Robert McKay, received 100,000 acres of their own in the Shenandoah Valley. This was the beginning of the German influx into the Shenandoah Valley. Coming originally from Germany (and later from the English borderlands) these white, Protestant, yeoman farmers were ideal settlers to act as buffers between the British Virginians, and the Indians and French. Many of them had fighting experience acquired from their original homelands.[27]

Planning ahead for the defense of the colony was not the only reason Gooch was aggressive in granting land. In 1649, as a political payoff for support, King Charles II had granted all the land in Virginia between the Rappahannock and Potomac rivers, known as the Northern Neck, to Lord Culpepper. This area later reverted to the Fairfax family through marriage. There had always been a dispute between the Northern Neck proprietors and the Council in Virginia on who could allot the land in this area. Gooch was aggressive in giving the land away as a means of asserting the Council's authority for that function. His strategy was to grant land and require settlement to assure government control. The proprietor fought back, and soon the contest was between the proprietor and the local government on how to distribute land. This gave the governor incentive to grant as much land as he could to confirm colonial control. Land that was once thought to be waste was now being fought over.[28]

Gooch's land grants increased German migration south, but not only to Virginia. In November of 1730 the Virginia Council granted up to 30,000 acres around the Potomac River near the Northern Neck. The problem was that some of these grants were on the north side of the Potomac, in Maryland. In one of the grants Gooch even acknowledged that this might be the case. At one point Gooch claimed there was uncertainty about the source of the Potomac River and therefore much of western Maryland and Pennsylvania were part of Virginia. He was clearly being aggressive in claiming western lands for Virginia. These latter claims were challenged and rejected, but he did cause the Maryland proprietor, Lord Baltimore, to take notice. Baltimore not only saw the danger in possibly losing those lands, but now saw the value in the western Maryland lands when he hadn't seen it before.[29]

Up to this time most of the land activity in Maryland was confined to the Tidewater and tobacco production. There was no natural entry, rivers for example, into the Maryland Piedmont and backcountry, but things were changing for the Maryland west in the 1730s. Virginia's push to occupy the Northern Neck, the stream of German settlers crossing Maryland to get to the Shenandoah Valley, the growing scarcity of desirable land in the Tidewater, and the interest of Marylanders who saw the value in those lands came together to boost interest in western Maryland settlements. In 1732 Lord Baltimore made a move to open the backcountry. He offered 200 acres of land to any family who would settle there within three years with a quitrent payable at the end of the three years; to single people he offered 100 acres. Even as late as the mid-eighteenth century, land was still being used as an inducement for settlement. This offer was not successful, but more land activity was to come.[30]

One of the reasons that western Maryland land was not developed, was that some speculators had patents on western Maryland land but saw no profit in developing it. For example, Benjamin Tasker had patented 7,000 acres on the Monocacy River, a tributary of the Potomac, but did nothing with it for years. Later a land developer named Daniel Dulany became interested in the west. He was a member of the Maryland Assembly, former judge, and businessman. He owned land in the Tidewater and also some on the Monocacy. He was one who had encouraged Lord Baltimore to settle the western lands in order to protect them from Virginia expansion. Dulaney now saw the German immigrants streaming south to Virginia and decided to do some developing. He bought 7,000 acres from Tasker and consolidated his land north and south of the river. He divided the land and sold it in 100- to 300-acre units. He sold most of it, five-sevenths, at a loss, but profited on the remaining two-sevenths. Some of those sales were to squatters who were already farming the land. He was acting on his own advice to the proprietor when he told him that the original feudal concept of holding land tight and charging high fees and rent would not work for the backcountry.[31]

He was a speculator; he made good profits from the land, but he was also a developer because he was getting small farmers to settle on the land and thus increase its value.

> The operation was as simple as it was profitable. Dulany patented the land for £5 sterling per hundred acres plus fees; he turned the land over to the buyers in small tracts at £30 sterling per hundred acres. No money changed hands in most transactions; the purchaser simply obligated himself to pay parts of the principal at stated intervals with interest at 6 percent. In a single one hundred acre deal the landlord "created" added value of £25, or five times the original cost, secured against unimpeachable assets, the land itself. Land speculation was easily the most profitable enterprise in Maryland for those persons who had the initial capital.[32]

He then went into more intensive development. He set up a town on the east side of the Monocacy and surveyed 350 to 400 feet by 60 feet lots. He offered them to artisans and tradesmen for small fees. Most of the lots went to German immigrants. He donated lots to both the Lutheran and Reformed churches. This town became Frederick, Maryland, one of the first, if not the first, planned, for-profit towns in the country.[33]

Western Maryland soon became German farm country. There were some immigrants from the Tidewater, but most were Germans from Pennsylvania. There was a nativist backlash at first, because the Germans tended to maintain their language and customs. However, that dissipated as Marylanders soon admired the Germans well-built barns and well-maintained farms. Even Benjamin Franklin, who expressed some anti-immigrant concerns at first, came around to admire their positive impact. He was susceptible to observing facts and changing his mind accordingly.[34]

Many of the German immigrants came through Philadelphia, headed west through Lancaster, turned left at the mountains, and headed south into Maryland either through the west, crossing the Potomac at what is now Harper's Ferry into the Shenandoah Valley, or through central Maryland to Frederick. Many who were heading for Virginia decided to stay in the fertile Monocacy Valley of Maryland. The trickle became a flood, so that there was now a strong German presence in Maryland as well as in the Shenandoah Valley of Virginia. The route they followed, the Great Valley Road or the Great Wagon Road, eventually went down through the Great Appalachian Valley, the head of which is the Shenandoah Valley, all the way down to Roanoke. From there a branch went down to the Carolinas and Georgia. It was a natural path, and the Germans were not the only ones to use it. In a contemporaneous migration the Scots-Irish also used it to get to the backcountry. Some Germans did eventually make it to North Carolina but had to settle for poorer land because others, notably Scots-Irish, preceded them and claimed the best land.[35]

Scots-Irish

Another large influx of immigrants to America in the eighteenth century, comparable in size to the German immigration, was the Scots-Irish (or Scotch-Irish) immigration. This was a large migration, over 250,000, that came in waves from about 1716 until the Revolution. They came for the same reasons the Germans came, paralleled the German migration patterns in America, and settled in the same places. Scots-Irish is the common designation that has taken hold although, as Fischer has pointed out in *Albion's Seed: Four British Folkways in America*, it is really too narrow a definition; a better designation would be the Borderlanders. The term Scots-Irish stuck because a significant portion did come from the Ulster Plantation in northern Ireland.[36]

The borderlands between England and Scotland had been the scene of wars and feuds for centuries. English and Scottish kings would invade the other's land and in turn be invaded by the other across the border.

"For seven centuries, the kings of Scotland and England could not agree who owned it, and meddled constantly in each other's affairs."[37] Part of the problem was the poor soil in the Scottish Lowlands, especially in the west. The lowlanders would plant and harvest what they could, but then would often be stripped of these meager returns by clans from the Highlands, which had an even worse environment for agriculture. So, at the borderlands there was both external conflict, and in Scotland, internal conflict. "Border violence also made a difference in patterns of association. In a world of treachery and danger, blood relationships became highly important. Families grew into clans, and kinsmen place fidelity to family above loyalty to the crown itself."[38] The lack of protection at the border regions by the government led to a disdain for government. They concluded they had to look after themselves through family and clan. The violence and poor harvests caused them to assume nothing was permanent and constant moves were necessary to survive.[39]

It was very similar in Ireland in the same era. "Throughout five centuries, ever since the Norman King of England, Henry II, invaded Ireland, the English had tried repeatedly to subdue the island, whose people steadfastly resisted subjugation." Anglo-Norman families given land in Ireland, would after time, be absorbed by the Irish; peace remained elusive. Eventually some progress was made by Elizabeth in controlling some of Ireland, but most of the Irish were outside this Pale. They were considered barbaric "and civilized Englishmen regarded them, as they did the Highlanders, as little better than savages." England controlled Ireland by right of conquest, but could do little to control the Irish.[40]

Both of these started to change when James VI (1566–1625) became king of Scotland in 1567 and later, king of England as James I after Elizabeth died in 1603. Lawlessness on the border was no longer tolerated. It was, for example, no longer possible for a criminal to simply move across the border to avoid prosecution. By 1610 James had tamed the border, although during the reign of Charles I hostilities between England and Scotland resumed, and the border again reverted to violence.[41] In Ireland, given the choice by one of his ministers "to plant strong 'colonies of civil people of England or Scotland' or else drive the wild Irishmen to the waste lands." James chose the former.[42] Through lands that reverted (were escheated) to him in northern Ireland, he established a plantation sponsored by the city of London. In January 1610 the city agreed to invest £20,000 for the project. The idea was to protect that land and encourage English settlers.[43]

Originally the settlers were to be English, but Scots were not excluded; they were both to mingle with the Irish of the area. In fact, many from the border regions of England and Scotland moved to this northern Ireland

Chapter Four. Populating the Land II 133

plantation, called Ulster, to avoid the borderland violence. Pushed out by repressive land measures, including enclosures for sheep as had been done in England, and attracted by more fertile land than existed in the lowlands they left, and with the welcoming protection of the English army, the Scots moved to Ulster in great numbers.[44] A linen industry was introduced and, along with a woolen industry, thrived. "The success of the settlers induced many of their friends from Scotland to follow."[45] The Ulster Plantation thrived at first, and the inhabitants became known as Scots-Irish. Hereafter the term "Scots-Irish" will collectively refer to those from Ulster as well as those from the borderlands between England and Scotland. The Ulster Plantation was established at the same time as Jamestown, Virginia, so they grew in parallel.

Circumstances changed in Ulster by the end of the seventeenth century, partly because of their own success. The wool produced in Ulster was of a good quality and became coveted worldwide. This threatened the English wool industry, which reacted by getting the subservient Irish Parliament to pass the Woollens Act in 1699, which prohibited the exportation of wool to any place except England, where they could set their own price. This was a disastrous blow for the primary industry in Ulster.[46]

There were other *push* factors that led to the mass exodus of Scots-Irish from Ulster. When they first came to Ulster from Scotland, many had reasonable leases, some of them long term. However, as these leases ran out the landlords took advantage of the settlers, who had been there for years and had improved the property, and they raised the rents substantially, some say double or even triple the original ones. This was called rack-renting. Some increase in rent would seem reasonable, but these were looked on as unreasonable. They could turn farmers from landowners into laborers or tenants. This played a major role in the movement of many from Ulster to America. Interestingly, the question of land was again at the center of the controversy. "Almost every civil war, rebellion, insurrection, and disturbance in Ireland, from the time of the Tudors downwards, arose more or less, directly from questions connected with the possessions of lands."[47] This seems to be a more universal concept than one associated only with the Tudors. Once people are settled on land, they become very concerned about keeping it or losing it when changes are in the air. We will see this later when it comes up late in eighteenth-century America.

There were two other strong push factors putting pressure on Ulstermen and getting them to think about moving. One was the Test Act imposed during the reign of Queen Anne in 1703. It required all officeholders to conform to the established Church of England practices. Although aimed at Catholics, this act threatened the religious freedoms of the Presbyterian Scots, who protested vigorously. They had been loyal to the British government but now felt betrayed. Finally, "when the fourth successive year of drought ruined the crops in 1717, serious preparations began to be made for a migration.... More than five thousand Ulstermen that year made the journey to the American colonies."[48]

This started the waves of Scots-Irish from Ulster, and the English and Scottish borderlands, immigrating to America, mostly for economic reasons such as rack-renting, depression in the wool industry, drought, and also religious reasons. The emigrants from Ulster were mostly Scots; the English and Irish tended to remain in Ulster. In the second wave, starting in 1725, the departures were so great that Parliament started to worry they would lose the whole Protestant element of Ulster. Some of the most skilled people left. One estimate was that between 1729 and 1750, Ulster lost a quarter of its population that had been engaged in manufacture. "From 1771 to 1773, 'the whole emigration from Ulster is estimated at thirty thousand, of whom ten thousand were weavers. Thus, was Ulster drained of the young, the enterprising, and the most energetic and desirable classes of its population.'... 'so that, making ample allowance for the increase of population between the years 1731 and 1768, we shall still find that one third of the whole Protestant population of Ireland emigrated within that disastrous period.'"[49] By some estimates the migration averaged 12,000 annually. The experience of the Scots-Irish was similar to that of the Germans. Although many had the skills and money to pay for the passage, many did not. These latter then did what other immigrant groups had done: paid for their passage through indenture for a few years. They also became advocates for the new land and wrote home encouraging others to follow, which they did in large numbers.[50]

Although the waves of Scots-Irish started in earnest in 1717, there had been some immigration to the colonies prior to that, to Maryland in 1680, to South Carolina in 1682, to Pennsylvania in 1708, and even to New England in 1718. These were relatively small migrations. The Puritans in New England had a sympathetic connection with those in Ulster, because of their understanding of religious intolerance. There was an active migration from Ulster to New England from 1714 to 1720, but as Henry Jones Ford so succinctly puts it in *The Scotch-Irish in America*, "so far as the disposition of the Ulster people was concerned New England would have been their American home, but their reception and experiences were such that the main stream of Ulster immigration soon turned toward Pennsylvania."[51] In retrospect it seems obvious that the Puritan culture and the borderland culture of North Britain and Ulster would not be a good fit.

Although some Scots-Irish came to various settlements along the seaboard, such as New England, South Carolina, and Maryland, the primary ports for the main waves of immigrants were Newcastle, now in

Chapter Four. Populating the Land II

Delaware, and Philadelphia. Many settled in southeastern Pennsylvania, including the area contested by Pennsylvania and Maryland, an area others had avoided because of the confrontations having to do with that border.[52] They quickly moved west through the same counties occupied by the contemporaneous German immigrants. They were moving toward the frontier, which was a familiar environment for them, only now the land they were in was much more fertile than that which they had left in the Old World.

Their ideas of acquiring land, however, were different from those of any other group of immigrants; many basically assumed it was theirs for the taking. This was a habit they had acquired while battling for lands on the English-Scottish borderland. James Logan, secretary of the province at the time, noted that they rarely approached him with a proposal for purchase. He refers to them as "bold and indigent strangers, saying as their excuse, when challenged for titles, that we had solicited for colonists and they had come accordingly." A frustrated Logan later was quoted as saying, "I must own from my experience in the land office, that the settlement of five families from Ireland gives me more trouble than fifty of any other people."[53] Another extreme, or perhaps typical, expression of this attitude happened when they moved west to the Susquehanna River into Conestoga tract. Logan complained of "the Scotch-Irish as having in an 'audacious and disorderly manner' possessed themselves about that time of the whole of Conestoga Manor, a tract of about 15,000 acres, which had been reserved by the Penns for themselves, as it contained some of the best land in the Province. In taking this land by force Logan says that the Scotch-Irish settlers alleged that 'it was against the laws of God and nature, that so much land should be idle while so many Christians wanted it to labor on and raise their bread.'"[54] As they moved west, this Conestoga land grab was a harbinger of what was to come.

Although he intended to sell land to increase his wealth, Penn, as Baltimore, intended to set up manors, keeping some of the best land for himself.

> Penn, though a believer in freedom of conscience, was never a republican or a democrat.... Though he believed in popular representation, and provided for it with sagacity beyond the lights of his time, he yet wished to reserve a power and prerogative beyond the people's reach.... For example, his land system, if carried out on its original lines, could not have resulted in anything but a landed gentry. He proposed a town and a province. Any purchaser of 5,000 acres in the province was entitled to 100 acres in the town; of 10,000 acres in the province to 200 acres in the town. The province was practically without limit in acreage, but the town *was* limited to 100 shares of 100 acres each. Had this scheme been carried out to the letter as Penn had framed it ... the result

must have been the elevation of one hundred families or less to the status of a landholding aristocracy separate and distinct from the mass of the people in privileges, which could not fail to produce distinction of caste in fact if not in name.[55]

Events have shown that this scheme did *not* play out. The Scots-Irish takeover of Penn's Conestoga tract was one event that put an end to that intention. We have noted previously that a feudal aristocracy never took root in this country precisely because there was so much land available to people who were interested in it. On the one hand, Penn's land distribution system was very unorganized. This can be seen by his inability to preclude the Scots-Irish immigrants from taking the land of one of the manors he had reserved for himself. On the other hand, the availability of the unoccupied land, not farmed by anyone, was seen as open by these Scots-Irish immigrants. As the Scots-Irish moved west toward the frontier it became even more difficult to control the distribution of land. There were advantages and disadvantages to the Quaker government in this westward move. The Quaker government was glad to see this group, accustomed to fighting on the frontier, as a buffer between the eastern Quakers and the Indians. However, they were also a problem, because they would routinely take over Indian lands that had not been cleared by the proprietors, which was against Penn's principle of always compensating Indians for their land.

Thus, a new method of acquiring land, besides the proprietor's grant and sales through the land office, became common. It was known as settlement right or "tomahawk" right. The settlers who were inclined to assume they had a right to the land without compensating anyone for it moved to the frontier, beyond the range of the land office, and would indicate the boundaries of the land they chose to squat on by marking trees on the boundaries with tomahawks. These boundaries would be respected by other settlers who had moved out with them and there would be a market in these properties. There would eventually be clashes with the authorities, and many of these settlers would acknowledge they had taken the land without paying for it, and would move on farther west. Some, though, would not; they would stay and rebuild after the authorities burned their homes in order to get them to move off the land. These squatters would almost exclusively be the Scots-Irish rather than the German settlers. The latter were much more interested in securing title to the land legally so it would be secure for their descendants.[56]

Squatting changed everything.

> The tendency toward small holdings became fixed, however, not so much through the law as by the practice of the colonists in the actual occupation of the land. Squatting, although discouraged by the proprietors, as it defrauded them of quitrents, soon became the most popular and regular method of

Chapter Four. Populating the Land II 137

acquiring land. Squatter's rights forced their way from presumptive titles to an established position, first as personality and finally as reality. They became the basis of land transfers through the customary alienation of improvements instead of legal title. Toward the middle of the eighteenth century the proprietors were forced to recognize them in the so-called settlements rights as a legitimate mode of obtaining title to land throughout the province. The early prevalence of squatters' rights is seen in the fact that of the 670,000 acres of land occupied between 1732 and 1740 400,000 acres were settled for which no grants had [sic] issued.[57]

Many of these squatters had come from Ulster, where they had been encouraged to migrate from Scotland and northern England. They had over the years improved the land in Ulster and built farms. When their original lease had expired, the landlords had increased the rents so high that they could not remain, and they therefore immigrated to Pennsylvania. After they had settled by squatting on lands in western Pennsylvania, they improved those lands also. So they were particularly sensitive to being moved off lands they had improved a second time; they resisted. The disorganization of the Penn land system and the reality of the squatters' settlements led to the acceptance of squatters' titles.

It finally dawned upon the proprietors that little could be done to eject squatters from their lands. Through a hardy perseverence [sic] and industry the squatter gained his point and was given a special legal protection. The old time "tomahawk title" gave way to the "law of improvements" and the power of preemption protected his rights of priority as a settler. Time has erased to a very great extent the disrespect which the term "squatter" seems to have called forth and we may now justly look upon the squatter as the pioneer among homesteaders who later play such an important role in the development of our nation.[58]

Ironically, after less than 150 years the ideas on land and property ownership had diverged widely in America. In the Tidewater and Piedmont regions of Virginia, large tracts of land had been acquired by relatively few wealthy planters who had been given preference for the land, which ended up in large plantations. Their definition of property expanded to now include property in people, chattel slavery, as well as land. They had established an aristocracy based on control of this property. The members of this American aristocracy were descendants of the feudal aristocracy of England, although they owned the land rather than holding it as a fief from the king or superior lord. It was through their membership in this nobility that the Cavaliers, royalists, of Virginia had access to large amounts of land for their private use. It was different in other parts of the country.

In the late fifteenth century, when John Cabot made his voyage of discovery for Henry VII, any lands that were discovered were to be held of the king, and Cabot was to be a vassal of the king. This was an extension of the English feudal system in which the king held all the land. However, with Elizabeth, things changed slightly but consequentially. She was interested in populating the North American mainland, primarily to deny it to Spain. She sponsored Sir Humphrey Gilbert's expedition to Newfoundland and gave him the right to claim the land in fee simple. "Fee simple" is equivalent to what we now call "ownership." His claim on the land was the beginning of the concept of private ownership of land. He would have complete control of the land; it was not a fief bestowed by the queen. Land became something that could be "owned" by a person as private property, instead of land held of the king or queen as a fief. Linklater, in *Owning the Earth*, claimed it started with this claim by Sir Humphrey Gilbert on Newfoundland in the late sixteenth century.[59]

Thus, the precedent was set that if a person or company was awarded land in English North America, that person or company could use it as he or it wished, and would own it. James I, who envisioned himself as an absolutist, reverted in the first charter for the London Company of Virginia when he insisted on assigning the land to the settlers. However, that changed in the second charter and thereafter, when the government and use of the land was turned over to the colonizing company. From then on, as the settlers looked west from the Atlantic seaboard to the empty land, except for the indigenous people whom they pushed aside, they claimed it as theirs.

In western Pennsylvania squatters were claiming land they saw as open and free to anyone who could use it, which was land that they did not pay for nor had access to by way of aristocratic connections. In one sense squatting was not much different from what kings had done previously. Seeing the east coast of America unoccupied, or occupied by indigenous people who were not "using it appropriately," they squatted on it, claiming it by "right of discovery" or by "conquest." The act of granting some of this land to Penn was a continuation of this artifice to the next level. The squatters were trying to turn the clock back to the time of Gilbert, claiming land for themselves that they said belonged to no one. Their claim was not for title to the land, since they didn't care much about titles, but to be able to use the land to support their families. Some scholars, such as Fullerton in "Squatters in Early Western Pennsylvania," saw this as a positive development. "They pressed into the interior of the province beyond the settlements of other immigrants because land was more easily acquired even if they did take it without the formality of securing a title to it. For the apparent disregard of existing land laws and for their courage and spirit of reckless adventure we are indebted to them for frustrating an absentee landlord system in America."⁶⁰ Within 50 years of its founding, Pennsylvania was filling up with both German and Scots-Irish settlers. The latter, those who didn't stay to claim their squatted land by the "law of improvements," continued to move to the far west to what became Cumberland County, just at the edge of the mountains. Then they did what the Germans had done previously: they turned left and headed south. They went past the German settlements in Maryland at the Monocacy and continued across what is now Harper's Ferry into the Shenandoah Valley of Virginia.

This is what Leyburn, in *The Scotch-Irish: A Social History*, calls the third wave of 1740–1741, "the first movement of Scotch-Irish in any numbers beyond the confines of generous Pennsylvania to the southwest."⁶¹ These were not only those previously living in Pennsylvania, but new immigrants coming from Ulster, leaving because of famine. They were now to share the Shenandoah Valley with the Germans, although not mingling with them.

We have seen that Lieutenant Governor Gooch had started granting lands to Germans in 1730 to speed up settlement of the Shenandoah Valley for defense purposes. Gooch continued his push to get the right type of settlers. For the Scots-Irish it started in 1736 with a grant to William Beverley, a native Virginian prominent in government affairs. The grant, 118,000 acres, was for the Manor of Beverley in the Shenandoah Valley in the present Augusta County. "A letter written by Colonel Beverley, August 8, 1737, to Captain James Patton at Kircubright, Scotland shows that they were endeavoring to induce immigrants from the north of Ireland, and, if necessary, from Pennsylvania, to settle these Valley lands. In this they were highly successful."⁶² Similarly, in 1736 Gooch made a grant of 500,000 acres to Benjamin Borden on the condition that he settle 100 families on it before receiving title. He met the conditions, and much of the initial settlement under this grant was made by direct immigration from Ulster.⁶³ This paved the way for the third wave from Ulster, which started in 1740.

Even before these grants, a number of Scots-Irish had come down from Pennsylvania and squatted on the land. As in Pennsylvania, they made up their own rules for keeping order, including recognition of land claims by "tomahawk right." Beverley worked with them amicably because he wanted to fill the Valley with settlers. Many of the "better" families took pains to have their titles cleared. He "gave legal title to those living in his Manor at the rate of one English pound for forty acres."⁶⁴ As the Valley filled up, Virginia struggled to keep up by creating new counties for this previous wasteland.

Some of the Scots-Irish continued their move southward and southwest toward the mountains, not only because the Valley was filling up but also because many of them led a peripatetic life, so they were used to moving. Many of them, having grown up on the agriculturally deficient, violence-prone borderlands between England and Scotland, knew mostly fighting and moving; they got restless if they stayed in one place too long. Their homes were what might be called shacks, meant to be temporary so they could move easily. Their land was not as well cared for as that of the Germans. Many of them moved through the southern mountains, eventually moving throughout Appalachia and west through Georgia, Alabama, Mississippi, and even as far as Texas. They would eventually form what Colin Woodward, in *American Nations*, would call Greater Appalachia.[65]

The Shenandoah Valley filled rather quickly over a few decades with both German and Scots-Irish farmers. Now the middle colonies of Pennsylvania, Maryland, and Virginia had expanded from coastal settlements all the way out to the Appalachian Mountains. Although some hardy souls ventured across the mountains, most did not. Not only was it a difficult trip, but it was known that New France claimed control of that country. Immigration was still strong, and as the immigrants came through Pennsylvania, they found the land too expensive, so they continued south down the Great Valley Road through the now mostly filled Shenandoah Valley, and then spread out again. Some came east into the Piedmont of Virginia, reversing the westward movement of Virginians up to that time. Others crossed the Alleghenies into present-day West Virginia. Most however, continued to the Piedmont area of North Carolina. Although the Germans were first into the Shenandoah Valley, followed by the Scots-Irish. The Scots-Irish, always ready to move, were earlier into North Carolina than the Germans and therefore claimed the best land. These immigration waves continued until the Revolution.

Land in North Carolina was originally granted in 100-acre headrights by the proprietors, and later sold by the proprietors. Later, after the crown took over in 1729, the land was sold.[66]

> Until 1729, both North and South Carolina had been owned by great English Proprietors, few of whom had taken active steps to develop their American holdings—certainly not to the extent that Penn had done. It was after the cession of these proprietary estates to the crown in 1729 that the frontier regions began to receive active attention from the government.... Official indifference to the up-country gave place, after 1730, to a policy of definite encouragement to settlers. The doors of both provinces were now thrown open to Protestants of all nations. Several governors even took active steps to induce European Protestants to come to the two Carolinas.[67]

Gabriel Johnson, who was governor from 1734 to 1751, oversaw an increase in population of North Carolina from 50,000 to 90,000. "Inhabitants flock in here daily, mostly from Pennsylvania and other parts of America who are overstocked with people and some directly from Europe. They commonly seat themselves toward the West and have got near the mountains."[68]

Lewis Family

The Lewis family ancestors, English Quakers, Germans, and Scots-Irish, were part of many of the major migrations of the seventeenth and eighteenth centuries; they typified their migrant kinsmen. As covered in the previous chapter, the earliest Lewis family ancestors to emigrate were Quakers from England and Wales who emigrated most likely for religious freedom. They appeared to be middle to upper income and were able to acquire land in Pennsylvania. These immigrations were in the late seventeenth and early eighteenth centuries. The Lewis family ancestors are even more fully represented in the waves of immigrants from Germany and Great Britain in the eighteenth century.

Johan Georg Arnold was born in 1702 in southwest Germany, where his family had lived for generations. He died in 1769 in Frederick County, Maryland. He appears to have been in the third wave of German immigration that started in 1716. As discussed previously, Frederick, Maryland was the center of the German farming settlements that were so common in central Maryland. Many of his descendants lived in York County, Pennsylvania, which is perhaps where he lived before moving to Frederick. Another German ancestor on the same side of the family was Johann Jacob Bender, who was born in 1721 in Eschelbach Germany, in the west near the Rhine. He died in 1786 in Menallen Township, Pennsylvania. He clearly was in the third wave of German immigrants. Menallen Township was a Quaker settlement, so most likely he was a German Quaker and perhaps met some of the other Lewis Quaker ancestors in Pennsylvania that were from England. His family remained in the Pennsylvania area.

William Weyerman was another German Quaker. He was born in Germany, probably southwest, around 1700 and died in 1764 in Pennsylvania. He was said to have befriended William Penn on one of his trips to Holland. Some of the dates given in his background regarding his arrival in this country are inconsistent, but he was friendly with the Penn family and acquired a lot of land in Pennsylvania once he arrived. As a Quaker he also settled in Menallen Township in Adams County. He was granted several tracts of land by the Penns, 500 acres in 1738, 300 acres in 1739, 300 acres in 1743, and 1049 acres in 1750. Other accounts add up to different totals, but clearly, he was allotted a great deal of land. He became a prominent, well-to-do member of the community. His descendants apparently stayed in Pennsylvania at least through the third generation. The last of the Lewis family German ancestors was the George Heiges family. Heiges was born in Swopeland Germany in 1726. It is not clear if he came to America himself, before or after the Revolution, or if it was his son or grandson.[69]

The Lewis family also had many ancestors of Scots-Irish descent from Great Britain aside from the English and Welsh Quakers we met previously. Not surprisingly, from our knowledge of the peripatetic nature of the Scots-Irish and borderlanders of England and Scotland, the families from these ancestors eventually ranged over a much wider area, from Pennsylvania to North Carolina to Texas and to Oregon. John Brandon was born in London in 1662; he came to America in the 1690s and died in Pennsylvania sometime between 1704 and 1752. He had five sons. We know for sure that two, Thomas and William, were born in London and one, George, was born in York County, Pennsylvania. The other two, John and James, were born either in London or in Pennsylvania. It seems likely that John (b. 1691) was probably born in London because he got married in England sometime between 1715 and 1717. The younger John Brandon and his three brothers William, George, and James were all living in Lancaster County in the early 1740s. It is likely they all came early in the Scots-Irish migration which started in 1717. Lancaster County was an entry way into Pennsylvania for the Scots-Irish as well as for the Germans. The name Brandon goes way back in Norman England and possibly to Anglo-Saxon England. However, it also has origins in Ireland and Scotland. We don't know the origins of the Brandon family, but their subsequent moves would suggest they traveled on the Scots-Irish migration paths. There is no hint of Quakerism in their story, as with other Lewis ancestors, but instead the Presbyterianism strongly associated with the Scots-Irish.[70]

John Brandon (b. 1691) was a fairly successful husbandman in Lancaster, holding various offices. However, for reason unknown, perhaps because he needed more land and it was now expensive in Lancaster, or he felt it was time to move on as was the bent of many of the Scots-Irish, "in 1748 (or early spring of 1749), Brandon took his leave of the rolling hills of the Susquehanna Valley and conducted his small army of Locks and Brandons along the wagon road to the fertile fields beyond the Yadkin."[71] He had been a widower, and his second wife Elizabeth Lock also had children from a previous marriage. This fertile land in the Yadkin Valley in Rowan County, North Carolina, was a favorite destination for many of the Scots-Irish. John Brandon received a 640-acre grant in 1753. His son, John Junior, received four grants from 1753 to 1780 totaling 1310 acres. His other sons, William and Richard, also received grants in the same area totaling 2587 acres. Their land was also near that of the Lock family and the Cathey family. Elizabeth Cathey was Brandon's first wife. Apparently, they had all migrated as a group to Rowan County. The 4,500 acres of land granted to just these four Brandon family members would have been prohibitively expensive in Lancaster, Pennsylvania, had it been available at all. The attraction of large amounts of land was clearly a pull factor that encouraged many of the Scots-Irish, in particular the Lewis family ancestors, to move to North Carolina. Besides the Brandons that moved to Rowan, there were Brandons that stayed in Pennsylvania. However, true to their Scots-Irish roots, descendants from both these family branches moved still farther out, including to Preston County, (now) West Virginia, and Sumner County, Tennessee, which was then still part of North Carolina.[72]

The Brandon family migration from Pennsylvania to North Carolina represents only a fraction of the moves made by other Lewis Scots-Irish ancestors. They were part of general movement of people looking for more and better land. Thomas Gillespie, a Scotsman whose family was from Ulster, was born in Pennsylvania, moved to the Shenandoah Valley where he met and married his wife, and then moved down to Rowan County, North Carolina, where his land was near the Brandons'. His children also moved on to Sumner County, Tennessee, where his son George received a land grant of 3,030 acres. Another Scottish ancestor, George Follis, was born in Philadelphia in 1698. His descendants moved first to Virginia, then to North Carolina, and finally owned land in Allen County, Kentucky.

John Day was born in 1748 or 1749 in Stafford, Virginia. The name can be of English or Scottish origin, but the travels of his descendants suggest the yen to move on was strong in this family. Stafford is near the Potomac River, not in the Shenandoah Valley where most of the Scots-Irish migrated, so it is unclear if he came from the Valley or perhaps from Pennsylvania directly. He moved to Caswell County, North Carolina, and then to Sumner County, Tennessee, where he died. His son Henry was born in Caswell and also moved to Sumner. Henry's descendants continued moving farther away, mostly west, including to Missouri, Florida, Virginia, Kentucky, Texas, and Oregon.[73]

The Lewis family was well represented in the German and Scots-Irish migrations of the eighteenth century. What motivated them to move was the same thing that motivated others in those migrations—more and better land. They moved from the then-crowded Pennsylvania to the rich Shenandoah Valley of Virginia, and when that overflowed, to the fertile valleys of North Carolina. The flow continued west to Tennessee, which was then part of North Carolina, and to Kentucky, which was then part of Virginia. Both these groups, from Germany and Great Britain, had suffered land problems in their native lands; it was too expensive, too crowded, too poor. When they arrived here, they kept moving and looking for land to satisfy their desire to farm it for their families. It was worth moving farther and farther west to achieve that.

Land Companies

We have seen Virginia grow in the seventeenth century by means of relatively small, 50-acre headrights, and larger sales by treasury right to groups who started their own plantations. This slowly filled the Tidewater region and started into the Piedmont region. It was in these latter stages that the wealthy members of the governing class favored their wealthy friends with choice lands in the Piedmont. This took the occupation of Virginia lands up to the Blue Ridge Mountains; it continued into the eighteenth century when things started to change. Tensions started to increase between Great Britain and France, and tensions also increased between the Virginia Council and the crown. In the former case the Virginians thought it prudent to extend their western borders, across the Blue Ridge into the Shenandoah Valley. They wanted to preclude French encroachment into Virginia land. Although there was no well-defined boundary between New France and the British colonies, it was well known that New France claimed all the land from Canada to Louisiana, with the Appalachian Mountains as an undefined but de facto border. Tensions with the crown were the result of disagreement over who had the authority to grant land in northern Virginia's Northern Neck grant.

For both these reasons the Virginia Council made large grants, thousands of acres, to fill up the Shenandoah Valley as quickly as possible. Besides these factors there was another one that came into play. "Writing in 1705, Robert Beverley, the historian of Virginia, described his compatriots as people 'not minding anything but to be masters of great tracts of land—lords of vast territory.'"[74] British sociologist Harriet Martineau, in *Society in America*, observed that

> the possession of land is the aim of all action ... and the cure for all social evils, among men in the United States. If a man is disappointed in politics or love, he goes and buys land. If he disgraces himself, he betakes himself to a lot in the west. If the demand for any article of manufacture slackens, the operatives drop into the unsettled lands ... that there was no character of permanence in anything:—all was fluctuation, except the passion for land, which under the name of enterprise, or patriotism, or something else that was credible, would last till his countrymen had pushed their out-posts to the Pacific.[75]

Land had now become big business, and land speculators became an important factor in the business of acquiring and reselling land. The seventeenth-century peasants from Europe were the amateurs. They were hungry for land they couldn't get in Europe and, when they arrived here, land seemed so cheap they sometimes took on too much.[76] As a result they sometimes bit off a bit more than they could farm and paid the price later. The professional speculators were also around early. In the early seventeenth century, they included the sea captains who would claim headrights for their sailors and then sell the land, and the speculators who purchased the land earned by an indentured servant who didn't have the means to farm the land he just received, and then sold it at a profit. In the southern colonies speculation was controlled by the Virginia and Carolina elite, and hundreds of free grants were made in the Piedmont and Shenandoah Valley to these same elites. The grants from the legislatures, controlled by the planters, were in the range of 10,000 to 50,000 acres. The crown and royal officials protested this land giveaway, but it went on.[77] The tract, even greater than 50,000 acres, in the Shenandoah Valley given to William Beverley discussed above was one of these.

As usual, the Virginians led the way west; at first it was up to the Blue Ridge Mountains. They then moved over these rather low mountains to fill the Shenandoah Valley, bounded on the west by the more formidable Allegheny Mountains, the Ridge and Valley system of the Appalachian Mountains. As the population pressure built up toward the middle of the eighteenth century, it reached the eastern edge of the mountains. This presented more opportunity for the professional land speculators. Instead of just operating off the lands given to individuals, there was now an attempt to form large investment companies, who would request large land grants to survey and sell to individuals. The scarcity of land east of the mountains forced these companies to go past the eastern ridge of the mountains into some of the mountain valleys. This was a riskier venture. Not only did the settler have to move across some mountains, but he had to be aware he was getting closer to the undefined mountain border that separated the British colonies from the claims of New France.

There were three of these companies that had their start prior to the Seven Years' War, or the French and Indian War in the Americas, which started in 1754. Virginia offered speculators 1,000 acres of land for each family they settled into or beyond the Allegheny Mountains, and allowed them four years instead of the usual two to meet their requirements. The first of the companies formed to take advantage of this offer was the Greenbrier Company in 1745, which was offered a grant of 100,000 acres in the Greenbrier Valley in southwest Virginia beyond the Shenandoah Valley. In 1748, just after King George's War, even before the Greenbrier Company started to lay out land, settlers were moving into the Greenbrier Valley. "In 1750 Thomas Walker reported several 'plantations' and asserted that prospective settlers had already purchased much of the land from the Greenbrier Company."[78] "By 1754 its surveyor, Andrew Lewis, had laid off more than fifty thousand acres."[79] Several of the family names were of Scottish origin, which is to be expected, since the Scots-Irish were not only just east of the mountains in the Shenandoah Valley, but were always the first on the frontier. They were used to the fighting that this position sometimes entailed, which was a useful attribute at that time and place. This was not an auspicious a time to move to the frontier. Several families became causalities of Indians raids, which were heating up in the 1750s as war edged closer.

The other company that was formed early and received land in the same general area was the Loyal Company. In July 1749 Virginia granted 800,000 acres in southwest Virginia, down to the North Carolina border, to Thomas Walker and John Lewis, who headed the Loyal Company. "By 1754, the Loyal Company had seated about two hundred families on its lands, mostly in southwestern Virginia, but a few apparently settled along the New and Bluestone rivers in present West Virginia."[80] These settlers also felt the depredations of the Indians leading up to and throughout the French and Indian War.

The last of the three land companies out of Virginia at the time was the Ohio Company of Virginia. This company was unique from many points of view. First, its founders were some of the most well known in Virginia's commercial and government community, including Thomas Lee, Robert Carter, George Fairfax, Richard Lee, Robert Dinwiddie, George Mason, and Lawrence and Augustine Washington; these names are writ large in Virginia history. Second, it sought land that was located toward the north rather than in southwest Virginia. The land sought was not in the mountain valleys but on the other side of the mountains, on the Appalachian Plain at the Forks of the Ohio. This is where the Monongahela and Allegheny rivers meet to form the Ohio River, in present-day Pittsburgh; it is the Ohio Country. The company billed itself as a trading and settlement company. Individual traders had been moving back and forth across the mountains for many decades trading with the Indians, but the company intended to increase this trade as well as to sell land on the west side of the mountains.

It was a boldly speculative venture for at least two reasons. This land was clearly fully in the domain that New France claimed, not on a fuzzy border such as the Appalachian Mountains. It was also in an area claimed by both Pennsylvania and Virginia, and the Iroquois Six Nations. The Pennsylvania western border, although vaguely defined, did appear to clearly include the Forks. Virginia claimed the land as theirs based on their assumption that all the land to the "south sea" to the west and northwest was theirs based on the charter of 1609. The Ohio Valley was seen as a rich prize as the speculators in the increasingly populated British colonies looked for more land to settle.[81]

The company made their first request for land from Governor Gooch and the Virginia Council in October 1747. They requested 200,000 acres

Chapter Four. Populating the Land II 147

of land around the Forks of the Ohio, specifying the boundaries of the requested grant. Gooch hesitated; although he was normally quite generous in granting land, he was concerned about the location of this land, in territory clearly claimed by the French. He backed it though, and sent it to the Board of Trade to ask permission from the king. The company also requested help in London from John Hanbury to lobby for this grant. In their petition to the king and council they requested a total of 500,000 acres, with 200,000 to be granted immediately and the remainder to be awarded after the first 200,000 had been settled. The request was well received, but during the negotiations a requirement was put in that the company had to erect a fort near the Forks. This most likely was a nod to the potential risk involved with claiming land in the territory claimed by New France. In March 1749 the king's council ordered Gooch to make the grant, which he did in July of that year. The company request included the phrase "or in such other parts to the west of the said mountains as shall be adjudged most proper by your petitioners for that purpose." It appears they were thinking of land beyond the mountains even further west than their present request.[82]

The land in the Ohio Country was just a vague concept to the company members; they had no personal knowledge of it. They employed a well-known woodsman and surveyor, Christopher Gist, to explore the region for them and to identify good lands for settlement. Gist made two journeys, one in 1750–51 and one in 1751–52. In the first he started at Oldtown on the upper Potomac River, present-day Cumberland, Maryland, looped through Pennsylvania, then to Ohio up to the Miami River, and back through Virginia (Kentucky). He identified good farmland near the Miami River. The company ultimately decided not to go as far as the Miami River, probably because it was too far to be defensible; they decided to stay with the land near the Forks. On his second journey he went more directly from Oldtown through southwest Pennsylvania to the Monongahela River. He returned via the Ohio River and Virginia as previously. His route to the Monongahela was the path they planned to expand into a full-fledged road, one that would be the route across the mountains to their land in Ohio. It became the well-known road across the mountains to the Ohio Country that much later would be the main road into the Ohio Country, the Cumberland Road.[83]

It wasn't only the French they had to worry about. The Indians had an even stronger claim on the land, and they were becoming more concerned as the British moved west. On his journeys Gist had to be careful to hide his compass lest the Indians think, correctly, that he was scouting more land for the British. There had been clashes with the Indians in the Shenandoah Valley about a decade earlier. A conference had been called in

Lancaster, Pennsylvania, in 1744 to end the raids. The conference included representatives from Pennsylvania, Maryland, Virginia, and the Iroquois Six Nations confederation, who claimed the land by right of conquest. The Iroquois did give up the Shenandoah Valley for gold in that conference, but that is all they thought they were giving up. Either purposely, or because of misunderstanding, the British thought the Iroquois had given up more land. In their petition to the king, Hanbury claimed the Iroquois "did yeild [sic]…and forever quit claim to your majesty all the lands west of Virginia with all the rights thereto, so far as your Majesty should at anytime thereafter be pleased to extend the said colony."[84]

Gist was challenged by the Indians. The Iroquois started pushing back as some settlers, including Gist, started to move into the Ohio Valley. The company decided it was now time to clarify the terms of the Lancaster Treaty, so they called for a meeting with the Indians at Logstown, a town on the Ohio River downstream of the Forks. This conference was called strictly for the benefit of the Ohio Company; they needed to secure their claim to the land in the Ohio Country. There was a very close connection between the members of the Virginia Council and the members of the Ohio Company; many were members of both. "About the same time the Ohio company began to function, Thomas Lee, its manager, became president of the Executive Council and acting lieutenant-governor of Virginia."[85] Money had been secured from London as a follow-up to the Lancaster Treaty, and that money was used to "purchase [£500] from the Six Nations peaceable possession by the Ohio Company of their huge tract of land on the Ohio."[86] Surprisingly, the Six Nations agreed to allow the settlement of the Ohio Company on the south side of the Ohio River, for very little money, just £500.[87]

It was important for these early land companies to have settlers on the land as soon as possible to solidify their claim to the land. It was no different for the Ohio Company of Virginia. "Christopher Gist agreed at the time of his employment by the company to colonize the new settlement with 150 families. The company promised that all families should receive 100 acres for each person up to four and 50 acres for each person in excess of four. Within three years after settlement each settler should pay the company four pounds sterling for every hundred acres; the land should be free of quit rents for the first five years.... Gist reported that 50 families would move during the fall of 1752 and the spring of 1753."[88]

It is not known how many families did settle there, not many, but the best indication is that they were Germans from Pennsylvania. Some Germans agreed they would settle 50,000 acres of the land with 200 families if they could get exemption from the taxes to support the Church of England; nothing came of that proposal. The Gist family, and the accompanying families, settled on the east side of the Monongahela below the Forks of the Ohio. While all this was going on the Ohio Company, in March 1754, sent a new request directly to the king, bypassing the Virginia Council. This was a request for a much larger grant. It included the original grant, but went much farther down the Ohio River to the intersection with the Kanawha River in present-day West Virginia. This grant, if it had been awarded, would have been for approximately seven million acres, over 10 times the original request. If it seemed like a desperate request by a company in trouble, it was. It arrived at the Board of Trade in London in April 1754. Needless to say, it was overtaken by events.[89]

The lure of more land and the profit to be gained from it now stretched into the Ohio Valley. It was land claimed by Pennsylvania, Virginia, the Iroquois Six Nations, and New France, a provocation that would become a spark for a new war. By crossing an unofficial, but de facto mountain border, it was only a matter of time before hostilities broke out. When they did, in 1754, all the advanced settlers in the lands of the Greenbrier, Loyal, and Ohio Companies would either be killed by Indian raids or forced back farther east. Although all three companies made an attempt to recover after the war, none really did. That did not stop the quest for more land in the west; it only intensified it, as we shall see in the next chapter.

Land speculation by Virginians seemed to naturally flow from the culture; from the 50-acre grant for a headright to the large grants provided to wealthy planters. These grants generally allowed people, including individuals, to settle where they would. It was different in New England, where the government allotted land for townships to groups, and these groups of the same Puritan persuasion would allocate the land in the townships to families. It did not seem like a place where land speculation could thrive, but finally it did. Land speculation was so strong that even the Puritans on the rock-bound coast entered the practice despite their carefully planned settlements. This land accumulation fever started within 50 years of their first settlements. The fact that land in their area was much less fertile than in the south was an indication of how strong the land speculation fever really was to these transplanted Englishmen.[90] Land originally was given out generously to groups to form townships, with the idea that newcomers would be provided land when available. As the townships increased in population, the land became more valuable, and conflicts arose between the original proprietors of the land and the newcomers. As a result, some of the newcomers started to move west as individuals rather than as religious communities as was originally the case. This was then a fertile area for land speculators; they looked for cheaper land farther west to sell to those willing to move west. One company that came out of this was the Susquehannah Company, which was formed in Connecticut in 1753. It wanted to speculate in land farther west, but to retain the same method of distribution as before, that is to allot the land to townships for them to distribute, not to individuals as the Virginia land companies were doing.[91]

The Susquehannah Company tried to take advantage of a favorable reading of the Connecticut Charter (1662) which originally gave Connecticut land all the way west to the "south sea." A map will show that this cuts through a major portion of northern Pennsylvania. They had their eyes on the Wyoming Valley of Pennsylvania. This is the first, or one of the first, instances of speculators from one chartered colony seeking land in another colony. It had been reserved as a hunting ground for the Six Nations but had not yet been purchased by Pennsylvania. (Penn's objective was to clear title to all land with the Indians before selling it.) They wanted to purchase it directly from the Iroquois. The company managed to negotiate with the Six Nations for an area west of the Susquehanna River, 120 miles wide from the forty-first to the forty second parallel, about 8,400 square miles (about five million acres) in the Wyoming Valley, for £2,000 New York currency. They did this at the Albany Conference of 1754, at which they joined six other colonies and the Iroquois. The conference was called for the purpose of trying to keep the Iroquois allied with Great Britain during the imminent hostilities with France. This purchase was not part of the conference but was done in side meetings, in an underhanded way; the Six Nations' delegates were plied with liquor to get them to agree. The war made moot the settlement of the Wyoming Valley for its duration. The company records went dark between 1755 and 1761, although there was an unsuccessful attempt to reestablish the company after the war, as will be discussed in a succeeding chapter.[92]

> The Pennsylvania authorities ... had no intention of letting Connecticut speculators acquire title to millions of acres of proprietary lands and dispatched their own Indian diplomat, Conrad Weiser, to negotiate a cession of all remaining claims in Pennsylvania. Weiser ... succeeded in obtaining a deed to hitherto unceded Iroquois lands—in this case everything west of the Susquehanna between 41° 31' north latitude and the Maryland boundary—in return for a nominal sum (four hundred pounds New York currency) and the promise of further payments to follow.

Note that this claim included everything to the Pennsylvania border, thus it included the area around the Forks of the Ohio, Ohio Country. This claim was in conflict with the Susquehannah Company claim and caused bitterness between the two colonies for years. Both of these claims did result in the transfer of vast amounts of Indian land to the colonies.[93]

There was another proposal for the land in the Ohio Country, contemporary with these land companies, but not specifically by a company. As discussed above, the Albany Congress of 1754 was called to work with

Chapter Four. Populating the Land II

the Iroquois to ensure their support in what seemed to be an impending war. There was also a secondary purpose, a proposed Plan of Union in which there would be a union between many of the colonies so they could act together, especially under emergency conditions like war. "Imperial officials saw the advantages of bringing the colonies under closer authority and supervision, while colonists saw the need to organize and defend common interests."[94] It was *not* an early attempt to separate from Great Britain, but a way for the colonies to cooperate more closely. Benjamin Franklin was the Pennsylvania representative at the conference and the driver behind the effort. At, or near, the conference he proposed a "Plan for settling two Western Colonies with Reasons for the Plan, 1754." He extolled the Ohio Country, specifically what was to become the State of Ohio.

> THE [sic] great country back of the Apalachian [sic] mountains, on both sides [of] the Ohio, and between that river and the lakes is now well known both to the English and French, to be one of the finest in North America for the extreme richness and fertility of the land; the healthy temperature of the air, and mildness of the climate; the plenty of hunting, fishing, and fowling; the facility of trade with the Indians; and the vast convenience of inland navigation or water-carriage by the lakes and great rivers, many hundred [sic] of leagues around.[95]

He was concerned that the French would take it, and all numbers of mischief would follow. The English would be confined east of the mountains and wouldn't be able to expand; the French would increase and "become a great people behind us"; many debtors and "loose" English people would desert to the French; they would cut us off from trade with the Indians; and in time of war would set the Indians on us to harass our frontiers. To counter these potential problems, he proposed to establish two strong English colonies between the Ohio River and Lake Erie. They would have the beneficial effect, first, of providing a buffer between the French and the western parts of Pennsylvania, Maryland, Virginia, and the Carolinas. Second, the "dreaded junction of the French settlements in Canada with those in Louisiana would be prevented.... In case of war it would be easy to annoy Louisiana from these colonies by going down the Ohio and Mississippi rivers, and by using the lakes. We would secure the friendship of the Miamis" who live in that area and are already predisposed to be friendly with the English. Finally, through the Ohio and Mississippi rivers and the lakes, trade with the Indians in the far west would be enhanced.[96]

Franklin was a man with a reputation for practical wisdom and common sense, but this proposal was a bit naïve. Just a few years prior, the French had specifically claimed that land with the Celeron expedition, and for the English to walk into Ohio and establish two new colonies would have expedited the imminent war. Nevertheless, he persisted. He said the present colonies were too long and narrow, and that new colonies should be set up in the west. If the Albany Plan passed, he could see these member colonies establishing one or more new colonies in the west. However, if that union did not pass, he proposed "two charters be granted, each for some considerable part of the lands west of Pennsylvania and the Virginia mountains" and a number of the "nobility and gentry of Britain" could contribute to the settlement of those lands by individuals such that "every actual settler be intitled [sic] to a tract of acres for himself, and acres for every poll [head] in the family he carries." He was thinking of how to get settlers beyond the mountains using new inland colonies as opportunities for new settlement beyond the mountains. This may have been the first time inland colonies were seriously proposed. Both the Albany Plan and Franklin's proposal for inland colonies failed, but they would be a major topic for expansion after the impending war was over.[97]

End of Peace—End of Expansion

The population had grown rapidly for 90 years of the seventeenth century, mostly by natural growth and immigration from England, but in the eighteenth century it virtually exploded. In 1700 the estimated population of the English North American colonies was approximately 275,000; by 1750 it was 1,207,000, quadruple the 1700 number.[98] The population in the seventeenth century was concentrated in a thin sliver of land along the Atlantic coast, confined to the Tidewater in Virginia and Maryland, eastern Pennsylvania, the Hudson Valley and coast in New York, and the seaboard Puritan settlements of Massachusetts and Connecticut. Some of the early colonists and early colonial settlement companies realized early that the vast expanse of land to their west represented a resource that could be utilized to enhance the wealth of the colonies as well as personal wealth.

Late in the seventeenth century economic opportunity in England picked up and English migration to America slowed. However, in America the pace picked up, starting with the Quaker immigration late in the seventeenth century. By the early years of the new century the slave-owning aristocracy had been well established, and slaves were being imported from Africa. The migrations from Germany, the Ulster Plantation, and English-Scottish borderlands, starting early in the eighteenth century, contributed tens of thousands to the population of the colonies. These massive migrations always had both push and pull factors associated with them. The push factors in all the cases included religious persecution, but in most cases lack of land, or very expensive land, was the primary driver for migration. Complementary to that was the pull factor of cheap, or even free, land in America. Religious intolerance was strong in America; if you moved for religious reasons, you wanted to live with your co-religionists without interference from others, but that intolerance was never as strong as it was in the Old World because there was always enough land, so settlers could spread out, increase the separation and give the others more space.

Since both the push and pull factors involved land it became very important to own land in America. Very few of the immigrants had owned land in the Old World, so they saw the ownership of land worth the trouble it was to obtain it. This included the costly, arduous voyage, the willingness to accept indenture, and the difficulty of clearing the land once they acquired it. Land became an obsession, not only for the opportunity it provided to feed one's family, but also because it provided a freedom they hadn't experienced in the Old World. One did not have to answer to the lord of the manor or the prince of the state. This was especially true in America early on, and truer the farther out one moved toward the frontier; there was very little provincial control on the frontier. This was one of the reasons the Scots-Irish moved so readily to the farthest frontiers. They resisted government control, and depended on family and clan for all their needs.

The first settlement was often satisfactory for the early settlers, but as the areas filled, the new immigrants could not find reasonably priced land in them, and were forced to leapfrog over these to lands farther west, often on the more dangerous frontier. When the original settlers could not find land nearby for the next generation, they also picked up to move. Moving west for better or cheaper land became a habit, and it was usually done by traveling with fellow kinsman from Germany or Ulster. This process was rapid; in approximately 50 years the population had increased and expanded from a thin sliver hugging the east coast all the way to the Appalachian Mountains in the west. The 13 colonies had filled up all the land recognized as British colonial territory by 1750; there appeared to be no place left to go.

As we have seen, one Virginia company did have an idea for how to acquire more land. It would entail a move to take over land now claimed by another empire, New France. As difficult as it had been to move and take over the land of the indigenous people to get up to the mountains, this next move would prove even more difficult.

The lure of the land both to local colonists and those from Europe, such as the Germans and Scots-Irish, had a social impact beyond just the acquisition and settlement of the land. Most of the colonists in the seventeenth century were of English or Welsh stock, a rather homogeneous group. "During the eighteenth century, however, the ethnic homogeneity was rudely and finally shattered, as Germans, Swiss, Scotch-Irish, Africans and peoples of other stocks migrated or were imported in such substantial numbers that by the time of the Revolution half the population south of New England was non–English."[99] This churn of cultures introduced more groups comfortable with religious dissent, such as the German Pietists and Scots-Irish Presbyterians, as well as the latter who were also used to pushing back on government. These traits would have consequences later. The availability of land was still the key to forming a middle class, one based on widespread ownership of land rather than on shopkeeping and industry. There was too much land for it to be sold extortionately; men of modest skills could acquire substantial holdings. It was relatively easy to become a landowner; so easy, in fact, that some governors around 1750 complained it was difficult to recruit for the army because there were so few landless individuals to draw on.[100]

Chapter Five

War for Empire: Still More Land

> The Seven Years' War was about the control of territory, not thrones; it created a seismic shift in Europe's alliance system and balance of power; and its first shots were fired not on a European, but an American frontier.[1]

This quote from Anderson's *Crucible of War* contains two salient phrases to the topic at hand: "control of territory'" and "American frontier." These made it different from previous recent wars and especially important for the people of North America at the time. The prior 100 years saw three wars between England and France; dynastic wars, all of which started in Europe but had spillovers in North America. King William's War (1689–1697), Queen Anne's War (1702–1713) or the War of the Spanish Succession, and King George's War (1744–1748) or the War of the Austrian Succession all ended with treaties that left North America around New England, and the maritime provinces around Canada only slightly changed, although of course they had profound impacts on the people of those areas. The last one, King George's War, was settled by the Treaty of Aix-la-Chapelle in 1748, which was about the time the British colonies had pushed all the way to the Appalachian Mountains. The fourth, and last of these wars, the French and Indian War as it was known in America, started in 1754. It is often equated with the Seven Years' War, 1756–1763, as it was known in the rest of the world, but it started and ended earlier. It had a much greater impact regarding the ownership of land in North America than all the previous wars combined.[2]

New France

The preliminary steps in establishing New France were not dissimilar to those establishing the British colonies, nor was the time frame dissimilar. Jacques Cartier (1491–1557), the French explorer and would-be colonizer, made three explorations to North America, starting with the first one in 1534 to the Gulf of St. Lawrence. On his second voyage, in 1535, he found his way down the St. Lawrence to present-day Quebec and Montreal. He was, of course, looking for the Northwest Passage to the east, as were others. Although he did not find the Northwest Passage, he concluded that this land would be a good source of fur, which later became the primary objective for claiming it. He attempted an unsuccessful settlement on his third voyage, which was in 1541. His explorations were within the decades between Cabot's claim on Newfoundland, and Gilbert's and Raleigh's unsuccessful settlement attempts later in the sixteenth century. His explorations at these northerly latitudes might have been his consideration of the Cabot claim on Newfoundland a few decades previously; he perhaps wanted to stay clear of any conflict.

The successful permanent settlements of New France were also very close in time to the first English settlements in the early seventeenth century. In December 1603 the French king, Henry IV (1553–1610), granted to Pierre du Gast, Sieur de Monts, an exclusive charter, for 10 years, for land in Acadia for the purpose of trading with the natives for fur.[3] The grant covered the area from the fortieth parallel to the forty-sixth parallel, roughly from the latitude of New Jersey and central Ohio to New Brunswick, Canada. Ironically the northern boundary did not include the present-day city of Quebec. Du Monts took Samuel de Champlain with him to start a colony on the island of Sainte Croix, located between present-day Maine and New Brunswick. The harsh weather made the location untenable, so in 1605 Champlain moved the colony to Port Royal on what is now Nova Scotia. Although the land was more fertile and the climate more pleasant, the colony still did not survive because the company had failed; the colonists moved back to France in 1607. Champlain persisted. He got another grant from the king in 1608, this time with a monopoly of only one year. He sailed to the St. Lawrence and set up the first permanent French colony at Quebec. New France was to be colonized to support the fur trade.[4]

The French presence in America was in some ways similar to that of the Spanish and English, yet vastly different in other ways. All three had the original intention of finding their way to the east for trade. The Spanish discovery of a New World during that quest, and the fortunate discovery of gold in this New World, caused them to abandon their quest for the Far East and exploit this precious metal. Gold became the "one trick pony" that allowed them to vastly increase their wealth. The early French expeditions of Cartier identified fur as the commodity that would increase wealth, their own "one trick pony." When Champlain settled in Quebec, the object of the settlement was to increase the value of the fur trade. In this the Spanish and French had similar success, a profitable commodity that exploited the resources of the New World. Neither of these required the importation of a large labor force from Europe. The Spanish dominated the native inhabitants, deemed them "vassals," and used their labor to extract the minerals and farm the lands. By trading with the Indians and using their own *coureurs de bois*, or "runners of the woods," the settlers of New France collected the furs for shipment back to France. Completing the similarity, both the Spanish and French operations in the New World were top-down operations run by the respective crowns; the land was held in the name of the king. Both also had the intention of Christianizing the indigenous people.

The English colonization efforts differed significantly from the other two. The colonizers were not sent by the crown, but by private trading companies chartered by the crown for the purpose of making a profit through trade. The idea was to use the resources of the colonies, ships' masts, timber, tar, potash, and iron to trade with the mother country to increase wealth, a mercantilist objective. They neither worked with the Indians (New France) nor dominated them (New Spain); rather, they tried to move them aside as irrelevant to their objectives. Without the resources provided by the Indians, and no special commodity like gold or furs, they were in a bind regarding the labor necessary to implement their trading objectives. They squeaked through when tobacco became profitable, but never really overcame a shortage of labor; land was plentiful, but labor was scarce. They made progress when they started to use the land as an inducement to increase the population, and therefore the labor supply. This is when the colonizing objectives of the English changed whereas those of New Spain and New France remained the same. New France and New Spain never reached the stage where a large population would lead to a vibrant economy.

Champlain's Quebec settlement was never large, but he managed to maintain an active network of fur traders for years. However, by the mid-1620s, population had not increased, and that would start to become a problem as the world was changing in the midst of the Thirty Years' War (1618–1648) raging in Europe. Things were changing in North America also, as England was increasing the population in Virginia and Massachusetts during this time. "In the winter of 1627–28, Champlain wrote that '55 people, men, women and children depended on the habitation for subsistence, not including the native inhabitants.' Other European settlements, by comparison, were expanding rapidly. By 1628, the Dutch had 270 colonists in New Netherland. The English Pilgrims at Plymouth were 300 strong in 1629.... New France had dangerous neighbors and tensions were building."[5] Louis XIII (1601–1643) became king at age nine in 1610 when his father was assassinated. The queen mother became the regent until he became of age in 1614, but she continued to govern for three more years. Louis had a difficult relationship with his mother, but eventually became friendly with her advisor Armand-Jean du Plessis, later Cardinal Richelieu, and took him on as the Secretary of State.[6]

Richelieu saw the potential of New France but was probably, rightly, concerned about the fragility of the colony, so he took some actions to boost population. In 1626 he decided "the best way to build the colony was to abolish the rival trading companies and create one new company." The new company was the Company of New France, but was called the Company of One Hundred Associates because of the number of investors he recruited. The company was given title to land all the way from the Arctic to Florida, essentially all of New France at the time. They were mandated to bring in 4,000 settlers to New France by 1653, and for this they were given monopoly rights over trade. Although it seems to be a significant increase over the less than dozens of settlers then in New France, these numbers are very small when compared to the robust growth of the British colonies at the time.[7]

Richelieu introduced other changes to increase population and increase crown control. In 1627 he introduced the seigneurial system into New France. "Technically a seigneur was anyone entitled to an oath of fealty for land held from him. The king was a seigneur because all the land in Canada was held ultimately from him."[8] This was the transfer of the still existent, but declining, feudal system of France to New France. "The axiom at the heart of French feudalism, 'no land without a seigneur,' was assumed from the beginning to be the basis of any land distribution in New France.... And when, in 1627, the Company of New France (the Company of One Hundred Associates) was granted most of eastern North America.... French feudalism, in theory at least, had been transported to New France."[9] The Company of One Hundred Associates was a seigneur and had seigneurial rights to grant land. Seigneuries were granted to influential and prominent people, but not necessarily nobles, as was the case for seigneuries in France. The stipulation for a seigneur was that he was to bring immigrants to work the land of the seigneurie, thus increasing population. These workers, known as habitants, would sign a contract with the seigneur stipulating their obligations and the rent they were to pay to the seigneur. There was a social gap between the seigneur and the habitant, but not as great as the one between the respective parties in France. In this frontier area the seigneur and habitant had to work side by side to make it work. The habitants had a choice of which seigneurial lands to settle.[10]

The seigneuries were usually five- by 15-kilometer lots fronting on the river. Most of the land between Montreal and Quebec along the St. Lawrence was taken up by these properties. Most of the people of New France lived in these rural areas. One estimate was that there were only about 220 seigneuries granted during the French regime. The seigneurial system in New France was just not an effective means of populating a vigorous colony; it was relatively static and "was largely irrelevant to the early geography of Canada."[11] There was not much incentive to become a seigneur, except perhaps the lure of the title, and less to become a censistaire, or known colloquially as a habitant, the one who paid rent (*cens*) to his feudal lord, the seigneur. The habitant could pass the land he was granted on to his family, but he could not regrant it. The climate could be harsh, especially in the winter when the St. Lawrence River froze up for several months, precluding commerce with France, and adding another disincentive to emigrate.

The population was not diverse as it was in the British colonies; it was constrained by law. It was written into the patent of the Company of One Hundred Associates that only Catholics could inhabit New France. Thus in 1627, when the Huguenots were defeated and fled France, they were specifically barred from New France. This is in stark contrast to the diversity of the British colonies, who welcomed those pushed out of Europe for religious or economic reasons. Charles Prestwood Lucas, in *A Historical Geography of the British Colonies*, considers this the fatal flaw in the development of New France.

> The most fatal mistake made by the French in regard to North America was the exclusion of the Huguenots. The men who wished to leave England went to the present United States. The men who wished to leave France were not allowed to go to Canada, and went in considerable numbers to England and her colonies. The effect, therefore, of Roman Catholic exclusiveness was that, though France had a far greater population than England, the greatest French colony failed for want of colonists. Nor was it only a matter of quantity, but a matter of quality also. The Huguenots were the type of men who would make homes, create business, and build up communities beyond the seas. They were of the same strong fibre as the New England Puritans. In the competition of the coming time, New France was doomed in consequence of being closed to the French Protestants.[12]

New France was also denied English Quakers, German Pietists, Scots-Irish Presbyterians, and other diverse groups; there was no *pull* in New France for these groups that were being *pushed* out of Europe. Likewise, the pull for Catholics from France was not strong, especially since they would still be moving into a feudal system imported from France, and the living conditions could be harsh. No population pressure in New France meant there was no reason to move on, move west for more or better land. The population lived mostly in the rural seigneuries, lying in the strip between Quebec and Montreal, which remained stable and small.

The Company of One Hundred Associates was not successful. Even though the population started to grow slowly, in 1663 it was still only about 2500, 800 of whom were in Quebec. It lost money and eventually failed in 1663, when it was taken over by the French crown under Louis XIV (1638–1715). In order to boost the population, he paid for hundreds of young unmarried women to move to New France to become wives of the male settlers already there. This program, the *Filles du Roi*, or Daughters of the King, helped, but was not itself the solution to the problem of low population.[13]

In 1665 Louis XIV appointed Jean Talon (1626–1694) as Intendant of New France, which is a post just below that of governor. Talon, who had two tours in Canada, 1665–1669 and 1670–1672, was ambitious with regard to claiming more land for New France. He may have been motivated by an opportunity the governor of New France had missed earlier by losing the area around the Hudson Bay to the English. Originally two Frenchmen, Pierre-Esprit Radisson and Medard Chouart, Sieur Des Groseilliers, had come across some Cree Indians who had shown them some prime furs said to have come from the north. Radisson and Groseilliers tried to interest the governor in an expedition to find the source of the furs. He refused, and eventually Radisson and Groseilliers were able to interest Prince Rupert of Batavia, a cousin of Charles II of England, in what turned out to be a successful trading mission to Hudson's Bay. Rupert and other investors organized the Hudson's Bay Company, which was chartered by Charles in 1670. The land, known as Rupert's Land, included the entire drainage of the Bay all the way west to the Rocky Mountains and south to present-day Minnesota and North Dakota, 1.5 million square miles. This was a critical missed opportunity for a country that depended on the fur trade.[14]

Talon was an expansionist; he wanted to claim as much land as he could and seal the borders of the empire.

> In particular Talon felt the full weight of the presence of the English on the continent. He had in fact been disturbed about it from the time of his first administration. On 13 Nov. 1666, for example, he had suggested to Louis XIV and Jean Colbert, Secretary of State, the conquest or the acquisition of New Holland in order, he said, to provide a second way of access to Canada and to prevent pelts from being diverted to Manhattan and Orange; moreover, he added, this would be the means of putting the Iroquois at the mercy of the French and of shutting the English up inside the boundaries of their territories.[15]

Had they been successful, it would have changed the face of North America and probably encouraged more emigration. Looking in the other

Chapter Five. War for Empire

direction, west, he sent out explorers such as Daumont de Saint-Lusson. By June 1671, Saint-Lusson had reached Sault Ste. Marie at the edge of Lake Superior, where he raised his sword and a sod of earth and claimed

> in the name of the Most High, Mighty, and Redoubted Monarch, Louis, Fourteenth of that name, Most Christian King of France and of Navarre, I take possession of this place, Sainte Marie du Saut, as also of Lakes Huron and Superior, the Island of Manatoulin, and all countries, rivers, lakes, and streams contiguous and adjacent thereunto: both those which have been discovered and those which may be discovered hereafter, in all their length and breadth, bounded on the one side by the seas of the North and of the West, and on the other by the South Sea: declaring to the nations thereof that from this time forth they are vassals of his Majesty.... *Vive le Roi*.[16]

Clearly, neither Talon nor Saint-Lusson lacked for ambition. This statement extended the French claim of New France from the St. Lawrence all the way to the west coast, including some land that overlapped with Rupert's land. It is doubtful, however, that the indigenous inhabitants gave it much thought at the time, if they even knew about it.

Talon still believed that by moving south he would find the South Sea; however, he was anticipated by René-Robert-Cavelier, sieur de La Salle. La Salle was born in Rouen, France in 1643. He started in a Jesuit seminary but soon sought more adventure in New France, where he was assigned a seigneury near Montreal. He heard about a river in the south that supposedly led to the South Sea and started on an expedition to find it in 1669, the year prior to Talon's second tour as Intendant. Traditionally he has been given credit for being the first European to discover the Ohio River, but there is doubt that he did. There is very compelling evidence that a Dutch trader named Arnold Viele was the first European to discover the Ohio, and that was in 1692.[17] Nevertheless, La Salle's purported discovery of the Ohio led to the French claim on the Ohio Valley. This was in the era when the British colonial population still hugged the Atlantic coast; the Pennsylvania charter wasn't issued until 1681.[18]

In 1670, Talon sent La Salle on a mission to find the South Sea via the Mississippi River. Again, although tradition has him following Lake Michigan to the Illinois River to the Mississippi, there is little evidence he did so. Talon wasn't finished. He commissioned Louis Joliet (Jolliet) and Jesuit Jacques Marquette to find the river that flowed to the South Sea, the Mississippi, and follow it to that sea. It is not clear if he still thought it was the way to the South Sea or if he was just concerned about the proximity of New Spain to the mouth of the river, later to become New Orleans, and he wanted to claim that area on the Gulf. Joliet and Marquette did canoe down the Mississippi as far as the Arkansas River, where they turned back after being warned by some Indians about hostile Spanish or Indians at the terminus of the river. Still later, in 1682, La Salle finally did make it to the mouth of the Mississippi, and claimed the whole river basin for France, naming it Louisiana in honor of Louis XIV.[19]

The Mississippi River Valley drains the upper west, the Midwest, and the Ohio Valley all the way down to the Gulf of Mexico. The territorial claims by Saint-Lusson and La Salle now completed the French claim on North America. The claim included land from the northeast such as Acadia, the St. Lawrence Valley, down the Ohio Valley to the Mississippi Valley and to the Gulf of Mexico. In the west it went as far as Montana, Colorado, and Texas. By 1690 New France, along with Spanish Florida, had completely surrounded the British colonies in North America. The conquest was painless, it did not take the force of arms; it is doubtful the existing inhabitants were aware of it. New France was also easily traversed, as one could travel from Montreal, with very few portages, by canoe all the way to the Gulf of Mexico; there were no mountain barriers to cross. They established several forts in the territory but no new cities; there were no cities south of Montreal. It is not clear if they had any plan to exploit this grand expanse except possibly for extended fur trading. There were not enough people in France, willing to emigrate, to populate New France; immigrants were limited to Catholics from France. "By the end of the seventeenth century the French had three spheres of influence and colonization in North America.... To join them and encircle the English colonies was the aim of French statesmanship. It was an impossible aim, inevitably frustrated by geographical conditions and by want of colonists; but the conception was a great one, large as the new continent in which it was framed, and able men tried to work it out, but tried in vain."[20] What they did do by their claim on the Ohio Valley was to set the unofficial but de facto border between New France and the English colonies: the Appalachian Mountains. The border didn't mean much for several years. It was at the turn of the century that English fur traders, mostly from the southern colonies such as Virginia, started their trading with the Indians in the Ohio Valley. Competition with French traders in the same area escalated over the next several decades. Although the Virginians had always assumed that they had the right to everything in the west, they had not yet settled the Shenandoah Valley east of the Alleghenies by 1690. Pennsylvania was just starting its settlements.[21]

The population of New France had increased by 1690, but only slightly, to about 12,000. On the other hand, the English colonies had about 214,000 at this time, and they were growing. It was after the turn of the century that the British colonial population started to rise rapidly because of immigration of Germans and Scots-Irish; English America was becoming an immigrant country. By mid-century the leaders of New France were becoming concerned. English traders were well ensconced in the Ohio Valley, and the English colonies had expanded all the way to the mountains; a Virginia company was considering crossing the mountains. The most ominous sign was the population differential. While New France now had around 55,000 colonists, the English colonies were up to 1.2 million. This would prove decisive in the coming war.[22]

Contest for the Ohio Country

The claims on the Ohio Valley and Mississippi Valley provided the French with what they sought, an expanded trading empire, one that went from Canada all the way to the Gulf of Mexico. There was easy access within this empire through its network of rivers and lack of mountain barriers. They saw the mountains as an effective barrier that would preclude the British from moving west, denying them access to the trading possibilities of the interior. Everything depended on geography. This barrier would provide additional benefits. Once the British colonists reached the mountains they would be bottled up, and the British would be forced to use their naval and military forces to defend these colonies and would be, therefore, hobbled in Europe. Similarly, the British were concerned that French control of the Ohio Country would inhibit colonial expansion, thus slowing the economy and inhibiting trade between the colonies and England. This might permit the colonies to produce goods more cheaply, thereby undercutting the British mercantilist economy. It was clear that neither side wanted the other to control the Ohio Country.[23]

Although the French claimed the Ohio Valley in the Ohio Country, they did not have the resources to control it; they depended on Indian control of the Valley, specifically by the Iroquois. Although the British did not have an immediate interest in the Ohio Valley for the first half of the century, they hadn't yet reached the mountains; they fully expected to move in that direction eventually. They also were content to allow the Iroquois to control the Ohio Valley as long as the French did not try. For the first decades of the eighteenth century the Iroquois were able to deftly play off both the French and English and maintain relative peace in the Ohio Valley, which they had claimed by conquest. However, as was seen in the previous chapter they made a miscalculation at the Treaty of Lancaster in 1744 when they seemed to cede the Ohio Country to the English. This was the opening for the Ohio Company of Virginia's claim for land at the Forks of the Ohio, where the Allegheny and Monongahela rivers meet to form the Ohio River.

The Iroquois confederation fractured further during King George's

War, 1744–1748. During this war the Mohawks allied with the New Yorkers against the French and suffered heavy losses, which made them suspicious of the New Yorkers. "King George's War thus proved a disaster for the Mohawks specifically and gravely diminished the coherence of Confederation policy-making. This in turn weakened Iroquois neutrality and accelerated the pace of Anglo-American trading and land speculation in the Ohio Valley."[24] The Iroquois were losing control of the Ohio Valley just when both the French and British were increasing their interest. "During the generation preceding 1754 the most dynamic and significant phase of the Anglo-French rivalry in the Indian trade was in the central and upper Ohio Valley and in the region south of Lake Erie."[25]

The economy of New France was built on the fur trade. It depended on successful trade with the Indians and maintenance of a vast land empire in which to exploit this trade. It also depended on the waterways between Canada and Louisiana, the St. Lawrence and Mississippi, which allowed them to use either end for shipment of trade goods in and out. The St. Lawrence was the more important of the two because it was near the center of population. Control of this trade meant keeping control of all the rivers between the St. Lawrence and Mississippi, especially the Ohio. The St. Lawrence was frozen for many months of the year, thus restricting access to the most populous parts of New France. They didn't have access to all the British ports on the coast, which provided easy access all year long.

They were more concerned about the integrity of the Ohio Valley than they were about the British Fort Oswego on Lake Ontario. They were fearful that a British post on the Ohio would possess more opportunities for damage.

> They would have much greater opportunities there than at Chouegen [Oswego], to seduce the Indians.... They would possess more facilities to interrupt the communication between Canada and Louisiana, for the Beautiful river [Ohio] affords almost the only route for the conveyance from Canada to the River Mississippi of detachments capable of securing that still feeble colony against the incursions of the neighboring Carolina Indians, whom the English are unceasingly exciting against the French.... If the English ever become strong enough in America to dare to attempt the conquest of Mexico, it would be by this Beautiful river, which they must necessarily descend.[26]

They had reason to be concerned. Virginia and Pennsylvania traders were becoming more aggressive in trading with the Indians of the Ohio Valley, even though it was much more difficult for these traders to cross the mountains than it was for the French already in the Valley. Additionally, the English had an advantage in the price of trade goods. The French had a more difficult path for their goods, coming through the St. Lawrence, frozen for many months. On top of that "during King George's War

Chapter Five. War for Empire

the operations of the British navy made it so difficult for the French to secure goods for the Indian trade that prices advanced as much as one hundred and fifty percent."[27] This was a real peril for the French because they depended on this trade in this one-product economy. The British colonies, on the other hand, had a more diverse economy, including agriculture and some small manufacturing capability; plus, they had trade access to English manufactures and the empire. Their trade goods were much cheaper for the Indians. "When, during King George's War, the highest French officials came to realize the peril of this quiet penetration of English power, they determined at any cost to secure sole and absolute control of the entire Ohio country."[28]

The French "thus entered the valley of the Ohio with territorial and no longer purely commercial intentions," since the empire was being threatened.[29] They had neglected the valley for decades after La Salle's claim on it; they never claimed it by settlement. One could claim a land by discovery, but the claim could not be complete until the land was occupied. The French then tried an intermediate step.

The Treaty of Aix-la Chappelle of 1748 ended King George's War, but it is likely both the British and French anticipated this would be but a lull in the contest for North America. In 1749, a year after the treaty, the Governor-General of New France, Marquis de la Galissoniere, sent one of his officers, Celoron de Bienville, on an expedition to ensure New France's claim to the Ohio Valley. They needed to make a statement that the Ohio Valley belonged to New France. Celoron left Montreal on June 15, 1749, with a company of 200 officers, soldiers, and Indians. Their objective was to claim the Ohio Valley by planting lead plates with inscriptions at the mouths of the major tributary rivers of the Ohio, known to the French as la Belle Riviere, but by the Iroquois as Oyo, which is the name Celoron used. The inscription claimed the Valley for France, citing the recent treaties between France and England, including the Treaty of Aix-la-Chapelle. They buried their first plate on the upper Allegheny River, which was then known as the Ohio, at the confluence of the Conawango (Kanaaiagon) Creek and the Allegheny in northern Pennsylvania.[30]

Besides claiming the land, their purpose was to reassure the Indians of their intentions to maintain peaceful trade with them. However, they noticed that as they approached an Indian village, it would often be deserted. The Indians had been trading with the English, and had assumed this large French force was there to punish them for that. Persistently, but without success, Celoron tried to convince them otherwise. He insisted the Indians were free to trade with the English but only on English land not on French land. At one point he came across a village that was flying three French flags and one English flag, which he ordered taken down.

The point he tried to make was the French intention of sharing the land with the Indians in contrast to the English desire to take the land. The idea he wanted to get across was that the English hide their intentions to take Indian land, and would do so if the French didn't stop them.[31] He was correct. For 150 years the English colonists had striven to expel Indians from any land the colonists desired. By the time of the expedition, the Ohio Company had received their grant from the king, which undoubtedly the French were apprised of, and the company was about to send an explorer to look for suitable land in the Ohio Valley.

Celoron was frustrated that the Indians didn't see the long-term issue, coming to the conclusion that the king of England was subsidizing the trade which made it possible for the English to offer lower prices for trade goods, as low as one-fourth of the French price.[32] As we saw previously, a subsidy by the crown to gain market share was probably not necessary because of the favorable trade advantages of the colonial economy, but that is how Celoron saw it.

In July and August Celoron continued his journey, burying plates at various rivers along the Ohio, including the Muskingum and Kanawha. They moved past the Indian village at the Scioto River, and left the Ohio River at the Great Miami River, where they planted the last of their six plates. They moved up the river to Pickawillany, a trading town, near present-day Piqua, Ohio. From there they went to Detroit and on to Montreal, completing the trip in September.[33]

It was obvious to Celoron that the Indians he hoped to reassure along the way felt almost universal fear of his party. He knew he had failed.

> The journey is twelve hundred leagues. I was still more happy in my own esteem and in that of my officers of the detachment. All I can say is, that the nations of these localities are very badly disposed to the French, and are entirely devoted to the English. I do not know in what way they could be brought back.... A solid establishment would be useful in the colony, but there are many inconveniences in being able to sustain it.... I am in doubt as to the feasibility of the undertaking without incurring enormous expenses, I feel myself obliged on account of the knowledge I have acquired of all these places, to put these reflections at the end of my journal, so that one may make use of them as shall judge proper.
> Signed
> Celoron[34]

He had put his finger on the vulnerability of the French in the Ohio Country. He recognized that a larger French population would be necessary to hold it, and he knew that was probably not going to happen. Some of the six plates he buried have been recovered; they did absolutely no good in protecting the territory for New France. It was as if someone had surveyed a plot of land that remained empty and inviting, but provided no deterrent from someone finding that land desirable and just moving in. The stage was now set for others, besides the Indians, the original occupiers, to contest for control of the Ohio Valley. The French and English rivalry sprung up to contest the Ohio Valley. The Indians were being squeezed out and they knew it. Their hunting grounds and living areas were being subjected to possession by others. They watched the French and English surveying both sides of the river. If the land was all being claimed for France and England the question came up: "where is the land that belongs to the Indians[?]"[35] Events were beginning to move quickly in the Ohio Valley after the Celoron mission. In July the Ohio Company received its grant from the king and started to look for land. Cristopher Gist made his two trips to the Ohio Country in 1750–51 and 1751–52 for that purpose, and later moved to the Valley himself. The Logstown conference discussed in the previous chapter, which ostensibly gave the British permission to occupy the south bank of the Ohio, was held in June 1752. It was only about a week after that conference, one can argue, that the first shots of the French and Indian war were fired.

Pickawillany was a trading town established by the Miami Indians on the Great Miami River in Ohio, a tributary of the Ohio River. In 1747 George Croghan, a Pennsylvania trader, built a fortified trading post at Pickawillany. This English trading post may have been the proximate reason for Glassoniere to send Celoron on his mission. The post was in a good location to draw trade from many tribes, including some as far away as Detroit. It was used by both the French and English traders, the latter mostly from Pennsylvania. The chief, known as La Demoiselle (for some unknown reason) by the French, and Old Briton by the British, was called by many Indian names, including Memeskia. He promoted a vigorous trading practice. Celoron had visited the post on his trip but impressed neither Memeskia nor the English traders. Desiring to clear Ohio of English traders, Celoron asked the Miami to move back west to the Maumee River in present-day Indiana from whence they had come; they refused. This English presence in what they considered their territory was clearly a provocation to the French. The next step was an escalation by New France.[36]

It was only a week after the Logstown conference in June 1752 that a 250-man French force of Ottawa, Ojibwa, and Potowatomi Indian allies led by Charles Langlade attacked Pickawillany. They attacked while the men were out hunting and the women were working in the fields. They took a few prisoners, but were more interested in making a statement, which they did rather ruthlessly. They killed one of the English traders and ate his heart; they also killed, boiled, and ate the chief La Demoiselle. They had made their point; the Miami got the message and moved back to the west. The English traders moved back to Pennsylvania. The French now had regained control of the Ohio Country.[37]

The new Governor-General of New France, Ange Duquesne de Menneville, Marquis de Duquesne, took additional steps in 1752 to consolidate French control of the Ohio Country. He had arrived in Quebec in July and was under orders "to make every possible effort to drive the English from our lands." He was to "make our Indians understand … that we have nothing against them [and] that they are at liberty to go and trade with the English in the latter's country, but that we will not allow them to receive the [English] on our lands." He then started efforts to fortify the Ohio Country by first ordering the Canadian militia of 11,000 men to start drilling every week.[38]

Duquesne's intention was to build a string of four forts in the Ohio Country to enforce French control. The first two were under construction in spring of 1753. One was at Presque Isle on Lake Erie near present-day Erie Pennsylvania, while the second, Fort Le Boeuf, near present-day Waterford Pennsylvania, was a portage away on the upstream part of French Creek, which is a tributary of the Allegheny River. The third fort, Fort Machault at present-day Franklin, Pennsylvania, was started in the fall of 1753 near the village of Venango at the confluence of French Creek and the Allegheny. The fourth fort was to be built in 1754 at the Forks of the Ohio and named Fort Duquesne. Fort Duquesne was ultimately built, but not before hostilities had begun.[39]

Robert Dinwiddie was Lieutenant Governor of Virginia when he arrived in Virginia 1751. He was also a shareholder in the Ohio Company. Mixing personal and government business was not unusual at the time, but he had to make sure his actions on behalf of Virginia could not be construed to be for the benefit of the private company alone. Nevertheless, he had decided to act against the French incursion into the Ohio Country when they decided on their fort building program.

He had the backing of London, of sorts, when he and other governors received word "to repell any hostile attempt by force of arms; and you will easily understand, that it is in his majesty's determination, that you should defend to the utmost of your power, all his possessions within your government, against any invader. But at the same time, as it is the king's resolution, not to be the aggressor. I am, in his majesty's name most strictly to enjoin you, not to make use of the force under your command, excepting within the undoubted limits of his majesty's province."[40] London wanted it both ways. They wanted the colonies to "repell any hostile attempt" and "defend to the utmost of your power" but did not intend to use royal troops to help. The last sentence, to not use force "except within the undoubted limits of his majesty's province," is very ambiguous. Was the Ohio Valley "within the undoubted limits of his majesty's province," or was it the province of New France? Dinwiddie decided to act despite this ambiguity.

In late 1753 he sent an inexperienced major in the Virginia Regiment, George Washington, along with Christopher Gist, on a diplomatic mission to Fort Le Boeuf with a stern letter from Dinwiddie to order the French off his majesty's land. "The lands upon the Ohio River are so notoriously known to be the property of the Crown of Great Britain." The French commander, Captain Jacques Legardeur de St. Pierre, received him cordially, but not the letter. In his letter to Dinwiddie he responded that "the lands situated along the Ohio [were] incontestable," they belonged to New France. He did, however, promise to forward the Dinwiddie message to the Marquis Duquesne.[41]

Still aggressive in his attempt to stop the French forts in the Ohio Valley, in the spring of 1754 Dinwiddie sent Washington with 160 men from the Virginia Regiment to stop the French from building a fort at the Forks of the Ohio. Washington was too late to stop the construction, but on this trip, he encountered a French patrol seeking to make diplomatic contact with his force in order to determine its intentions. Not knowing the French intentions, Washington led a surprise attack on the French patrol, headed by Ensign Joseph Coulon de Villiers de Jumonville. During the attack the inexperienced Washington lost control of the situation, and a friend of his, an Ohio Indian named Tanaghrisson (Tanacharison), put a hatchet to the head of Jumonville. Tanaghrisson had his own issues with the French prior to this, which were most likely the cause of his attack on Jumonville. This attack on Jumonville turned a diplomatic mission into an act of war. On hearing of this attack, the French commandant at the Forks, Captain Contrecoeur, sent troops after Washington's force. After some indecision, a move forward, and then a retreat, Washington tried to make a stand at Great Meadows, at a makeshift fort he called (aptly) Fort Necessity. Great Meadows is a clearing between two ridges in the Alleghenies, Laurel Ridge and Chestnut Ridge in southwest Pennsylvania. In another unforced error the inexperienced Washington built a flimsy stockade fort in the meadow, against the advice of Tanaghrisson, who rightly called it a deathtrap. The French force under Louis Coulon de Villiers, brother of Jumonville, surrounded the fort and fired on it from the surrounding trees. After a short battle, on July 3, 1754, Washington capitulated. After he signed the papers of capitulation, he and his force were allowed to return home. The French force then burned Fort Necessity, and also Gist's plantation on the Monongahela, thus tightening their control of the Ohio Valley.[42]

This was the start of the French and Indian War. It was considered part of the war between Great Britain and her allies and France and her allies, known as the Seven Years' War, 1756–1763, which raged over Europe and other theaters for the duration. The war is chronicled by many, including by Fred Anderson, in *Crucible of War: The Seven Years' War and the Fate of Empire in British North America*. In the previous wars between France and England over the prior 100 years the wars in America were considered sideshows to the main engagements in Europe. This war was different; North America was now a major theater of operation, and France was fighting for her empire there.

The British thought that it could be a quick war if they could take Fort Duquesne quickly. They were wrong; they could not take it, and the war was longer and more consequential than originally imagined. As Anderson notes,

> in fact, events had reached a stage at the beginning of 1755 that made war between Britain and France all but inevitable.... [Many factors] would take such comparatively minor episodes as Jumonville's death and the Battle of Fort Necessity and make of them something much larger, much more dangerous, than even Newcastle at his most pessimistic could have foreseen. How the clash of tiny numbers of men in a frontier conflict would grow into a world war, how the war would redraw the map of Europe's empires, and how it would transform the relationship between England and her American colonies—such a chain of events would have defied the most exuberant imaging.[43]

The French and their Indian allies pushed the war into the western settlements of the British colonies, all the way to the Susquehanna River in Pennsylvania. Settlers on the western frontier, especially in Pennsylvania, Maryland, and Virginia had to move back east to avoid the devastation. The ultimate outcome, however, was never really in doubt. The British colonists had a population advantage over New France of more than 20 to one, and the combination of colonial troops, British royal troops, and their Indian allies eventually prevailed. The last major battle in North America, the Battle of Quebec on the Plains of Abraham where General James Wolfe defeated General Louis-Joseph, Marquis de Montcalm, was over in 1759. Both Montcalm and Wolfe perished in the battle. By 1760 the war in North America was over and The Seven Years' War ended with the Treaty of Paris in 1763. The territory west to the Mississippi was now part of the British empire.

The French had ignored "the injunction of Louis XIV, given to Frontenac in 1676, not to turn his intention to new discoveries without necessity and a very great advantage, as it was better to occupy less territory and to people it thoroughly, than to have feeble colonies of large territorial extents and easily destroyed." Frontenac was the Governor of New France when La Salle claimed the Ohio Country for France. New France had claimed more territory than it could inhabit or defend. Their desire to maintain just a trading empire was not feasible for the era. Although it appeared to start as a trade dispute with Pennsylvania and Virginia traders in Ohio, it was much more than that for the colonies. The colonies had pushed the population all the way to the mountains and there were companies, Loyal and Greenbrier, with settlements in the mountains. The Ohio Company was clearly attempting settlement in the Ohio Valley itself, unequivocally claimed by New France. Control of territory was the objective of the war, not trade.

For 150 years the British colonists had gotten the message that land was abundant, free or cheap, and just a little bit farther west. It was now part of the culture and they felt entitled to that western land to the Mississippi now wrested from France.

Rush for More Land

The Seven Years' War would end with the Treaty of Paris in 1763, but by 1760 the war in North America was over. The changes wrought by the war were dramatic. For the first time in 150 years there was no official French presence in North America. Great Britain now controlled North America from Canada down the coast to Florida, which was under Spanish control, and to the west as far as the Mississippi River, well more than double the original colonial lands. Any collective sigh of relief was welcome but brief.

The end of the war led to two separate, but intersecting, movements, one public and one private. The public one had to do with the policy of the home government in London. They knew they had to rethink their colonial policy. What would they do with the newly acquired western lands? How would they deal with the Indians who claimed the land? How would they defend the new land and pay for the defense? The second, or private one, was the response by the colonials to the apparently available new land to the west. The farmers and speculators saw it as unclaimed, except by the Indians, whom they still saw as unworthy of land claims because of their savage nature and their inappropriate use of the land. To them, this was free land.

These two visions were in competition for the next 12 years after the end of the war and would eventually lead to separation of the colonies from Great Britain in 1776. This sequence of events leading to the separation will be covered in the next chapter. In the meantime, there would be a continuous push by the colonists to claim that land, sell it, and occupy it. This process would start in 1760, even before the Treaty of Paris was signed.

Even though the population had been expanding dramatically for decades, the end of the war brought an additional surge.

> In the years after the cessation of the war in North America in 1760, the colonies experienced an extraordinary burst of expansion. By 1775 British North America, for all its remoteness, simplicity and exotic strangeness, had become a place of interest for Britain, and to a lesser extent for Western Europe.... The British North American colonies, still viewed as primitive outlands at the edge of civilization, were now immense in extent, and they were known to be potential gold mines in "futures"; futures in land values, in consumer markets, and supplies of colonial goods. Most important of all, they had acquired a powerfully intensified social role as a magnet and a refuge for the threatened, the discounted, the impoverished, and the ambitious of the western world.[44]

Immigration had been high for most of the century, but now with the cessation of the war it turned into a flood. Between the end of the war and 1775, over 55,000 Protestant Irish emigrated to America, along with over 40,000 Scots, and over 30,000 Englishmen, making up 125,000 from the British Isles alone. In the same years at least 12,000 German speakers came and 84,000 enslaved Africans were imported. Thus, approximately 221,500 came during the period or about 10 percent of the entire population of the British colonies in 1775. The Scots influx represented about 3 percent of the entire population of Scotland, and the Irish about 2.3 percent of the Irish population. Immigration "had a direct and peculiar impact on the leading edge of expansion, the frontier. It is in fact, as much transatlantic migration as domestic population movements that accounts for the speed and extent of frontier expansion." "[T]his surge of innumerable farming families from all over North America and from western Europe, could not be contained within the existing colonies, or even within the newly extended boundaries of permissible white settlement outside the established provinces. Settlers defied all legal constraints."[45] The common denominator among these immigrants was land; they came to farm the abundant land they had heard about.

Even in 1759, during the last battles of the war, the Scots-Irish and German migration from Pennsylvania to the Shenandoah Valley resumed. Farmers were also settling around the forts, including Fort Pitt, which had replaced Fort Duquesne at the Forks, in present-day Pittsburgh. This not only provided them protection, but it worked to provide the forts with provisions, an advantage for both farmer and soldier. These, of course, were illegal settlements; no one had purchased the land, and the home government had not yet decided on what to do with western lands. "Thus the forts furnished markets that helped stimulate the movement of the population to the west, and an ironic symbiosis emerged between forts and settlers that placed contradictory pressures on commanders ... who sought to discourage the squatters on whom their garrisons were coming to rely."[46]

Even in these early years, as the war was still officially in progress, the settlers moved into the Ohio Valley. It wasn't only settlers but traders and hunters. The traders moved back into Ohio very early, as soon as it seemed safe. The trade goods were plentiful, but now that the Indians had no leverage between the French and British, they were forced to pay much higher prices for the goods, and they had to go to the English forts to do the trading. Hunters from Virginia started pouring over the mountains and taking game and hides, which caused shortages for the Indians trying to live off the land. "Precisely when these men, mostly Virginians, began to enter the region is uncertain, but judging from the Indian reactions and the army reports, by autumn 1761 this invasion had become impossible to ignore." Both the trade and hunting would lead to conflicts later.[47]

The pressure from the settlers became so intense that Colonel Henry Bouquet, commander at Fort Pitt, complained to the governor of Virginia that the Monongahela was being "over run by ... Vagabonds, who under pretense of hunting were making settlements."[48] Bouquet was still trying to abide by the Treaty of Easton, 1758. At that conference General John Forbes tried to repair relations with the Indians to gain support for his march to try to take Fort Duquesne. He claimed that they, the English, would not take Indian land west of the Alleghenies once they took Fort Duquesne from the French. Bouquet's attempt to stop the invasion of the Ohio Country was a proclamation in October 1761. "Whereas by a Treaty held at East Town in the year 1758 ... the Country to the West of the Allegany [sic] Mountains is allowed to the Indians for their Hunting Ground, and as it is of the Highest Importance to his Majesty's service, the preservation of the peace and a good understanding with the Indians, to avoid giving them any just cause of Complaint, this is therefore to forbid any of his Majesty's subjects to Settle or Hunt to the west of the Allegany [sic] Mountains on any Pretence [sic] Whatsoever...."[49] It didn't work. People were on the move all along the frontier from Nova Scotia to the Carolinas. As Anderson points out, "the fundamental force at work in them all, was the dynamism of a farming population seeking opportunity.... American farmers moved to take up new lands regardless of virtually every factor but the safety of their families.... With the defeat of the French accomplished and the Indians unlikely to mount effective military resistance, therefore, both governments and private enterprises tried to position themselves to take advantage of population movements that no one could control."[50] Up to this time the British home government did not have a land policy, which made it difficult to impose one when they now thought it necessary. The original provinces were established by grants to private companies or to proprietors, and the granting of land in these provinces was left to the provinces themselves. Land was granted, given away, or sold cheaply by these provinces. After 160 years it became clear that land distribution was a local prerogative and that it was abundant and free, or almost free. It seems clear by this time that most colonists and immigrants thought they were entitled to land. Most expected to pay for it, although squatters were among the first over the mountains, and were willing to challenge the Indians for the land.

Even before the war was officially over in 1763, when the French were defeated in North America in 1760, the eyes of the settlers and speculators were looking west. The 15 years between the end of fighting in North America and the start of the Revolution saw numerous attempts to stake out legal land claims in what was assumed to be the open lands of the west, the Ohio Country. These claims, some of which were ambitious but none of which were successful, were in process right up to the time of the Revolution.

The Ohio Company was one whose settlers in the Ohio Country suffered during the war. "Then after more than five years of forced inactivity, the Ohio Company renewed its interests and vigorously explored all avenues which might led to a legal title or patent to a huge tract of land on the Ohio." There now was a large British presence in Fort Pitt, "yet the Company to all intents and purposes had lost its great land grant 'west of the Alleghenies.'" The clock had also run out on the time for them to settle their grant. In July 1759 they ordered their secretary to draw up the case on why they should get their original grant back.[51]

The company was trying to start again, and proposed settling some Virginia and Maryland families on the Ohio. They approached Colonel Bouquet, commander of Fort Pitt, perhaps for military protection for these families. He refused the request. In the summer of 1760, he was offered a share of 25,000 acres of company land by Thomas Cresap, an officer of the company, if he would push the company's interest, and later, George Mercer of the company offered to sell him a share; he refused both offers. Bouquet continually referred to the Treaty of Easton, which reserved that land for the Indians. "In 1761 the British government officially accepted the principle of the Easton treaty, The Board of Trade ... proclaimed the policy on November 11, 1761.... By this decree, all rights of granting Indian lands were removed from the powers of the governor and turned over to the Crown. This act was to last only for the duration of the war at which time a new policy was to be determined."[52] The company continued to try to renew their grant for several more years but failed, primarily because of the post-war Royal Proclamation of 1763. The Royal Proclamation of 1763 was a major policy statement prohibiting settlement beyond the mountains. It will be considered in the next chapter.

Another speculative land company was started in 1763 by many of the same investors of the Ohio Company, perhaps because the Ohio Company's requests to renew their grant were going nowhere. The Mississippi Company was looking for a grant of 2.5 million acres along the Mississippi River. They took a long time to get organized and only submitted the petition for a grant in 1768. The company was a complete failure; George Washington, for example wrote off his investment as a total loss. This was another company Del Papa, in "The Royal Proclamation of 1763," claimed was a victim of the Proclamation of 1763.[53]

Still another land company formed after the war was composed of traders motivated to request reparations for damages sustained in the war from either the colonial governments or the home government in London, or both. They called themselves the Suffering Traders and sought reparations for goods lost in both 1754 and 1763 in the form of either cash payments or land. It is difficult to see how one could make legitimate claims for war damages for one particular group, but they tried. The land, more realistic than cash, they sought was to be called Indiana and the company was called the Indiana Company. It was to be located on 1.2 million acres in what is now northern West Virginia, just south of the Ohio River. The Indian agent, Sir William Johnson, had secured a promise of this land cession from the Indians in the Treaty of Fort Stanwix (1768). The treaty will be discussed in the next chapter. There were issues of course; one was that this was land still claimed by Virginia, and another was that it was land claimed by the Iroquois based on their conquest of the Cherokees. In early 1769 the company sent two of their members, William Trent and Samuel Wharton, to London to press for royal confirmation for this grant; hopes were high for approval.[54]

The approval was not quick because the Trent and Wharton mission was overtaken by events: a more grandiose land scheme was proposed that would be much larger than Indiana, but would encompass it. The original request for the new project was to be for 2.4 million acres, but early on, Lord Hillsborough, Secretary of State for the Colonies, proposed the petitioners ask for much more, 20 million acres, large enough for a new western colony. His intentions were not clear, and some suggested he made this suggestion in order to preclude the deal from going through, because of the increased cost this would entail. Nevertheless, Trent and Wharton gained the support of the prominent London banker Thomas Walpole, and the company became known unofficially as the Walpole Company, but officially as the Grand Ohio Company. (Not to be confused with the Ohio Company of Virginia.) The land grant was to be bounded by a line from the Ohio and Scioto River intersection down to the Cumberland Gap, and from there northeast through the Greenbrier River Valley, following the mountains up to the Pennsylvania border and then west to the Ohio River. This was estimated to be about 20 million acres. A proposed name for the new colony was to be Pittsylvania in honor of the Prime Minister. Later names such as "Charlottina" or "Charlotta" were proposed to honor the queen. Eventually the name Vandalia was chosen because the queen claimed descent from the Vandals. Clearly the queen was interested in the project.[55]

This was not to be an ordinary grant, but a new colony, the fourteenth one, and Samuel Wharton was angling to be the governor. Presumably the new colony would have the same land granting privileges as the other 13 colonies. The process was not smooth, however, and many changes took place over the years it went on. One step taken to ease opposition was to bring in the Ohio Company and incorporate their land claims. As the process went on the size of the proposed land grant changed more than once. First the southern boundary was moved down to the Virginia–North Carolina border and followed that east to the Alleghenies and then followed them up to the western boundaries of Pennsylvania and Maryland. Eventually land in the west, to the Kentucky River was added. Ultimately it "included all of the trans–Allegheny West Virginia, the part of Pennsylvania between the Monongahela and Ohio rivers, and all of Kentucky east of the Kentucky River."[56] All of this land was west of the mountains, new land so to speak, and it was west of the Proclamation Line of 1763. It was land that Virginia claimed in her second charter (1609), so naturally the colony pushed back. In normal times, that is before the war, had there not been a French threat, Virginia would have acted independently and moved to grant lands on the other side of the Alleghenies. The justification would have been the second charter. These were no longer normal times; the home government was now intending to take charge of western lands. Abernethy, *Western Lands and the American Revolution*, covers Vandalia in detail.[57]

There was a great deal of optimism at first; the speculators were ready to move in as soon as the new colony was approved. Wharton had claimed that 30,000 people were already settled on it. However, the size of the project, the opposition from Virginia, and London politics, described well by Alvord in *The Mississippi Valley in British Politics, Vol. II*, all caused the process to drag on. "Here the history of Vandalia really ends. Wharton struggled on manfully until the outbreak of the Revolution, and in the spring of 1775 the draft of the grant was actually completed, but laid aside pending settlement of the dispute with the colonies."[58]

The last significant land claim after the war came late, and it included land that was set aside for the Indians by various treaties after the war. It involved negotiations by the developers directly with the Cherokee. It was as bold a step as the Vandalia project, an attempt to establish a new proprietary colony. It was an early indication of the cracks that appeared between the colonies and the mother country regarding the control and disposition of land that had become available after the war.

After the war, settlers started pouring into the Clinch River Valley in southwest Virginia and farther beyond, that into Cherokee country. Following Lord Dunmore's war with the Indians (next chapter), when the fighting had quieted down in the area, speculators, first from Virginia and later from North Carolina, sought to take advantage of the migration and moved to buy lands from the Cherokee to start what they hoped would be a new colony. On August 27, 1774, Richard Henderson of North Carolina organized Richard Henderson and Company. Within months they approached the Cherokee to buy Cherokee land. In January 1775 the company reorganized under the name of the Transylvania Company, and on March 17, 1775, they negotiated the Treaty of Sycamore Shoals with the Cherokee, paying for a large area of land that encompassed most of present-day Kentucky and a major part of present-day Tennessee. The treaty was seen as a fair deal for the Cherokee, but private treaties with the Indians were illegal. Even before the treaty was completed, Henderson had Daniel Boone lead a party through the Cumberland Gap to start settlements, blazing what would be known as the Wilderness Trail from the Great Valley Road into Kentucky. "Surveyors, prospectors, and settlers swarmed into the new region during the spring of 1775."[59]

The original agreement between the Transylvania Company and the Cherokee was for all the land below the Ohio River and between the Kanawha and Tennessee rivers. These boundaries were unsustainable; for one thing, the Kanawha was in the middle of the grant sought by the Vandalia Company. The Transylvania Company finally settled on the Kentucky River as the eastern limit, the Ohio River as the northern limit, and the Cumberland River watershed as the western and southern boundary. This put Transylvania west of Vandalia, well into previous Cherokee territory.

Their ambitions were high. "Plans were now made for establishing a new colony in the west. The intention of the partners was to pay quit-rents if the King would recognize their title; otherwise they would declare their independence of him. In any event they meant to establish their own government and administer their own laws."[60] Transylvania was to have a democratic government, but it was to be a proprietary one, with the proprietors having veto power over the legislature. They had yet to figure out how to deal with Virginia, the Continental Congress, and his majesty's government.[61]

Transylvania elected a legislature in 1775 and named two delegates to the Continental Congress in 1775, hoping to be considered as the fourteenth colony, but it is unlikely they were noticed or their cause considered. At that time, the Congress was in the middle of a war that had started in April, only a month after the Treaty of Sycamore Shoals between the Transylvania Company and the Cherokee. They also had problems with Virginia and the home government. As might be expected, Virginia opposed a new colony on land Virginia had claimed for over 150 years. Lord Dunmore, the decidedly royalist governor of Virginia, acted first, however. Just days after the Sycamore Shoals treaty was announced, he sent a proclamation denouncing Henderson and his colleagues. In this proclamation he referred to Board of Trade restrictions that he had received more than a year earlier. In these the crown was now claiming control over the western lands and intended to make money in the process. "The vacant lands of the colony were to be surveyed in lots of one hundred to one thousand acres, and put up at public sale for the highest bidders, subject to the reservations of one half-penny sterling quit rent per acre."[62] The Henderson claim was being rejected by the royal governor. This claim was fought by the Ohio and Loyal Companies, rejected by both the crown and Virginia, and ignored by the Continental Congress. As with the other companies, it did not survive the imminent Revolution.[63]

By mid-century, and at some places before, the original 13 colonies had expanded to the Appalachian Mountains. Land across the mountains, in the Ohio Valley, was seen as available to anyone who could take it and hold it. The mountains, though difficult to cross, were not seen as a hindrance to the occupation of the Valley. There was concern about the French threat, however, which caused some, but not all, to hesitate. There were two concurrent movements across the mountains from 1747 to 1754. One was by speculative land companies, such as the Ohio Company of Virginia, who were interested in claiming the land and selling it for a profit. There were several companies, at least three of them well known, Greenbrier, Loyal, and Ohio, who had made claims and settled a few people on the other side of the mountains by 1754. The other movement was one of individuals and families who saw the opportunity to obtain free land by simply moving over the mountains and squatting on it; there were thousands of these. Most of them were Scots-Irish who had hundreds of years of experience fighting along the Scottish-English border and were willing to contest the Indians for this land. Many of them held the view that the Indians were savages that had to be destroyed. Most of the settlers in these transmontane settlements were killed or driven back by the French and their Indian allies in the French and Indian War, which started in 1754. As bad as it was, it turned out to be a temporary setback for the idea of western expansion.

The fighting in North America ended in 1759, but the world war between France and Great Britain didn't end until the Treaty of Paris in 1763. In the meantime, Great Britain was trying to prosecute the war and catch its collective breath in North America. In one respect, everything had been changed by the war; Great Britain, for example, was now the dominant empire in North America, having defeated France. On the other hand, regarding land, nothing had changed in that, after the war was over, thousands now saw an opportunity to once again claim lands in the transmontane region, and started to move there despite dangerous conditions. And similar to a decade earlier, there were companies organized to claim land in the west for profit. In the latter case, the ambitions included the intent to establish whole new colonies west of the mountains. All this was happening while Great Britain was struggling with a policy for how to deal with this new-found bounty of western lands.

The British policy derived from the war, and the colonial response to that policy, would determine events for the next 12 years and would lead to still another war, one which would separate the colonies from Great Britain. The question of who controlled the lands in the west would be at the heart of the struggle and would be a major factor in the separation.

Taking Indian Land

Up to this point we have been talking about the granting or selling of the land in North America as if it was free and uninhabited and the only issues were whether it would be assigned by a settlement company, given as a headright as an inducement to increase the labor force, or sold cheaply to a European immigrant willing to move to the backcountry. Of course, the land was inhabited by an indigenous people even though the population density was low. The continual expansion of English settlements, people who wanted to own the land, meant there was a constant effort by the colonists to take over land from these people, for whom ownership of land was meaningless.

From the very beginning of colonization, the English settlers had no respect for the indigenous people, the Indians. The attitude was that the land belonged to those who could use it, and the Indians were not using the land appropriately, as civilized Europeans would. They were seen as savages who were to be pushed aside and possibly converted to Christianity and civilized, although that was not their first priority. It started at Jamestown and happened in other colonies, although later men, such as William Penn, took a more reasoned view, paying the Indians for land Penn wanted. But even Penn expected the Indians would yield the land to him.

Indian land was acquired through a variety of means, including force, trickery, and sometimes peacefully through sale. This land acquisition history started in the colonial period and continued through the nineteenth-century history of the United States. This history is beyond the scope of this book but is covered in many classic history texts. It happened in all the colonies, from New England, through Pennsylvania, and into Virginia. A few examples demonstrate this acquisition process.

In New England a bloody war was fought in a contest for land.

King Philip is the English name given to the son of Massasoit, the Wampanoag who had greeted the Pilgrims at Plymouth decades earlier. Although the New England colonists and the Indians had lived in an uneasy peace for about 55 years, there were tensions based on land ownership and occupation. "The sale of land was regulated by law, but unfortunately the Indian's idea of what he sold and the white man's idea of what was bought were entirely at variance.... While 'the Indian little appreciated the value of the land until he felt the pressing want of it,' there is no doubt but that the English settler was greedy, for 'land is one of the Gods of New England, of which, the living and most high Eternal' will punish the transgressor. Wrote Roger Williams."[64]

King Philip's War started in 1675; the proximate cause was the execution of three of Philip's warriors after their trial for murder. That incident was the last straw for Philip. Another "cause of [the] war was the frequent demands of the settlers for the purchase of his lands. Philip was too wise not to discover that if these continued, he would not have a home in all the territories which his father had governed. From a period before the death of Massasoit, until 1671, no year passed in which large tracts were not obtained by the settlers."[65] The war killed thousands of Indians and many were sold into slavery or indentured servitude. Six hundred English soldiers were killed, and 17 white settlements destroyed and 50 others damaged before the war ended with the death of Philip in 1676. Although the war was "won" by the New Englanders, per capita, it was the deadliest war in American history.[66]

In Pennsylvania a more subtle fraud was perpetrated to acquire land in the Delaware Valley.

The infamous Walking Purchase occurred in 1737 in Pennsylvania when some Penn family members agreed to purchase some land west of the Delaware River from the Delaware tribe. The land was to be defined by the distance a man could walk in a day and one-half. This seemed reasonable because the Delaware knew how much ground could be covered by walking for this time. The Penn's had a plan that could only be called a fraud. They had fast runners run straight out from the river for the time allotted, and then simply drew a line from the end of the run, perpendicular to it, back to the river. The area enclosed was approximately 1,100 square miles, clearly an impossible distance for one man to cover in a day and one-half. This fraudulent deal was to be addressed 20 years later, near the end of the war, when the British needed the help of the Indians. It also meant that many of the Delaware went to fight for the French in the impending French and Indian War.[67]

In Virginia a succession of treaties with the Indians was used to progressively move the colonial boundary to the west.

By 1722 there were several tribes in Virginia with friendly relations with the colony, known as client tribes. About this time there was a problem with Iroquois raids on these tribes in the west, in and near the Shenandoah Valley. This was one of the reasons for a conference in Albany between the governors of New York, Pennsylvania, and Virginia. Lieutenant Governor Alexander Spotswood of Virginia was seeking to end these raids on the Virginia client Indians. At the conference he proposed "that the great River of the Potowmak & the High Ridge of Mountains which extend all along the Frontiers of Virginia to the Westward of the present Settlements of that colony shall be for ever the established Boundaries between the Indians subject to the dominion of Virginia & the Indians belonging to and depending on the 5 Nations."[68] Spotswood's "High Ridge of Mountains" was intended to be the Allegheny Ridge Mountains, west of the Shenandoah Valley, not the lower Blue Ridge Mountains east of the Shenandoah Valley. Spotswood also claimed the boundaries were intended for the *client Indians*, not the Virginia colonists, implying the latter were not limited by these boundaries.[69]

Six days later the Five Nations replied they would agree to the boundaries, but "in their terms the line became the 'Frontiers of Virginia,' ... the Five Nations' restatement implied plainly that Virginia's colonials also were to stay inside the line."[70] Later the ambiguity about which mountains were the boundary became an issue; the Five Nations considered the easternmost Blue Ridge to be the boundary, not the westernmost Allegheny Ridge. This was only the first time that the colonial push for land to the west would end up in an ambiguous treaty, interpreted differently by the two parties, but not the last. This treaty was between the colonies and the Indians, not between the Indians and the imperial crown. The crown was not particularly interested in pushing the boundaries at this time.[71]

We know that it was in the 1730s that Virginians started to fill the Shenandoah Valley, between the Blue Ridge and the Appalachian Ridge. The Iroquois had used the Valley to travel to conduct attacks against the southern Indians, so there was bound to be conflict because of the ambiguity of who controlled the land in the Valley based on the Treaty of Albany of 1722. Maryland also had a dispute about the Iroquois presence in western Maryland. These grievances engendered the need for another conference, which was held at Lancaster, Pennsylvania, in 1744. Attending were representatives from Pennsylvania, Maryland, and Virginia. The Virginia delegation included Thomas Lee who a few years later would be the head of the Ohio Company of Virginia, and William Beverly, a landowner in the Valley; both had significant personal interest in moving the boundary west.

The Virginians accused the Iroquois of violating the Spotswood line of 1722 by traveling in the Shenandoah Valley east of the Appalachian Ridge. The Iroquois countered that at Albany "you took a Belt of Wampum, and made a Fence with it on the Middle of the Hill."[72] In their interpretation the "Hill" was the Blue Ridge. Thus, the ambiguity of Albany became an issue again. Nevertheless, they agreed to move their road further west "to the Foot of the Great Mountain [Allegheny Ridge], where it now is; and it is impossible for us to remove it any further to the West, those parts of the Country being absolutely impassible by either Man or Beast."[73] They moved to the foot of the mountains they now thought to be the limit of the Virginia colony claim; they had acknowledged that the Shenandoah Valley was part of Virginia. That is *all* they thought they were giving up, and acknowledged in the deed signed at the conference that "they the said Sachims or chiefs on behalf of the said Six Nations Do hereby renounce and disclaim not only the Right of the Six Nations but also *recognize* and acknowledge the Right and Title of our Sovereign the King of Great Britain to all the land within the said Colony as it is now or hereafter may be peopled and bounded by his said Majesty ... his Heirs and Successors."[74] That seemed to settle it for now. The Iroquois gave up what they thought was the Shenandoah Valley for £400, a reasonable price considering the Virginians were already settling the Valley. However, the Virginia delegation didn't inform the Iroquois that they still had designs on land beyond the mountains based on the 1609 charter, which covered all the lands beyond the mountains, including all of Ohio. Thomas Lee, the future founder of the Ohio Company of Virginia, certainly interpreted "all the land within said colony" to include the Ohio Country, because in the Ohio Company request for land at the Forks they cited the Lancaster Treaty as justification.

A further extension of Virginia's land claims in the west came just a few years later. We saw that the Ohio Company of Virginia requested a land grant in the Ohio Valley, at the Forks of the Ohio, which was on the *other side*, that is west, of the Allegheny Ridge. The request was made of the governor in 1747. This claim was more sensitive than other land claims because it was in the disputed Ohio Country. Governor Gooch, who normally dispensed land grants easily, was concerned, so he sent the request to London for approval. The king saw a way to advance British interests in the west without involving the crown itself, as they had just concluded a war with France, but through the use of the colonies; he approved the grant in 1749.

The Ohio Company continued its work in preparation for setting up trading posts and settlements in Ohio Country near the Forks by sending Christopher Gist on his expeditions to the country in 1751–1752. Prior to any move, they thought it prudent to reaffirm the terms of the Treaty of Lancaster. Primarily for the benefit of the company, a conference was set up with the Indians at Logstown (Loggstown), Pennsylvania in June 1752. Logstown was on the Ohio River a few miles downstream from the Forks. Christopher Gist of the Ohio Company was a member of the Virginia delegation, clearly indicating the thrust of the meeting was to benefit the company.

After the traditional gift giving by the English, the Virginia delegation stated their desire that the Treaty of Lancaster be confirmed and then stated the most recent request. "Brethren, it is the Design of the King, our Father, at present, to make a Settlement of British Subjects on the South East Side of Ohio [River], that we may be united as one People, by the strongest Ties of Neighbourhood as well as Friendship." They then pitched the trade advantage it would give the Indians if the English had a trading post at the Forks. They believed they had purchased these lands at Lancaster, but were willing to repurchase them. Every effort would be made to secure access to these lands. They went on to claim, "brethren, be assur'd that the King our Father, by purchasing your Lands, had never any Intention of *taking them from you*, but that we might live together as one People, & *keep them from the French*, who wou'd be bad neighbors" (emphasis added). It is not clear if the Virginia delegation believed their own words, but this statement was disingenuous; history had shown that the English colonists had every intention of continuing to take Indian lands in their move westward.[75]

The Indian delegation acknowledged the Lancaster Deed and responded, "we assure you we are willing to confirm any Thing our Council has done in Regard to the Land, but we never understood, before you told us Yesterday, that the Lands then sold were to extend further to the Sun setting than the Hill on the other Side of the Allegheny Hill, so that we can't give you a further Answer now." They were surprised that the British thought the Lancaster Treaty had given them the right to land west of the Allegheny Ridge. Nevertheless, they accepted it but said they could not dispose of any land until they consulted with the Onondagas, the diplomatic arm of the Six Nations. Though later the same day, June 13, they had agreed to allow an English settlement on southeastern parts of the Ohio River, and "do further promise that the said Settlement or Settlements shall be unmolested by us, and that we will, as far as is in our power, assist and Protect the British Subjects there inhabiting." This was the tract that the Ohio Company had requested at the Forks. So, although the Indians did not agree to sell the land, they did agree to an English settlement on it.[76]

This was a major step in the Virginians' continuous westward movement. They now had an agreement with the Indians to occupy lands west of the mountains, although the land was still disputed by the French. Supposedly, the Indians repudiated this Logstown Treaty about a year later. However, that is largely irrelevant, because at that time tensions were quickly building toward a full-scale war starting in 1754. The settlers who had moved to the Forks were either killed or moved back east during the war, erasing any settlements in Ohio. The next time there would be discussions with the Indians about the lands in the west would be during the war, in 1758, when General John Forbes needed their support for his assault on Fort Duquesne.[77]

Chapter Six

End of Expansion: Rebellion and Break

The seven-year interval between King George's War, which ended in 1748, and the French and Indian War could have been characterized as a "cold war." Both belligerents remained in place and continued to claim and counterclaim parts of North America to which they felt entitled. It is likely both France and Great Britain anticipated there would be another battle for the continent, which is exactly what happened. Gipson, in *The American Revolution as an Aftermath of the Great War for Empire, 1754–1763*, called it the Great War for Empire.

The Great War for the Empire, 1754–1763, started in America in 1754 and was known here as the French and Indian War; it ended in 1760. The other part of the war, 1756–1763, was known in Europe and beyond as the Seven Years' War; it ended in 1763 with the Treaty of Paris. They were both part of a war that was the most consequential war of the eighteenth century. This war changed the map of the world and especially the map of North America. Prior to the war there had been three major empires with footprints in North America: Spain, France, and Great Britain. Following the war, New France had disappeared from the map of North America. "Great wars in modern times have too frequently been the breeders of revolution. The exhausting armed struggles in which France became engaged in the latter half of the eighteenth century led as directly to the French Revolution as did the First World War to the Russian; it may be said as truly that the American Revolution was an aftermath of the Anglo-French conflict in the New World carried on between 1754 and 1763."[1]

One would think that after an exhausting war the resulting peace would last for generations, there being nothing left to fight for. This was not to be the case.

The 12-year interval from 1763 to 1775 did not see a cold war, but was an interval with very different dynamics, even though it still ended with a war which started in 1775. Despite the different dynamics, there is one issue that was a factor in the French and Indian War which continued to simmer during these 12 years. The one issue, the one dynamic, was land and who would control it. As we have seen, the French and Indian War originally started as a trade dispute to decide who would control the trade with Indians. This was important for Great Britain, which depended on trade to power its mercantile economy. The immediate *casus belli* for the war was the British colonial determination to cross the mountains for the purpose of enlarging trade prospects and for settlement in the Ohio Valley. Thus, the war was fought for control of the Ohio Country, a war for territory.

One issue in the struggle between the crown and the colonists during these 12 years was land—how was it to be used and who would control the western lands acquired by Great Britain at the 1763 Treaty of Paris. The crown's attempt to control those lands and deny colonial access to them was a contravention of 160 years of colonial history in which the colonies controlled their own land, and granted it or sold it to settlers on a frontier that was moving west.

Ending the Fighting

In the spring of 1755, General Edward Braddock led a force from Maryland, across what was to be named Braddock's Road, moved up the Monongahela River, and planned to take Fort Duquesne from the French. He made what turned out to be a costly mistake, one that would cost him the battle and his life. He was offered the support of the Ohio Indians, including Shingas, a Delaware war chief, who were anxious to see the French removed from the Ohio Valley. "When the Delaware chief stood before him and asked the only question that mattered to the Ohio Indians—'what he intended to do with the land if he Could drive the French and their Indians away'—Braddock summoned all his considerable reserves of arrogance, and replied, 'that the English Shou[l]d Inhabit and Inherit the Land.... No Savage Should Inherit the Land.'" This of course angered and alienated the Indians, who deserted Braddock leaving him without any Indian support. Many of them joined the French.[2]

Braddock and his army moved down the Monongahela, near present-day Pittsburgh, where on July 9, 1755, they were surprised by the French forces and their Indian allies and completely routed in the Battle of the Monongahela. The surviving British army made their way back to Fort Cumberland, Maryland, from which they had started. General Braddock was mortally wounded and buried on the road by George Washington, a colonial officer attached to Braddock's staff. It was too late for Braddock to learn a lesson about the Indians, but others learned it. If it wasn't obvious before, it was now: there were three parties interested in the Ohio Valley, not only the British and French, but the Indians who had called it their home for centuries.

The war in the western part of the British colonies was carried on mostly by the Indian allies of the French, who considered themselves to be fighting for their homeland, not for the French, whom they also wanted out of the Valley. The colonial western frontier was pushed back east as far as Harris's Ferry on the Susquehanna River. "Canadian governor-general Pierre de Rigaud, marquis de Vaudreuil complained that raiders entering the Susquehanna Valley near Shamokin in mid-1757 found nothing to attack: the region contained only abandoned farms."[3] The area was devastated and the western settlers had moved back east for protection and food. Clearly the Indians were enraged and sought to regain land lost over the years. "Years later, John Heckewelder, on his way to the new Moravian mission in the Ohio Country, passed through Carlisle and entered a 'howling wilderness' where, in every direction, the 'blackened ruins of houses and barns, and remnants of chimneys' confronted him."[4] If nothing else, this savage war meant that whichever European empire won the war, it would have to deal with the legitimate claims of the Ohio Indians on the land.[5]

One British general who had learned the lesson of Braddock's mistake in alienating the Indians, and which was undoubtedly reinforced by the Indian attacks in Pennsylvania, Maryland, and Virginia, was Acting Brigadier General John Forbes. Forbes had been appointed to take Fort Duquesne in the summer of 1758. He was in Carlisle, Pennsylvania, at the time and decided to march directly west to the fort rather than take the Braddock Road from Fort Cumberland, Maryland to the fort as Braddock had done. He knew he would need the help and support of the Indians in crossing the territory and building a road at the same time. Although "no more culturally sensitive than any of the other British commanders, he was virtually unique among them in that he grasped the strategic importance of the Indians and ... never ceased to seek accommodation with them." He had learned from Braddock's mistake.[6]

It was for this purpose that he called a conference with the Indians at Easton, Pennsylvania, in the fall of 1758; he wanted their support. The conference followed one the previous summer, which had been called to try to remedy some of the previous fraudulent land deals perpetrated against the Indians. The eastern Delaware Indians had been trying to reverse the Walking Purchase deal perpetrated in 1737, and to secure a permanent Delaware reservation in the Wyoming Valley of Pennsylvania, land previously acquired by the Susquehannah Company at the Albany Congress of 1754. Those objectives were not secured in 1757, although a promise was made to submit the Walking Purchase for review by higher authorities, and reconsider the Susquehannah Company purchase. Now, however, in 1758, the Indians had something Forbes wanted: the possibility of a stand-down by the western Delaware, Ohio Indians fighting with the French. The conference was large and included many groups, both colonial delegates and Indians, with conflicting goals. The bottom line, however, was that "everyone at Easton realized that the Ohio Indians would never make peace with the English unless they were satisfied that the Ohio Country would remain theirs once the war was over."[7]

At this point the Pennsylvania agent, Conrad Weiser, made a shrewd move to appease the Delaware. He "formally returned to the Iroquois all the land from the Albany purchase that lay *west* of the Allegheny Mountains." All the land *west* of the Allegheny Mountains was in the Ohio Country. So, he returned the Ohio Country to the Iroquois, but retained the land between the Susquehanna and the mountains for Pennsylvania. At the Albany Conference, Weiser had negotiated with the Iroquois and got them to cede all the lands west of the Susquehanna River, which included the Ohio Country. (See Chapter Four.) This was the only part of Pennsylvania that was in the Ohio Country, so Pennsylvania retained most of its land, and the Iroquois retained their status as lords of the valley.

One more concession was necessary. Pennsylvania Governor William Denny made a pledge on behalf of the proprietor to negotiate *directly* with the western Delaware (and the Ohio Indians in general), thus removing them from the domination of the Iroquois, who had considered them tributary Indians to that time; the Iroquois still held sway over the eastern Delaware. The Treaty of Easton concluded on October 26, 1758, with feasting and gift giving. Easton was the last time the British would see the Indians as allies rather than as impediments to their own plans in their quest for land. This treaty cleared the way for peace between the Ohio Indians and the British under General Forbes. Forbes took Fort Duquesne on November 24, 1758.[8]

The decisive battle of the war was the Battle of Quebec in the fall of 1759, in which General James Wolfe defeated the Marquis de Montcalm on the Plains of Abraham just outside Quebec. The fall of New France took place in 1760, when the newly appointed head of British forces in America, General Jeffery Amherst, took Montreal. This ended the fighting between the British and French in North America, but it didn't end all the fighting.

The British government still had to deal with the war in progress abroad. While they acknowledged they had to make some changes regarding both the colonies and the new land they had just won, they thought little about it and did less in the subsequent three years. Amherst, on the

Chapter Six. End of Expansion

other hand, as the military commander and the only one with a comprehensive view of the country, had to take some steps to control a vast country with a diverse population.

The major issue at the end of the contest between the French and British, although Amherst didn't seem to realize it, was the claim the Indians had on the land, especially the land in Ohio Country. They made that clear at the beginning of the war. "Tanaghrisson ... told the French at the start of the war: 'Fathers, both you and the English are white, we live in a Country between; therefore the Land belongs to neither one nor t'other: But the Great Being above allow'd it to be a Place of Residence for us; ... I am not afraid to discharge you off this Land.'"[9] The Indians never thought they were fighting for the French or the British, but rather for their country, their homeland. That is why originally the Ohio Indians fought with the French to keep the British out of the Ohio Country, and why after Easton they agreed to stay neutral while the British moved against Fort Duquesne. They were consistent and determined. "Three days after Fort Duquesne fell in 1758, the Delaware chief Tamaqua (Beaver) had advised General Forbes 'in a most soft, loving and friendly manner, to go back over the mountains and stay there.' Another was more blunt, and warned that if the British settled west of the mountains, 'all the nations would be against them.' It would, he said 'be a great war, and never come to peace again.'"[10] This was a warning that the British must heed the agreement at Easton, which assured the Indians all the land beyond the mountains. It must be upheld or there would be another war, this time with the Indians.

Rather than cooperating with the Indians as some had suggested, Amherst took a vindictive approach. He was there to enforce order over the Indians that he assumed had been on the losing side and, therefore, needed to submit to British rule, especially on trade and land. He, as many other British officers, had nothing but disdain for the Indians; he thought them indolent and in need of direction. His measures were enforced despite the fact that "the articles of Capitulation agreed upon by General Amherst and French Lieutenant-Governor Marquis de Vaudreuil at Montreal in 1760 stated that France's allies were to 'be maintained in the lands they inhabit, if they chose to remain there; they shall not be molested on any pretence [sic] whatsoever, for having carried arms, and served his most Christian Majesty.'"[11]

Amherst had a large area to control, from the mountains to the Mississippi, so he consolidated control around British forts. The Indians were required to do all the trading at the forts rather than in trading posts scattered conveniently throughout the country. This caused great hardship for those living at distances from the forts. Another burden was the rise in prices of trading goods. Without French rivalry the traders had no competition, so prices increased dramatically. He ended gift giving to the Indians, thinking it no longer necessary. Along with this pressure on Indian cultural life, he started the promotion of white settlements. As early as 1759 he had agreed to grant land to officials and officers in the vicinity of military posts. This occurred from New England down to Virginia. Land was granted in Connecticut, Quebec, New York, and Pennsylvania, for example, near forts along the Forbes road. When Fort Duquesne was destroyed in late 1758, the land on the Forks, in Ohio Country, should have been returned to the Indians to conform to the Treaty of Easton. Instead, Fort Pitt was erected, more substantial than Fort Duquesne. Land around the fort was widely settled and Pittsburgh grew rapidly.

Amherst saw these settlements as addressing two problems. One was that they could supply food to local garrisons which would not have to be brought in from distant sources. Secondly, he saw it as the only way to control the movement of farm families migrating to the frontier. This latter policy showed the disarray of western policy at the time. While he was allowing these settlers on the frontier, his commandant at Fort Pitt was complaining about the large and rapid flow of settlers beyond the mountains in contravention of the Easton Treaty. As we have seen, Colonel Henry Bouquet issued a proclamation in 1761 against this movement, saying he was trying to uphold Easton.[12]

While Amherst saw all these measures as necessary to exert military control over a conquered people over a large area, the Indians clearly saw it as the intent to colonize land they thought they had been finally promised at Easton. Between 1760 and 1763 tensions rose as Indians became more impatient with the colonial settlement of Indian lands. One example is the story of the Wyoming Valley in Pennsylvania.

As we saw in a previous chapter, the Connecticut Susquehannah Company purchased, by subterfuge, Delaware land in the Wyoming Valley at the 1754 Albany Congress. The eastern Delaware remained in the valley during the war. However, in 1760, after the fighting in middle Pennsylvania barely settled down, Teedyuscung, the Delaware chief, found that 20 settlers from Connecticut and the Susquehannah Company had started a settlement on the west bank of the Delaware River. They indicated a much larger group of settlers would be coming also. This started the legal battle between Pennsylvania and Connecticut over that land that would last for years. Meanwhile the settlers kept coming, scores of them, building houses, blockhouses, and roads.

By the fall of 1762, the settlers had cut their way through from the Delaware to the Susquehannah River. When they started to move in, they laughed at Teedyescung when he warned them off. In the meantime, he was losing legal battles to keep them out and could not gain support from

Chapter Six. End of Expansion

even the western Delawares. Yet he had garnered some support and gathered with his warriors to wait for the settlers to come back in 1763. When they did return, in the spring of that year, they met no resistance because Teedyescung was dead, murdered, and his people scattered. They took advantage of the circumstances and planted corn and built houses. They didn't stay long though, because by summer they had heard of an Indian uprising farther west, and most decided to return to Connecticut. About 30 or 40 remained in the blockhouse to wait and harvest the corn. Teedyescung's son, Captain Bull, led a war party that wiped out these settlers in the valley. The Susquehannah Company settlers would not reappear until 1768. The Indian absence was permanent; they lost another five million acres.[13]

The contest for the Ohio Country between the British and French was over by 1760, but the war continued in the rest of the world until it ended in 1763. In this interim the British government basically ignored North America. It knew it would have to make some changes, but it was naturally distracted until the war's end. They expected the status quo to be maintained. The colonists were to remain in place, Amherst was to control the frontier, and the Indians were to retire to prewar positions. No policy changes were implemented to cover how this vast new territory was to be handled; that is, no new discussions were held with the Indians. The Easton Treaty of 1758 was left over to guide any settlement actions. Colonel Bouquet's proclamation in October 1761, accepted in principle by the British government in November, was meant to enforce the Easton Treaty prohibition of white settlement beyond the mountains. Everything had to wait until the end of the war. Except it couldn't.

The next war started as a war for independence. The Indians, especially the Ohio Indians, were angry. They were angry because they were being treated as a conquered people in their own land. "Minavana, an Ojibwa chief … told trader Alexander Henry in 1761 that 'although you have conquered the French, you have not yet conquered us! We are not your slaves.' 'The Indians were not governed by the French,' a Huron chief reminded a British colonist in 1763, 'but were free all over the world.'" Neolin, a Delaware prophet, put a spiritual base under this anger. He basically said if they can't live with us, we should separate from them; we should become independent. He proposed going back to the old ways before the white man came, and becoming independent of all their goods—going back to the bow and arrow and living as their forefathers did. He had a vision of a heaven with only Indians and no white men.[14]

There is little or no evidence that they returned to the austere lifestyle he proposed, but there is clear evidence that he ignited a pan–Indian movement across the west; he predicted a war in the west. In the winter of

1762–63 it was not a question of whether there would be war, but where and when it would begin. Old leaders who had dealt with the British previously lost influence and nativist leaders emerged. "The western Indians made no secret of their discontent with Amherst's trade and settlement policies and could not conceal the ascendency of nativist leaders." The war started on April 27, 1763, when Ottawa war chief Pontiac invoked Neolin's teaching and inspired an attack on a British garrison near Detroit. It was probably not coincidental that this uprising started only two months after the Treaty of Paris was signed, ending hostilities between the French and British. The Indians had no say in the treaty, which, rightly, enraged them.[15]

The war was known as Pontiac's War or Pontiac's Rebellion, although he did not lead it. It was a spontaneous uprising all over the west and into the east. Tribes not normally on friendly terms with one another cooperated to attack settlements and British garrisons. Many hundreds, if not thousands, were slain, including Indians, British troops, and settlers. It seemed to many a reprise of the war that had just ended, or maybe a continuation of it. It was a war that the Indians could not win. For one thing, they had no support for food and weapons since the French were out of the picture. Clearly it was an eruption of pent-up rage on being suppressed and facing the loss of their homeland. So, at the heart it was a war for territory; who would control the land beyond the mountains?

The fighting continued through 1763 and into 1764. "At its height, the war encompassed a vast region between the Great Lakes, the Appalachians, and the Mississippi." The Indians had captured many British forts, excepting the three major ones of Fort Niagara, Fort Detroit, and Fort Pitt. In 1764 Amherst organized thrusts by two armies into the west, using these major forts as the basis, and finally put down the uprising. By the fall of 1764 the conflict was basically concluded. Pontiac formally surrendered in July 1766. There would be more Indian wars, but this at least was the end of the fighting of the French and Indian War.[16]

The basic problems remained. How would the Indian trade be controlled? What land would be allotted to the Indians? Would colonial expansion to the west be allowed? How would the colonists and the Indians be separated?

The contest for the land west of the mountains would continue for the next 12 years.

Coping with Peace

Complicated negotiations to end the war started in 1762, during which Great Britain had captured Havana and therefore Cuba; a tentative agreement was reached late in the year. In November France had ceded the Louisiana Territory to Spain. On February 10, 1763, the Treaty of Paris was signed between Great Britain, France and Spain. Spain retained Cuba but ceded Florida to Great Britain. France was not willing to give up both Canada and the sugar islands, especially Guadeloupe. "In Britain a long debate and a pamphlet war raged over the wisdom of holding on to snowy Canada, with its annual exports of £14,000, and returning Guadeloupe, which produced more sugar than all the British West Indies combined, with exports of £6,000,000...."[17] "At that time the men who held the opinion that the chief value of the colonies consisted in the production of staple and raw materials which might be returned on British ships to the mother country argued for the retention of Guadaloupe, [sic] whereas those who thought of colonies as markets where the manufactured articles of the mother country could be sold preferred Canada."[18] Both sides of this latter argument express clearly the mercantile policy pursued by Britain with her colonies.

There was fear that another war would break out if the French held Canada, so the security argument won out and France ceded not only Canada, but everything east of the Mississippi, and kept Guadeloupe. Great Britain now controlled the eastern half of North America, from Canada down to Florida east of the Mississippi.

The island nation was in a unique position now, having imperial control over vast swaths of land, whereas prior to the war she had very light control of 13 coastal colonies with which she had a rather simple mercantile relationship. This latter situation was about to change. Britain faced a couple of difficult dilemmas, somewhat different but certainly related. It appeared the size of the problems would require imperial control by the crown, rather than by any colonial actions.

The most prominent problem, the one that has received the most attention, was the cost of the war. The war had almost doubled England's debt between 1755 and 1766 to £145 million.[19] Not all of that was spent in North America, but a substantial amount was. Over 100,000 men were under arms by the war's end, and it was anticipated many would stay in America. This latter force, of perhaps 10,000, would incur a yearly expense of three to four hundred thousand pounds. The British plans to pay for the war seemed to reasonably expect the colonies to pay some of the expenses through various taxes or fees, because it was waged for the protection of the colonies. Or at least the argument seemed reasonable. The thread, from the imposition of the Sugar Act in 1764 through the Stamp Act of 1765 through all other revenue raising measures, to the final break between Great Britain and the colonies, has been thoroughly covered by many historians in the succeeding years, and need not be repeated here. However, a factor, just as important, had to do with the British policies dealing with land in the American west. The attempt to block access to the western lands by the imperial government became the final straw in the break between Great Britain and her American colonies.[20]

Faced with these large challenges after the war, Great Britain made a conscious shift in her policies from a low-key mercantilist policy to a take-charge imperialist policy.

Britain's mercantilist policies were manifested in the way the colonies were established. All the colonies had been established by private companies or proprietors on grants by the crown; none had been established by the crown. It was not interested in the risk of investing directly in colonies and therefore eschewed the income from quitrents; the companies took all the risks and incurred all the expenses. At first the crown controlled the influx of settlers, but very quickly allowed the companies to determine who would settle. The companies took charge of distributing the land, and eventually a form of private ownership evolved. The crown reaped the benefit of the colonies through trade, collecting raw materials and shipping back manufactured products.

The crown encouraged the westward expansion of the colonies, at least to the mountains, because this expansion would enlarge the entire economic pie to the benefit of both colonies and crown. Local governance evolved, albeit with royally appointed governors, allowing the colonies to become self-sufficient. This low-key approach to the colonies worked well for both the colonies and the home government. It contrasts well with that of New France, which with its top-down government approach, never worked well. The population of New France was never more than a fraction of that of British America.

By 1763 everything had changed. Great Britain knew that major changes would be necessary in the wake of the war and the new land available in the west, but was not afforded the luxury of time. The Treaty of Paris had been signed in February, Pontiac's War had started in May, and word of it was received in London in the summer. The war weighed heavily on the ministries, and they knew that some measure was necessary rather quickly, to help allay the fears of the Indians and at the same time address some of the land issues. The result was the hastily drawn Royal Proclamation of 1763, issued on October 7.

The Proclamation had two objectives. The first was to define "four distinct and separate Governments, styled and called by the names of Quebec, East Florida, West Florida and Grenada." These four areas, three on the mainland and one on an island, were carved out of the land just acquired by the Treaty. The intention was to try to persuade new settlers to move into these areas to keep them out of Indian lands. Quebec,

Chapter Six. End of Expansion

meaning "narrow strait" in Algonquin, was a wedge of land with the point just below present-day Montreal and going northeast, encompassing the St. Lawrence River Valley. It was apparently drawn to include the mostly French residents to keep them separate from the English colonists.

The second objective was to set off an area of land that was to be an Indian reserve. The Proclamation deemed it "just and reasonable, and essential to Our Interest and the Security of Our Colonies" that all lands west of the Appalachian ridge be reserved for the Indians, at least "for the present, and until Our further Pleasure be known." This latter provision was a direct attempt to appeal to the Indians still in Pontiac's War, which was to end the following year. The governors in these areas and the other colonies were allowed to grant land in their provinces, but not in Indian territory. It is worth noting that western Pennsylvania was west of the line, so Pennsylvania did not have access to its own western lands.[21]

There was a flaw in the Proclamation, which Alvord, in "Genesis of the Proclamation of 1763," attributes to the change in British ministers just prior to its release. After governors and assemblies were established for the new provinces, they were given the powers to "ordain Laws, Statutes, and Ordinances for the Publick Peace, Welfare, and Good government of Our said Colonies, and of the People and Inhabitants thereof, as near as may be agreeable to the Laws of England." This phrase indicates that the four new government areas, including Quebec, were to be governed by the laws of England, which included laws having to do with the Church of England. The problem was that the Treaty of Paris stipulated that "His Britannick Majesty, on his side, agrees to grant the liberty of the Catholick religion to the inhabitants of Canada." It is probable that the odd shape given to Quebec was intended to include all French inhabitants and few others, and the further intent was that it be governed according to the stipulations of the Treaty. Instead, a last-minute (accidental?) change in the Proclamation included Quebec with the other new governments to be governed by the laws of England. This problem of conflicting governing forms for Quebec was recognized early and an attempt was later made to correct it, but that attempt had unintended consequences that helped lead to the final break between the colonies and Great Britain. We will come back to this later in the chapter.[22]

The British knew they had an explosive mixture on their hands. The colonists had pushed up to the mountains, and with the Ohio Company a little beyond, but it was clear the intentions were to move farther west for more free land. This was obvious just from the nature of the organized efforts covered in the previous chapter. It included, among others, the Ohio Company, the Loyal Company, the Indiana Company, the Vandalia colony, and the Transylvania Company. All of these were staking a claim for land beyond the mountains, and a couple were looking to start inland colonies, not tethered to the seaboard. These organized adventures were all handled through regular channels and many drew out for years.

The immediate problem was the pioneer settlers who were willing to move west as squatters, or on dubious claims, and were already doing so. Many of these, mostly Scots-Irish, were anxious to take on Indians, whom they detested. The Proclamation of 1763 had almost no effect on these people, despite its directive that those on these western lands must return to the east of the mountains. "These 'Frontier People' sought not accommodation with the Ohio Indians but rather their removal. Compromise did not enter their thoughts, and magnanimity never governed their actions.... Respecting personal freedom more than the law and advocating their right to take unused land rather than to await negotiated settlements with the trans–Appalachian Indians, these frontier people moved relentlessly into the Ohio Valley and soon cast covetous eyes to the rich land west of the River."[23] The purpose of choosing Canada over Guadeloupe was security. There would be no fear of the French attacking again; the Spanish in the west were no threat. This choice of Canada over Guadeloupe turned out to be a two-edged sword. It is true there was no longer a French threat, but the lack of an external threat made it more difficult to contain the colonists who saw this new land as free. They considered free land to be their birthright.

The other challenge they faced was what to do about the western Indians and the land in the west. The Proclamation boundary was defined in haste and was only meant to be temporary, until they were able to work out something else. This is what transformed the British policy from simple mercantile to imperial.

> Conditions had made necessary the centralization of the control over all relations with the Indians. The former policy of permitting each colony to settle these delicate affairs had proved a failure; and if the Indians were to receive a fair treatment in the future—and this they deserved as much as the colonists—a radical change of policy had to be adopted ... so that the preservation of the empire required that those interests which were general should be assumed by some power superior to the separate colonies, and be conducted with greater regularity and consistency.[24]

This quote from Alvord matter-of-factly states "and this they deserved as much as the colonists" as if it were an obvious and long-standing principle. That was far from the case. The Proclamation was the first time the British ever accepted that they had any moral obligation to the Indians. From the beginning the English colonists were anxious to remove the Indians, either because they represented a threat to their well-being or were in the way of the land they wanted. Most of the time they were forced out of the way, defrauded, or bought out. Even those who wanted to do right by the Indians, such as William Penn, and paid for the land, expected the Indians would eventually accept the payment and move out of the way. Land had become the basis of wealth, and the Indians were not going to stand in the way; the land they occupied was still seen as free to the British colonist.

The home government decided that the colonies had made a mess of dealing with the Indians, as well as with Indian trade. This plus the fact that the scale of land was too much for any one colony to handle, led to the crown taking control of western land and Indian affairs, including trade, into imperial hands. Hereafter, London would control relations with the Indians and decide how to dispose of the western lands. The last point is key. There was never any thought that the western lands would permanently remain the domain of the Indians, but only *how* they would be acquired from the Indians.

The control of Indian trade was made explicit in a supplement to the Royal Proclamation issued in 1764. The trade was to remain free and open but under new orders. The two Indian superintendents, Sir William Johnson in the north and Colonel John Stuart in the south, would be responsible for management of the trade. Also, the plan called for the concentration of all Indian trade at Forts Pitt, Niagara, Detroit, and Michilimackinac in the north, and towns in the south designated by Stuart. The purpose was to separate the populations of settlers and Indians. Only licensed traders would be allowed across the Proclamation line. This concentration of trade at the approved forts made it extremely difficult for the Indians to get what they needed without traveling long distances, even as it made the imperial control more efficient. It was a continuation of the policy initiated between 1760 and 1763.[25]

The Proclamation of 1763 was supposed to be a temporary expedient until they determined a new policy. However, years went by without resolution, because it was tied up in British politics. "The chief point of contention was whether to permit the colonists to expand westward as they had always done, develop the land resources of the region and so increase the Imperial revenues, or to confine them to the seaboard where they would best serve the interest of the British economy, and reserve the great interior region as hunting grounds for the Indians and so preserve the source of supply for the valuable fur trade."[26]

Expanding west into free land had been the experience for over 160 years; it was a cultural expectation. At first it had been done in small increments by single families or groups, but by this time the western expansion was being driven by land speculators from both the northern merchants and the southern planters, including George Washington, Thomas Jefferson,

Patrick Henry, George Mason and others. The Virginia elite, two to five percent of powerful Virginians, used land speculation to maintain money and power.[27] Washington thought the Proclamation was temporary and continued to look for land in the west. He wrote to his friend William Crawford, "I can never look upon that Proclamation in any other light ... than as a temporary expedient to quiet the Minds of the Indians & must fall of course in a few years especially when those Indians are consenting to our Occupying the Lands."[28] The land speculators were stymied, temporarily, but Washington was prescient.

The speculators might have been temporarily stymied, but the settlers kept moving west into the Ohio Country. The Virginians already at Redstone in the Monongahela Valley, beyond the Proclamation line, did not view the line as the final boundary.

> In the winter of 1765-1766, anti-Indian violence increased exponentially in the Redstone Creek region.... In the summer and fall of 1765, a detachment of troops from the 42nd Regiment at Fort Pitt swept the Redstone settlements and ran out the Virginia settlers, but, once the troops returned to garrison duty, the squatters returned to their tomahawk claims.... In September 1766, Shelburne ordered Fauquier to take more aggressive measures to curb the illegal Redstone settlements.... By early 1768, Johnson claimed there were 'above 500 Familys' [sic] domiciled at Redstone Creek, and that most of the squatters were Virginians.... The Virginia backcountry careened out of control, and neither the army nor the Indian superintendents possessed the wherewithal to halt the cycle of violence."[29] [Lord Shelburne was Secretary of State for the Southern Department. Francis Fauquier was the lieutenant governor of Virginia.]

The army was costing the royal treasury and it still could not control the situation. As a cost cutting measure the regulation of Indian trade was now returned to the provinces. They had even less capability to manage this process than did the army. As a Virginia Gazette essayist pointed out in 1773, "not even a second Chinese wall, unless guarded by a million soldiers, could prevent the settlement of the Lands on the Ohio and its dependencies.'"[30] Something else had to be done.

For most of a century the policy of New France was to keep the British bottled up east of the mountains so they would have to expend military land forces and sea power to protect these colonies, leaving France to operate more freely in Europe. It didn't work; the French then lost their North American empire. The west was open, but now being closed off by British policy, no longer by French occupation. The British were now bottling up the colonies on the east coast. Or as Alvord, in *The Mississippi Valley in British Politics,* noted, "circumstances had changed. Through the exigencies of politics, a British ministry had now established the same limits [as the French] to colonization. In trying to maintain these boundaries did Great Britain, like France, lose an empire?"[31] An interesting question. The answer is yes.

Boundaries Move Westward

The years from the Proclamation in 1763 to 1767 were years in which the American west was not a live issue in Britain. The British ministries were consumed by the attempts to raise money from the colonies to help reduce the war debt. First there was the American Duties Act, or Sugar Act of 1764, and then the Stamp Act of 1765. Both were repealed, but numerous other revenue acts were enacted in this era of conflict between the colonies and Great Britain. This political strife was occupying the attention of the colonial leaders in the east. In the meantime, the British regulars were patrolling the west and trying to enforce the trade policies with the Indians, while illegal squatters were contesting the Indians for control of the western land. The west finally received some attention in 1767. The western instability was a prod to action to finally move the Indian boundary west from the temporary one imposed by the Proclamation of 1763, as had always been intended. Indian concurrence in moving the line west was always assumed.

Clearly there was an intense interest in moving the line westward by both the northern and southern land speculators. These were now the people who had the most interest in acquiring land in the west, which they could then sell to smaller landholders. Thus, there was an incentive for them to get involved with the process of moving the boundary. This was especially true for speculators interested in land that Virginia claimed, land that was to later become West Virginia, and Kentucky. Some of them would become involved with the process of negotiating the treaties that would move the boundary west, a process that would include self-serving dealings, which we would now call conflict of interest.

It was the autumn of 1764, the same year the Sugar Act was passed, when the first steps were taken to fix the Indian boundary line set by the Proclamation. The Indian superintendents were authorized to start negotiations with the Indians. Sir William Johnson, Superintendent of Indian Affairs for the Northern Department, and Colonel John Stuart, Superintendent of Indian Affairs for the Southern Department, set about meeting with the Six Nations and Cherokee respectively. By the spring of 1765, Johnson had successfully negotiated a line across that each party had agreed to.[32] "By 1767 Stuart had an agreement with the Cherokees on a southern line 'beginning at a point near the southern boundary of

Virginia, running south and west at the back of the Carolinas, bending somewhat toward the east in Georgia, and including the tide-water limits of East Florida.'"[33] This point at the southern border of Virginia was at Chiswell's Mine (present Austinville) on the upper Great Kanawha River, now known at that point as the New River. This southern line put a "back" to the colonies south of Virginia, but not yet on Virginia. Putting a western boundary on Virginia would be controversial because Virginia claimed all the lands to the west. Putting a back on the western end of all the colonies, though, was one of the goals of the Earl of Shelburne, Secretary of State for the Southern Department. These were as yet unofficial boundaries.

"In the spring of 1767 Shelburne instructed Stuart to establish Virginia's western boundary." After more delays, Shelburne ordered that the line be completed and run from Chiswell's Mine on the Kanawha to "'that point from whence the northern provinces set out.' This was interpreted to mean the southwest corner of Pennsylvania, but this point had not yet been determined." If this had been the Virginia western boundary, it would have meant that the boundary line would have moved very little westward. This was not to be the case. Southwest Pennsylvania was never seriously considered to be the western boundary of Virginia. Before the end of the year the meeting of the northern line and southern line would be determined to be the intersection of the Great Kanawha and Ohio rivers.[34]

It was in these years that the land speculators started to get involved with the boundary line as they urged the line be moved west to open the lands for settlement. Two of the speculators were Dr. Thomas Walker and Colonel Andrew Lewis, heads of the Loyal and Greenbrier Companies, respectively. These two companies had land in southwest Virginia which was beyond the Proclamation line and therefore unavailable for settlement. The "Suffering Traders" group, which was seeking land, called Indiana, in what is now northern West Virginia, was also pressing for changes since their land was also beyond the boundary line. The latter group included George Croghan, Johnson's deputy. They set to work after Shelburne's directive on January 5, 1768, in which he ordered the line to be made final. He dictated that the northern and southern boundaries would meet at the intersection of the Great Kanawha and Ohio rivers, and official negotiations then commenced.[35]

Billington, in "The Fort Stanwix Treaty of 1768," and Abernethy, in *Western Lands and the American Revolution,* lay out plausible scenarios on the sequence of events. Walker and Lewis managed to convince the governor of Virginia to put them on the negotiating team with Stuart to work with the Cherokee. However, Stuart didn't trust them, and managed to complete the Treaty of Hard Labor (South Carolina) on October 14, 1768,

Chapter Six. End of Expansion 201

before either of them could get to the meeting. "Here he negotiated a treaty whereby the natives consented to a boundary line that would run from Chiswell's Mine directly to the mouth of the Great Kanawha [the point directed by Shelburne.] This line was northwest from Chiswell's Mine. According to previous plans the line was expected to follow the river, but Stuart's arrangement gave Virginia appreciably more territory than the river boundary." This was because the river bowed east in flowing north from Chiswell's Mine to its mouth at the Ohio River. More land that could be squeezed out was the name of the game. Stuart had now put a western limit to Virginia and the other southern colonies; the first western limit since the Treaty of Paris had made the Mississippi River the western boundary of British North America, but the Loyal and Greenbrier Companies were still on the outside of the boundary line. There was more work to be done on the southern boundary by Walker and Lewis.[36]

The establishment of the northern boundary was a little more complicated. In the early negotiations in 1765, the Six Nations offered to cede more territory than just down the Ohio to the Kanawha. They offered *all* the territory below the Ohio River up to the Tennessee River, then known as the Cherokee River, which was almost all the way to the Ohio River intersection with the Mississippi River. This would have included most of present-day Kentucky. They had claimed that area by conquest and offered it as a token of their friendship. The conquest claim was tenuous, and the Six Nations might have wanted to get clear of the land before any conflicts with the Cherokee arose. It was not land that they used, but belonged to the tributary tribes, for whom they had little regard. Also, the cession could have been because they saw the writing on the wall and expected the Virginians to move west to Kentucky anyway, so they wanted to get what they could at the time. They saw this as an opportunity to steer the settlements away from their northern homelands. They were protective of these northern lands around the Mohawk River and would not agree with Johnson on some lands he desired in that area.[37]

Johnson convened the parties for the final treaty arrangements at Fort Stanwix in September 1768. They were all there, hundreds of members of the Six Nations, colonial government officials, and land speculators, including George Croghan, Samuel Wharton and William Trent of the Indiana Company, Andrew Lewis of the Greenbrier Company, and Dr. Walker of the Loyal Company; Walker was also an official representative of Virginia. Before the start of the negotiations, the Six Nations said they wanted to compensate the Suffering Traders or Indiana Company with land for the losses they had claimed. The land they wanted to "sell" was between the Ohio, Monongahela and Little Kanawha Rivers, the Laurel Mountains and the southern boundary of Pennsylvania, which is in present-day West Virginia. The "sale" of this nearly two million acres was complete on November 3. Wharton and Trent of the Indiana Company had spent the summer lobbying the Indians and plying them with gifts to get to this deal. Sir William was amenable to this deal also.[38] The conference got underway in October and continued into November.

This deal with the Indiana Company was unusual in that it involved land below the Ohio River in western Virginia, which was not in Johnson's bailiwick and not within the purview of the Six Nations, either. It was in land that could have been claimed by the Cherokee, and was land that should have been dealt with by Colonel Stuart, the Superintendent of the Southern Department. All parties knew the location of the intersecting lines. They knew that Stuart would be setting the line at the back of Virginia in October and that it would go from Chiswell's Mine to the mouth of the Great Kanawha, which would include this Indiana land. Johnson had good relations with the Six Nations, all the parties were agreeable, so they decided to go ahead with it. This gift of the Six Nations of land that they did not own, that was made to a private company, apparently slid under the radar. Stuart made no objection.

One person at least should have had an objection to the Indiana grant: Dr. Walker, head of the Loyal Company, and representing Virginia at the Fort Stanwix conference. This grant was in territory Virginia claimed. His signature would be necessary on any treaty that came out of the conference. Walker, however, was playing a longer game. He wanted the boundary to run directly to the mouth of the Tennessee and not stop at the Great Kanawha. He would accept the Indiana Company grant if Johnson would allow the boundary to run to that point. Johnson would have violated his orders if he did. Walker was willing to give up mountainous land in the north if it would open the possibility of obtaining better land near the Clinch and Holston Rivers where his land was, and to the rich lands to the west in Kentucky. However, that would have required Colonel Stuart to reopen negotiations to move his line farther west. If the line had moved, it would have opened the lands of the Loyal and Greenbrier Companies. Stuart did not reopen negotiations to move this line to the Tennessee River.[39]

Johnson violated his orders and accepted the offer of the Six Nations to extend the line to the Ohio and Tennessee rivers. The line violated the orders in many areas. It went farther north than ordered, although that was limited by Mohawk resistance; exempted more land for settlers in Pennsylvania; and finally, went too far along the Ohio, almost to the Mississippi River. In Pennsylvania and Connecticut, settlers were moving into the upper Susquehanna Valley, so he bowed to reality in that case. He was excoriated by Lord Hillsborough, who had succeeded Shelburne, because he had violated the orders. Johnson stood his ground,

Chapter Six. End of Expansion

consistently claiming that the Six Nations *forced* him to accept this line, and to try to return it would be an insult. This does not stand up, but Johnson claimed that westward expansion was inevitable. Johnson, a strong loyalist, assumed getting more land from the Indians was always in the best interest of the empire. He also surmised that the opening of Kentucky would draw more settlers from the coast to the interior, which would make them more dependent on royal protection. This also appealed to the loyalist Johnson. The ministry eventually accepted the new status quo. The Treaty of Fort Stanwix was signed on November 5, 1768.[40]

Had Johnson followed his orders there would have been one continuous Indian boundary line across Pennsylvania to the Ohio River, through the Great Kanawha and Ohio River junction south across the back of the southern colonies. However, as it stood at the end of 1768, there was a northern line from New York, through Pennsylvania, down the Ohio River and west to the Tennessee River, and a southern line from the Ohio and Great Kanawha rivers as Stuart had negotiated. Thus, the lines formed a T with the intersection at the Ohio and Kanawha rivers with the east-west Fort Stanwix line the top of the T, and the north-south Stuart line the vertical part of the T. All land to the right and under the T was colonial land or land acquired by Great Britain. To the left under the T was still Indian land, which included Kentucky. There was a gap under the T between the Great Kanawha and the Tennessee rivers, which led to a lot of confusion. The cession of the land below the Ohio by the Iroquois did not account for the Cherokee claims in this area. Stuart was asked to renegotiate his line and extend it all the way to the Tennessee; he refused. Land company speculators, often acting as representatives of colonial governments, had influenced the ceding of Indian land and the extension of Indian cessions well beyond imperial orders. This land fever was to get even more intense.

> The colony most immediately interested in the "imperial line," as it was called, was Virginia. Her citizens had already made settlements beyond the mountains, and some of them had marked out claims and built homes a considerable distance beyond the limits established at the treaty of Hard Labour. In the territory of the upper branches of the Tennessee River there were several such settlements situated on the extensive land claims of Walker and Lewis who had been the representatives of Virginia at Fort Stanwix; but the speculators had ambitions that went far beyond the securing of these Holston River settlements. Their success in securing the cession of all the land south of the Ohio from the Iroquois and their allies paved the way for enterprises throughout this region, and they made preparations to utilize this opportunity to the utmost.[41]

Immediately after the Fort Stanwix conference, Governor Botetourt of Virginia asked Lewis and Walker to petition for more western land from

Stuart. Stuart was willing to try, and the Cherokee were willing to sell. They did not try to get all the land ceded by the Six Nations south of the Ohio to the Tennessee River, but only enough to include the Virginia lands on the Holston River. This meant that the Loyal company (Walker) and the Greenbrier Company (Lewis) land would be in Virginia and lie east of the boundary line. This area was defined by extending the Virginia-North Carolina border west to the Holston River, and then running the line back northeast to the mouth of the Great Kanawha, a triangular addition to Virginia. This cession was formalized in the Treaty of Lochaber in October 1770. Virginia paid the Cherokee £2,500 for this land. The royal treasury paid out £10,460 for the other land gained in the two main treaties of Stanwix and Hard Labor.[42]

The final Indian boundary line defined by the Stanwix, Hard Labor and Lochaber Treaties did not really settle the issues at hand. For one thing, even though the line was farther west than the Appalachian Ridge, the prohibition of the Proclamation of 1763 against settling west of the mountains was still in effect. Hillsborough was angry at Johnson and refused to allow settlement beyond the 1763 Proclamation line, even though much of that land was now in Virginia. Thus, the western policy remained confused. What was clear was that it was no longer possible to acquire lands through private or colonial treaties. Legal title was not possible that way; now one had to go through the crown, so crown connections were now necessary.[43] This is the reason that many of the land companies described in the previous chapter sought the support of London investors after 1763. It is the reason, for example, that William Trent and Samuel Wharton sought to partner with London banker Thomas Walpole to further the interests of the Indiana Company, later the Grand Ohio Company or Vandalia colony.

The Fort Stanwix treaty was expected to end the Proclamation of 1763, but instead it set off a land rush in Virginia.[44] In 1769 Thomas Jefferson had asked the Loyal Company for 5,000 acres of land, and he also joined two other syndicates, seeking 1,000 acres from each. At the same time Patrick Henry bought 3,335 acres on the Holston and Clinch rivers. In December 1769 the Virginia House of Burgesses asked the British government to let Virginia have Kentucky. Virginia speculators had received preliminary grants from Virginia west of the Cherokee line totaling six to seven million acres. The area also included nearly 50,000 square miles of additional land that would be available for Virginia speculators to sell in the future if the Privy Council agreed, nearly double its current land area. However, government officials were watching the Indians, not Virginia.[45]

The Cherokee knew the implications of the Stanwix treaty; they knew a land rush into what is now Kentucky would deprive them of all their

Chapter Six. End of Expansion

hunting land. Not only the Cherokee, but the Ohio Indians as well were concerned. There were about 7,200 Cherokee, 600 Mingo, 1,800 Shawnee, 3,500 Delaware, and potentially the southern nations of Creeks, Choctaws, and Chickasaws totaling about 28,000 who might also be aroused. This would be a major Indian confederation that greatly exceeded the one in Pontiac's rebellion, the strongest the British ever faced. The tribes in the confederation made peace among themselves to face the Virginia threat. They met at the Scioto River in the summer of 1769 to devise a diplomatic strategy. In January 1770, John Stuart expressed concern that the Stanwix land deal would cause a break with all the tribes. In June when Lord Hillsborough, secretary of state for the colonies, received the letter, he assured Stuart that he understood. In a quid pro quo, he promised the Cherokee chiefs that the British would meet with them to run a line that left Kentucky in Cherokee country. Although the Stuart line existed, the Stanwix treaty was later in time, and the Cherokee became concerned. Even before this, British officials began to block implementation of the Fort Stanwix land deal. The Privy Council denied the House of Burgesses petition for Kentucky and refused to revoke the Proclamation of 1763. Hillsborough told Johnson to tell the Iroquois that the British would *not* occupy the land south of the Ohio and west of the mouth of the Great Kanawha, the north end of Stuart's line.[46]

The great speculators' land rush after the Stanwix treaty proved futile; they were left holding worthless surveys. Even bounty lands promised to veterans of the French and Indian War were denied west of the Proclamation line. However, this did not stop the squatters from their continued movement westward. They squatted on land from which the speculators could not eject them. In the years following, the Indian confederation held its ground and generally maintained peace, although there were many skirmishes along the border. Virginians decided to launch an attack on Shawnee and Mingo towns in the Ohio Valley in the fall of 1774 with the hope of forcing them to turn over Kentucky to the land dealers.[47] However, they needed a pretext for such a raid, and managed to come up with one.

They received some friendly help from John Murray, fourth Earl of Dunmore, who was appointed governor in 1771, the last royal governor of Virginia. Dunmore was a strong supporter of Virginia's western land movement, and as such had received the support of men like George Washington, who held land in the west. Dunmore's first interest was in claiming land in the upper Ohio Valley, land that had been in dispute by both Pennsylvania and Virginia because it seemed to be included in both the 1609 Virginia charter and the 1681 Pennsylvania grant. This dispute went on with the two colonies almost coming to blows with one another. It escalated when in early 1774, Dunmore ordered his representative, Dr.

John Connolly, to seize Fort Pitt, which he did. The fort had been abandoned in 1772 by the British as being too expensive to maintain. This abandonment was one of the reasons the tensions between the settlers and the Indians were so high—there was no force on the border to maintain order.

In April 1774, two Virginia Indian-hating groups lured some Indians across the Ohio near Yellow Creek and killed them. Following that raid, the Mingo John Logan retaliated by attacking the Virginians. These attacks did not lead to the full-scale uprising that some feared, because both sides tamped down the tensions. However, the latter raid by Logan was the pretext Dunmore needed to go after the Indians in the Ohio Country with the hope of opening up more land. Dunmore assembled two armies of about 1,000 men each, one led by himself and one led by Colonel Andrew Lewis. The intent was to meet at the Hocking River at the Ohio River and move up it to attack Indian towns together. Lewis moved down the Kanawha to the Ohio at Point Pleasant where, before Dunmore's army could arrive, he was attacked by men of the Shawnee Chief Cornstalk. The Battle of Point Pleasant was on October 10, 1774. Lewis's army managed to hold off Cornstalk and prevailed. Cornstalk retreated up the Hocking Valley and was followed by Dunmore. Dunmore set up a temporary camp, Camp Charlotte, and forced Cornstalk into a treaty which "deeded all the land east of the Ohio river—including all of Kentucky—to Virginia." This concluded Dunmore's War, a war by and for Virginia's land. They intended this to persuade the Privy Council to revoke the Proclamation of 1763. The British government and the Indians agreed, however, that any treaty signed under duress was invalid, and the Proclamation remained in place. By the end of 1774 the Proclamation still held, and other events in 1775 would overtake this latest attempt to expand the Virginia land west.[48]

"English leaders could not make up their minds between westward expansion and confinement of the colonists to the east coast."[49] Until the war they had encouraged westward expansion, so this attempt to stop expansion was a complete reversal from the previous policy, in which the colonies distributed their own western lands. For some colonies, such as Maryland, which had fixed western borders this was of little consequence because they had no western territory to exploit. Pennsylvania had lost some territory to the Proclamation but did not look beyond that. It was Virginia which stood to lose the most because of the presumed western lands Virginians hoped to occupy. It confused and angered the colonists, especially the land speculators, who expected a continuation of westward expansion after the war on land gained by Great Britain from France. The colonists presumed this land would be theirs by the 1609 charter; this included planters like Thomas Jefferson, George Mason, George Washington, Patrick Henry.

Chapter Six. End of Expansion

It had been decided that the land acquired by the crown through the Indian treaties would be disposed of by the crown, and not by the colonies. Income was needed to support the troops who were still in the field, and land sales would be used to do this. In 1773, an order was issued blocking all royal officials from making land grants of any kind, punishable by removal from office.[50] The screws were being tightened on the control of land just as things were heating up in the east. In 1774, Great Britain announced the reform of the land system.

This reform was based on some very explicit instructions from the crown. All previous instructions were annulled. The royal officials in each province were to lay out the lands most likely to draw interest and seen as desirable for settlement. The land was to be laid out in lots from 100 to 1,000 acres and numbered on a map. These lands were to be offered for sale by these officials and sold to the highest bidder after being advertised for four months. The price was set at six pence per acre and would carry an annual quitrent of one-half penny per acre. These were very detailed instructions indeed.[51]

This was a dramatic measure. First, it went back to claim lands for the crown that were *already in* the colonies, something that hadn't ever been done previously. The sectioning of lots to between 100 and 1,000 acres, and setting a minimum price, meant it would lock out the land speculators. The new owner was also charged a quitrent of one-half penny per acre. This was new because the land was now not sold outright. Quitrents had been charged in the colonies sporadically over the years, but often they were ignored. Now they were going to be reintroduced and collected by the crown. The sales and rent proceeds were to go to the crown, which was trying to find the funds to pay for the war, because the various revenue acts back east weren't going very well. All of this was to be implemented by the governors, royal officials under crown control.[52]

In June 1774, George Mason petitioned the governor and council for permission to take up land "upon the western waters" that he had apparently purchased at great expense. He argued that this method of acquiring land had been authorized by the Virginia charter of 1609 and reaffirmed by Charles II. Much land had been granted in this manner, and he felt the king would have observed the law of the 1609 charter.[53] He claimed that the 1609 charter gave Virginia the right to the land, and therefore this latest instruction was out of place. He was unsuccessful, and events in 1775 eventually overtook his claim, but his argument would resurface later.

This put an end to the expectations of the colonists concerning western land. It did not stop the squatters, but it certainly stopped the land speculators, both the northern merchants and southern planters. The former expected to claim and sell the land, and the latter planned not only to sell but to expand on the land. It had the effect of aligning these two groups, read Massachusetts and Virginia, in their views of the new relationship with the crown. It broke the close relationship between the crown and the business community that was behind the successful colonial expansion. Instead, it brought the northern and southern colonies closer together. Tight imperial control of western lands was now the order of business. It was the same imperial control sought back east with all the revenue acts. The stated objective was to bring in revenue to help with the war debts. Although true, it was also a plan to separate the colonists from the Indians, and from one another. The British government did finally feel some obligation to the Indians in this regard after all these years, but it was still unsure of how to address the issue. They still felt it was inevitable that the Indians must concede their lands, but how that would happen was unclear. The final attempt to manage the western lands, bring order to Indian relations, and bring the colonies under stricter imperial control was the promulgation of the Quebec Act.

Quebec Act

The year 1774 was a turning point. It started in February with the restrictive land reforms. That legislation was quickly followed by Parliamentary acts intended to punish Boston for the December 1773 Tea Party. In the spring, from March to June, Parliament enacted four acts called the Coercive Acts by Parliament, but the Intolerable Acts by the colonists. Thomas Jefferson quickly followed with his paper, "A Summary View of the Rights of British America," which attacked these acts as an infringement of colonists' rights as British citizens. In June, Parliament passed the last of the Intolerable Acts, the Quebec Act, the most draconian of them all.

The first of these Coercive Acts was the Boston Port Act, passed by Parliament on March 31, 1774, because "dangerous commotions and insurrections have been fomented and raised in the town of Boston.... And whereas, in the present condition of the said town and harbour, the commerce of his Majesty's subjects cannot be safely carried on there" the port of Boston was to be closed in June. No commerce, in or out, would be allowed. If satisfactory reparations were made to the East India Company for the tea, the king could authorize the reopening of the harbor. This was a drastic and ruinous step, as Boston did most of its commerce by sea.[54]

On May 20, Parliament passed two more acts specifically aimed at Boston, the Massachusetts Government Act and the Administration of Justice Act. The first was passed because the Massachusetts Bay government

Chapter Six. End of Expansion

"hath, for some time past, been such as had the most manifest tendency to obstruct and, in great measure, defeat, the execution of the laws ... and to encourage the ill-disposed among them to proceed even to acts of direct resistance." Parliament recommended the locally elected Council be dissolved, and the governor be appointed by the king. The second act, passed the same day, was the Administration of Justice Act. This act deemed that an accused, especially for rioting or impeding the execution of a law, could be sent to another province or even to Great Britain if the governor felt that "an indifferent [impartial] trial cannot be had within the said province." Although it is not uncommon in a notorious, well-publicized case in the present day that a change of venue be requested to help ensure a fair trial by one's peers, that was not the situation proposed. The provinces, now states, were all separate entities with their own laws and legal systems. It would be equivalent to a move to another country. A move of a trial to Great Britain would mean the defendant would have no ties to the local citizenry and, therefore, it would not be a trial by one's peers. This right went back centuries.[55]

The first three of these acts were directed at Massachusetts Bay and specifically Boston. The fourth, the Quartering Act, passed on June 2, was directed at all the colonies, although it pertained mostly to New England. This act required the colonies to provide quarters for any royal troops sent to the colonies for any reason. There were barracks in the colonies, but they were often not located close to where the troops were needed. These were not to be private homes, as is commonly thought, but "uninhabited houses, out-houses, barns, or other buildings." Ironically, this act had a sunset clause; it was to expire on March 24, 1776.[56]

These four acts were intended to bring pressure on the colonies to make them conform to the imperial stance Great Britain had taken with respect to the colonies. They were aimed primarily at Massachusetts Bay and Boston because that is where they saw the most physical resistance, such as the Boston Tea Party. "With this dramatic expression of open defiance against the authority of the British legislature, the tension between the colonies and the mother country, mounting for almost a decade, reached a peak."[57] They had reason to believe that Boston was alone in its resistance, and by isolating it, they could stamp out any resistance. They knew of the seeming incompatibilities between the southern provinces and the northern provinces. These incompatibilities were soon to be narrowed, especially with Thomas Jefferson's "A Summary View of the Rights of British America."

This paper was a plea to the king written at the time of the Coercive Acts in 1774. Starting with the role of the king, "he is no more than the chief officer of the people ... circumscribed with definite powers ... subject to their superintendence." Jefferson poses some radical thoughts for the time, ones that would eventually make it into the Declaration of Independence. He claimed that the motherland of the Saxon ancestors of the English never claimed superiority over them and thus, similarly, the English should not claim superiority over the British Americans. "And it is thought that no circumstance has occurred to distinguish materially the British from the Saxon emigration. America was conquered, and her settlements made and firmly established, at the expence [sic] of individuals, and not of the British public." He goes on to complain about Virginia being dismembered, for example, the establishment of Maryland from the land of the original Virginia grant, and about free trade being denied to the colonists. The latter was the consequence of the strict mercantilist policy, which required the province to trade only with Great Britain.[58]

He then addresses the issue of land tenure going all the way back to the Saxons again. He claims the Saxons held their land under allodial tenure, that is, they were not subservient to any feudal lord above them who granted the land to them; it was theirs to own in absolute right. "Our Saxon ancestors held their lands as they did their personal property, in absolute dominion, disencumbered with any superior, answering nearly to the nature of those possessions which the Feudalists term Allodial."[59] When William I became king,

> A general principle indeed was introduced that "all lands in England were held either mediately or immediately of the crown": but this was borrowed from those holdings which were truly feudal, and only applied to others for purposes of illustration. Feudal holdings were therefore but exceptions out of the Saxon laws of possession, under which all lands were held in absolute right.... America was not conquered by William the Norman, nor its lands surrendered to him or any of his successors. Possessions there are undoubtedly of the Allodial nature. Our ancestors however, who migrated hither, were laborers [farmers], not lawyers. The fictitious principle that all lands belong originally to the king, they were early persuaded to believe real, and accordingly took grants of their own lands from the crown. And while the crown continued to grant for small sums and on reasonable rents, there was no inducement to arrest the error and lay it open to public view. But his majesty has lately taken on him to advance the terms of purchase and of holding to the double of what they were, by which means the acquisition of lands being rendered difficult, the population of our country is likely to be checked. It is time therefore for us to lay this matter before his majesty, and to declare that he has no right to grant lands of himself.[60]

In other words, Americans hold their lands as allods, in absolute right, because they were not conquered by the king; they were not assigned under a feudal tenure. The last part refers to the recent land reforms in which the crown controls the distribution of land and is charging double the previous rate for it. Jefferson foresees this as stifling the population growth of the colonies.

He addresses all the Coercive Acts at one point or another. He spends several paragraphs on the Boston Port Act in which he complains that "a large and populous town, whose trade was their sole subsistence, was deprived of that trade, and involved in utter ruin." This is significant because he now links his concern about the land with the trade of Boston. He links the interests of Boston and Virginia, which was not always easy to do. The land reforms enacted early in the year were not part of the Coercive Acts, although they could be considered in the same category. Nevertheless, Jefferson managed to link this land reform with these acts.

Some of his rhetoric was radical for the time. "The true ground on which we declare these acts void is that the British parliament has no right to exercise authority over us.... Can any one reason be assigned why 160,000 electors in the island of Great Britain give law to four millions in the states of America, every individual of whom is equal to every individual of them in virtue, in understanding, and in bodily strength? ... every society must at all times possess within itself the sovereign powers of legislation." Later these ideas would also show up in various forms in the Declaration of Independence.

Virginia was the most vocal about the restrictions on western lands because, since 1609 and the second charter, she had expected to continually move west. Her citizens had been doing this for over 160 years. Other states with definite western borders, such as Maryland, had little concern about the western lands. (Later, after independence, Maryland would take a strong stance on the future of those western lands.) But as Virtue notes in "British Land Policy and the American Revolution," prior to the Revolution, Virginia was the only colony to complain about British land policy, and at the time it was ignored. The grievance appears in the Declaration of Independence, but had been omitted in the Declaration and Resolves of the first Continental Congress.[61] "He has endeavored to prevent the population of these States; for that purpose obstructing the Laws for Naturalization of foreigners; refusing to pass others to encourage their migrations hither, and raising the conditions of new Appropriations of Lands."[62] Here Jefferson was referring to the limitation on the population of Virginia if these western lands were not available to Virginia. "Raising the conditions" refers to the doubling of cost of the lands now under crown control. It is possible, probable even, that Jefferson also had in mind the Quebec Act, which was pending that spring.

Great Britain had solved only one of the problems she had after the French and Indian War. With the land reform policy in 1774, she had decided how she would dispose of the new territory acquired through the

Indian treaties. This land reform policy never did come into effect; it was overtaken by the Revolution. In 1774 there were still three distinct imperial goals to be addressed by the forthcoming Quebec Act. One was to redress the accidental inclusion of the French population of Quebec under English laws in the Proclamation of 1763. At that point they were in violation of the Treaty of Paris, in which all parties agreed that the people in the conquered lands of Canada would be able to practice their own religion instead of being forced to obey the laws of the Church of England. A second issue was control of the Indian trade. When it reverted to the colonies, they were unable to come up with one coherent policy which would suffice for all Indian trade.

The last issue had to do with getting imperial control over the upper Mississippi Valley, north and west of the Ohio River, all the way to the Mississippi River. There were still clashes in the west between the illegal settlers and the Indians, and the royal army could not patrol the area indefinitely. There needed to be some civil government over the area that would deal with the Indians, distribute land, guard the borders, and bring civil law to the upper Mississippi Valley. The Quebec Act, passed in June 1774, was intended to address these issues. "The Quebec Act turned out to be the final imperial attempt to resolve one of the most intractable American problems faced by the king's various ministries since the end of the Seven Years' War: how to curb backcountry lawlessness."[63] The Quebec Act passed in June and was the last of the Intolerable acts of 1774.

"The main provisions of the Quebec Act were designed to facilitate the three imperial goals.... The four principal sections of the Act dealt with boundaries, religion, civil law, and legislative assembly." The first thing the Quebec Act did was dramatically change the boundaries of Quebec. This was done to enable the implementation of the goals of the act. The first definition of the province of Quebec, as proclaimed in the Proclamation of 1763, had the area as a triangular shaped province, with the point near Lake Nipissing moving to include Montreal and then extending northeast around the St. Lawrence Valley. This was clearly to incorporate the bulk of the French Catholic population in one province. It was a very small province. The *new* boundary of Quebec started at the Bay of Chaleurs north of Nova Scotia, moved down the highlands separating the rivers that flow into the Atlantic and the St. Lawrence, to the forty-fifth parallel, west to the St. Lawrence, down that river around Lakes Ontario and Erie, down the western border of Pennsylvania until it reached the Ohio River. It continued along the Ohio River until it reached the Mississippi River, and went north along the Mississippi until it reached the Hudson Bay Company land. Note that it excluded Pennsylvania because it wasn't supposed to affect the boundaries of other colonies.[64] See Map 1.

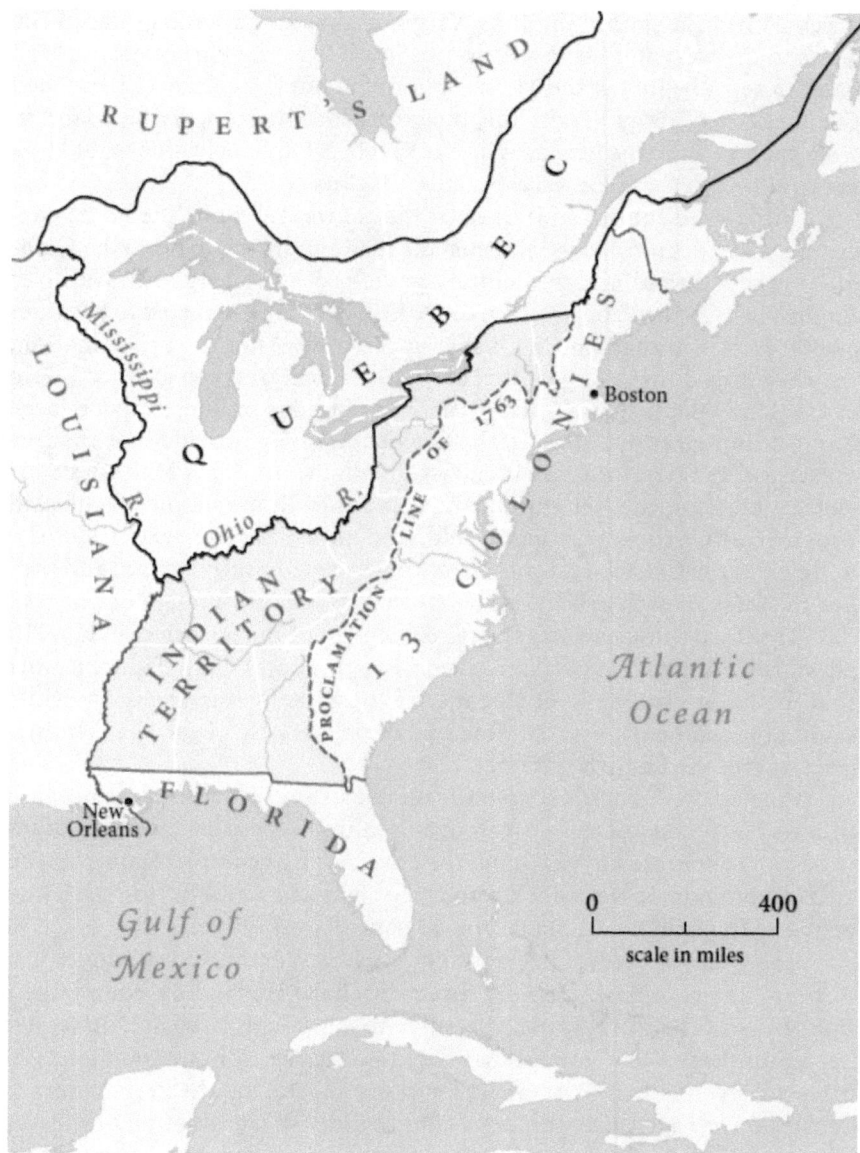

Map 1. Quebec Act, 1774 (David Deis, Dreamline Cartography).

This was a vast territory and, after independence, most of it became the Northwest Territory, which eventually became the states of Ohio, Indiana, Michigan, Illinois, Wisconsin, and part of Minnesota. The claim that Quebec would not infringe on any other colony was specious; it impinged on the Virginia claim. The 1609 Virginia charter gave Virginia all the lands to the west and northwest to the South Sea. The Paris treaty of 1763 had limited Virginia at the Mississippi River, but the colony still claimed the northwest. Many Virginians, including Washington, claimed land in what then became the new province of Quebec. Obviously, this would be a sore point with the colonies, especially Virginia.

The second subject addressed by the act was religion. The home government had acknowledged the mistake made by trying to place the Catholic French-Canadians in a colony governed by clearly anti–Catholic English laws in the Proclamation of 1763. There were estimated to be about 65,000 French-Canadians in Quebec at the time. After the Proclamation, they had hoped that a large influx of English immigrants to Quebec would cause these people to assimilate. That did not happen; there was no large English immigration. Thus, in the Quebec Act they provided for the free exercise of religion for these French-Canadians: "That his Majesty's Subjects, professing the Religion of the Church of Rome of and in the said Province of Quebec, may have, hold, and enjoy, the free exercise of the Religion of the Church of Rome." The king was still the sovereign, and they had to swear an oath to him, but it was a civil oath, not a religious one.[65]

The third provision was the reinstatement of the French civil law. "In all Matters of Controversy, relative to Property and Civil rights, Resort shall be had to the Laws of Canada, as the Rule for the Decision of the same"; the seigneurial system was also reinstated. However, the criminal law was still the English system.[66]

Finally, the French were seen as unable to govern themselves because they had no history of self-government, so the governor and the legislature were to be appointed by the king; the governor had complete control. The citizens of Quebec were denied the free right of assembly "for the Time being."[67] Thus, the crown had ultimate control over Quebec.

The Quebec Act was deemed the "most intolerable of the Intolerable Acts" by the colonials. One Virginian, Richard Henry Lee, complained that this was the worst thing to happen to American citizens.[68] Jefferson in "A Summary View" claims that the king "has no right to grant lands of himself." Even in Britain there was opposition. During the Parliamentary debates on the act, Lord Camden "after the fullest examination of the Act in question … found it so thoroughly impolitic, pernicious, and incompatible with the religion and constitution of our country, that no amendment, nor anything short of a total repeal of it would be sufficient."[69] The following spring, in Edmund Burke's "Speech on the Conciliation with the Colonies" in Parliament, he railed against the government for all the recent attempts to bring force to colonial control. He reminded them how lucrative the trade had been with the colonies and that the peaceful, fruitful policy should be continued.[70] Besides the conciliation of the French-Canadian population and the intent to meet the treaty obligations, the "imperial goal of bringing the Mississippi Valley under the control and supervision of the Crown was included in the boundary provision.... The land west and north of the Ohio River to the Mississippi River belonged to Canada and was part of the Quebec provinces." This would allow revenue to be raised from the sale of land and enable the government to maintain peaceful relations with the Indians, thus enabling their other goal of settling the trade with the Indians. Control of Indian trade, fur trade, seemed to be an easy call. When the colonists were reassigned control of the Indian trade in 1768, they didn't do well, failing to take responsibility and coming close to another Indian war. To forestall any further problems with Indian trade, the crown decided to put it all under the new Quebec province. This seemed reasonable, since the French had always done well with the Indian fur trade. It would avoid direct British supervision but still be under strong crown control, because the colony was under strong imperial control through the appointed royal governor.[71]

The boundary provisions helped meet subsidiary goals also. The entire province was now under French civil authority. The crown thought that this would deter settlers, especially from Virginia, from trying to enter, not only because of the animosity between the Protestant Virginians and French Catholics, but also because there was now a civil authority to enforce the law in the province. Prior to this there was no law, no civil authority, to hold the squatter to account when he moved out of a province like Virginia into the western Indian country; now there would be. In the Parliamentary debates, Solicitor-General Wedderbourne stated that

> one of the objects of the measure was to deter Englishmen from settling in Canada, and that one of the great advantages of the extension of territory would be that the other inhabitants of North America "will have little temptation to stretch themselves northwards." He added moreover, "I think this limitation of the boundary (i.e., of the older colonies) will be a better mode than any restriction laid upon government. In the grant of lands we ought to confine the inhabitants to keep them according to the ancient policy of the country along the line of the sea and river."[72]

In other words, it was an attempt to sever the west from the shore colonies by putting this colony above and in back of the other colonies, and to confine the other colonies to the coast.

The establishment of the colony of Quebec was an indication that the mercantilist policies of the previous 160 years were starting to fray. All the colonies up to now had been established by private companies, with the blessing of the crown, which was glad to encourage an exclusive trade link between the home country and the colonies, a mercantile economic system. No colony was established by the crown, until now. During this mercantilist time Great Britain was hostile to colonial manufactures, preferring the colonies to supply the raw materials and the manufacturing be done in Britain. For that reason, she preferred colonies to be on the shore, the Atlantic coast, and not too far inland. If they were too far inland, they might find it necessary to manufacture their own goods and thus break the trade link with Britain. This had not been a problem up to now because the inland spread was relatively slow, and eventually the mountains would block the way.

Quebec was the first, and only, colony established by the crown, and it was consistent with the new imperial policy Britain was demonstrating after the war. The crown would have complete control of Quebec through the royally appointed governor and his council, but would not have to handle the day-to-day details. The army could be removed from the back country because now the civil government in Quebec would take civil control. The new colony was itself a shore colony via the St. Lawrence River, reasonably accessible by sea for most of the year. There "was a strongly rooted preference of shore to inland colonies; a preference based on the belief that the further the colonists removed themselves from the ocean and the mother country, the more inevitably would they be led to manufacturing enterprises and the less easy would it be for Great Britain to restrain this activity." This reluctance to allow the existing colonies to expand, and attempt to keep them penned to the coast, was also probably the reason the proposed inland colonies of Vandalia and Transylvania, although encouraged at first, were allowed to die on the vine. They both expired at the start of the Revolution.[73] When the first Continental Congress met in the autumn of 1774, they "alleged that the extension of Quebec's boundary and the act's religious provisions threatened to deprive Americans, particularly Virginians and Pennsylvanians, of what they believed was their birthright: western land."[74]

Rebellion

By the end of the war in 1763, the colonists were optimistic. The war was over, the French had been defeated, and new land would be open to them. They had suffered large losses but they remained in good shape, having prospered in the war years, partly through illegal trade with the French. The population had grown 33 percent during the worst war years of 1750 to 1760, and another 38 percent between 1760 and 1770, both naturally and through immigration.[75] They were looking to resume the commercial ties with the mother country and to resume westward expansion.

Chapter Six. End of Expansion 217

They had grown more confident politically, and even with the appointment of the governors by the crown, had learned to govern themselves. There were some who started to think they no longer needed Great Britain. Nevertheless, a strong exclusive, mercantile relationship between the mother country and the colonies still prevailed. The colonies provided raw materials and the mother country did the manufacturing. This would become even more pronounced as Great Britain entered the Industrial Revolution in the 1760s. The colonies would not enter the Industrial Revolution until the nineteenth century, but they had started to increase their manufacturing capability by this time. All these factors would play out over the next few years.

Despite the optimism at the end of the war, the following dozen years played out differently; they went in the opposite direction. Partly this was because of some legitimate issues that followed the peace treaty, such as what to do with the western lands and the Indians, and partly it was because Britain, which seemed to be concerned about the relative independence of the colonies, decided to swing from a soft mercantile trade policy with them to a hard imperial policy, which it deemed necessary to solve all their problems at once.

It started with the Proclamation of 1763 limiting the colonists to lands east of the Appalachian Ridge to keep them separate from the Indians in the west. Everyone considered this to be a temporary expedient, a time to catch one's breath after the recent war. However, this was quickly followed by a series of acts to not only produce revenue to pay for the war, but also to demonstrate the primacy of Parliamentary rule over colonial rule. The first was the Sugar Act of 1764, which was followed by the Stamp Act of 1765. The Townshend Acts of 1767 not only taxed lead, glass, paper, paint, and tea, but also put in some punitive measures such as suspending the New York Assembly until it complied with the financial requirements of stationing troops in the colony. The last of this series was the Tea Act of 1773. An "effort to help the financially troubled British East India Company sell 17,000,000 pounds of tea stored in England, the Tea Act rearranged excise regulations so that the company could pay the Townshend duty and still undersell its competitors." In other words, the Tea Act was created to support the company. This was the motivation for the Boston Tea Party of December 1773, when hundreds of chests of East India Company tea were dumped into Boston harbor by the protesting Bostonians. The Boston Tea Party led to the previously discussed Coercive and Quebec acts.[76]

The resistance to the Quebec Act fell into two broad categories, religious and economic, or political. The colonists were incensed that the largest of all the colonies would be operated under the detested

French-Catholic civil law. They had defeated the French, but now it seemed as though the French would be back in charge. This cut deeply in Puritan New England and with the irreligious. Alexander Hamilton reacted strongly and extremely when he said "by giving a legal sanction to the accustomed dues of the priests" it would lead to "first the subjugation of the colonies; and afterwards, that of Great Britain itself.... The pre-eminent advantages secured to the Roman Catholic religion, will discourage all Protestant settlers, of whatever nation; and on these accounts, the province will be settled and inhabited by none but Papists ... will attract droves of immigrants from all the Roman Catholic States in Europe."[77] In the Parliamentary debates, Lord Camden also expressed concern about the anxiety this religious issue has raised in the colonies. "Nor can we forbear mentioning the jealousies which have been excited in the colonies by the extension of the limits of the province of Quebec, in which the Roman Catholic religion has received such ample support."[78]

If the fervent, anti–Catholic Protestants of New England were incensed by the religious aspect of the act, the land speculators of Virginia felt just as strongly about the prohibition against access to western land. Virginia speculators had hoped that the Proclamation would be just temporary, but their hopes were dashed quickly in 1774 when, in quick succession, the new land reform policy abolished land grants; grants to war veterans were stopped; the continued enforcement of the Proclamation line was announced; and the Quebec Act was passed. It looked hopeless that the Proclamation would ever be repealed, and that caused economic distress to many of Virginia's elite, the ones who speculated in land. George Mason lost his Ohio Company land and 50,000 acres he hoped to get in Kentucky. Richard Henry Lee saw his Mississippi hopes dashed by both the Proclamation and Quebec Act. Washington was counting on selling bounty lands in the affected area. Thomas Jefferson was expected to get about 17,000 acres of Indian land, but was now precluded by the restrictions. Patrick Henry had at least five ventures which he knew now were worthless.[79] The Quebec Act was the last straw for the colonials. In September 1774 representatives from 12 of the 13 colonies, all except Georgia, gathered in Philadelphia in what would become known as the First Continental Congress. In their "Declaration and Resolves," of October 14, 1774, they threatened peaceable measures such as to "enter into a non-importation, non-consumption, and non-exportation agreement," between the colonies and Great Britain unless these coercive acts were removed.[80]

These events are well-known and well-documented, but the emphasis is usually on Parliament's taxing authority, "taxation without representation." However, predating that issue was the issue of western land and who would control it. The first proclamation after the war, the Proclamation of

1763, had the impact of putting up an effective "iron curtain" at the Appalachian Ridge that precluded any motion westward by the colonies. (Colonel Bouquet's similar proclamation in 1761, before the end of the war, predated even this.) So, the first stone thrown in the lead-up to the Revolution was based on an order prohibiting colonists from moving west on land they thought they controlled.

All the discussions, wars, and negotiations between the crown, the colonists and the Indians between 1763 and 1770 involved western land boundaries. Some progress was made late in the decade with the Treaties of Fort Stanwix, Hard Labor, and Lochaber in moving the boundary line with the Indians slightly further west of the Appalachian Ridge. The much larger western territory beyond this new boundary was still reserved for the Indians. Surprisingly though, even after the Indian cessions in these treaties, the home government *would not allow settlement even in these newly acquired lands*; they were wary of a strong Indian uprising, which had been threatened. The last section of the wall sealing off the west from eastern colonies was the redefinition of the new boundaries of Quebec, which would now control all the land north and west of the Ohio River. Although the governor and assembly were appointed and controlled by the crown, the civil law was left to the French-Catholics in Quebec. "By granting them French laws, the customs of Canada, and the free exercise of their religion, the measure was an inducement to the Roman Catholic subjects of Quebec as well as the other colonies to migrate to the interior."[81] It was also meant to discourage the fervent Protestant English from even going into the province to seek land.

By the end of 1774 the new British imperial policy was essentially complete. The original seaboard colonies had been truncated, limited to east of the Appalachian Ridge from upper New York down to East Florida. The new Quebec province was as large in area as all the now-truncated original 13 Atlantic colonies. It stretched from Nova Scotia along the Saint Lawrence River around the Great Lakes to the Ohio River to the Mississippi and back north. It touched only upper New York and Pennsylvania of the original 13 colonies. Land between Quebec and the other colonies was still reserved as Indian country. It was in this Indian country that Britain expected the Indians would cede or sell their land to the crown, not to land speculators, which in turn would sell it in 100-to-1,000-acre parcels to the highest bidder.[82]

This map would provide Britain with the strong imperial control she sought after the war. It would limit the original colonies to the seaboard, force them to trade with Great Britain, provide civil control over the vast northwest through the Quebec province controlled by a royal governor and his council, and provide for crown control of any land acquired from the Indians in the Indian territory. It would totally eliminate any land speculation. It would also bring the colonies to heel, so they would be in reach of the crown on the seaboard and could not stray further.

The First Continental Congress met in September 1774, just three months after the Quebec Act was passed. The meeting was a direct result of the five Intolerable Acts: the four Coercive Acts and the Quebec Act. In the Declarations and Resolves from the Congress, they addressed these acts as "impolitic, unjust, and cruel, as well as unconstitutional, and most dangerous and destructive of American rights." Note the term "American" rights as contrasted with "British American" rights which Jefferson had used only a few months earlier. These acts had managed to bring the colonies together as nothing had done before. The northern and southern colonies seldom agreed on anything, and as separate entities never had need to. The interests of the merchant north and slave-holding south were very different, so that anything that brought them together was very unusual.

Events were moving quickly in 1774, and although Jefferson wrote his "Summary View" mostly to attack what he saw as the unjust attack on Virginia land policies, he also attacked the Coercive Acts, which seemed mostly to impact the north. He correctly foresaw that these were a threat to all the colonies. The Quebec Act sealed the deal. As Curtis, in "Riches, Real Estate, and Resistance," points out, there were five different groups that had often opposed each other but were brought together by the changing British land policy: southern planters, northern merchants engaging in land speculation, small-scale farmers, frontier squatters and the fur trappers. Members of the social elite led the movement, but they needed buy-in from all these other classes. This elite couldn't do it themselves, they needed buy-in from the working class, a larger class of people. They got this buy-in through the Quebec Act; everybody was now on board.[83]

So, the final step in the break between the colonies and the mother country came down to land, acts truncating the colonies to the eastern seaboard, and prohibiting any colonial expansion beyond the mountains; a reversal of the policy in effect for over 160 years. As Victor Coffin notes in *The Province of Quebec and the Early American Revolution*,

> disastrous as the Quebec Act proved, no part of it I think was more shortsighted or more disastrous than this treatment of the Western lands. Following up the Proclamation of 1763, it seemed an attempt to indefinitely maintain in the great heart of the continent, when apparently thrown open for Anglo-American expansion, the policy of monopoly and restriction against which the colonies on the coast were chafing so sorely. It was natural that the latter should imagine themselves threatened and impeded more malignly and seriously than could have proven to be the case; it was on this side, I have little doubt, that the Quebec Act figured most prominently amongst the colonial grievances.[84]

Chapter Six. End of Expansion 221

The war started in April 1775, a month after Edmund Burke made his plea in Parliament to stop the vindictive path Britain was on, and a month before the Quebec Act was to take effect. In response to a conciliatory proposal by the king, the Virginia House of Delegates Virginia Resolution of June 1775 complained that not enough had been done and again cited the Quebec Act. "The Commons only resolve to forbear levying pecuniary taxes on us; still leaving unrepealed their several Acts passed for the purposes of restraining the trade and altering the form of Government of the Eastern Colonies; extending the boundaries and changing the Government and Religion of *Quebec*."[85] Tom Paine's *Common Sense* in January 1776 provided the moral support for the coming colonial activities. In the Virginia Constitution of June 29, 1776, the Virginians were still adamant about their rights to land under the second charter. The 1776 Constitution of Virginia stated that "the western and northern extent of Virginia shall, in all other respects, stand as fixed by the Charter of King James I in the year one thousand six hundred and nine, and by the public treaty of peace between the Courts of Britain and France, in the Year one thousand seven hundred and sixty-three."[86]

All these led to Jefferson's Declaration of Independence in July, in which there were three references to grievances on the land issue. The first, quoted previously, talked about limiting the population of the colonies. The others were more specific regarding the Quebec Act, and limiting land granted under Crown charters. "For abolishing the free system of English Laws in a neighboring Province, establishing therein an Arbitrary government, and enlarging its Boundaries so as to render it at once an example and fit instrument for introducing the same absolute rule into these colonies.... For taking away our Charters, abolishing our most valuable Laws, and altering fundamentally the Forms of our Governments."[87] The road to American independence after the French and Indian War was short, but complicated, as evidenced by the long list of grievances in the Declaration. They included taxes, jury trials, trade, quartering acts, and harbor closings. A short road, because up until the conclusion of the French and Indian War, there was relative harmony between the colonies and the mother country. Because of the exigencies of the war's aftermath, Great Britain felt the need to apply a much stronger imperial control over the colonies, including dropping an iron curtain on any colonial western land expansion. It included the draconian Quebec Act, which was the last brick in the wall which was to separate the colonies from Great Britain. Land which had been free in North America for over 160 years was no longer free; it was no longer available in the west. The western land, for which the British fought the French in the French and Indian War, was the *same* land for which the colonies fought the British in the War for Independence.

Summary and Conclusion

A contemporary UK website claims that "land is free—as free as sunshine air and water.... It is here when we arrive, and we cannot take it with us when we leave."[88] Although the latter claim is certainly true, the former has been disputed for centuries. The concept of free land is paradoxical. It could mean free to anyone who can use it, but is not owned exclusively by anyone; this is the land concept of the indigenous people of North America. Or it could mean land, originally free, claimed by conquest for personal ownership and use. In this case the land is no longer free but is claimed by the conqueror, as William I did in eleventh-century England. This set the pattern for land tenure in England for over 700 years, ownership by one or a few. Similarly, land claimed by discovery can be allotted by the discoverer, for example the English Crown as the discoverer of North America, to enhance the wealth of the crown as it sees fit. This was done by James I when he chartered free grants of land in North America to encourage trading companies to settle, and thereby contribute to the wealth of the crown. This in turn set the pattern for land tenure for the English colonies in North America for the following 160 years. In the latter case it was individual land ownership rather than feudal tenure. Both cases reject the free land concept of the indigenous people.

The land that William I claimed by conquest in 1066 was sparsely settled. There was a lot of empty land available, but also land owned by local lords or villages. These lands were allodial, which means they had no obligation to an overlord; in this sense these lands were free. William changed all that; he claimed the whole island by right of conquest. Land tenure was no longer allodial but feudal. No one except William owned land. The barons to whom he awarded fiefs owed him fealty, but did not own their land. Although the feudal system defined the political hierarchy, the manorial system was the social system of the time. The vassals of the king were the lords of the manors on their fiefs. The serfs, bound to the manor, labored for the lord of the manor but had no rights of their own, not even the right to personal possessions, let alone any right to land. This rigid hierarchy lasted for three centuries, until the scourge of the Black Death. The loss of so much life disrupted the system and led to a more fluid society. This fluidity was a two-edged sword.

Many serfs lost their land and became beggars in the now emerging villages and cities. Others gained some rights, and with these proprietary rights, essentially owned their land as yeomen farmers. These rights were tenuous, however, and when the lords started to enclose the land for sheep farming in the fifteenth through eighteenth centuries, many lost their land. The era of the large landowner returned. The purpose of enclosing farms was to encourage sheep farming and an emerging wool industry. The wool industry led to England becoming a trading nation in the fifteenth and sixteenth centuries. Thus, from the eleventh into the nineteenth centuries there was little to no concept of individual land ownership in England. By the end of the eighteenth century only 10 percent of the land belonged to owner-occupying farmers. Land ownership by a few wealthy families was the only land concept known to the first English immigrants to North America. Even today, land ownership in the greater part of Great Britain is claimed by relatively few families.

The fifteenth and sixteenth centuries were also the age of discovery, when Portugal and Spain were discovering new trading partners in the far east and Spain was finding new land in the west. A late comer to the exploration party, England did lay a tenuous claim to North America in the late fifteenth century through Cabot's discovery of Newfoundland. This was a land claim by discovery. The claim was tenuous, because a claim by discovery implies occupation of the land to validate the claim, which Cabot did not do. Decades later, failed attempts at colonization were made by Sir Humphrey Gilbert and Sir Walter Raleigh on grants given by Queen Elizabeth. The remarkable thing about these grants is that they were grants for personal ownership, non-feudal grants, perhaps the first ones. She had assumed sovereignty in North America and decided to give *ownership* in land to two of her favorite subjects, ownership in land in North America, ownership that was limited to an elite few in England where feudalism had only recently collapsed.

Serious English colonization started early in the seventeenth century with James I, who had succeeded Elizabeth in 1603. English colonization was a unique enterprise compared to Spanish colonization in the southern Spanish American empire. The Spanish Crown directed the colonization of New Spain, and retained ownership of the land. For whatever reason, lack of funds, fear of debt, risk avoidance, or any other reason, England did not attempt any crown colony in North America; she used a different approach. By this time, she had become a major trading nation with trading companies, joint stock companies, in full flower looking for trading opportunities around the world. Although reluctant to involve the crown directly in colonization, James was very happy to give a grant to a joint stock company that was interested in setting up trading posts in North America. He gave a grant in 1607 to the Virginia Company, which intended to set up a trading colony on the coast of North America, to be known as Virginia. He assumed sovereignty, by the claim of prior discovery; assumed it was free, not held by another Christian prince; and therefore, assumed he could give it away in a grant.

The first grant in Virginia in 1607 was modest in size, just 100 miles square. It was also characterized by a great deal of royal control; the king would decide who the settlers would be. This was apparently too much trouble, so when a second charter was issued, only two years later in 1609, the terms were dramatically changed. First, the chartered area was extended from the lower end of the Chesapeake Bay all the way up to around the present-day Atlantic City. From this northern point it was extended inland northwest. Both these boundaries were from "sea-to-sea." Second, the company was now given the right to allot the land as it saw fit; no longer would it be the king assigning land holdings. These two factors were to have an enormous impact 160 years later during the crises between 1763 and 1775. The area covered by this second charter covered most of North America, including the Ohio Country. It would be the basis for Virginia land claims after the French and Indian War, and even past the War for Independence. In granting the company the right to allot land, James was essentially ceding sovereignty over the land. It was a right Virginia assiduously guarded and exercised over the following 160 years. The crown no longer had control over the land, a fact neither party recognized until Thomas Jefferson pointed it out 160 years later.

At first a quitrent was imposed on the American colonies, but it never took hold except in one or two colonies. A quitrent was a holdover from feudalism. When feudalism was breaking down, the serf or tenant farmer no longer paid a feudal duty in service to the head of the manor, but instead this service was converted to a money rent, a quitrent, essentially a land tax. In the "American colonies it was imposed as an initial charge upon new soil … [it] emphasized their relation to the mother-country as fiefs of the crown."[89] Even in early Virginia, when the law of 1618 required everyone whose land was based on a headright to pay an annual rent of 12 pence, it wasn't applicable for the first seven years. It wasn't until 1637 that first steps were taken to collect quitrents in Virginia.[90] Some colonies never bothered to collect them at all, and eventually the collection fell into disuse. This is another indication that, even in the early colonial history, the crown was losing control of land in the colonies. This did not seem to be a problem as long as the trade flowed regularly.

The Virginia Company soon learned that the settlers they imported to work for the company became much more productive when they received a small plot of their own for their own use, rather than just working for the company on company land. The same rise in productivity occurred in the Plymouth colony when settlers were given their own private land to own and cultivate. Now, for the first time, poor and middle-class farmers could own their own land to use as they wished, and could pass it down to heirs. This was not possible back in England, where they would have been tenant farmers at best, or laborers at least.

The first few years in Virginia were very difficult, with little output and a high death rate. The company needed to increase the population if the original trading company, now an agriculture colony, was to survive and make a profit. They finally decided to take advantage of a bountiful resource that they did have—land. They gave away land as headrights, 50 acres to every "head" that could get himself or another to Virginia; free land just for coming over to work the land. In Virginia the headright was an attractive way for young, single males, ones who might have had a hard time finding work in England, to come over for a new start. The headright system started to make the colony viable by increasing population. Later in the century, especially during the English civil war, royalists were enticed to immigrate, but with promises of much greater parcels of land. The land allocation process worked slightly differently in New England. There the company would allocate land to establish towns, which in turn allotted the land to families. The effect, however, was the same; immigrating families would end up with farms of their own.

There was now a real, but imperceptible, culture change in how one viewed the land. In England, where 90 percent of the farmers were tenants on someone else's land, there was little hope of owning one's own land. In America, the view was the opposite. "If I don't own my land now, I soon will be able to, or I can get more by moving west." The American culture now accepted the fact that land, if not free, was cheap, and there was always more to the west. Even if one had to pay for it, access to land came to be seen as a right, not just a privilege, such a right that squatters, who were always plentiful on the western frontier, assumed they could simply take any land that they could find and farm, regardless of who else might have claimed it.

Free or cheap land was not only an inducement for English emigrants, but drew in thousands from other countries, including the Scots-Irish from the Ulster Plantation, the England-Scotland borderlands, and Germans from Germany, places where land was scarce or burdened by rackrents. Land was used to implement policy. William Penn sold land, but he also gave some away to his co-religionist Quakers. He encouraged the aggressive Scots-Irish from Ulster and the borderlands to settle in western Pennsylvania to act as a buffer between the heavily Quaker colony and the Indians. Similarly, land in great quantities was given away in the Shenandoah Valley to Scots-Irish and German farmers to solidify the Virginia claim to the Valley and act as a buffer against Indians.

All 13 colonies were founded by private companies for profit, and some for the additional purpose of religious refuge. They existed comfortably in the British mercantile system with trade profitable to both parties, the colonies and the mother country. There was little imperial control, so the individual colonies grew in population and self-government, and expanded in size through the distribution of colonial land.

The land beyond the mountains had been claimed by England when the charters for Virginia and the other "sea-to-sea" colonies had been granted. In the ensuing years, New France had claimed the Ohio and Mississippi valleys, so that land was now in dispute. When Great Britain defeated New France in the war, she claimed that land for the crown by right of conquest. After the war, "it has been said, quite often and with good reason, that 'Americans were never more British than in 1763.' They relished their part in the defeat of the old enemy and looked forward to a golden age in which the blessings of British political civilization would be extended west."[91] However, on the other side of the Atlantic, some Britons saw a huge new empire and were concerned about the cost and military forces that would be needed to maintain it. They "were perplexed by the problem of having acquired too much power too quickly over too many people."[92] Their response was to clamp down on the increasingly independent colonies, and control the new lands and Indian relations by switching from a relatively relaxed approach to the colonies to a strict imperial control. The first impact would be on the western lands. The "blessings of British political civilization would [not] be extended west."

It was reasonable for the colonists to assume that the status quo ante in the colonial empire would again hold; that is, the colonies would resume their western land policies and continue to make western land available for settlement as part of the colony. This was certainly the expectation of Virginia; after all, the Ohio Company of Virginia had already been granted land in the Ohio Country in 1748, well before the war, but even this land was now being walled off. The precedent for giving free land in America had been set in 1607 and followed for over 160 years. Thousands had immigrated based on that premise, settlers, who were given or purchased the land from the colonies. It was logical to think that this precedent constituted settled law, and colonial land rights should pick up after the war as they had been practiced prior to the war. As Thomas Jefferson put it in his Summary View, "From the nature and purpose of civil institutions, all the lands within the limits which any particular society has circumscribed around itself, are assumed by that society, and subject to their allotment only. This may be done by themselves assembled collectively, or by their legislature to whom they may have delegated sovereign authority; and, if they are allotted neither of these ways, each individual of the society may appropriate to himself such lands as he finds vacant, and occupancy will give him title."[93] These are the words of Jefferson, the lawyer and wealthy land speculator, expounding on land rights a "particular society has circumscribed around itself," in this case Virginia, all the way down to the

Chapter Six. End of Expansion

importance of land to the individual. The humbler farmer or squatter might have used different words, such as the words of a John Steinbeck tenant farmer when expressing the importance of land to the individual farmer. "Funny thing how it is. If a man owns a little property, that property is him, it's part of him, and it's like him. If he owns property only so he can walk on it and handle it and be sad when it isn't doing well, and feel fine when the rain falls on it, that property is him, and some way he's bigger because he owns it. Even if he isn't successful he's big with his property. That is so."[94] These thoughts felt by thousands over 160 years, would lead one to believe that one had a right to the land. Once the access to western land is seen as a right rather than a privilege, it is easy to see that the colonial land seekers saw their rights as British citizens being infringed.

In "Why Have Americans Always Been So Obsessed with the Land?" historian H.W. Brands claims that

> something about land lies deep in the American psyche.... The history of America's land is the history of the country itself. America grew into its defining institutions even as it grew into its land. The land inspired American independence; it spawned American democracy; it undergirded America's rise to world power. Land symbolized opportunity to generations of Americans, starting with colonists who never had a chance of owning property in Europe; the vast continent gleamed in their eyes and its frontier drew them west.[95]

As the early colonists individually received free land, either as a headright from the Virginia Company or from the township in Massachusetts, they were undoubtedly pleased, but probably did not think much of it collectively; they were too busy defending and cultivating it. Eventually, though, they had to think of it collectively. As the population grew both naturally and by immigration, they were forced to consider where the new people would live and how they would apportion the land. This required collective action and led to the formation of civil compacts, such as the General Court in Massachusetts or the House of Burgesses in Virginia. Through these compacts they learned to govern themselves. It was during the growth in the seventeenth and eighteenth centuries that land entered into the American psyche. It was land that gave them the confidence that they could take care of themselves economically and socially, that is, become independent.

It was not only western land, but their political freedom they thought was endangered; political freedom was tied up in land. The early settlers, English and European, who came over came for a variety of reasons, including opportunities to get a new start, cheap land, and religious freedom. But once they arrived, the ownership of land sparked another feeling, the "awareness of government and political freedom." They knew they were different from their English neighbors, because in England very few owned land. The ownership of land in England was equated with the ownership of government. Once land was owned in America, the owners realized they, too, had new responsibilities, including local government. The prospect of loss of political freedom, because of loss of access to land, came through in all the grievances in the Declaration.[96]

The American Revolution cannot be attributed to a single cause; there were many grievances. When this last issue on land was added, motivated by the Quebec Act, these grievances coalesced into the Declaration of Independence. It was the last one on land that tipped the scale. As Curtis noted in "Riches, Real Estate, And Resistance," it was one of the most important acts to unite the north and south, the elites and farmers, to agree it was time to separate. As Gordon Wood noted in *The Radicalism of the American Revolution,* "men were equal in that no one of them should be dependent on the will of another, and property made this independence possible. Americans in 1776 therefore concluded that they were naturally fit for republicanism precisely because they were 'a people of property; almost every man is a freeholder.'"[97] So, it is fair to say that the colonies, originally started with land given away as an inducement to settle, free land, eventually saw access to land as a right, and when the right was taken from them, saw it as an abridgement of their liberty. When it was added to the other injustices they saw, they rebelled.

Free land eventually did lead to a free country.

Epilogue:
Free Land in the Move West

The negotiations leading to the Treaty of Paris in 1783 that ended the war, and finally acknowledged American independence, were long and difficult. Acknowledgment of independence was of course the first American goal, but the establishment of satisfactory borders was also critical. Various proposals were advanced that would have limited the area of the new United States to much less than what would actually be achieved. A French proposal would have limited the western boundary to the Allegheny Mountains, essentially the Proclamation line of 1763. Another proposal would have given all the territory north of the Ohio River to Great Britain. This would have maintained the Province of Quebec in Canada. Of course, it worked the other way also; the American negotiators wanted to include Canada in its new territory. Under the strong leadership of John Jay and John Adams, the American negotiating team worked out an advantageous deal that extended the western boundary to the Mississippi River and kept the bulk of the Quebec Province in the United States. This included everything north of the Ohio River and west to the Mississippi; it became the Northwest Territory. The original Quebec Province remained in Canada, which was retained by Great Britain.[1]

The war was the first priority of the colonies engaged in rebellion, especially during the first three years. That does not mean, however, that the land issues had gone away; in fact, in some ways they became more intense. Once independence was declared, although not yet secured, all the strictures imposed by the Crown were seen to be dissolved.

> A great change was effected in the land-system of America between the years 1775 and 1795.... In the first place, royal restrictions on the acquisition of land fell into abeyance. The king's proclamation of 1763 ... and those provisions of the Quebec Act which in a similar sense restricted westward expansion.... Now these checks were removed. Moreover, all the vast domains of the Crown fell into the hands of the states, and were at the disposal of the state legisla-

tures, and it was certain that these popular assemblies would dispose of them in some manner that would be agreeable to popular desires.[2]

There was almost a giddiness in the state assemblies, assemblies that tended toward populism anyway. (These legislatures were almost too "democratic," for example, responding to debt relief from their constituents at the expense of creditors. Protection of private property was one of the reasons the Founders proposed and recommended the passage of the Constitution.)

Other restrictions fell after the Declaration also. Quitrents, never popular, were abolished, as were restrictions on cutting down large white pines in New Hampshire for masts for the Royal Navy. Within 10 years after independence, most states had abolished entail, and within 15 years, all states had abolished primogeniture in favor of more equal inheritance laws.[3]

The greatest emphasis, however, was on land. One aspect of this was the confiscation of Tory lands, 28 estates in New Hampshire, for example. The largest confiscation was by Pennsylvania of the Penn family lands. The Penn heirs were deprived of their proprietorship and not all, but most of the land. "The Penns estimated their loss at more than 21,500,000 acres with a value of nearly £1,300,000. To indemnify them for the lost land, the Assembly voted £130,000 sterling to be paid one year after the end of the war at the rate of £15,000 per year."[4] "By 1782 the state of New York had confiscated royalist property in land valued at $2,500,000 in hard money."[5] Confiscated land, however, was a small part of the land issue.

The states realized that with restrictions removed they could use their own wild lands as a resource and look to western lands also. This caused land to be more valuable and led to many boundary disputes, attempts to claim the land of neighboring states. The boundary dispute between Virginia and Pennsylvania over the Ohio Country land that both claimed was the first to be reignited. It eventually settled down in order to prosecute the war more successfully, but not before a Pennsylvania official had a Virginia official arrested and incarcerated.[6] "Since the end of the colonial regime no land office had been opened and no lands had been granted in Virginia. Yet settlers were daily filtering in and establishing themselves upon soil to which it was impossible at the time to gain title. The claims of the great land companies were so extensive and, in the case of the Virginia companies, so vague as to boundaries, that any settler was in danger of eviction whenever the companies might find it possible to push their pretensions." These squatters finally put pressure on the Virginia constitutional convention of May 1776, and were promised preemption rights if the lands they settled were later put on the market. This meant that the squatter had the first right to the land if he could pay for it. The claim limit was up to 400 acres.[7]

Jefferson proposed some progressive changes in 1776 with regard to land. In the third draft of the Virginia Constitution, he proposed that "every person of full age neither owning nor having owned [50] acres of land, shall be entitled to an appropriation of [50] acres or to so much as shall make up what he owns or has owned [50] acres in full and absolute dominion, and no other person shall be capable of taking an appropriation."[8] It was his attempt to expand Virginia with the yeomen farmers he often extolled, by providing everyone who didn't have land with a way to get some. It was a domestic revival of the old headright system used to populate the colony 157 years previously. He wasn't successful.

Finally, on June 22, 1779, George Mason had the land office bill passed that he and Jefferson, now as governor, had been working on. Consistent with his earlier efforts to offer the land to the typical yeoman farmer, Jefferson included in the bill he submitted some far-sighted policies; he "advocated use of western lands for those who would settle there, for opposing monopoly and exploitation, for attracting immigration, for supporting the credit of the state, and for strengthening the bonds of the union by securing the adoption of the Articles of Confederation." The bill, however, was hijacked in the legislature and "it was deflected from its original purposes and altered to suit the desires of land companies and large speculators." For this reason, Abernethy, in *Western Lands and the American Revolution,* called the land office act of 1779 "a colossal mistake ... the act by which democracy was defeated in Virginia at the moment when it might have had its birth. The result was that within a few years Robert Morris came to own one and a half million acres, and Alexander Walcott a million acres of Virginia's Western lands, and most of that remaining fell into the hands of absentee speculators."[9]

"No group of people in America was more deeply affected by the declaration of independence [sic] than were the land speculators." These speculators needed to be able to look ahead in a stable environment to be able to invest successfully. Following the Declaration, the environment was anything but stable; there was a war on. Even during the war, the competition for land continued. "It was ... a contest between certain States claiming Western lands for themselves, on the one side, and those claiming it in the interest of certain land companies on the other." Virginia fell into both of these categories, having a great many speculators and a lot of land claimed. Speculators had outsized influence on land issues; many even tried to influence the peace commissioners to limit the boundaries of the new United States to enhance their own opportunity for western land. However, Blaakman, in "The Marketplace of American Federalism," saw moving across state lines to speculate as a good idea. He said that "land speculation across state lines helped lash the federal union together during an era of persistent fears that it might splinter.... 'A firm union is absolutely necessary, from one end of the states to the other,' one leading member of the New England Mississippi Land Company wrote to a Georgia senator. 'Removing a number of men and families from New England to Georgia' would be an 'incalculable advantage' to the republic, 'strengthen[ing]' a state that marked 'an extreme of the national boundary.'"[10]

Some of the other, smaller states, like Maryland, became concerned. Maryland had fixed western borders and no prospect of gaining western land. She reasoned that if Virginia successfully claimed all the western land she sought, Maryland would be too small to compete. Virginia could sell the land and thus lower her taxes, leaving Maryland with higher taxes and a population draining to Virginia. She pursued her concerns with the Confederation Congress, as seen in the following.[11]

In June 1776, the Second Continental Congress established a committee to form a confederation of the colonies, soon to become states, in order to provide a framework for cooperation to prosecute the war. By mid–July, just after the Declaration was signed, the first draft of the Articles of Confederation was ready. The Continental Congress became the Confederation Congress and named themselves "The United States of America." One purpose of the Confederation was to present the United States to the world in order to seek both legitimacy and allies in their fight with Great Britain. The Confederation was a loose one, with each state jealously guarding its sovereignty. It did not have the power to tax. The states had just declared their independence based on what they saw were unjust taxes by Parliament, and were not about to let a confederation impose taxes on them. It also required unanimous consent to pass any legislation. Because of these weaknesses the Confederation struggled through the war and afterwards until the adoption of the new Constitution in 1788. Despite its weakness, there were some significant steps taken by the Congress regarding the western lands.

Maryland was the first to act regarding the land issue. On October 15, 1777, Maryland proposed that Congress have the power to fix the western boundaries of the states that claimed land west to the Mississippi River, and that the land beyond the mountains should be made into "separate and independent states." However, the Articles of Confederation stipulated each state held the right to its own sovereignty and therefore to its own borders, so the Maryland proposal died; hers was the only vote in favor. The argument now started to change to *asking* the states to cede their land to the Confederation, since the issue could not be forced. Even though her proposal was defeated, Maryland still held up the ratification of the Articles on the land issue. On May 21, 1779, just 16 days after Delaware became the 12th state to ratify the Articles, Maryland held firm, saying the land should be made "into free, convenient and independent governments." This was the first proposal to have the Northwest Territory divided into states. This was the same month Virginia had set up its land office, presumably to sell land in Ohio. Finally, in 1780, Virginia, led by Joseph Jones and James Madison, started to consider cession of Virginia western lands to the Confederation. In January 1781, Virginia offered to cede "all lands north-west of the Ohio," and as a result, on March 1, 1781, Maryland ratified the Articles of Confederation. The Virginia land cession was completed on March 1, 1784, three years after the ratification of the Articles and six months after the Treaty of Paris.[12]

"One of the most noteworthy features of American Social history in the period immediately succeeding the Revolution is the prodigiously rapid migration of settlers into the new West ... in 1783, when news of peace came to America, the stream of westward migration assumed proportions unknown before.... In 1783 there were probably twenty-five thousand in the settlements west of the Alleghenies." These squatters, George Washington called them "Banditti," were threatening to overrun the west. There was a growing fear that these western settlers, far removed from the Confederation government, could not be controlled by the Confederation, but could fall under the influence of the British, who were still there in the west, or by the Spanish, or possibly set up their own governments. However, this surge of peasant squatters also precluded the possibility of anyone setting up large landed estates in the Northwest Territory. Instead, the United States was to be a land of "peasant proprietors."[13]

Congress recognized this surge, and lack of control, as dangerous, and took uncharacteristically rapid action. A series of land ordinances were enacted in 1784, 1785, and 1787 to address the issue. This area, north of the Ohio River, to the Mississippi and north to Canada, was now known as the Northwest Territory and was to be divided into new states. The Land Ordinance of 1784 did not determine the number of states, but did decide they would be laid out in a rectilinear pattern using longitude and latitude (undoubtedly due to the influence of Thomas Jefferson, who headed the committee). The Ordinance also declared these states would be part of the Confederacy with rights equal to those of the original 13 when they were admitted to the Confederation. When a territory met certain population requirements it could call a convention, establish a republican government, and apply for statehood.[14]

The Land Ordinance of 1785 decided how the land would be divided, laid out, and sold. It was to be surveyed in a rectangular grid, with the starting point for the grid at the point the Ohio River crossed the Pennsylvania border. The grid was composed of six-mile-square townships running north-south and east-west. Most townships were to be divided into one-mile-square sections of 640 acres per section. The minimum sale price for a section, which was the minimum lot for sale, was to be one dollar per acre. It was known that this was a high price for an individual, so it was expected that companies would buy the sections and subdivide them for individual sale. This brought large land companies back into the land business, now not as speculators, but as purveyors of government land. The six-mile-wide vertical strips were called ranges. The first set of ranges, known as the Seven Ranges, was located in southeast Ohio and took a long time to lay out, three years. Eventually all the states would be laid out in this pattern, except the ones that had first been independent republics, such as Vermont and Texas. It would become known as the United States Public Lands Survey System (PLSS).[15]

The land survey went very slowly, with only four ranges surveyed in the first two years. "Impatient to sell public lands and bring revenue into the treasury, Congress ordered the completed townships auctioned in the fall of 1787. Not one township was sold and only 108,431 acres were bid for." Indian troubles and distances from agricultural markets were some of the reasons for this slow sale. "Desperate for revenue, the Confederation abandoned the Land Ordinance of 1785 and contracted to sell public lands without competition, to two speculative companies."[16]

One such company was the Ohio Company of Associates. (It had no connection with the Ohio Company of Virginia.) This company was started in 1783 by Rufus Putnam, a war veteran in Boston, before the war was even over. It appears to have been the first group from New England, outside the middle or southern colonies, that took an interest in Ohio. They weren't successful at first, but by 1787 they agreed with Congress to purchase 1.5 million acres in Ohio. As a private organization they surveyed the land themselves. As per the Land Ordinance of 1785: "in each six-mile square township, section 16 was to be reserved for support of public schools, section 29 to support religion, sections, 8, 11, and 266 for later disposition by Congress, and two entire surveying townships (72 square miles) in perpetuity for support of a university." The company had trouble meeting their obligations for payment, and eventually settled with the government by paying in severely depreciated Continental securities for about twelve and a half cents per acre, considerably below what land sold for in the Seven Ranges. "But Congress was being practical instead of doctrinaire. It wanted the west settled." The other sale was to John Cleves Symmes for a one-million-acre tract in southeast Ohio. This also was sold for less than one dollar per acre.[17]

Even before the survey was completed, Congress drafted the Land

Ordinance of 1787. The purpose of the ordinance was to establish a method of governance for the territories and a process for applying for statehood. To ensure order in the territory, the ordinance provided for an appointed governor for three years and an elected legislature over which the governor would have veto power. These were to be only temporary, until the territory fulfilled the requirements for statehood. It did state that "the states that may be formed therein, shall forever remain a part of this Confederacy of the United States of America, subject to the Articles of Confederation." They identified an eastern state, a middle state and a western state, roughly corresponding to Ohio, Indiana, and the western part of the territory. When it had "sixty thousand *free* inhabitants" it would be admitted "on an equal footing with the original states in all respects whatsoever." Of course, it had to write its constitution consistent with the Articles of Confederation. Congress specifically repealed the Land Ordinance of 1784 to avoid confusion over similar actions in both. The timeliness of this action cannot be overstated. The Confederation Congress was meeting in New York in 1787 at the same time the Constitutional Convention was meeting in Philadelphia. Reginald Horsman, in "The Northwest Ordinance and the Shaping of an Expanding Republic," points out that "without the writing of a new constitution in the summer of 1787, the Northwest Ordinance might well have been a futile effort of a disintegrating nation rather than the keystone of a continental republic."[18]

The series of land ordinances enacted by the Confederation Congress brought some order to the settlement of western lands. It put down a marker that it would retain control over the Northwest Territory by ensuring a government structure was established, but also allowing settlement under that structure. Thus, it precluded a headlong rush into the west in an uncontrolled manner. The settlers had to look back to the Confederation for direction and were precluded from drifting into the orbit of a foreign country, such as Great Britain or Spain. Virginia had already found it hard to govern the distant west from Richmond, which is one reason for the cession of its western lands to the Confederation. Thus, the control of the new territory was ensured by establishing a federal system which provided for new states under the Confederation as settlement would allow. Underlying this was the expectation of income from the sale of land in these new states, which could be used to retire the war debt.

When the Confederation was replaced by the Constitution in 1788, the Land Ordinance of 1785 was no longer in effect. The Land Ordinance of 1787 was renewed by Congress in its first session, but the one from 1785 was not, so a new policy for land sales had to be determined.

When General Anthony Wayne defeated an Indian confederation in 1794 in northwest Ohio, it started another flood of settlers in the now safer

Ohio territory. The territorial governor, Arthur St. Clair, warned the federal government they were in a "use it or lose it" situation when he wrote, "but it is my duty to inform you Sir, that in my opinion, if they [the lands] are not disposed of soon, such numbers of People will take possession of them, as may not be easily be removed." This spurred Congress to act.[19]

The first of several land laws was enacted in 1796 by the Congress of the new republic. The Land Law of 1796 was enacted specifically for land in Ohio, northwest of the Ohio River and "above the mouth of the river [sic] Kentucky." The law kept the grid approach and the 640-acre sections of the 1785 act. The intent was still to bring revenue into the treasury. The tracts were to be sold at a public auction at a minimum of one section, or 640 acres, and for a price not less than two dollars per acre. There was no maximum sale; they could be sold in unlimited amounts.[20]

Although the intent to increase revenue was still there, the thinking now started to shift as to whom the land should be sold. Alexander Hamilton wanted the lands to be sold to capitalists, speculators, to achieve the maximum sale price. It could then be resold by them in smaller lots to the settlers. Thomas Jefferson and his colleagues, including Pennsylvania Congressman Albert Gallatin, wanted it to go to smaller farmers. Gallatin hoped the settlers would pool their resources and buy the land directly. He spoke of the importance of land to the nation and its citizens. "If the cause of the happiness of this country was examined into ... it would be found to arise as much from the great plenty of land in proportion to the inhabitants, which their citizens enjoyed, as much as from the wisdom of their political institutions."[21] This observation once more linked the availability of land as important to the American psyche as the new political state. His colleague from Pennsylvania, William Findley, also from western Pennsylvania, also spoke up for the small farmer when he said, "they ought not only to keep a wholesale but a retail store." As usual, the monied interests had the advantage. These ideas about distributing the land would become more prominent in later land laws when land again was given away.[22]

The results from the first year of the land law operation were disappointing; less than 50,000 acres were sold. At two dollars per acre the price was high for a 640-acre section, and it had to be paid within a year. Congress reacted to the poor performance and revised the law. The Land Law of 1800 made the provisions more friendly to the westerners. It kept the two dollar per acre fee but lowered the minimum purchase to a half-section of 320 acres, and extended credit to up to four years. It also provided four new land offices *in Ohio*, rather than those in Philadelphia and Pittsburgh. This stimulated the land business, so that by the end of 1802 more than 750,000 acres had been sold. Another revision in 1804 extended credit payments and reduced the size of the tracts to 160 acres.[23]

No states were admitted for the duration of the Articles of Confederation. However, soon after the republic was born, they started to fill up rapidly and enter the Union. Vermont entered in 1791, Kentucky in 1792, Tennessee in 1796, and Ohio in 1803. Given the popularity of the Northwest Territory, one might have expected the next state to enter the Union to be from that area, Indiana perhaps. However, another major addition to the United States territory intervened—the Louisiana Purchase of 1803. Thomas Jefferson thought long and hard about purchasing Louisiana from France, because permission to buy land outside the United States did not seem to be addressed in the Constitution. He swallowed any doubts and finally decided to purchase the 800,000 plus square-mile tract for 15 million dollars, almost doubling the size of the country. As a result, Louisiana was the next state to enter the Union in 1812. Indiana entered in 1816.

Jefferson's acquisition of this new land was perfectly in sync with the psyches of first, the British colonists, and then with that of the Americans. For about 200 years the quest for land in North America was seen as means to become self-sufficient, perhaps to become wealthy, certainly to become independent of others, and finally to become an independent nation. The availability of all this new western land only intensified the drive to move to occupy these lands, now all public land. The creation of wealth was still seen as the productive use of these new lands. Thus, there were incentives for settlers to purchase land and move west.

One of the first of the new incentives was *An Act making provision for the sale of the public lands,* or the Homestead Act of 1820. This act reduced the minimum purchase to 80 acres and the price to one dollar and 25 cents per acre. Thus, one could purchase 80 acres for only 100 dollars. The catch was that it had to be in cash; credit was no longer allowed. Despite the cash constraint, sales boomed. "The average annual acreage sold from 1820 to 1862 was about 3.3 million acres compared to an average of only 649,983 acres sold per year from 1800 to 1820. The average receipts after 1820 were nearly $3.6 million per year, a 273 percent increase over the average annual revenues of the preceding period.... After 1820, receipts from land sales became a major component of federal revenues." This latter fact had been a goal of the new republic since the Revolution. "From the program's beginnings in 1796 until 1862, privatization of the public lands via sales to the private sector scored several major successes."[24]

Although the sales were successful, as in 1835 the national debt temporarily went to zero under Andrew Jackson, the goals regarding land distribution were starting to change. Part of the change was due to the ever-present squatters, who, as usual, were getting ahead of the process. Another reason was the conviction that the wealth of the country could be increased by settling open lands and increasing the population on them.

There was also the fear of possible confrontations in the south and west with Mexico, and the northwest with Great Britain. The ever-present fear about losing control of westerners to foreign powers was still there also. All these combined to increase incentives for rapidly populating the west. We saw this above as smaller land parcels were made available to farmers and the price per acre was dropped.

In 1841 Congress passed the Preemption Act. The first part provided that 10 percent of the proceeds of the public land sold in the new states would go to those states. It also granted 500,000 acres of public land in the state for internal improvements. These states were not permitted to sell any of this land for less than one dollar and 25 cents per acre. The second part of the act is more important for this discussion; it was a protection for squatters. Squatters, by definition, would take land that did not belong to them, mostly because they couldn't afford it in the first place, and improve the land by cultivation and home building. However, they were always at risk of having the land taken away by someone who could claim it and pay for it. This act protected their labor investment in the land by giving them preemptive rights to buy the land before it could be sold to anyone else who claimed it. The land had to be clear of Indian title and surveyed in the usual pattern. To be eligible, a person had to be "the head of a family, or widow, or a single man, over the age of twenty-one years," and be a citizen, or intend to become one. The land wasn't free; the squatter still had to pay the minimum price for the land, but this went a long way toward protecting the small farmer. The government finally recognized the importance of the pioneer settler who was willing to take the chance and extend the frontier.[25]

The race to populate the west was now on. The term "manifest destiny" was coined in 1845, the same year Texas entered the Union. Manifest destiny quickly caught on and was taken to mean that God had intended the people of the United States were to occupy the land between the two coasts. This was all many needed to justify their movement west. By this time the pretense of using the sale of the land to reduce the debt was abandoned, and the idea was to populate it as quickly as possible.

The land rush to the west was on by the early 1840s, especially to Oregon via the Oregon Trail. The Oregon Trail started at Independence, Missouri, and went for about 2,000 miles to Oregon City. There were offshoots of the trail that went to the southwest and to California. The lure was free land offered by the provisional government of Oregon. Married couples were allowed to claim up to 640 acres at no cost. This offer continued until Congress passed the Donation Land Claim Act (1850), or the Oregon Donation Land Act. This law legitimized the 640 acre claims of the provisional government for married couples but separated it into 320 acres for the husband and 320 acres for the wife, a recognition that the wife could own land in her own right. The requirements were the same as in previous grants; the settlers had to be white, and the Indian title to the land had to be extinguished. Thus, the impact of "manifest destiny" was the same as the land policy had been for over 200 years, displacement of the Indian by the white settler. "By the time the law expired in 1855, approximately 30,000 white immigrants had entered Oregon Territory, with some 7,000 individuals making claims to 2.5 million acres of land." After 1855 the price was one dollar and 25 cents per acre.[26]

The mass migrations to Oregon were an indication that many people were on the move to the west. These included ancestors of the Lewis family, whom we had met in Chapter Four. They had moved from places like England, Germany, and Ulster to provinces on the east coast, and some, ultimately to Tennessee. They were typical of the early settlers who were continually looking for better land and moved west to find it. We were introduced to some of these ancestors: the Gillespies, Brandons, and Days. All these families stayed in Tennessee for a while until some moved on. Jacob Gillespie moved to Missouri and had a daughter, Agnes, who eventually moved to Oregon. John Day, a blacksmith born in 1823, left Tennessee to move to Oregon, where in September 1852 he married Agnes Gillespie, and together they had seven children. The timing of their travels makes it likely they were part of the movement on the Oregon Trail, and probably received free land.[27] "Preemption Laws helped placate frontier demands for land but what pioneer farmers really wanted was 'free land.' They argued that free land was their due. They transformed the public lands from wilderness to farmlands. They were the bulwark against Indian hostilities. And upon their efforts rested the country's economic, political and social strength."[28]

The movement west continued, and finally Congress capped it off with the Homestead Act of 1862—free land. "From the program's beginnings in 1796 until 1862, privatization of the public lands via sales to the private sector scored several major successes. By 1862, acreage equaling about 67 percent of the public domain in 1802 had been sold, and land sale receipts provided a significant, although fluctuating, fraction of total federal revenues."[29] Although sales were proceeding, Congress wanted to move faster to occupy the west, especially during the war.

The Homestead Act was similar to, and very much an extension of, the Preemption Act of 1842. Any person that was the head of a family, over 21, and had never borne arms against the United States was "entitled to enter one quarter section [160 acres] or a less quantity of unappropriated public lands ... for the purpose of actual settlement and cultivation ... and on the payment of ten dollars, he or she shall thereupon be permitted to enter the quantity of land specified." If they reside on the land for five years, they "shall be entitled to a patent."³⁰

Debate over a Homestead Law started in 1840, when the southern states were a major component of Congress. Northern industrialists were against the law because they worried it would empty the cites and deprive them of their control over labor. "The South also worried. The delicate political balance between the slave and free states in the Senate could be undermined by opening the undeveloped territories to small, independent farmers opposed to slavery." A compromise was reached in 1860 in which settlers could purchase land very cheaply if they lived on it for five years. President James Buchanan vetoed it, claiming it would reduce the revenues from selling public land—on this, he was correct. The Republicans passed the bill in 1862, in the middle of the Civil War, which is why it contained the stipulation that the homesteader "had never borne arms against the United States."³¹

Just before the end of the Civil War, in January 1865, General William T. Sherman had a meeting with 20 black leaders in Savannah. "The conversation revealed that these black leaders possessed a clear conception of the meaning of freedom. Garrison Frazier, a Baptist minister ... defined freedom 'as placing us where we can reap the fruit of our own labor.' The best way to accomplish this, he added, was 'to have land, and ... till it by our own labor.'" Only days later Sherman issued a Special Field Order setting aside the Sea Islands and part of coastal South Carolina below Charleston and 30 miles inland exclusively for the settlement of blacks. Each family would be given 40 acres. He also authorized the army to loan them mules. This was the origin of the phrase "forty acres and a mule," which rang out across the south for years as a rallying cry for more land. It was never officially adopted as government policy, but it clearly indicated the relationship all people saw between the land and freedom.³²

In the 246 years since Virginia started to give out 50-acre headrights to encourage settlers to come from England to settle, we had now come full circle. The United States government was giving out free land to encourage population of the west. The reasons were exactly the same in each case: free land to attract settlers for the purpose of increasing the wealth of the province or country. In both cases it was deemed that increasing the population of vacant lands was more important than trying to hold back and sell the lands.

This was certainly one of the largest, if not the largest, land giveaway programs in history. The sale of land did not stop, either. However, "for every acre of land sold between 1796 and 1923, over two acres were transferred to states, firms and individuals in the form of grants. Almost all of this transfer activity occurred after 1862.... The federal government

Epilogue: Free Land in the Move West 241

disposed of almost 592 million acres of public land using several different types of transfers. The most important transfer program, involving approximately 213.9 million acres, was the granting of homesteads." The rush continued with sales also. "For every 160 acres granted by the government to homesteaders, settlers and speculators purchased 400 acres of the public domain for cash." Most of the homesteading took place in the first three decades of the twentieth century. By that time "approximately 783,000 men and women 'proved up' and completed the homesteading process" although "roughly sixty percent of the homesteader never received title." Congress repealed the Homestead Act in 1976, but allowed for some homesteading in Alaska until 1986. Grants to homesteaders were not the only grants of land by the federal government. "Between 1850 and 1923, approximately 129 million acres were granted to states and corporations for railroad purposes"; that is a story to be covered elsewhere.[33]

After the 1890 census, Frederick Jackson Turner declared that there was no longer a discernible frontier; it no longer existed.

Chapter Notes

Introduction

1. Frederick Jackson Turner, *The Frontier in American History*, New York: Henry Holt and Company, 1920, http://www.gutenberg.org/files/22994/22994-h/22994-h.htm#Page_1.
2. "Estimated Population of the American Colonies," https://web.viu.ca/davies/H320/population.colonies.htm; Daniel Wunderlich Nead, *The Pennsylvania-German in the Settlement of Maryland*, Lancaster: Pennsylvania-German Society, 1914, p. 33.
3. "Estimated Population of the American Colonies."
4. Thomas D. Curtis, "Riches, Real Estate, and Resistance: How Land Speculation, Debt, and Trade Monopolies Led to the American Revolution," *The American Journal of Economics and Sociology*, Vol. 73, No. 3 (July 2014), pp. 445–626, p. 566, Map 8.
5. Curtis, p. 563.
6. Peter Epp, "How Property Ownership Led to the American Revolution," *Today's Farmer*, June 26, 2012. Provided to the author by Paul Mahon of the *Ontario Farmer*, London, Ontario.
7. H.W. Brands, "Why Have Americans Always Been So Obsessed with the Land?" March 7, 2018, https://www.history.com/news/american-land-frontier.

Prologue

1. William Blackstone, *Commentaries on the Laws of England, Book the Second*, Oxford: At the Clarendon Press, 1775, p. 51; J.F.C. Harrison, *The Common People: A History from the Norman Conquest to the Present*, London: Flamingo, Published by Fontana Paperbacks, 1984, p. 30.
2. Mary A.M. Marks, *Landholding in England: Considered in Relation to Poverty*, London: A.C. Fifield, 1908, pp. 8–12; Marc Bloch, *Feudal Society*, London: Routledge, 2014, p. 53.
3. David C. Douglas and George W. Greenway, *English Historical Documents 1042–1189*, London: Routledge, 1981, p. 20.
4. The Domesday Book was a census of all the people, and an accounting of all the land, in England in 1086. Cynthia L. Puryear, "The Effects of the Norman Conquest on the Anglo-Saxon Aristocracy," Honors Thesis, 1976, Paper 711, http://scholarship.richmond.edu/honors-theses, pp. 10–11; Benaiah W. Adkin, *Copyhold and Other Tenures of England*, London: The Estates Gazette, Ltd., 1911, pp. 6, 11; George C. Brodrick, *English Land and English Landlords*, London: Cassell, Peter, Galpin & Co., 1881, p. 8.
5. Adkin, p. 8.
6. Bloch, p. 155, *passim*; David Herlihy, ed., *The History of Feudalism*, New Jersey: Humanities Press, 1970, pp. 68–69. Harrison, p. 30.
7. Bloch, p. 253, *passim*.
8. Herlihy, p. xvii; George Burton Adams, "Anglo-Saxon Feudalism," *The American Historical Review*, Vol. 7, No. 1 (Oct. 1901) pp. 11–35, pp. 18–20, https://www.jstor.org/stable/1832530; Thomas Walker Page, *The End of Villeinage in England*, London: Macmillan Company, published for the American Economic Association, 1900, pp. 3–99, pp. 6, 7, 10–12, 15, https://www.jstor.org/stable/2485861; Bloch, p. 253, 285, *passim*; Doug-

las C. North and Robert Paul Thomas, "The Rise and Fall of the Manorial System: A Theoretical Model," *The Journal of Economic History*, Vol. 31, No. 4 (Dec. 1971), pp. 777–803, pp. 801–802, *passim*; Adkin, pp. 76–77, *passim*; Fredric William Maitland, *Domesday Book and Beyond: Three Essays in the Early History of England*, Cambridge: At the University Press, 1897, *passim*; Robert L. Bloom, Basil L. Crapster, and Harold A., Dunkelberger, "3. Manorialism," *Section II: Medieval, Political and Economic Development: Feudalism and Manorialism*, The Cupola Scholarship at Gettysburg College, pp. 23–27, http://cupola.gettysburg.edu/contemporary_sec2.

9. Arrush Choudhary, "From the Light and into the Dark: The Transformation to the Early Middle Ages," *Humanities and Social Studies, College of Arts and Science, Vanderbilt University*, Vol. 10 (Fall 2015), p. 5.

10. Bloch, p. 256.

11. Page, pp. 14, 19, 88, 37; Mark Bailey, *The Decline of Serfdom in Late Medieval England: From Bondage to Freedom*, Woodbridge, UK: The Boydell Press, 2014, http://ebookcentral.proquest.com/lib/umdcp/detail.action?docID=1334325; pp. 16–19.

12. Page, p. 6; Maitland, pp. 142, 337–339, 346, 379, 396; Bloom, *et al.*, pp. 24–26; Simon Fairlie, "A Short History of Enclosure in Britain," *The Land Magazine*, 2017, http://www.thelandmagazine.org.uk/articles/short-history-enclosure-britain; Harrison, p. 32.

13. Bloch, p. 262.

14. Brodrick, p. 15.

15. Page, pp. 40, 48, 51, 56,76–77; Jane Whittle, ed., "Introduction: Tawney's Agrarian Problem Revisited," *Landlords and Tenants in Britain, 1440–1660: Tawney's Agrarian Problem Revisited*, Woodbridge, UK: Boydell and Brewer, 2013, p. 13, http://www.jstor.org/stable/10.7722/j.ctt31nh5b.9; Harrison, pp. 76–77, 80–81; Bailey, 13, 32, 44, 65, 67, 70, 76; North and Thomas, p. 798; "Medieval Sourcebook: Tables on Population in Medieval Europe," *Fordham University*, 2020, https://sourcebooks.fordham.edu/source/pop-in-eur.asp.

16. Page, pp. 83–84.

17. R.H. Tawney, *The Agrarian Problem in the Sixteenth Century*, London: Longmans, Green and Co., 1912, p. 292; Brodrick, p. 19; Henry Charles Taylor, *The Decline of Landowning Farmers in England*, PhD thesis, University of Wisconsin, 1901, p. 9; Page, p. 88; Bailey, pp. 21–22.

18. Robert C. Allen, *Enclosure and the Yeoman*, Oxford: Clarendon Press, 1992, p. 65; Tawney, pp. 213–214; Page, pp. 24, 47, 56–58, 72, 75, 83; Bailey, p. 12.

19. Edwin F. Gay, "Inclosures in England in the Sixteenth Century," *The Quarterly Journal of Economics*, Vol. 17, No. 4 (Aug. 1903), pp. 576–597, p. 587, https://www.jstor.org/stable/1885511.

20. Tawney, pp. 262, 265.

21. Page, *passim*; Tawney, p. 9; Allen, pp. 47–48, 65; Harrison, pp. 125–132; Whittle, p. 16; Bailey, pp. 5, 24.

22. Allen, p. 66.

23. Allen, p. 68.

24. Allen, pp. 76–77; Harrison, p. 127.

25. Allen, p. 77.

26. Allen, pp. 78–79, 85–86.

27. Allen, p. 101.

28. Allen, p. 1.

29. W.J. Ashley, "The Early History of the English Woollen Industry," *Publications of the American Economic Association*, Vol. 2, No. 4 (Sep. 1887), pp. 12–85, pp. 13, 80, http://www.jstor.org/stable/2696712.

30. Allen, pp. 55, 101; Tawney, pp. 183, 401; Taylor, p. 23.

31. Allen, pp. 55, 79, 85.

32. Richard White, *The Republic for Which It Stands: The United States During Reconstruction and the Gilded Age, 1865–1896*, New York: Oxford University Press, 2017, p. 458.

33. Kevin Cahill, *Who Owns Britain*, Edinburgh: Canongate, 2001, p. 6.

Chapter One

1. Stanley L. Engermann and Kenneth L. Sokoloff, "Once Upon a Time in the Americas: Land and Immigration Policies in the New World," *National Bureau of Economic Research: Understanding Long-Run Economic Growth: Geography, Institutions, and Knowledge Economy*, Conference date: November 7–8, 2008, Published August 2011 by University of

Chicago Press. p. 1, http://www.nber.org/chapters/c11994.

2. Richard Hakluyt, *Discourse of Western Planting*, 1584, http://nationalhumanitiescenter.org/pds/amerbegin/exploration/text5/hakluyt.pdf; Gerald Roe Crone, "Richard Hakluyt, British Geographer," *Encyclopædia Britannica*, 2020, https://www.britannica.com/biography/Richard-Hakluyt.

3. Jean Brown Mitchell, "European Exploration: The Age of Discovery," *Encyclopædia Britannica*, 2019, https://www.britannica.com/topic/European-exploration/The-Age-of-Discovery; "Silk Road," *Encyclopædia Britannica*, 2019, https://www.britannica.com/topic/Silk-Road-trade-route.

4. National Park Service, "Unit 1-Spain in the New World to 1600," 2019. https://www.nps.gov/fora/learn/education/unit-1-spain-in-the-new-world-to-1600.htm.

5. J.H. Elliott, *Empires of the Atlantic World: Britain and Spain in America, 1492-1830*, New Haven: Yale University Press, 2007, p. 19.

6. Henry William Elson, *History of the United States of America*, New York: The Macmillan Company, 1904, pp. 23–24; R.A. Skelton, "Cabot, John," *Dictionary of Canadian Biography, Vol. 1*, 2019, http://www.biographi.ca/en/bio/cabot_john_1E.html.

7. George McCutchen McBride, *The Land Systems of Mexico*, New York: American Geographical Society, 1923, pp. 42–43.

8. Elliott, p. 18.

9. Charles Gibson, *Spain in America*, New York: Harper & Row Publishers, 1966, pp. 7–11; Peter Hinks and Mick McKivigan, eds., *Encyclopedia of Antislavery and Abolition, Volume 2: J-Z*, Westport, CT: Greenwood Press, 2007, p. 571.

10. McBride, pp. 43–44.

11. George Brown Tindall and David Emory Shi, *America: A Narrative History*, New York: W.W. Norton, 1999, p. 26.

12. Gibson, *Spain in America*, pp. 24–25; Lyle N. McAlister, *Spain and Portugal in the New World*, Minneapolis: University of Minnesota, 1984, p. 94.

13. Elliott, pp. 3–4.
14. Elliott, p. 4.
15. Elliott, pp. 4–5.
16. Elliott, p. 20.
17. Elliott, p. 19.
18. Tindall, p. 31.
19. Elliott, pp. 37–38; Stanley L. Engerman and Kenneth L. Sokoloff, "Once Upon a Time in the Americas: Land and Immigration Policies in the New World," p. 16, https://economics.yale.edu/sites/default/files/files/Workshops-Seminars/Economic-History/engerman-090412.pdf.

20. Elliott, p, 21.

21. Placido Gomez, "The History and Adjudication of the Common Lands of Spanish and Mexican Land Grants," 25 *Natural Resources Journal*, 1039 (1985), p. 1055, https://digitalrepository.unm.edu/nrj/vol25/iss4/11.

22. Andro Linklater, *Owning the Earth: The Transforming History of Land Ownership*, New York: Bloomsbury, 2013, p. 77.

23. Elliott, p. 21; "*Encomienda*: Spanish Policy," *Encyclopædia Britannica*, 2019, https://www.britannica.com/topic/encomienda; "*Repartimiento*: Spanish-American History," *Encyclopædia Britannica*, 2019, https://www.britannica.com/topic/repartimiento.

24. Elliott, pp. 39–40; "Cortez himself claimed to have been granted authority over more than 25,000 square miles and 23,000 of the region's 115,000 inhabitants," Gomez, p. 1055 fn.

25. Charles Gibson, *The Aztecs Under Spanish Rule: A History of the Indians of the Valley of Mexico 1519-1810*, Stanford CA: Stanford University Press, 1964, pp. 58, 78.

26. McAlister, p. 162.
27. Elliott, p. 123.

28. Robert G. Keith, "Hacienda and Corregimiento in Spanish America: A Structural Analysis," *The Hispanic American Historical Review*, Vol. 51, No. 3 (Aug. 1971), p. 433 fn, https://www.jstor.org/stable/2512690.

29. "Corregidor, Spanish Government Official," *Encyclopædia Britannica*, 2019, https://www.britannica.com/topic/corregidor-Spanish-official.

30. McAlister, pp. 162–163.

31. Gibson, *Spain in America*, p. 63. Another estimate was "In a period of 36 years, from 1532 to 1568, the Indian population of Mexico was reduced from almost 16.9 million to slightly over 2.6 million." Gomez, p. 1052, fn.

32. Keith, p. 443.

33. Gibson, *The Aztecs Under Spanish Rule*, p. 275.
34. James Lockhart, "The Evolution of the Great Estate in the Spanish Indies," *The Hispanic American Historical Review*, Vol. 49, No. 3 (Aug. 1969), p. 416, https://www.jstor.org/stable/2511778.
35. Gibson, *Spain in America*, p. 152.
36. Keith, p. 444.
37. Gibson, *The Aztecs Under Spanish Rule*, p. 275.
38. Gibson, *Spain in America*, pp. 152–155.
39. Lockhart, pp. 416–417. For the Zavala reference see footnote one on page 411.
40. Lockhart, p. 422.
41. Lockhart, p. 421 fn.
42. Lockhart, p. 427.
43. Lockhart, pp. 419–420, *passim*.
44. Lockhart, p. 426.
45. Gibson, *Spain in America*, p. 155.
46. Stanley L. Engerman and Kenneth L. Sokoloff, "Colonialism, Inequality, and Long Run Paths of Development," *National Bureau of Economic Research*, Working Paper 11057, January 2005, pp. 20–21, http://www.nber.org/papers/w11057.
47. Lockhart, p. 424.
48. John Butman and Simon Targett, *New World, Inc.: The Making of America by England's Merchant Adventurers*, New York: Little, Brown and Company, 2018, p. 3.
49. Butman and Targett, pp. 3–4.
50. W.J. Ashley "The Early History of the English Woollen Industry," *Publications of the American Economic Association*, Vol. 2, No. 4 (Sep. 1887), p. 15, http://www.jstor.org/stable/2696712.
51. Ashley, p. 38.
52. Ashley, pp. 38, 40, 45, 50, 56, 58–59.
53. Ashley, p. 67.
54. W. E Lingelbach, *The Merchant Adventurers of England: Their Laws and Ordinances with Other Documents*. 1902, p. xxiv. The company was re-chartered in 1505 by Henry VII, p. xxvi: "Merchant Adventurers," *Encyclopædia Britannica*, 2019, https://www.britannica.com/topic/Merchant-Adventurers.
55. Ashley, p. 68.
56. Ashley, p. 69.
57. Lingelbach, p. xxvi.
58. Ashley, p. 71.
59. Ashley, p. 80.
60. Ashley, p. 80.
61. R. H. Tawney, *The Agrarian Problem in the Sixteenth Century*, London: Longmans, Green and Co, 1912, pp. 6–9.
62. "Chartered Company, Economics," *Encyclopædia Britannica*, 2019, https://www.britannica.com/topic/chartered-company.
63. Tu Kha Tran, "Growth of Joint Stock Companies in the Seventeenth Century," *San Jose State University, SJSU ScholarWorks*, Master's Thesis, 2008. p. 14.
64. Tran, p. 36.
65. Michael J. Braddick, *State Formation in Early Modern England, c. 1550-1700*, Cambridge: Cambridge University Press, 2000, p. 398.
66. Cheesman A. Herrick, *History of Commerce and Industry*, New York: The Macmillan Company, 1817, p. 207.
67. Edward P. Cheyney, *An Introduction to the Industrial and Social History of England*, New York: The Macmillan Company, 1921, p. 117.
68. Herrick, pp. 207–214.
69. D. W. Prowse, *History of Newfoundland from the English, Colonial, and Foreign Records*, London: Macmillan Company, 1805, p. 8.
70. Prowse, p. 8.
71. "1497: John Cabot's Voyage to America," *The National Archives*, 2019, https://www.nationalarchives.gov.uk/museum/item.asp?item_id=10.
72. "Patent Granted by Henry VII to John Cabot and His Sons, March 1496," *Heritage: Newfoundland and Labrador*, https://www.heritage.nf.ca/articles/exploration/1496-cabot-patent.php.
73. Prowse, pp. 9–11.
74. Prowse, pp. 19, 59.
75. Thomas B. Costain, *The White and the Gold: The French Regime in Canada*, Toronto: Doubleday Canada Limited, 1954, Chapter II, Section 2.
76. "Juan Ponce de Leon, Spanish Explorer," *Encyclopædia Britannica*, 2019, https://www.britannica.com/biography/Juan-Ponce-de-Leon.
77. "Hernando de Soto, Spanish Explorer," *Encyclopædia Britannica*, 2019, https://www.britannica.com/biography/Hernando-de-Soto.
78. Costain, Chapter II, Section 2.
79. Costain, Chapter II, Section 2.
80. "Cartier, Jacques," *Dictionary of Canadian Biography*, 2019, http://www.

biographi.ca/en/bio/cartier_jacques_1491_1557_1E.html; "The Explorers, Jacques Cartier, 1534–1542," *Canadian Museum of History, Virtual Museum of New France*, 2019, https://www.historymuseum.ca/virtual-museum-of-new-france/the-explorers/jacques-cartier-1534-1542/.

81. "Giovanni de Verrazzano Letter to King Francis 1 of France, 8 July 1524," 2019, http://nationalhumanitiescenter.org/pds/amerbegin/contact/text4/verrazzano.pdf.

82. Brendan Wolfe, "The Roanoke Colonies," *Encyclopedia Virginia, Virginia Humanities*, 2019, https://www.encyclopediavirginia.org/roanoke_colonies_the.

83. "The Letters Patents Graunted by Her Maiestie to Sir Humfrey Gilbert (June 11, 1578)," *Encyclopedia Virginia, Virginia Humanities*, 2019, https://www.encyclopediavirginia.org/Letters_Patents_graunted_by_her_Maiestie_to_Sir_Humfrey_Gilbert_June_11_1578_The; David B. Quinn, "Gilbert, Sir Humphrey," *Dictionary of Canadian Biography* 2019, http://www.biographi.ca/en/bio/gilbert_humphrey_1E.html.

84. "Gilbert (Gylberte, Jilbert), Sir Humphrey," *Dictionary of Canadian Biography*, 2019, http://www.biographi.ca/en/bio/gilbert_humphrey_1E.html\.

85. Edward Hayes, *Sir Humphrey Gilbert's Voyage to Newfoundland*, eBook, 2019, p. 7, http://www.gutenberg.org/ebooks/3338.

86. Elliott, p. 30.

87. Ken MacMillan, *Sovereignty and Possession in the English New World: The Legal Foundations of Empire, 1576–1640*, New York: Cambridge University Press, 2006, p. 115; Lauren Benton and Benjamin Straumann, "Acquiring Empire by Law: From Roman Doctrine to Early Modern Practice," *Law and History Review*, Vol. 28, No. 1 (February 2020), pp. 1–38, *passim*, https://www.jstor.org/stable/40646121.

88. "Alexandrine Bulls." *New Catholic Encyclopedia*, July 8, 2019, https://www.encyclopedia.com/religion/encyclopedias-almanacs-transcripts-and-maps/alexandrine-bulls.

89. Elliott, p. 35.

90. "The Letters Patents Graunted by Her Maiestie to Sir Humphrey Gilbert."

91. Hayes, p. 7; "Fee-farm," *The Law.com Dictionary*, 2019, https://dictionary.thelaw.com/fee-farm-2/.

92. Brendan Wolfe, "Sir Walter Raleigh's Patent to Settle Virginia," 2019, https://encyclopediavirginia.org/entries/sir-walter-raleighs-patent-to-settle-virginia-1584/; "Charter to Sir Walter Raleigh: 1584," *The Avalon Project: Yale Law School*, 2019, http://avalon.law.yale.edu/16th_century/raleigh.asp.

93. Wolfe, "Sir Walter Raleigh's Patent to Settle Virginia."

94. Wolfe, "Sir Walter Raleigh's Patent to Settle Virginia."

95. Wolfe, "Sir Walter Raleigh's Patent to Settle Virginia."

96. MacMillan, p. 3.

97. "The Early Stuarts and the Commonwealth, England in 1603," *Encyclopædia Britannica*, 2019, https://www.britannica.com/place/United-Kingdom/The-early-Stuarts-and-the-Commonwealth.

98. Carl Bridenbaugh, *Vexed and Troubled Englishmen, 1590–1642*, New York: Oxford University Press, 1968, pp. 22, 355.

99. Allan Kulikoff, *From British Peasants to Colonial American Farmers*, Chapel Hill: The University of North Carolina Press, 2000, pp. 23–24.

100. Thomas J. Wertenbaker, *The Planters of Colonial Virginia*, Princeton: Princeton University Press, 1922, pp. 7–10.

101. "The Early Stuarts and the Commonwealth, England in 1603," *Encyclopædia Britannica*, 2019, https://www.britannica.com/place/United-Kingdom/The-early-Stuarts-and-the-Commonwealth.

102. Nicholas Canny, *The Origins of Empire: British Overseas Enterprise to the Close of the Seventeenth Century*, Oxford: Oxford University Press, 1998, p. 4.

103. Canny, p. 4.

104. MacMillan, p. 5–6.

105. John C. Appleby, "War, Politics, and Colonization, 1558–1625," Chapter 3 from *The Origins of Empire: British Overseas Enterprise to the Close of the Seventeenth Century*, Ed. by Nicholas Canny, Oxford: Oxford University Press, 1998, p. 55.

106. Appleby, p. 67.

107. Butman and Targett, p. 216.

108. Butman and Targett, pp. 233–245.

109. Appleby, p. 70.
110. Alexander Brown, *The Genesis of the United States, Volume II*, Boston: Houghton, Mifflin and Company, The Riverside Press, Cambridge, 1897, pp. 799–802.
111. MacMillan, p. 9; Anthony Pagden, "The Struggle for Legitimacy and the Image of Empire in the Atlantic to c. 1700," Chapter 2 from *The Origins of Empire: British Overseas Enterprise to the Close of the Seventeenth Century*, Ed. by Nicholas Canny, Oxford: Oxford University Press, 1998, p. 42.
112. Pagden, p. 41.
113. MacMillan, pp. 9–10.
114. Nicholas P. Canny, "The Ideology of English Colonization: From Ireland to America," *The William and Mary Quarterly*, Vol. 30, No. 4 (Oct. 1973) pp. 575–598, pp. 576, 578–579, 586, 588–589.
115. Canny, "The Ideology of English Colonization: From Ireland to America," pp. 593–594.
116. Canny, "The Ideology of English Colonization: From Ireland to America," p. 596.
117. John Locke, *Two Treatises of Government, Book II, Chapter V, Of Property*, London: Printed for Whitmore and Fenn, Charging Cross; and C. Brown, Duke Street, Lincoln's-Inn-Fields, 1821, https://play.google.com/books/reader?id=K5UIAAAAQAAJ&pg=GBS.PR3.w.2.0.0.

Chapter Two

1. Philipp Blom, *Nature's Mutiny: How the Little Ice Age of the Long Seventeenth Century Transformed the West and Shaped the Present*, New York: Liveright Publishing Corporation, A Division of W.W. Norton, 2017. p. 24.
2. Blom, p. 131.
3. "Mercantilism," *Encyclopædia Britannica*, 2019, https://www.britannica.com/topic/mercantilism.
4. Marshall Harris, *Origin of the Land Tenure System in the United States*, Ames: The Iowa State College Press, 1953, p. 76.
5. Alexander Brown, *The First Republic in America*, Boston: Houghton, Mifflin and Company, New York: The Riverside Press, Cambridge, 1898, p. 4.
6. Brown, *The First Republic*, pp. 5–6.
7. The whole east coast of North America was known as Virginia, having received that title years before during the Raleigh expeditions.
8. "The First Charter of Virginia; April 10, 1606," *The Avalon Project, Lillian Goldman Law library, Yale Law School*, 2019, http://avalon.law.yale.edu/17th_century/va01.asp; "The First Virginia Charter 1606," *American History: From Revolution to Reconstruction and Beyond*, 2019, http://www.let.rug.nl/usa/documents/1600-1650/the-first-virginia-charter-1606.php.
9. Brown, *The First Republic*, p. 7.
10. Brown, *The First Republic*, p. 7.
11. "The First Charter of Virginia; April 10, 1606," *The Avalon Project*; "The First Virginia Charter 1606," *American History: From Revolution to Reconstruction and Beyond*, 2019, http://www.let.rug.nl/usa/documents/1600-1650/the-first-virginia-charter-1606.php.
12. W. Stitt Robinson Jr., *Mother Earth, Land Grants in Virginia, 1607–1699*, Virginia 350th Anniversary Celebration Corporation, Williamsburg, Virginia, Historical Booklet, No. 12, 1957, p. 11, https://babel.hathitrust.org/cgi/pt?id=uc1.b000866728&view=1up&seq=19.
13. "Socage, Law" *Encyclopædia Britannica*, 2019, https://www.britannica.com/topic/socage.
14. "'N. N.': On the Tenure of the Manor of East Greenwich, 6 January 1766," *National Archives-Founders Online*, 2019, https://founders.archives.gov/documents/Franklin/01-13-02-0006#BNFN-01-13-02-0006-fn-0002.
15. William Reynolds Vance, "Quest for Tenure in the United States," *Yale Law Journal, Yale Law School Legal Scholarship Repository, Yale Law School*, 1923, p. 256.
16. Susan M. Kingsbury, *An Introduction to the Records of the Virginia Company of London*, Library of Congress, Washington: Government Printing Office, 1905, p. 12.
17. Kingsbury, p. 12.
18. Wesley Frank Craven, *The Southern Colonies in the Seventeenth Century 1607–1689*, The Louisiana State University Press and The Littlefield Fund for Southern History of the University of Texas, 1991, pp. 60–61.
19. Norman MacDonald, "English Land Tenure on the North American Continent:

A Summary," *Contributions to Canadian Economics*, Vol. 7 (1934), p. 21, https://www.jstor.org/stable/136552.

20. Brown, *The First Republic*, p. 40; Henry Elson, *History of the United States of America*, New York: Macmillan, 1904, p. 62.

21. Kingsbury, pp. 19–20.

22. Alexander Brown, *The Genesis of the United States, Volume I*, Boston: Houghton, Mifflin and Company, 1890, p. 84.

23. Robinson, p. 15.

24. Harris, p. 84.

25. Kingsbury, p. 12; Robinson, p. 12.

26. Robinson, pp. 11–12.

27. Harris, 32, p. 180.

28. L.D. Scisco, "The Plantation Type of Colony," *The American Historical Review*, Vol. 8, No. 2 (Jan. 1903), p. 261, https://www.jstor.org/stable/1832925.

29. Robinson, p. 15.

30. Charles E. Hatch, *The First Seventeen Years: Virginia, 1607–1624*, Charlottesville: The University of Virginia Press, 1957, pp. 7–8, https://www.gutenberg.org/ebooks/30780.

31. Hatch, p. 10.

32. Robinson, p. 14; Harris, p. 86.

33. "The Second Charter of Virginia; May 23, 1609, "*The Avalon Project*, Lillian Goldman Law library, Yale Law School, 2019, https://avalon.law.yale.edu/17th_century/va02.asp.

34. Robinson, p. 13.

35. Bernard Bailyn, *The Barbarous Years: The Conflict of Civilizations, 1600–1675*, New York: Vintage Books, a Division of Random House, 2013, pp. 69, 77–79; Hatch, p. 7, 17.

36. Hatch, pp. 17–18; Bailyn, p. 79.

37. Hatch, pp. 15.

38. Harris, pp. 74–75.

39. Harris, pp. 74–81.

40. "Council for New England," *Encyclopedia Britannica*, 2019. https://www.britannica.com/topic/Council-for-New-England.

41. "Council for New England," *Encyclopedia.com*, 2019, https://www.encyclopedia.com/history/dictionaries-thesauruses-pictures-and-press-releases/council-new-england; "Petition for a Charter of New England by the Northern Company of Adventurers: March 3, 1619/20," *The Avalon Project*, Lillian Goldman Law library, Yale Law School, 2019, https://avalon.law.yale.edu/17th_century/charter_002.asp; "The Charter of New England: 1620," *The Avalon Project*, Lillian Goldman Law library, Yale Law School, 2019, https://avalon.law.yale.edu/17th_century/mass01.asp.

42. Samuel Eliot Morison, "The Plymouth Colony and Virginia." *The Virginia Magazine of History and Biography*, Vol. 62, No. 2 (Apr. 1954), pp. 147–165, p. 149.

43. Morison, pp. 149–158; Susan Myra Kingsbury, *The Records of the Virginia Company of London, Volume I*, Washington: Government Printing Office, 1906, p. 303. The original northern boundary of the Virginia Company of London was at forty-one degrees north latitude. However, the northern boundary of the second charter, 200 miles north of Cape Comfort, seems to place the new northern boundary at just under forty degrees. Thus, their target landing place of the Hudson (40.7 degrees) would still have been north of the Virginia Company of London's northern boundary. However, it is likely they all assumed that the 200 miles north point was the forty-first latitude. Edward M. Douglas, *Boundaries, Areas, Geographic Centers and Altitudes of the United States and the Several States*, United States Department of the Interior Bulletin 817, Washington D. C.: United States Government Printing Office, 1930, p. 138.

44. Morison, pp. 156–158; Harris, pp. 103–105; Peggy M. Baker, "The Plymouth Colony Patent: Setting the Stage," *Pilgrim Hall Museum*, 2007, https://pilgrimhall.org/pdf/The_Plymouth_Colony_Patent.pdf; "The Pierce Patent," *The Plymouth Colony Archive Project*, http://www.histarch.illinois.edu/plymouth/piercepat.html Note: The May 1620 date that appears in the introductory paragraph appears to be in error. It should be 1621.

45. Tom Bethell, "How Private Property Saved the Pilgrims," *Hoover Digest*, No. 1, January 30, 1999. https://www.hoover.org/research/how-private-property-saved-pilgrims.

46. Samuel Eliot Morison, *Of Plymouth Plantation, 1620–1647, by William Bradford*, New York: Alfred Knopf, 2002, p. 121.

47. Morison, p. 120.

48. Harris, p. 274.

49. Harris, p. 274.

50. Carl Bridenbaugh, *Vexed and*

Notes—Chapter Two

Troubled Englishmen, 1590-1642, New York: Oxford University Press, 1968, p. 436-437.

51. "John Endecott, British Colonial Governor," *Encyclopædia Britannica*, 2019, https://www.britannica.com/biography/John-Endecott.

52. Bridenbaugh, p. 437.

53. Bridenbaugh, p. 437; "The Charter of Massachusetts Bay: 1629," *The Avalon Project, Lillian Goldman Law library, Yale Law School*, 2019, https://avalon.law.yale.edu/17th_century/mass03.asp; Henry William Elson, *History of the United States of America*, New York: Macmillan, 1904, p. 105.

54. Elson, p. 105.

55. Bridenbaugh, p. 441; Elson, pp. 104-105; "Massachusetts Bay Company," *Encyclopedia.com*, 2019, https://www.encyclopedia.com/history/united-states-and-canada/us-history/massachusetts-bay-company; "1629: Agreement of the Massachusetts Bay Company," *Online Library of Liberty*, 2019, https://oll.libertyfund.org/pages/1629-agreement-of-the-massachusetts-bay-company.

56. Bailyn, p. 371.

57. Elson, pp. 105-107.

58. Harris, p. 275; Melville Egleston, *The Land System of the New England Colonies*, Baltimore: N. Murray, Publication Agent, Johns Hopkins University, November and December 1886, included in Volume IV *Municipal Government and Land Tenure*, Herbert B. Adams ed., Baltimore: N. Murray, Publication Agent, Johns Hopkins University, 1886, pp. 18-19.

59. Egleston, p. 24-25; Harris, pp. 276-277.

60. Egleston, p. 27.

61. Virginia Dejohn Anderson, *New England's Generation: The Great Migration and the Formation of Society and Culture in the Seventeenth Century*, Cambridge: Cambridge University Press, 1991, pp. 31, 89-91; Egleston, pp. 27-28.

62. Egleston, pp. 29-30; Harris, p. 278-279; Anderson, pp. 92-99.

63. Anderson, pp. 93, 145, 147, 160-162, 172.

64. Harris, pp. 287-288.

65. Kenneth Lockridge, *A New England Town, the First Hundred Years*, New York: W.W. Norton, 1970, pp. 70-71.

66. Lockridge, pp. 71-72.

67. Family genealogy notes from Paul Cooper to the author. Jennie M. Holley (Scoville) and Homer Worthington Brainard, compilers, *Arthur Scovell and His Descendants in America, 1660-1900*, Rutland VT: The Tuttle Publishing Company, Inc., 1941. Reprinted by the Apple Manor Press, 2017, pp. 1-5.

68. Harris, pp. 113-114; "Charter of Connecticut-1662," 2019, *The Avalon Project, Lillian Goldman Law library, Yale Law School*, https://avalon.law.yale.edu/17th_century/ct03.asp.

69. Harris, pp. 109-112; "Charter of Rhode Island and Providence Plantations, July 15, 1663," 2019, *The Avalon Project, Lillian Goldman Law library, Yale Law School*, https://avalon.law.yale.edu/17th_century/ri04.asp.

70. Harris, p. 117; John Hrastar, *Breaking the Appalachian Barrier: Maryland as the Gateway to Ohio and the West, 1750-1850*, Jefferson NC: McFarland, 2018, pp. 34-43.

71. "The Charter of Maryland: 1632," 2019, *The Avalon Project, Lillian Goldman Law library, Yale Law School*, https://avalon.law.yale.edu/17th_century/ma01.asp.

72. Aubrey C. Land, *Colonial Maryland: A History*, Millwood, New York: kto press, A U.S. Division of Kraus-Thompson Organization Limited, 1981, p. 23.

73. Land, p. 23.

74. Newton D. Mereness, *Maryland as a Proprietary Province*, New York: The Macmillan Company, 1901, p. 50.

75. Aubrey C. Land, "Provincial Maryland," Chapter One in *Maryland: A History, 1632-1974*, edited by Richard Walsh and William Lloyd Fox, Baltimore: Maryland Historical Society, 1974, p. 9.

76. Land, "Provincial Maryland," p. 10.

77. David Hackett Fischer, *Albion's Seed: Four British Folkways in America*, New York: Oxford University Press, 1989, p. 459.

78. Fischer, p. 566; "Delaware was administered as part of New York until 1682, when the duke of York (the future James II) ceded it to William Penn, who wanted it so that his colony of Pennsylvania could have access to the ocean." "Delaware, the Colony," *Encyclopædia Britannica*, 2019, https://www.britannica.com/place/Delaware-state/The-colony.

79. Richard S. Dunn, "William Penn and the Selling of Pennsylvania, 1681–1685," *Proceedings of the American Philosophical Society*, Vol. 127, No. 5 (Oct. 14, 1983), pp. 322–329, p. 325, https://www.jstor.org/stable/986501; Fischer, p. 566.

80. Fischer, p. 567; Dunn, p. 324; John E. Pomfret, "The First Purchasers of Pennsylvania, 1681–1700," *The Pennsylvania Magazine of History and Biography*, Vol. 809, No. 2 (April 1956), pp. 137–163, pp. 146–147.

81. "Estimate Population of American Colonies," https://web.viu.ca/davies/h320/population.colonies.htm.

82. Harris, pp. 125–126.

83. Harris, pp. 92–93.

84. Harris, p. 94.

85. Harris, p. 97.

86. Harris, p. 96.

87. Harris, p. 128.

88. Harris, pp. 129–132.

89. Harris, pp. 134–135.

90. John L. Bell, "Fundamental Constitutions," *NCPedia, The Encyclopedia of North Carolina, University of North Carolina Press*, 2019, https://www.ncpedia.org/fundamental-constitutions.

91. Harris, p. 40, 95.

92. Harris, p. 135.

93. Harris, p. 135.

94. Harris, pp. 135–136.

95. "Colonial Settlement, 1600–1763, Establishing the Georgia Colony, 1732–1750," *Library of Congress*, 2019, http://www.loc.gov/teachers/classroommaterials/presentationsandactivities/presentations/timeline/colonial/georgia/; Harris, p. 139.

96. Harris, p. 140.

Chapter Three

1. "The Population in the Colonial and Continental Periods," 2019, p. 9, https://www.census.gov/history/pdf/colonialbostonpops.pdf; Wesley Frank Craven, *Dissolution of the Virginia Company: The Failure of a Colonial Experiment*, Gloucester MA: Peter Smith, 1964, pp. 300–303; "History of Immigration, 1620–1783," 2019, https://immigrationtounitedstates.org/548-history-of-immigration-1620-1783.html.

2. "The Population in the Colonial and Continental Periods," p. 10.

3. "The Population in the Colonial and Continental Periods," p. 10.

4. Thomas Malthus, *An Essay on the Principle of Population*, London: Printed for J. Johnson, in St. Paul's Church-Yard, 1798, p. 7.

5. "The Second Charter of Virginia; May 23, 1609," 2020, *Yale Law School, Lillian Goldman Law Library, The Avalon Project*, https://avalon.law.yale.edu/17th_century/va02.asp.

6. W. Stitt Robinson, Jr., *Mother Earth, Land Grants in Virginia, 1607–1699*, Published by The Virginia 350th Anniversary Celebration Corporation, 1957, p. 11.

7. Marshall Harris, *The Origin of the Land Tenure System in the United States*, Ames: The Iowa State College Press, 1953, p. 86.

8. Harris, p. 91.

9. Alexander Brown, *The First Republic in America*, Boston: Houghton, Mifflin and Company, 1898, pp. 76–77.

10. "Nova Britannia: Offering Most Excellent Fruites by Planting in Virginia. Exciting all such as be well affected to further the same," London Printed for Samuel Macham, and are to be sold at his Shop in Pauls Churchyard, at the Signe of the Bul-head," 1609, http://www.virtualjamestown.org/exist/cocoon/jamestown/fha/J1051; Fairfax Harrison, *Virginia Land Grants: A Study of Conveyance in Relation to Colonial Politics*, Westminster MD: Heritage Books, 2007, pp. 12–13; Philip Alexander Bruce, *Economic History of Virginia in the Seventeenth Century*, New York: Macmillan, 1896, pp. 502–503.

11. Harris, p. 86.

12. Harris, p. 87; Robinson, pp. 14–15. Note: Harris has the date as 1618 instead of 1616.

13. Harris, p. 88; Brown, *The First Republic*, pp. 74–75.

14. Robinson, p. 16.

15. *A Brief Declaration of the Present State of Things in Virginia, and of a Division to Be Made, of Some Parts of Those Lands in our Actual Possession*, reprinted in Alexander Brown, *The Genesis of the United States Volume II*, Boston: Houghton, Mifflin and Company, 1897, pp. 775–779.

16. *A Brief Declaration of the Present State of Things in Virginia*, pp. 775–779.

17. Robinson, pp. 12, 30.
18. Harrison, p. 43; Brown, *The Genesis of the United States, Volume 1*, New York: Houghton, Mifflin and Company, The Riverside Press Cambridge, 1890, p. 471.
19. Brown, *The Genesis of the United States, Volume II*, New York: Houghton, Mifflin and Company, The Riverside Press Cambridge, 1897, p. 549 fn.
20. Brown, *Genesis, Vol. II*, p. 774; Harrison, p. 14. Note: The slight discrepancy in dates could be due to the date of the Codrington Bill of Adventure date, or the date of the Declaration acknowledged by Brown to be included within a range.
21. Bruce, pp. 509–511.
22. Robinson, p. 17.
23. Harris, p. 188. Note: Bruce claimed, "Certain associations of persons were allowed to engross enormous bodies of land in Virginia by purchasing many shares in the original Company, which carried with them the same privileges and the same obligations as those accompanying the purchase of a single share" (Bruce, p. 505). This is misleading. The shares were the same price as the company shares but were outside the company.
24. Robinson, p. 17; Harris, pp. 188–189.
25. Wesley Frank Craven, *Dissolution of the Virginia Company: The Failure of a Colonial Experiment*, Gloucester, MA: Peter Smith, 1964, p. 57–58.
26. Charles E. Hatch, *The First Seventeen Years, Virginia, 1607–1624*, Charlottesville: The University of Virginia Press, 1957, 1991 printing, http://www.gutenberg.org/files/30780/30780-h/30780-h.htm, p. 20; Robinson, pp. 17–20.
27. Craven, pp. 58–59; Harris, pp. 188–189; "Instructions to Governor Yeardley, 1618," *The Virginia Magazine of History and Biography*, Vol. 2, No. 2 (Oct. 1894), p. 160, https://www.jstor.org/stable4241805; W. Stitt Robinson, Jr., *Mother Earth: Land Grants in Virginia, 1607–1699*, Published by 350th Anniversary Celebration Corporation, 1957. p. 19.
28. Harris, pp. 188–190.
29. Bernard Bailyn, *The Barbarous Years: The Conflict of Civilizations, 1600–1675*, New York: Vintage Books, 2013, p. 111; Bruce, pp. 507–508; Harris, pp. 188–190; "The Population in the Colonial and Continental Periods," 2019, p. 9.
30. Robinson, pp. 17–20.
31. Craven, pp. 60–63.
32. Craven, p. 45, 59.
33. Harrison, p. 10.
34. Hatch, p. 21.
35. "Instructions to Governor Yeardley, 1618," *The Virginia Magazine of History and Biography*, Vol. 2, No. 2 (Oct. 1894), pp. 154–165, https://www.jstor.org/stable/4241805?seq=1#metadata_info_tab_contents.
36. Craven, pp. 54–56; Hatch, p. 22; Robinson, pp. 21–22; "Instructions to Governor Yeardley, 1618," *The Virginia Magazine of History and Biography*, Vol. 2, No. 2 (Oct. 1894), pp. 156–157, https://www.jstor.org/stable/4241805?seq=1#metadata_info_tab_contents.
37. "Instructions to Governor Yeardley," p. 161.
38. "Instructions to Governor Yeardley," p. 163–164.
39. "Instructions to Governor Yeardley," p. 164.
40. Bruce, p. 512–514; Harrison, pp. 16–17; "Instructions to Governor Yeardley," pp. 164–165.
41. Harrison, pp. 16–17; "Instructions to Governor Yeardley," pp. 164–165.
42. Bruce, p. 512–514.
43. Robinson, p. 40–41.
44. Edmond S. Morgan, "The First American Boom: Virginia, 1618–1630," *The William and Mary Quarterly*, Vol. 28, No. 2 (Apr. 1971), pp. 169–198, p. 176, https://www.jstor.org/stable/1917308.
45. Bailyn, p. 165.
46. Brendan Wolfe and Martha McCartney, "Indentured Servants in Colonial Virginia," *Encyclopedia Virginia*, October 28, 2015, https://encyclopediavirginia.org/entries/indentured-servants-in-colonial-virginia/.
47. Bailyn, p. 166–167.
48. Morgan, p. 184.
49. Morgan, p. 183.
50. Bailyn, p. 173.
51. Bailyn, p. 165. Note: Middlesex County is between the Rappahannock and York rivers.
52. Robinson, p. 39; Wolfe and McCartney, "Indentured Servants."
53. Morgan, p. 176, 179.
54. Thomas J. Wertenbaker, *The Planters of Colonial Virginia*, Princeton: Princeton University Press, 1922. pp. 29–30.

55. Allan Kulikoff, *From British Peasants to Colonial American Farmers*, Chapel Hill: The University of North Carolina Press, 2000, p. 57; "The Cavalier Flight to Virginia," July 13, 2016, https://britishheritage.com/the-cavalier-flight-to-virginia; David Hackett Fischer and James C. Kelly, *Bound Away: Virginia and the Westward Movement*, Charlottesville: University of Virginia Press, 2000, pp. 35–37.
56. "The Population in the Colonial and Continental Periods," 2019, p. 9.
57. Fischer and Kelly, p. 28.
58. Bruce, p. 589.
59. Wertenbaker, p. 35.
60. Wertenbaker, p. 41.
61. Wertenbaker, p. 45.
62. Kulikoff, pp. 71, 74.
63. Wertenbaker, p. 43.
64. Wertenbaker, p. 71.
65. Wertenbaker, p. 46.
66. Wertenbaker, p. 75.
67. Wertenbaker, pp. 73–74.
68. Richard Middleton, *Colonial America: A History, 1607-1760*, Cambridge, MA: Blackwell, 1992, p. 81.
69. Fischer and Kelley, p. 95.
70. Wertenbaker, p. 84; "Navigation Acts, United Kingdom." *Encyclopædia Britannica*, 2020, https://www.britannica.com/event/Navigation-Acts.
71. Middleton, pp. 116–117.
72. Wertenbaker, p. 97.
73. Wertenbaker, p. 124; Middleton, p. 188.
74. Harrison, pp. 48–50; Harris, pp. 190–191.
75. Wertenbaker, pp. 108, 126, 137.
76. Fischer and Kelly, p. 8.
77. Fischer and Kelly, p. 299.
78. Fischer and Kelly, p. 75.
79. Wertenbaker, pp. 139–140.
80. Wertenbaker, pp. 141–142.
81. Fischer and Kelly, p. 47, 137; Wertenbaker, p. 140.
82. Fischer and Kelly, pp. 214–215.
83. Fischer and Kelly, p. 215.
84. "The Population in the Colonial and Continental Periods," 2019, p. 9.
85. Glenn T. Trewartha, "Types of Rural Settlement in Colonial America," *Geographical Review*, Vol. 36, No. 4 (Oct. 1946), pp. 568–596, p. 568, https://www.jstor.org/stable/211416.
86. Fischer and Kelly, p. 75.
87. Trewartha, p. 574.
88. David Grayson Allen, "*Vacuum Domicilium*: The Social and Cultural Landscape of Seventeenth Century New England," 2020, http://memorialhall.mass.edu/classroom/curriculum_12th/unit1/lesson2/allen.html.
89. Lois Kimball Mathews, *The Expansion of New England: The Spread of New England Settlement and Institutions to the Mississippi River, 1620-1865*, Boston: Houghton Mifflin company, 1909, pp. 27–29.
90. Mathews, p. 27.
91. Kulikoff, p. 114.
92. Mathews, p. 16.
93. Mathews, pp. 33–34.
94. Mathews, p. 54.
95. Mathews, p. 71.
96. Family genealogy notes from Paul Cooper to the author. Jennie M. Holley (Scoville) and Homer Worthington Brainard, compilers, *Arthur Scovell and His Descendants in America, 1660-1900*, Rutland VT: The Tuttle Publishing Company, Inc., 1941, Reprinted by the Apple Manor Press, 2017, pp. 1–5.
97. Trewartha, p. 578.
98. Trewartha, p. 579.
99. Mathews, p. 81.
100. Mathews, p. 85.
101. Eugene Irving McCormac, *White Servitude in Maryland, 1634-1820*, Baltimore: Johns Hopkins Press, 1904, pp. 11–13.
102. Russell R. Menard, *Economy and Society in Early Colonial Maryland*, New York: Garland Publishing, 1985, p. 117.
103. Abbot Emerson Smith, "The Indentured Servant and Land Speculation in Seventeenth Century Maryland," *The American Historical Review*, Vol. 40, No. 3 (Apr. 1935), pp. 467–472, p. 468.
104. Smith, p. 468.
105. McCormac, p. 22; Newton D. Mereness, *Maryland as a Proprietary Province*, New York: Macmillan, 1901, pp. 50–51.
106. John E. Pomfret, "The First Purchasers of Pennsylvania, 1681-1700," *The Pennsylvania Magazine of History and Biography*, Vol. 80, No. 2 (Apr. 1956), pp. 137–163, p. 147, www.jstor.org/stable/200088845.
107. Pomfret, p. 147.
108. Pomfret, p. 148.
109. Thomas J. Sugrue, "The Peopling and Depeopling of Early Pennsylvania:

Indians and Colonists, 1680-1720," *The Pennsylvania Magazine of History and Biography*, Vol. 116, No. 1 (Jan. 1992), pp. 3-31, pp. 17, 19, 20, https://www.jstor.org/stable/20092669.
  110. Sugrue, pp. 26-27.
  111. Charles Albert Lewis Jr., family genealogy provided by Mr. Lewis to the author; "John Gilpin," http://www.pa-roots.com/~armstrong/beeersproject/g/gilpinj.html 2002; Fischer, *Albion's Seed: Four British Folkways in America*, New York: Oxford University Press, 1989, p. 430.
  112. Charles Albert Lewis Jr., family genealogy provided by Mr. Lewis to the author.
  113. Harris, p. 227; Wesley Frank Craven, *The Southern Colonies in the Seventeenth Century, 1607-1689*, Louisiana State University Press, The Littlefield Fund for Southern History of the University of Texas, 1949, pp. 319-321, pp. 329-331.
  114. Stanley L. Engermann and Kenneth L. Sokoloff, "Once Upon a Time in the Americas: Land and Immigration Policies in the New World," *National Bureau of Economic Research: Understanding Long-Run Economic Growth: Geography, Institutions, and Knowledge Economy*, Conference date: November 7-8, 2008, Published August 2011 by University of Chicago Press. p. 16, http://www.nber.org/chapters/c11994.
  115. Engermann and Sokoloff, p. 18.
  116. Engermann and Sokoloff, p. 20.
  117. Engermann and Sokoloff, p. 17.
  118. Engermann and Sokoloff, pp. 17, 26.

Chapter Four

  1. "The Population in the Colonial and Continental Periods," 2019, p. 9, https://www.census.gov/history/pdf/colonialbostonpops.pdf.
  2. Ben Johnson, "The UK and Great Britain—What's the Difference?" *Historic UK*, 2020, https://www.historic-uk.com/HistoryUK/HistoryofBritain/The-UK-Great-Britain-Whats-the-Difference/.
  3. Aaron Spencer Fogleman, *Hopeful Journeys: German Immigration, Settlement, and Political Culture in Colonial America, 1717-1775*. Philadelphia: University of Pennsylvania Press, 1996, p. 17.
  4. "The Population in the Colonial and Continental Periods," 2019, p. 9.
  5. Philip Otterness, "The 1709 Palatine Migration and the Formation of German Immigrant Identity in London and New York," *Pennsylvania History: A Journal of Mid-Atlantic Studies*, Vol. 66, Explorations in Early American Culture (1999), pp. 8-23, pp. 8, 9, 17, 19, https://jstor.org/stable27774234.
  6. Fogleman, p. 44; Marianne S. Wokeck, "Part Four: German Settlements in the British North American Colonies: A Patchwork of Cultural Assimilation and Persistence," *In Search of Peace and Prosperity: New German Settlements in Eighteenth-Century Europe and America*, edited by Hartmut Lehman, Hermann Wellenreuther, and Renate Wilson, University Park, PA: The Pennsylvania State University Press, 2000, p. 201.
  7. Fogleman, p. 31.
  8. Fogleman, p. 35.
  9. Fogleman, pp. 37-38.
  10. Fogleman, p. 38.
  11. Fogleman, pp. 44-45.
  12. Fogleman, p. 45-46.
  13. R. W. Kelsey, "Exploring Diversity in Pennsylvania History: An Early Description of Pennsylvania," *The Historical Society of Pennsylvania, the Sower Letter*, 2021, https://hsp.org.
  14. Fogleman, p. 45-46.
  15. Fogleman, pp. 90-91; Wokeck, pp. 202-203.
  16. Wokeck, p. 205.
  17. James G. Leyburn, *The Scotch-Irish: A Social History*, Chapel Hill: The University of North Carolina Press, 1962, p. 201.
  18. Warren R. Hofstra, "'The Extensions of His Majesties Dominions': The Virginia Backcountry and the Reconfiguration of Imperial Frontiers," *The Journal of American History*, Vol. 84, No. 4 (Mar. 1998), pp. 1281-1312, pp. 1282-1283.
  19. "How Colonists Acquired Land in Virginia," 2020, http://www.virginiaplaces.org/settleland/headright.html#eight.
  20. Hofstra, "The Extensions of His Majesties Dominions," p. 1291.
  21. Hofstra, "The Extensions of His Majesties Dominions," 1292.
  22. Warren R. Hofstra, *The Planting of New Virginia: Settlement and Landscape in the Shenandoah Valley*, Baltimore: The

Johns Hopkins University Press, 2004, p. 114.

23. Hofstra, "The Extensions of His Majesties Dominions," p. 1298.

24. Hofstra, "The Extensions of His Majesties Dominions," p. 1298.

25. Hofstra, "The Extensions of His Majesties Dominions," p. 1298.

26. Hofstra, "The Extensions of His Majesties Dominions," p. 1298.

27. Charles E. Kemper, "The Early Westward Movement of Virginia, 1722–1734," *The Virginia Magazine of History and Biography*, Vol. 13, No. 2, October 1905, pp. 113–134; Hofstra, "The Extensions of His Majesties Dominions," p. 1296.

28. "The Fairfax Grant," 2020, http://www.virginiaplaces.org/settleland/fairfaxgrant.html; Hofstra, "The Extensions of His Majesties Dominions," p. 1299.

29. Kemper, pp. 129–137.

30. John Hrastar, *Breaking the Appalachian Barrier: Maryland as the Gateway to Ohio and the West, 1750–1850*, Jefferson, NC: McFarland, 2018, pp. 55; Frank W. Porter, III, "From Backcountry to County: The Delayed Settlement of Western Maryland," *Maryland Historical Magazine*, Vol. 70, No. 4 (Winter 1975), p. 334.

31. Aubrey C. Land, "A Land Speculator in the Opening of Western Maryland," *Maryland Historical Magazine*, Vol. 48, No. 3 (September 1953), pp. 196–198; Hrastar, p. 55.

32. Aubrey C Land., *Colonial Maryland: A History*, Millwood, New York: kto press, A U.S. Division of Krauss-Thomson Organization Limited, 1981, p. 200.

33. Hrastar, p. 57.

34. Hrastar, pp. 54–57.

35. Robert W. Ramsey, *Carolina Cradle: Settlement of the Northwest Carolina Frontier, 1747–1762*, Chapel Hill: The University of North Carolina Press, 1964, pp. 172–175.

36. Fischer, *Albion's Seed: Four British Folkways in America*, New York: Oxford University Press, 1989, pp. 608, 618; Bernard Bailyn, *Voyagers to the West: A Passage in the Peopling of America on the Eve of the Revolution*, New York: Alfred A. Knopf, 1986, p. 26.

37. Fischer, p. 623.

38. Fischer, p. 628.

39. Fischer, pp. 623–628; Leyburn, pp. 3–13.

40. Leyburn, pp. 83–84.

41. Leyburn, pp. 12–13; Fischer, p. 624.

42. Henry Jones Ford, *The Scotch-Irish in America*, Princeton: Princeton University Press, 1915, p. 21.

43. Ford, pp. 28–32.

44. Leyburn, pp. 99–101.

45. Charles A. Hanna, *The Scotch-Irish or The Scot in North Britain, North Ireland, and North America, Volume I*, New York: G.P. Putnam's Sons, The Knickerbocker Press, 1902. p. 502.

46. Leyburn, p. 159; Hanna, p. 614; Ford, p. 185.

47. Leyburn, pp. 162–163; Hanna, p. 148; Philip Bagenal, *The American Irish and Their Influence on Irish Politics*, London: Kegan Paul, Trench & Co., 1882, p. 7.

48. Leyburn, p. 164, 168; Hanna, p. 148; Ford, p. 187.

49. Hanna, p. 621–622.

50. Leyburn, pp. 169–174; Ford, p. 198.

51. Ford, p. 192; Leyburn, p. 185.

52. The southern boundary for the Pennsylvania grant had been inadvertently laid out south of the Maryland northern boundary. This resulted in a hotly contested strip between Pennsylvania and Maryland. Had the original boundary of Maryland held, Philadelphia would have been in Maryland. The Penns won the boundary dispute which was settled by the famous Mason-Dixon survey many years later.

53. Ford, pp. 264, 291; Hanna, p. 63.

54. Ford, p. 271; Hanna, p. 63.

55. Augustus C. Buell, *William Penn as the Founder of Two Commonwealths*, New York: D. Appleton and Company, 1904, p. 122.

56. James M. Fullerton, "Squatters and Titles to Land in Early Western Pennsylvania," *Western Pennsylvania Historical Magazine*, Vol. 6, No. 3, July 1923, pp. 165–176, pp. 169, 174; Leyburn, pp. 191–198, p. 205.

57. James Curtis Ballagh, "I–Introduction to Southern Economic History—The Land System," *Annual Report of the American Historical Association-the Year 1897*, Washington: The Government Printing Office, 1898, pp. 112–113. https://play.google.com/books/reader?id=xK4UAAAAYAAJ&printsec=frontcover&pg=GBS.PA112.

58. Fullerton, pp. 174–175.
59. Andro Linklater, *Owning the Earth: The Transforming History of Land Ownership*, New York: Bloomsbury, 2013, pp. 1–6.
60. Fullerton, p. 169.
61. Leyburn, p. 172.
62. Kemper, pp. 123–124 fn; Leyburn, pp. 201–204.
63. Wayland Fuller Dunaway, "Pennsylvania as an Early Distributing Center for Population," *Pennsylvania Magazine of History and Biography*, Vol. 55, No. 2 (1931), pp. 134–159, p. 144, https://www.jstor.org/stable20086765.
64. Leyburn, p. 205.
65. Colin Woodard, *American Nations: A History of the Eleven Rival Regional Cultures of North America*, New York: Viking, 2011, pp. 101–115.
66. "NC Land Records before 1800: 1663–1775," *State Library of North Carolina*, 2020, https://statelibrary.ncdcr.libguides.com/nclandrecords1800/1663-1775; Walbert, David, "Land Ownership and Labor in Carolina," Anchor, North Carolina History Online Resource, https://www.ncpedia.org/anchor/land-ownership-and-labor#:~:text=Headrights%20gave%20100%20acres%20of,per%20head%2C%20or%20per%20person.
67. Leyburn, p. 211.
68. Leyburn, p. 215.
69. Lewis family genealogy.
70. Lewis family genealogy.
71. Robert W. Ramsey, *Carolina Cradle: Settlement of the Northwest Carolina Frontier, 1747–1762*, Chapel Hill: The University of North Carolina Press, 1964, p. 40.
72. "North Carolina Land Grant Images and Data," 2020, http://www.nclandgrants.com/index/; Ramsey, p. 40; Lewis family genealogy on the Brandon family.
73. Lewis family genealogy.
74. Thomas Perkins Abernethy, *Western Lands and the American Revolution*, New York: Russell & Russell, 1959, p. 2.
75. Harriet Martineau, *Society in America, Two Volumes in One*, Paris: Baudry's European Library, 1842, pp. 203, 231.
76. Ray Allen Billington, "The Origin of the Land Speculator as a Frontier Type," *Agricultural History*, Vol. 19, No. 4 (Oct. 1945), pp. 204–212, p. 205.
77. Billington, p. 210.
78. Otis Rice, *West Virginia; A History*, Lexington: The University of Kentucky Press, 1985, pp. 20–21; Kenneth R. Bailey, "Greenbrier Company," 2013, https://www.wvencyclopedia.org/articles/2166.
79. Rice, p. 19.
80. Rice, p. 19; Stephen G. Smith, "Loyal Company," 2013, https://www.wvencyclopedia.org/articles/1462. Note: This John Lewis was not related to the Lewis family mentioned peviously.
81. Kenneth P. Bailey, *The Ohio Company of Virginia and the Westward Movement, 1748–1792*, Glendale, CA: Arthur H. Clark, 1939 *passim* (Reprinted by Isha, New Delhi, 2013); Hrastar, pp. 62–77.
82. Bailey, *passim*; Hrastar, p. 63.
83. Hrastar, pp. 69–73.
84. Lois Mulkearn, compiler and editor, *George Mercer Papers: Relating to the Ohio Company of Virginia*, Pittsburgh: University of Pittsburgh Press, 1954, p. 246. Spelling as in the original; Fred Anderson, *Crucible of War: The Seven Years' War and the Fate of Empire in British North America, 1754–1766*, New York: Alfred Knopf, 2000, p. 23.
85. Lois Mulkearn, "Why the Treaty of Logstown, 1752," *Virginia Magazine of History and Biography*, Vol. 59, No. 1 (Jan. 1951), pp. 3–20, p. 4, http://www.jstor.com/stable4245750.
86. Mulkearn, "Why the Treaty of Logstown, 1752," p. 7.
87. Hrastar, pp. 79–80.
88. David, B. Trimble, "Christopher Gist and Settlement on the Monongahela, 1752–1754," *The Virginia Magazine of History and Biography*, Vol. 63, No. 1 (Jan. 1955), pp. 15–27, 17–18, https://www.jstor.org/stable/4246087.
89. Trimble, pp. 19–21; Hrastar, pp. 92–93.
90. Billington, p. 206.
91. Billington, p. 207; Shaw Livermore, *Early American Land Companies: Their Influence on Corporate Development*, New York: The Commonwealth Fund, Oxford University Press, 1939, pp. 84–85.
92. Livermore, pp. 83–87; Hrastar, p. 105; "Charter of Connecticut, 1662," *The Avalon Project, Yale Law School Lillian Goldman Law Library*, 2020, https://avalon.law.yale.edu/17th_century/ct03.asp.
93. Anderson, pp. 78–79; The Pennsyl-

vania claim is described with different borders in another reference: "Proceedings of the Albany Congress, 19 June 1754–11 July 1754," *Founders Online National Archives*, https://founders.archives.gov/documents/Franklin/01-05-02-0096.

94. "Albany Plan of Union, 1754," *Department of State, Office of the Historian*, 2020, https://history.state.gov/milestones/1750-1775/albany-plan.

95. Benjamin Franklin, *The Complete Works in Philosophy, Politics, and Morals of the Late Dr. Benjamin Franklin, Vol. III*, London: Printed for J. Johnson, St. Paul's Church-Yard; and Longman, Hurst, Rees, and Orme, Paternoster-Row, 1806, pp. 41–42.

96. Franklin, pp. 43–45.

97. Franklin, p. 45.

98. "The Population in the Colonial and Continental Periods," 2019, p. 9.

99. Richard Hofstadter, *America at 1750: A Social Portrait*, New York: Alfred A. Knopf, 1974, p. 17.

100. Hofstadter, pp. 135, 160–161.

Chapter Five

1. Fred Anderson, *Crucible of War: The Seven Years' War and the Fate of Empire in British North America, 1754–1766*, New York: Alfred A. Knopf, 2000, p. 11.

2. Anderson, p. 11; "American Colonies: Contest with France," *Encyclopædia Britannica*, 2020, https://www.britannica.com/topic/American-colonies/The-contest-with-France.

3. The present-day Canadian Atlantic provinces.

4. "Charter of Acadia Granted by Henry IV of France to Pierre du Gast, Sieur de Monts; December 18, 1603," *Avalon Project, Yale Law School, Lillian Goldman Law Library*, 2020, https://avalon.law.yale.edu/17th_century/charter_001.asp; David Hackett Fischer, *Champlain's Dream*, New York: Simon & Schuster, 2008, pp. 221–222.

5. Fischer, *Champlain's Dream*, p. 405.

6. "Louis, XIII, King of France," *Encyclopædia Britannica*, 2020, https://www.britannica.com/biography/Louis-XIII.

7. John Boyko, "Company of One hundred Associates," *The Canadian Encyclopedia*, 2020, https://www.thecanadian encyclopedia.ca/en/article/compagnie-des-cent-associes; "Louis XIII, King of France," *The Encyclopædia Britannica*, 2020, https://www.britannica.com/biography/Louis-XIII.

8. R. Cole Harris, *The Seigneurial System in Early Canada: A Geographical Study*, Madison: University of Wisconsin Press, 1966, p. viii.

9. Harris, pp. 3–4.

10. Jacques Mathieu, "Seigneurial System," *The Canadian Encyclopedia*, 2020, https://www.thecanadianencyclopedia.ca/en/article/seigneurial-system#.

11. Harris, p. 193.

12. Charles Prestwood Lucas, *A Historical Geography of the British Colonies, Vol. V, Canada-Part I (New France)*, Oxford: Clarendon Press, 1901, p. 338.

13. "Early French Settlements, 1606–1691," *Statistics Canada*, 2020, https://www150.statcan.gc.ca/n1/pub/98-187-x/4064812-eng.htm#:~:text=1663%2D%2DPopulation%20of%20New,whom%20800%20were%20in%20Quebec.; "Filles du Roi," *The Canadian Encyclopedia*, 2020, https://thecanadianencyclopedia.ca/en/article/filles-du-roi.

14. Andre Vachon, "Talon, Jean," *Dictionary of Canadian Biography*, 2020, http://www.biographi.ca/en/bio/talon_jean_1E.html; Jack and Claire Nisbet, "Hudson's Bay Company," *HistoryLink.org*, 2020, https://www.historylink.org/File/9881.

15. Vachon, "Talon, Jean."

16. Francis Parkman, *La Salle and the Discovery of the Great West*, Boston: Little, Brown, and Company, 1879 p. 43.

17. George Thorton Fleming, *History of Pittsburgh and Environs: From Prehistoric Days to the Beginning of the American Revolution*, Volume One, New York: American Historical Society, 1922, pp. 157–158.

18. Parkman, p. 22; Celine Dupre, "Cavelier de la Salle, Rene-Robert," *Dictionary of Canadian Biography*, 2020, http://www.biographi.ca/en/bio/cavelier_de_la_salle_rene_robert_1E.html.

19. Parkman, p. 23; Jean Talon, Cavelier de la Salle, Rene-Robert; Vachon, Andre, "Jolliet, Louis," *Dictionary of Canadian Biography*, 2020, http://www.biographi.ca/en/bio/jolliet_louis_1E.html.

20. Lucas, p. 36.

21. Frank E. Ross, "The Fur Trade of the

Ohio Valley," *Indiana Magazine of History*, Vol. 34, No. 4 (December 1938), pp. 417–442, p. 417, http://www.jstor.com/stable/27787012.

22. "Estimated Population of Canada, 1605 to Present," *Statistics Canada*, 2020, https://www150.statcan.gc.ca/n1/pub/98-187-x/4151287-eng.htm; "Population in the Colonial and Continental Periods," 2020, p. 9, https://www.census.gov/history/pdf/colonialbostonpops.pdf.

23. Anderson, p. 17; The Ohio country was considered to be anything west of the mountains. The Ohio Valley is the valley of the Ohio River. For this time period they can be used interchangeably.

24. Anderson, p. 24.

25. Albert T. Volwiler, "George Croghan and the Westward Movement, 1741–1782, I. The Indian Trader," Reprint from *The Pennsylvania Magazine of History and Biography*, Vol. 46, No. 4, October 1922, p. 4.

26. Berthold Fernow, *The Ohio Valley in Colonial Days*, Albany, NY: Joel Munsell's Sons, Publishers, 1890, pp. 91–92.

27. Volwiler, p. 26.

28. Volwiler, p. 6.

29. Fernow, p. 85.

30. C. P. Galbreath, ed., *Expedition of Celoron to the Ohio Country in 1749*, Columbus, OH: F.J. Heer, 1921, pp. 13–18; John Hrastar, *Breaking the Appalachian Barrier: Maryland as the Gateway to Ohio and the West, 1750–1850*, Jefferson, NC: McFarland, 2018, pp. 80–82.

31. Galbreath, p. 33.

32. Galbreath, pp. 34–35.

33. Galbreath, *passim*.

34. Galbreath, pp. 57–58.

35. Galbreath, p. 9.

36. Anderson, p. 25–26; Douglas R. Hurt, *The Ohio Frontier: Crucible of the Old Northwest, 1720–1830*, Bloomington: University of Indiana Press, 1996, pp. 33–34.

37. Anderson, pp. 28–29; Hurt, pp. 33–34.

38. Anderson, p. 32.

39. Anderson, p. 32.

40. Kenneth P. Bailey, *The Ohio Company of Virginia and the Westward Movement, 1748–1792, A Chapter in the History of the Colonial Frontier*, Glendale, CA: Arthur Clarke, 1939, p. 202 (Reprinted by Isha, New Delhi, 2013).

41. Anderson, pp. 44–45.

42. Anderson, Chapter 5.

43. Anderson, pp. 72–73.

44. Bernard Bailyn, *Voyagers to the West: A Passage in the Peopling of America on the Eve of Revolution*, New York: Alfred A. Knopf, 1986, p. 7.

45. Bailyn, pp. 20, 26.

46. Anderson, p. 525.

47. Michael N. McConnell, *A Country Between: The Upper Ohio Valley and Its Peoples, 1724–1774*, Lincoln: University of Nebraska Press, 1992, pp. 161, 167.

48. Anderson, p. 524.

49. Douglas Brymner, archivist, *Report on Canadian Archives, 1889*. Ottawa, Printed by Brown Chamberlain, Printer to the Queen's Most Excellent Majesty, 1890, p. 73; Jack M. Sosin, *Whitehall and the Wilderness, The Middle West in British Colonial Policy, 1760–1775*, Lincoln: University of Nebraska Press, 1961, pp. 42–48.

50. Anderson, p. 526.

51. Lois Mulkearn, ed., *George Mercer Papers Relating to the Ohio Company of Virginia*, Pittsburgh: The University of Pittsburgh Press, 1954, p. 395.

52. Bailey, pp. 224–227; Eugene M. Del Papa. "The Royal Proclamation of 1763: Its Effect Upon Virginia Land Companies," *The Virginia Magazine of History and Biography*, Vol. 83, No. 4 (Oct. 1975), pp. 406–411, p. 408; Mulkearn, pp. 614–615.

53. Del Papa, p. 410; Shaw Livermore, *Early American Land Companies: Their Influence on Corporate Development*, New York: The Commonwealth Fund, Oxford University Press, 1939, pp. 102–105.

54. Livermore, pp. 113–115; James Donald Anderson, "Vandalia: The First West Virginia?" *West Virginia History*, Vol. 40, No. 4 (Summer 1979), pp. 375–392, http://www.wvculture.org/history/journal_wvh/wvh40-4.html.

55. Thomas Perkins Abernethy, *Western Lands and the American Revolution*, New York: Russell & Russell, 1959, pp. 40–58.

56. Otis K. Rice. *West Virginia: A History*, Lexington: The University of Kentucky Press, 1985, p. 31.

57. Abernethy, pp. 40–58.

58. Abernethy, pp. 43, 57; Clarence Walworth n, *The Mississippi Valley in British Politic: A Study of the Trade, Land Speculation, and Experiments in Imperialism*

Culminating in the American Revolution, Volume II, Cleveland: The Arthur H. Clarke Company, 1917, Chapter V.
59. Abernethy, p. 126.
60. Abernethy, p. 124.
61. Livermore, p. 93.
62. C. Herbert Laub, "British Regulation of Crown Lands in the West, the Last Phase 1773-1775," *The William and Mary Quarterly*, Vol. 10, No. 1 (Jan. 1930), pp. 52-55, http://www.jstor.com/stable/1921753 p. 54; Sosin, p. 227.
63. Abernethy, pp. 123-135; Livermore, pp. 90-97.
64. George W. Ellis, and John E. Morris, *King Philip's War: Based on the Archives and Records of Massachusetts, Plymouth, Rhode Island and Connecticut, and Contemporary Letters and Accounts*, New York: The Grafton Press, 1906, p. 21; Jason W. Warren, "King Philip's War, *Encyclopædia Britannica*, 2020, https://www.britannica.com/event/King-Philips-War.
65. Daniel Strock, Jr., *Pictorial History of King Philip's War*, Boston: Horace Wentworth, 1851, pp. 47-48.
66. Warren, "King Philip's War."
67. Daniel Gilbert, "What Ye Indians Call 'Ye Hurry Walk,'" 2020, http://pabook2.libraries.psu.edu/palitmap/WalkingPurchase.html.
68. "Early Recognized Treaties with the American Indian Nations, Ratified Treaty #1: The Great Treaty of 1722 Between the Five nations, the Mahicans, and the Colonies of New York, Virginia, and Pennsylvania," 2020, p. 670, http://treatiesportal.unl.edu/earlytreaties/treaty.00001.html.
69. Francis Jennings, *The Ambiguous Iroquois Empire: The Covenant Chain Confederation of Indian Tribes with English Colonies from Its Beginning to the Lancaster Treaty of 1744*, New York: W.W. Norton, 1988, p. 295.
70. Jennings, p. 295.
71. Jennings, pp. 295, 298; "Early Recognized Treaties with the American Indian Nations, Ratified Treaty #1: The Great Treaty of 1722 Between the Five nations, the Mahicans, and the Colonies of New York, Virginia, and Pennsylvania," 2020, p. 671, http://treatiesportal.unl.edu/earlytreaties/treaty.00001.html.
72. "Early Recognized Treaties with American Indian nations, Ratified Treaty #3: A Treaty Held at the Town of Lancaster, June, 1744," p. 56, http://treatiesportal.unl.edu/earlytreaties/treaty.00003.html.
73. "Early Recognized Treaties with American Indian Nations, Ratified Treaty #3: A Treaty Held at the Town of Lancaster, June, 1744," p.56, http://treatiesportal.unl.edu/earlytreaties/treaty.00003.html 2020.
74. "The Treaty of Lancaster, 1744," *The Virginia Magazine of History and Biography*, Vol. 13, No. 2 (Oct. 1905), p. 142.
75. "The Treaty of Logg's Town, 1752," *The Virginia Magazine of History and Biography*, Vol. 13, No. 2 (Oct. 1905), p. 161.
76. "The Treaty of Logg's Town, 1752," *The Virginia Magazine of History and Biography*, Vol. 13, No. 2 (Oct. 1905), p. 168, 174; Bailey, pp. 136-137.
77. Bailey, p. 137.

Chapter Six

1. Lawrence Henry Gipson, "The American Revolution as an Aftermath of the Great War for the Empire, 1754-1763," *Political Science Quarterly*, Vol. 65, No. 1 (Mar. 1950), pp. 86-104, p. 86.
2. 2 Fred Anderson, *Crucible of War: The Seven Years' War and the Fate of Empire in British North America, 1754-1766*, New York: Alfred A. Knopf, 2000, pp. 94-96.
3. 3 Michael M. McConnell, *A Country Between: The Upper Ohio Valley and Its People, 1724-1774*, Lincoln: University of Nebraska Press, 1992, p. 122.
4. McConnell, p. 122.
5. John Hrastar, *Breaking the Appalachian Barrier: Maryland as the Gateway to Ohio and the West, 1750-1850*, Jefferson, NC: McFarland, 2018, pp. 102-104.
6. Anderson, p. 268.
7. Anderson, pp. 205-207, 277-278.
8. Anderson, pp. 277-278; Jack M. Sosin, *Whitehall and the Wilderness, The Middle West in British Colonial Policy, 1760-1775*, Lincoln: University of Nebraska Press, 1961, p. 32.
9. Colin G. Calloway, *The Scratch of a Pen: 1763 and the Transformation of North America*, New York: Oxford University Press, 2006, p. 61.
10. Calloway, pp. 66-67.
11. Calloway, pp. 99-100.
12. Anderson, pp. 473-474.

13. Anderson, pp. 529–534.
14. Calloway, p. 77, 79.
15. Anderson, pp. 535–538.
16. Calloway, p. 81.
17. Calloway, p. 24.
18. Clarence W. Alvord, *The Mississippi Valley in British Politics, Volume I*, New York: Russell & Russell, 1959, p. 106.
19. Thomas Curtis, "Riches, Real Estate, and Resistance: How Land Speculation, Debt, and Trade Monopolies Led to the American Revolution," *The American Journal of Economics and Sociology*, Vol. 73, No. 3 (July 2014), pp. 445–626, p. 496.
20. Gipson, p. 96.
21. "The Royal Proclamation, 1763," *University of Toronto Libraries*, 2020, https://exhibits.library.utoronto.ca/items/show/2470.
22. "The Royal Proclamation, 1763," *University of Toronto Libraries*, 2020; Clarence Walworth Alvord, "The Genesis of the Proclamation of 1763," *Michigan Historical Collections, Volume 36, Michigan Pioneer and Historical Society*, Lansing: Wyncoop, Hallenbeck, Crawford Company, 1908, p. 21, *ad passim*, https://quod.lib.umich.edu/cgi/t/text/text-idx?c=moa;idno=0534625.0036.001; "Treaty of Paris 1763," *Lillian Goldman Law Library, Yale Law School, The Avalon Project*, 2020, https://avalon.law.yale.edu/18th_century/paris763.asp.
23. R. Douglass Hurt, *The Ohio Frontier: Crucible of the Old Northwest, 1720–1830*, Bloomington: Indiana University Press, 1996, p. 55.
24. Alvord, "The Genesis of the Proclamation of 1763," p. 35.
25. Matthew L. Rhoades, "Blood and Backcountry: Virginia Backcountry Violence and the Origins of the Quebec Act, 1758–1775," *West Virginia History*, New Series, Vol. 3, No. 2 (Fall 2009), p. 10, https://www.jstor.org/stable/43265120.
26. George O. Virtue, "British Land Policy and the American Revolution: A Belated Lecture in Economic History," *University of Nebraska Studies*, New Series No. 11 (Sept. 1953), p. 2.
27. Woody Holton, "The Ohio Indians and the Coming of the American Revolution in Virginia," *The Journal of Southern History*, Vol. 60, No. 3 (Aug. 1994), pp. 453–478, p. 456, https://www.jstor.org/stable/2210989.
28. "From George Washington to William Crawford, 17 September 1767," *Founders Online*, 2020, https://founders.archives.gov/documents/Washington/02-08-02-0020.
29. Rhoades, pp. 11–13.
30. Holton, p. 454.
31. Clarence Walworth Alvord, *The Mississippi Valley in British Politics: A Study of the Trade, Land Speculation, and Experiments in Imperialism Culminating in the American Revolution, Volume II*, Cleveland: The Arthur H. Clark Company, 1917, p. 91.
32. Ray A. Billington, "The Fort Stanwix Treaty of 1768," *New York History*, Vol. 25, No. 2 (Apr. 1944), pp. 182–194, p. 183, http://www.jstor.org/stable/23147791.
33. Max Farrand, "The Indian Boundary Line," *American Historical Review*, Vol. 10, No. 4 (Jul. 1905), pp. 782–791, p. 786.
34. Thomas Perkins Abernethy, *Western Lands and the American Revolution*, New York: Russell & Russel, 1939, p. 61.
35. Billington, pp. 189–190.
36. Abernethy, p. 64.
37. Billington, p. 186.
38. Billington, pp. 191, 192; Peter Marshall, "Sir William Johnson and the Treaty of Fort Stanwix, 1768," *Journal of American Studies*, Vol. 1, No. 2 (Oct. 1967), pp. 149–179, p. 176, https://www.jstor.org/stable27552784; Alvord, *The Mississippi Valley in British Politics, Volume II*, p. 69.
39. Billington, p. 192, 193.
40. Billington, pp. 186–188; Alvord, *The Mississippi Valley in British Politics, Volume II*, p. 76.
41. Alvord, *The Mississippi Valley in British Politics, Volume II*, p. 78.
42. Alvord, *The Mississippi Valley in British Politics, Volume II*, p. 78; Curtis, p. 548; Marshall, p. 176.
43. Curtis, p. 536; Alvord, *The Mississippi Valley in British Politics, Volume II*, p. 77.
44. Holton, p. 458.
45. Holton, pp. 458–460; "George Washington to Charles Washington, January 31, 1770," 2020, https://babel.hathitrust.org/cgi/pt?id=mdp.39015008921101&view=1up&seq=51.
46. Holton, pp. 461–468.
47. Holton, p. 473.
48. Holton, pp. 473–474; Douglas Hurt,

The Ohio Frontier: Crucible of the Old Northwest, 1720–1830, Bloomington: Indiana University Press, 1998, p. 59; Michael N. McConnell, *A Country Between: The Upper Ohio Valley and Its Peoples, 1724–1774*, Lincoln: University of Nebraska Press, 1992, pp. 268–279; Philip Sturm, "Battle of Point Pleasant," *The West Virginia Encyclopedia*, 2020, http://www.wvencyclopedia.org/articles/1889.

49. Curtis, p. 548.
50. Curtis, p. 551.
51. Virtue, p. 39.
52. Curtis, p. 552.
53. Virtue, pp. 39–40 fn.
54. "The Boston Port Act: March 31, 1774," *Lillian Goldman Law Library, Yale Law School, The Avalon Project*, 2020, https://avalon.law.yale.edu/18th_century/boston_port_act.asp; Caroline Eisenhuth, "The Coercive (Intolerable) Acts of 1774," *George Washington's Mount Vernon*, https://www.mountvernon.org/library/digital history/digital-encyclopedia/article/the-coercive-intolerable-acts-of-1774/.
55. "The Massachusetts of Government Act: May 20, 1774," *Lillian Goldman Law Library, Yale Law School, The Avalon Project*, 2020, https://avalon.law.yale.edu/18th_century/mass_gov_act.asp; "The Administration of Government Act; May 20, 1774," *Lillian Goldman Law Library, Yale Law School, The Avalon Project*, 2020, https://avalon.law.yale.edu/18th_century/admin_of_justice_act.asp.
56. "The Quartering Act; June 2, 1774," *Lillian Goldman Law Library, Yale Law School, The Avalon Project*, 2020, https://avalon.law.yale.edu/18th_century/quartering_act_1774.asp.
57. Sosin, pp. 239–240.
58. Thomas Jefferson, "A Summary View of the Rights of British America," *Lillian Goldman Law Library, Yale Law School, The Avalon Project*, 2020, https://avalon.law.yale.edu/18th_century/jeffsumm.asp.
59. Jefferson, "A Summary View."
60. Jefferson, "A Summary View."
61. Virtue, p. 42.
62. "Declaration of Independence: A Transcription," *National Archives: America's Founding Documents*, 2020, https://www.archives.gov/founding-docs/declaration-transcript.
63. Rhoades, p. 20.
64. Curtis, pp. 554–556; "The Quebec Act: October 7, 1774," *Lillian Goldman Law Library, Yale Law School, The Avalon Project*, 2020, https://avalon.law.yale.edu/18th_century/quebec_act_1774.asp; For a map of the area see "British Possessions in North America, 1775," *MAPS ETC, https://etc.usf.edu/maps/pages/2400/2425/2425.htm* or Hrastar, Map 11.
65. Maxime Dagenais, "Quebec Act, 1774," *The Canadian Encyclopedia*, 2020, https://www.thecanadianencyclopedia.ca/en/article/quebec-act; "The Quebec Act: October 7, 1774," *Lillian Goldman Law Library*.
66. "The Quebec Act: October 7, 1774," *Lillian Goldman Law Library*.
67. "The Quebec Act: October 7, 1774," *Lillian Goldman Law Library*.
68. Holton, p. 475.
69. William Cobbett, ed., *The Parliamentary History of England from the Earliest Period to 1803*, Vol. 18, London: T.C. Hansard, pp. 656–657, https://www.google.com/books/edition/Cobbett_s_Parliamentary_History_of_Engla/kqQ9AQAAMAAJ?hl=en&gbpv=1&dq=cobbett+parliamentary+history+of+england+from+the+earliest+period+to+1803+Volume+18+london&pg=PP9&printsec=frontcover.
70. Cobbett, 478; Jefferson, "A Summary View"; Edmund Burke, "Burke's Speech on Conciliation with America," *Project Gutenberg EBook*, 2021, https://www.gutenberg.org/files/5655/5655-h/5655-h.htm.
71. Curtis, pp. 554–557.
72. Victor Coffin, "The Province of Quebec and the Early American Revolution: A Study in English-American Colonial History," *The Bulletin of the University of Wisconsin, Economics, Political Science, and History Series*, Vol. 1, No. 3 (June 1896), pp. 275–562, pp. 420–421.
73. Coffin, p. 423.
74. Rhoades, p. 23.
75. "Population in the Colonial and Continental Periods," 2020, p. 9, https://www.census.gov/history/pdf/colonialbostonpops.pdf.
76. "Tea Act," *Encyclopædia Britannica*, 2020, https://www.britannica.com/event/Tea-Act.
77. John C., Hamilton, ed., *The Works of Alexander Hamilton*, Vol. II, New York: John F. Trow, Printer, 1850, pp. 136–137,

https://www.google.com/books/edition/_/OENMAAAAcAAJ?gbpv=1.
78. Cobbett, p. 654.
79. Holton, p. 476, 477.
80. "Declarations and Resolves of the First Continental Congress," *Lillian Goldman Law Library, Yale Law School, The Avalon Project*, 2020, https://avalon.law.yale.edu/18th_century/resolves.asp.
81. Sosin, p. 243.
82. "British Possessions in North America, 1775," *MAPS ETC, https://etc.usf.edu/maps/pages/2400/2425/2425.htm* See also Map1.
83. Curtis, p. 571.
84. Coffin, p. 431.
85. "Virginia Resolutions on Lord North's Conciliatory Proposal, 10 June 1775," *Founders Online*, National Archives, https://founders.archives.gov/documents/Jefferson/01-01-02-0106.
86. "Constitution of Virginia; June 29, 1776," *The Avalon Project, Lillian Goldman Law Library, Yale Law School*, 2020, https://www.law.gmu.edu/assets/files/academics/founders/VA-Constitution.pdf.
87. Declaration of Independence.
88. "Land is Free," 2020, https://www.landisfree.co.uk/.
89. Beverley W. Bond Jr., "The Quit-Rent System in the American Colonies." *The American Historical Review*, Vol. 17, No. 3 (Apr. 1912), pp. 496–516, p. 496, https://www.jstor.org/stable/1834386.
90. Philip Alexander Bruce, *Economic History of Virginia in the Seventeenth Century, Volume I*, New York: Macmillan, 1896, pp. 556–557.
91. Calloway, p. 26.
92. Calloway, p. 28; Linda Colley, *Britons: Forging the Nation 1707–1837*, New Haven: Yale University Press, 1992, p. 103.
93. Jefferson, "A Summary View."
94. John Steinbeck, *The Grapes of Wrath*, New York: The Viking Press, 1939.
95. H.W. Brands, "Why Have Americans Always Been So Obsessed with the Land?" 2021, https://www.history.com/news/american-land-frontier#:~:text=Land%20symbolized%20opportunity%20to%20generations,its%20frontier%20drew%20them%20west.
96. Peter Epp, "How Property Ownership Led to the American Revolution," *Today's Farmer*, June 26, 2012, p. 6. Provided to the author by Paul Mahon of the *Ontario Farmer*, London, Ontario.
97. Gordon S. Wood, *The Radicalism of the American Revolution*, New York: Vintage Books, 1990, p. 234.

Epilogue

1. Thomas Perkins Abernethy, *Western Lands and the American Revolution*, New York: D. Appleton-Century Company, 1937, pp. 274–287; Reginald Horsman, Reginald, "On to Canada: Manifest Destiny and the United States Strategy in the War of 1812," *Michigan Historical Review*, Vol. 13, No. 2 (Fall 1987), pp. 1–24, p. 7, https://www.jstor.org/stable/20173101.
2. J. Franklin Jameson, *The American Revolution Considered as a Social Movement*, Princeton: Princeton University Press, 1926, eBook edition: Papamoa Press, 2017, pp. 39–41, https://play.google.com/books/reader?id=9RkkDwAAQBAJ&num=19&printsec=frontcover&pg=GBS.PT1.
3. Jameson, pp. 39–46.
4. Anne M. Ousterhout, "Pennsylvania Land Confiscations During the Revolution," *The Pennsylvania Magazine of History and Biography*, Vol. 102, No. 3 (Jul.1978), pp. 328–343, p. 339, https://www.jstor.org/stable/20091279.
5. Jameson, pp. 41–42.
6. Abernethy, pp. 166–167.
7. Abernethy, p. 218.
8. "III. Third Draft by Jefferson. [Before June 1776]," National Archives, Founders Online., 2021, https://founders.archives.gov/documents/Jefferson/01-01-02-0161-0004.
9. "Editorial Note: Bills for Establishing a Land Office and for Adjusting and Settling Titles," *National Archives-Founders Online*, 2021, https://founders.archives.gov/documents/Jefferson/01-02-02-0045-0001; Abernethy, p. 228.
10. Abernethy, pp. 162, 172; Michael A. Blaakman, "The Marketplace of American Federalism: Land Speculation Across State Lines in the Early Republic," *Journal of American History*, Vol. 107, Issue 3 (December 2020), pp. 583–608, pp. 585–586, 607–608, https://doi.org/10.1093/jahist/jaaa340.
11. John Hrastar, *Breaking the Appa-*

lachian Barrier: Maryland as the Gateway to Ohio and the West, 1750-1850, Jefferson, NC: McFarland, 2018, pp. 126, 127.

12. Hrastar, pp. 124-128.

13. Jameson, pp. 51-53.

14. Hrastar, p. 129.

15. George W. Knepper, *The Official Ohio Lands Book*, Columbus, OH: Publication of the Auditor of the State, 2002, pp. 7-13, www.auditor.state.oh.us; Hrastar, p. 131.

16. "Opportunity and Challenge: The Story of BLM (Chapter 1)," *National Park Service, Department of the Interior*, 2021, https://www.nps.gov/parkhistory/online_books/blm/history/chap1.htm.

17. Knepper, *The Official Ohio Lands Book*, p. 28; George W. Knepper, *Ohio and Its People, Bicentennial Edition*, Kent, OH: The Kent State University Press, 2003, p. 61; Morris Bien, "The Public Lands of the United States," *The North American Review*, Vol. 192, No. 658 (Sep. 1910) pp. 387-402, https://www.jstor.org/stable/25106763.

18. "Northwest Ordinance; July 13, 1787," *Avalon Project, Yale Law School, Lillian Goldman Library*, 2021, https://avalon.law.yale.edu/18th_century/nworder.asp; Hrastar, pp. 132-133; Reginald Horsman, "The Northwest Ordinance and the Shaping of an Expanding Republic," *The Wisconsin Magazine of History*, Vol. 73, No. 1 (Autumn 1989), pp. 21-32, p. 21, https://www.jstor.org/stable/4636235.

19. Malcom J. Rohrbough, *The Land Office Business: The Settlement and Administration of American Public Lands, 1789-1837*, New York: Oxford University Press, 1968, p. 17.

20. Acts of the Fourth Congress of the United States, Session 1, Statute 1, May 18, 1796, Chap. XXIX—An act providing for the sale of the Lands of the United States, in the territory northwest of the river Ohio, and above the mouth of the Kentucky river; Bien, p. 390; "Opportunity and Challenge: The Story of BLM (Chapter 1)."

21. Rorhbough, p. 18.

22. "Opportunity and Challenge: The Story of BLM (Chapter 1)"; Rorhbough, p. 18.

23. "Opportunity and Challenge: The Story of BLM (Chapter 1)"; Rorhbough, pp. 22, 23.

24. Richard Peters, ed., *Public Statutes at Large of the United States of America, Vol. III*, April 24, 1820, Chap. LI, Boston: Little and Brown, 1850, https://digitalcommons.csumb.edu/hornbeck_usa_2_d/; Gary M. Anderson and Dolores T. Martin, "The Public Domain and Nineteenth Century Transfer Policy," *Cato Journal*, Vol. 6, No. 3 (Winter 1987), p. 907-908.

25. Richard Peters, ed., *The Public Statutes at Large of the United States of America, Vol. V*, September 4, 1841, Chap, XVI, Boston: Charles C. Little and James Brown, 1846, https://digitalcommons.csumb.edu/hornbeck_usa_2_d/.

26. William G. Robbins, "Oregon Donation Land Law," *Oregon Encyclopedia*, 2021, https://www.oregonencyclopedia.org/articles/oregon_donation_land_act/#.YCQWWmhKiUk; "Land Claims," *End of the Oregon Trail: Historic Oregon City*, 2021, https://historicoregoncity.org/2019/04/03/land-claims/#:~:text=Married%20couples%20were%20allowed%20to,and%20accept%20or%20reject%20them; "The Donation Land Claim Act (1850)," 2021, https://pages.uoregon.edu/mjdennis/courses/hst469_donation.htm.

27. Lewis family genealogy.

28. "Opportunity and Challenge: The Story of BLM (Chapter 1)," 2021.

29. Anderson and Martin, p. 908.

30. The Homestead Act of 1862, 37th Congress Session II 1862, Chapter LXXV—An act to secure Homesteads to Actual Settlers on the Public Domain, https://digitalcommons.csumb.edu/cgi/viewcontent.cgi?article=1011&context=hornbeck_usa_2_d; https://www.nps.gov/home/learn/historyculture/abouthomesteadactlaw.htm; "Opportunity and Challenge: The Story of BLM (Chapter 1)," 2021.

31. "Opportunity and Challenge: The Story of BLM (Chapter 1)," 2021.

32. Eric Foner, *A Short History of Reconstruction: 1863-1877*, New York: Harper & Row, 1990, p. 32.

33. Anderson and Martin, p. 908; "The Museum Gazette: The Homestead Act of 1862," *Jefferson National Expansion Memorial, National Park Service, U.S. Department of the Interior*, 2021, https://www.nps.gov/jeff/learn/historyculture/upload/homestead.pdf.

Bibliography

Abernethy, Thomas Perkins, *Western Lands and the American Revolution*, New York: Russell & Russell, 1959.

Acts of the Fourth Congress of the United States, Session 1, Statute 1, May 18, 1796, Chap. XXIX—An act providing for the Sale of the Lands of the United States, in the territory northwest of the river Ohio, and above the mouth of the Kentucky river.

Adams, George Burton, "Anglo-Saxon Feudalism," *The American Historical Review*, Vol. 7, No. 1 (Oct. 1901), pp. 11–35, https://www.jstor.org/stable/1832530.

Adkin, Benaiah W., *Copyhold and Other Tenures of England*, London: The Estates Gazette, 1911.

"The Administration of Government Act; May 20, 1774," *Avalon Project, Yale Law School, Lillian Goldman Law Library*, 2020, https://avalon.law.yale.edu/18th_century/admin_of_justice_act.asp.

"Albany Plan of Union, 1754," *Department of State, Office of the Historian*, 2020, https://history.state.gov/milestones/1750-1775/albany-plan.

"Alexandrine Bulls," *Encyclopedia.com*, 2019, https://www.encyclopedia.com/religion/encyclopedias-almanacs-transcripts-and-maps/alexandrine-bulls.

Allen, David Grayson, "*Vacuum Domicilium*: The Social and Cultural Landscape of Seventeenth Century New England," 2020, http://memorialhall.mass.edu/classroom/curriculum_12th/unit1/lesson2/allen.html.

Allen, Robert C., *Enclosure and the Yeoman*, Oxford: Clarendon Press, 1992.

Alvord, Clarence Walworth, "The Genesis of the Proclamation of 1763," *Michigan Historical Collections, Volume 36, Michigan Pioneer and Historical Society*, Lansing: Wyncoop, Hallenbeck, Crawford Company, State Printers, 1908, https://quod.lib.umich.edu/cgi/t/text/text-idx?c=moa;idno=0534625.0036.001.

———, *The Mississippi Valley in British Politics: A Study of the Trade, Land Speculation, and Experiments in Imperialism Culminating in the American Revolution, Volume II*, Cleveland: The Arthur H. Clarke Company, 1917, Chapter V.

———, *The Mississippi Valley in British Politics, Volume I*, New York: Russell & Russell, 1959.

"American Colonies: Contest with France," *Encyclopædia Britannica*, 2020, https://www.britannica.com/topic/American-colonies/The-contest-with-France.

American History: From Revolution to Reconstruction and Beyond, "The First Virginia Charter 1606," 2019, http://www.let.rug.nl/usa/documents/1600-1650/the-first-virginia-charter-1606.php.

Anderson, Fred, *Crucible of War: The Seven Years' War and the Fate of Empire in British North America, 1754–1766*, New York: Alfred Knopf, 2000.

Anderson, Gary M., and Dolores T. Martin, "The Public Domain and Nineteenth Century Transfer Policy," *Cato Journal*, Vol. 6, No. 3 (Winter 1987).

Anderson, James Donald, "Vandalia: The First West Virginia?" *West Virginia History*, Vol. 40, No. 4 (Summer 1979), pp. 375–392, http://www.wvculture.org/history/journal_wvh/wvh40-4.html.

Anderson, Virginia Dejohn, *New England's Generation: The Great Migration and the Formation of Society and Culture in the *Seventeenth Century*, Cambridge: Cambridge University Press, 1991.

Appleby, John C., "War, Politics, and Colonization, 1558–1625," Chapter 3 from *The Origins of Empire: British Overseas Enterprise to the Close of the Seventeenth Century*, Ed. by Nicholas Canny, Oxford: Oxford University Press, 1998.

Ashley, W. J., "The Early History of the English Woollen Industry," *Publications of the American Economic Association*, Vol. 2, No. 4 (Sep. 1887), pp. 12–85, http://www.jstor.org/stable/2696712.

Bailey, Kenneth P., *The Ohio Company of Virginia and the Westward Movement, 1748–1792*, Glendale, CA: Arthur H. Clark, 1939 (Reprinted in India by Isha, New Delhi, 2013).

Bailey, Kenneth R., "Greenbrier Company." *e-WV: The West Virginia Encyclopedia*, September 30, 2013, https://www.wvencyclopedia.org/articles/2166.

Bailey, Mark, *The Decline of Serfdom in Late Medieval England: From Bondage to Freedom*, Woodbridge, UK: The Boydell Press, 2014, http://ebookcentral.proquest.com/lib/umdcp/detail.action?docID=1334325.

Bailyn, Bernard, *The Barbarous Years: The Conflict of Civilizations, 1600–1675*, New York: Vintage Books, 2013.

———, *Voyagers to the West: A Passage in the Peopling of America on the Eve of the Revolution*, New York: Alfred A. Knopf, 1986.

Baker, Peggy M., "The Plymouth Colony Patent: Setting the Stage," *Pilgrim Hall Museum*, 2007, https://pilgrimhall.org/pdf/The_Plymouth_Colony_Patent.pdf.

Ballagh, James Curtis, "I-Introduction to Southern Economic History—The Land System," *Annual Report of the American Historical Association-the Year 1897*, Washington: The Government Printing Office, 1898, p. 112–113, https://play.google.com/books/reader?id=xK4UAAAYAAJ&printsec=frontcover&pg=GBS.PA112.

Benton, Lauren, and Benjamin Straumann, "Acquiring Empire by Law: From Roman Doctrine to Early Modern Practice," *Law and History Review*, Vol. 28, No. 1 (February 2020).

Bethell, Tom, "How Private Property Saved the Pilgrims," *Hoover Digest*, No. 1, January 30, 1999, https://www.hoover.org/research/how-private-property-saved-pilgrims.

Bien, Morris, "The Public Lands of the United States," *The North American Review*, Vol. 192, No. 658 (Sep. 1910), pp. 387–402, https://www.jstor.org/stable/25106763.

Billington, Ray Allen, "The Fort Stanwix Treaty of 1768," *New York History*, Vol. 25, No. 2 (April 1944), pp. 182–194, http://www.jstor.org/stable/23147791.

———, "The Origin of the Land Speculator as a Frontier Type," *Agricultural History*, Vol. 19, No. 4 (Oct. 1945), pp. 204–212.

Blaakman, Michael A., "The Marketplace of American Federalism: Land Speculation Across State Lines in the Early Republic," *Journal of American History*, Vol. 107, Issue 3, (December 2020), pp. 583–608, https://doi.org/10.1093/jahist/jaaa340.

Blackstone, William, *Commentaries on the Laws of England, Book the Second*, Oxford: At the Clarendon Press, 1775.

Bloch, Marc, *Feudal Society*, London: Routledge, 2014.

Blom, Philipp, *Nature's Mutiny: How the Little Ice Age of the Long Seventeenth Century Transformed the West and Shaped the Present*, New York: Liveright, 2017.

Bloom, Robert L., Basil L. Crapster, and Harold A. Dunkelberger, "3. Manorialism," Section II: Medieval, Political and Economic Development: Feudalism and Manorialism, The Cupola Scholarship at Gettysburg College, http://cupola.gettysburg.edu/contemporary_sec2.

Bond, Beverley W., Jr., "The Quit-Rent System in the American Colonies," *The American Historical Review*, Vol. 17, No. 3 (Apr. 1912), pp. 496–516, https://www.jstor.org/stable/1834386.

"The Boston Port Act: March 31, 1774," *Avalon Project, Yale Law School, Lillian Goldman Law Library*, 2020, https://avalon.law.yale.edu/18th_century/boston_port_act.asp.

Boyko, John, "Company of One hundred Associates," *The Canadian Encyclopedia*, 2020, https://www.thecanadianencyclopedia.ca/en/article/compagnie-des-cent-associes.

Braddick, Michael J., *State Formation in Early Modern England, c. 1550–1700*,

Cambridge: Cambridge University Press, 2000.

Brands, H. W., "Why Have Americans Always Been So Obsessed with the Land?" 2021, https://www.history.com/news/american-land-frontier#:~:text=Land%20symbolized%20opportunity%20to%20generations,its%20frontier%20drew%20them%20west.

Bridenbaugh, Carl, *Vexed and Troubled Englishmen, 1590–1642*, New York: Oxford University Press, 1968.

"British Possessions in North America, 1775," *MAPS ETC, University of South Florida*, https://etc.usf.edu/maps/pages/2400/2425/2425.htm.

Brodrick, George C., *English Land and English Landlords*, London: Cassell, Peter, Galpin & Co., 1881.

Brown, Alexander, *The First Republic in America*, Boston: Houghton, Mifflin, The Riverside Press, Cambridge, 1898.

———, *The Genesis of the United States, Volume I*, Boston: Houghton, Mifflin, 1890.

———, *The Genesis of the United States, Volume II*, Boston: Houghton, Mifflin, The Riverside Press, Cambridge, 1897.

Bruce, Philip Alexander, *Economic History of Virginia in the Seventeenth Century*, New York: Macmillan, 1896.

Brymner, Douglas, archivist, *Report on Canadian Archives, 1889*, Ottawa: Printed by Brown Chamberlain, Printer to the Queen's Most Excellent Majesty, 1890.

Buell, Augustus C., *William Penn as the Founder of Two Commonwealths*, New York: D. Appleton, 1904.

Burke, Edmund, "Burke's Speech on Conciliation with America," *Project Gutenberg EBook*, 2021, https://www.gutenberg.org/files/5655/5655-h/5655-h.htm.

Butman, John, and Simon Targett, *New World, Inc.: The Making of America by England's Merchant Adventurers*, New York: Little, Brown, 2018.

Cahill, Kevin, *Who Owns Britain*, Edinburgh: Canongate, 2001.

Calloway, Colin G., *The Scratch of a Pen: 1763 and the Transformation of North America*, New York: Oxford University Press, 2006.

Canny, Nicholas, "The Ideology of English Colonization: From Ireland to America," *The William and Mary Quarterly*, Vol. 30, No. 4 (Oct. 1973).

———, *The Origins of Empire: British Overseas Enterprise to the Close of the Seventeenth Century*, Oxford: Oxford University Press, 1998.

"Cartier, Jacques," *Dictionary of Canadian Biography*, 2019, http://www.biographi.ca/en/bio/cartier_jacques_1491_1557_1E.html.

"The Cavalier Flight to Virginia" *British Heritage Travel*, July 13, 2016, https://britishheritage.com/the-cavalier-flight-to-virginia.

"Charter of Acadia Granted by Henry IV of France to Pierre du Gast, Sieur de Monts; December 18, 1603," *Avalon Project, Yale Law School, Lillian Goldman Law Library*, 2020, https://avalon.law.yale.edu/17th_century/charter_001.asp.

"Charter of Connecticut-1662," *Avalon Project, Yale Law School, Lillian Goldman Law Library*, 2019, https://avalon.law.yale.edu/17th_century/ct03.asp.

"The Charter of Maryland: 1632," *Avalon Project, Yale Law School, Lillian Goldman Law Library*, 2019, https://avalon.law.yale.edu/17th_century/ma01.asp.

"The Charter of Massachusetts Bay: 1629," *Avalon Project, Yale Law School, Lillian Goldman Law Library*, 2019, https://avalon.law.yale.edu/17th_century/mass03.asp.

"The Charter of New England: 1620," *Avalon Project, Yale Law School, Lillian Goldman Law Library*, 2019, https://avalon.law.yale.edu/17th_century/mass01.asp.

"Charter of Rhode Island and Providence Plantations, July 15, 1663," *Avalon Project, Yale Law School, Lillian Goldman Law Library*, 2019, https://avalon.law.yale.edu/17th_century/ri04.asp.

"Charter to Sir Walter Raleigh: 1584," *Avalon Project, Yale Law School, Lillian Goldman Law Library*, 2019, http://avalon.law.yale.edu/16th_century/raleigh.asp.

"Chartered Company, Economics," *Encyclopedia Britannica*, 2019, https://www.britannica.com/topic/chartered-company.

Cheyney, Edward P., *An Introduction to the Industrial and Social History of England*, New York: Macmillan, 1921.

Choudhary, Arrush, "From the Light and Into the Dark: The Transformation to the Early Middle Ages," *Humanities and Social Studies, College of Arts and Science, Vanderbilt University*, Vol. 10 (Fall 2015).

Cobbett, William, ed., *The Parliamentary History of England from the Earliest Period to 1803*, Vol. 18, London: T.C. Hansard, pp. 656–657, https://www.google.com/books/edition/Cobbett_s_Parliamentary_History_of_Engla/kqQ9AQAAMAAJ?hl=en&gbpv=1&dq=cobbett+parliamentary+history+of+england+from+the+earliest+period+to+1803+Volume+18+london&pg=PP9&printsec=frontcover.

Coffin, Victor, "The Province of Quebec and the Early American Revolution: A Study in English-American Colonial History," *The Bulletin of the University of Wisconsin, Economics, Political Science, and History Series*, Vol. 1, No. 3 (June 1896), pp. 275–562.

Colley, Linda, *Britons: Forging the Nation 1707–1837*, New Haven: Yale University Press, 1992.

"Colonial Settlement, 1600–1763, Establishing the Georgia Colony, 1732–1750," *Library of Congress*, 2019, http://www.loc.gov/teachers/classroommaterials/presentationsandactivities/presentations/timeline/colonial/georgia/.

"Constitution of Virginia; June 29, 1776," *Avalon Project, Yale Law School, Lillian Goldman Law Library*, 2020, https://www.law.gmu.edu/assets/files/academics/founders/VA-Constitution.pdf.

Cooper, Paul, family genealogy notes provided to author by Mr. Cooper.

"Corregidor, Spanish Government Official," *Encyclopædia Britannica*, 2019, https://www.britannica.com/topic/corregidor-Spanish-official.

Costain, Thomas B., *The White and the Gold: The French Regime in Canada*, Toronto: Doubleday Canada Limited, 1954.

"Council for New England," *Encyclopedia Britannica*, 2019, https://www.britannica.com/topic/Council-for-New-England.

"Council for New England," *Encyclopedia.com*, 2019, https://www.encyclopedia.com/history/dictionaries-thesauruses-pictures-and-press-releases/council-new-england.

Craven, Wesley Frank, *Dissolution of the Virginia Company: The Failure of a Colonial Experiment*, Gloucester, MA: Peter Smith, 1964.

_____, *The Southern Colonies in the Seventeenth Century 1607–1689*, The Louisiana State University Press and The Littlefield Fund for Southern History of the University of Texas, 1991.

Crone, Gerald Roe, "Richard Hakluyt, British Geographer," *Encyclopædia Britannica*, 2020, https://www.britannica.com/biography/Richard-Hakluyt.

Curtis, Thomas D., "Riches, Real Estate, and Resistance: How Land Speculation, Debt, and Trade Monopolies led to the American Revolution," *The American Journal of Economics and Sociology*, Vol. 73, No. 3 (July 2014), pp. 445–626.

Dagenais, Maxime, "Quebec Act, 1774," *The Canadian Encyclopedia*, 2020, https://www.thecanadianencyclopedia.ca/en/article/quebec-act.

"Declarations and Resolves of the First Continental Congress," *Avalon Project, Yale Law School, Lillian Goldman Law Library*, 2020, https://avalon.law.yale.edu/18th_century/resolves.asp.

Del Papa, Eugene M., "The Royal Proclamation of 1763: Its Effect Upon Virginia Land Companies," *The Virginia Magazine of History and Biography*, Vol. 83, No. 4 (Oct. 1975), pp. 406–411.

"Delaware, the Colony," *Encyclopædia Britannica*, 2019, https://www.britannica.com/place/Delaware-state/The-colony.

"The Donation Land Claim Act (1850)," *University of Oregon*, 2021, https://pages.uoregon.edu/mjdennis/courses/hst469_donation.htm.

Douglas, David C., and George W. Greenway, *English Historical Documents 1042–1189*, London: Routledge, 1981.

Dunaway, Wayland Fuller, "Pennsylvania as an Early Distributing Center for Population," *Pennsylvania Magazine of History and Biography*, Vol. 55, No. 2 (1931), pp. 134–159, https://www.jstor.org/stable20086765.

Dunn, Richard S., "William Penn and the Selling of Pennsylvania, 1681–1685," *Proceedings of the American Philosophical Society*, Vol. 127, No. 5 (Oct. 1983), pp. 322–329.

Dupre, Celine, "Cavelier de la Salle, Rene-Robert," *Dictionary of Canadian*

Biography, 2020, http://www.biographi.ca/en/bio/cavelier_de_la_salle_rene_robert_1E.html.

"Early French Settlements, 1606–1691," *Statistics Canada*, 2020, https://www150.statcan.gc.ca/n1/pub/98-187-x/4064812-eng.htm#:~:text=1663%2D%2DPopulation%20of%20New,whom%20800%20were%20in%20Quebec.

"Early Recognized Treaties with the American Indian Nations, Ratified Treaty #1: The Great Treaty of 1722 Between the Five Nations, the Mahicans, and the Colonies of New York, Virginia, and Pennsylvania," 2020, http://treatiesportal.unl.edu/earlytreaties/treaty.00001.html.

"Early Recognized Treaties with the American Indian Nations, Ratified Treaty #3: A Treaty Held at the Town of Lancaster, June 1744," http://treatiesportal.unl.edu/earlytreaties/treaty.00003.html.

"The Early Stuarts and the Commonwealth, England in 1603," *Encyclopædia Britannica*, 2019, https://www.britannica.com/place/United-Kingdom/The-early-Stuarts-and-the-Commonwealth.

"Editorial Note: Bills for Establishing a Land Office and for Adjusting and Settling Titles," *National Archives-Founders Online*, 2021, https://founders.archives.gov/documents/Jefferson/01-02-02-0045-0001.

Egleston, Melville, *The Land System of the New England Colonies*, Baltimore: N. Murray, Publication Agent, Johns Hopkins University, November and December 1886, included in Volume IV *Municipal Government and Land Tenure*, Herbert B. Adams ed., Baltimore: N. Murray, Publication Agent, Johns Hopkins University, 1886.

Eisenhuth, Caroline, "The Coercive (Intolerable) Acts of 1774," *George Washington's Mount Vernon*, https://www.mountvernon.org/library/digitalhistory/digital-encyclopedia/article/the-coercive-intolerable-acts-of-1774/.

Elliott, J.H., *Empires of the Atlantic World: Britain and Spain in America, 1492–1830*, New Haven: Yale University Press, 2007.

Ellis, George W., and John E. Morris, *King Philip's War: Based on the Archives and Records of Massachusetts, Plymouth, Rhode Island and Connecticut, and Contemporary Letters and Accounts*, New York: The Grafton Press, 1906.

Elson, Henry William, *History of the United States of America*, New York: Macmillan, 1904.

"*Encomienda*: Spanish Policy," *Encyclopædia Britannica*, 2019, https://www.britannica.com/topic/encomienda.

Engermann, Stanley L., and Kenneth L. Sokoloff, "Colonialism, Inequality, and Long Run Paths of Development," *National Bureau of Economic Research*, Working Paper 11057, January 2005, http://www.nber.org/papers/w11057.

———, "Once Upon a Time in the Americas: Land and Immigration Policies in the New World," *National Bureau of Economic Research: Understanding Long-Run Economic Growth: Geography, Institutions, and Knowledge Economy*, Conference Date: November 7–8, 2008, Published August 2011 by University of Chicago Press, http://www.nber.org/chapters/c11994.

Epp, Peter, "How Property Ownership Led to the American Revolution," *Today's Farmer*, London, ON, June 26, 2012.

"Estimated Population of Canada, 1605 to Present," *Statistics Canada*, 2020, https://www150.statcan.gc.ca/n1/pub/98-187-x/4151287-eng.htm.

"Estimated Population of the American Colonies," https://web.viu.ca/davies/H320/population.colonies.htm.

"The Explorers, Jacques Cartier, 1534–1542," *Canadian Museum of History, Virtual Museum of New France*, 2019, https://www.historymuseum.ca/virtual-museum-of-new-france/the-explorers/jacques-cartier-1534-1542/.

"The Fairfax Grant," *Virginia Places*, 2020, http://www.virginiaplaces.org/settleland/fairfaxgrant.html.

Fairlie, Simon, "A Short History of Enclosure in Britain," *The Land Magazine*, 2017, http://www.thelandmagazine.org.uk/articles/short-history-enclosure-britain.

Farrand, Max, "The Indian Boundary Line," *American Historical Review*, Vol. 10, No. 4 (July 1905), pp. 782–791.

Fernow, Berthold, *The Ohio Valley in Colonial Days*, Albany, NY: Joel Munsell's Sons, 1890.

"The First Charter of Virginia; April 10, 1606," *Avalon Project, Yale Law School*,

Lillian Goldman Law Library, 2019, http://avalon.law.yale.edu/17th_century/va01.asp.

Fischer, David Hackett, *Albion's Seed: Four British Folkways in America*, New York: Oxford University Press, 1989.

_____, *Champlain's Dream*, New York: Simon & Schuster, 2008.

_____, and James C. Kelly, *Bound Away: Virginia and the Westward Movement*, Charlottesville: University of Virginia Press, 2000.

Fleming, George Thorton, *History of Pittsburgh and Environs: From Prehistoric Days to the Beginning of the American Revolution*, Volume One, New York: American Historical Society, 1922.

Fogleman, Aaron Spencer, *Hopeful Journeys: German Immigration, Settlement, and Political Culture in Colonial America, 1717-1775*, Philadelphia: University of Pennsylvania Press, 1996.

Foner, Eric, *A Short History of Reconstruction: 1863-1877*, New York: Harper & Row, 1990.

Ford, Henry Jones, *The Scotch-Irish in America*, Princeton: Princeton University Press, 1915.

"1497: John Cabot's Voyage to America," *The UK National Archives*, 2019, https://www.nationalarchives.gov.uk/museum/item.asp?item_id=10.

Franklin, Benjamin, *The Complete Works in Philosophy, Politics, and Morals of the Late Dr. Benjamin Franklin*, Vol. III, London: Printed for J. Johnson, St. Paul's Church-Yard; and Longman, Hurst, Rees, and Orme, Paternoster-Row, 1806.

"From George Washington to William Crawford, 17 September 1767," *National Archives-Founders Online*, 2020, https://founders.archives.gov/documents/Washington/02-08-02-0020.

Fullerton, James M., "Squatters and Titles to Land in Early Western Pennsylvania," *Western Pennsylvania Historical Magazine*, Vol. 6, No. 3 (July 1923), pp. 165-176.

"Fundamental Constitutions," *NCPedia, The Encyclopedia of North Carolina*, University of North Carolina Press, 2019, https://www.ncpedia.org/fundamental-constitutions.

Galbreath, C. P., ed., *Expedition of Celoron to the Ohio Country in 1749*, Columbus, OH: F.J. Heer, 1921.

Gay, Edwin F., "Inclosures in England in the Sixteenth Century," *The Quarterly Journal of Economics*, Vol. 17, No. 4 (Aug. 1903), pp. 576-597 https://www.jstor.org/stable/1885511.

"George Washington to Charles Washington, January 31, 1770," *Hathi Trust Digital Library*, 2020, https://babel.hathitrust.org/cgi/pt?id=mdp.39015008921101&view=1up&seq=51.

Gibson, Charles, *The Aztecs Under Spanish Rule: A History of the Indians of the Valley of Mexico 1519-1810*, Stanford CA: Stanford University Press, 1964.

_____, *Spain in America*, New York: Harper & Row, 1966.

Gilbert, Daniel, "What Ye Indians Call 'Ye Hurry Walk,'" 2020, http://pabook2.libraries.psu.edu/palitmap/WalkingPurchase.html.

"Gilbert (Gylberte, Jilbert), Sir Humphrey," *Dictionary of Canadian Biography*, 2019, http://www.biographi.ca/en/bio/gilbert_humphrey_1E.html\.

"Giovanni de Verrazzano Letter to King Francis 1 of France, 8 July 1524," *National Humanities Center*, 2019, http://nationalhumanitiescenter.org/pds/amerbegin/contact/text4/verrazzano.pdf.

Gipson, Lawrence Henry, "The American Revolution as an Aftermath of the Great War for the Empire, 1754-1763," *Political Science Quarterly*, Vol. 65, No. 1 (Mar. 1950). pp. 86-104.

Gomez, Placido, "The History and Adjudication of the Common Lands of Spanish and Mexican Land Grants," *25 Natural Resources Journal*, 1039 (1985), https://digitalrepository.unm.edu/nrj/vol25/iss4/11.

Hakluyt, Richard, *Discourse of Western Planting*, 1584, http://nationalhumanitiescenter.org/pds/amerbegin/exploration/text5/hakluyt.pdf.

Hamilton, John C., ed., *The Works of Alexander Hamilton*, Vol. II, New York: John F. Trow, 1850, https://www.google.com/books/edition/_/OENMAAAAcAAJ?gbpv=1.

Hanna, Charles A., *The Scotch-Irish or The Scot in North Britain, North Ireland, and North America, Volume I*, New York: G.P. Putnam's Sons, The Knickerbocker Press, 1902.

Harris, Marshall, *The Origin of the Land Tenure System in the United States*,

Ames: The Iowa State College Press, 1953.

Harris, R. Cole, *The Seigneurial System in Early Canada: A Geographical Study*, Madison: University of Wisconsin Press, 1966.

Harrison, Fairfax, *Virginia Land Grants: A Study of Conveyance in Relation to Colonial Politics*, Westminster, MD: Heritage Books, 2007.

Harrison, J.F.C., *The Common People: A History from the Norman Conquest to the Present*, London: Flamingo, Published by Fontana Paperbacks, 1984.

Hatch, Charles E., *The First Seventeen Years: Virginia, 1607-1624*, Charlottesville: University of Virginia Press, 1957, https://www.gutenberg.org/ebooks/30780.

Hayes, Edward, *Sir Humphrey Gilbert's Voyage to Newfoundland*, eBook, 2019, http://www.gutenberg.org/ebooks/3338.

Herlihy, David, ed., *The History of Feudalism*, New Jersey: Humanities Press, 1970.

"Hernando de Soto, Spanish Explorer," *Encyclopædia Britannica*, 2019, https://www.britannica.com/biography/Hernando-de-Soto.

Herrick, Cheesman A., *History of Commerce and Industry*, New York: Macmillan, 1817.

Hinks, Peter, and Mick McKivigan, eds., *Encyclopedia of Antislavery and Abolition, Volume 2: J-Z*, Westport, CT: Greenwood Press, 2007.

"History of Immigration, 1620-1783," *Immigration to the United States*, 2019, https://immigrationtounitedstates.org/548-history-of-immigration-1620-1783.html.

Hofstadter, Richard, *America at 1750: A Social Portrait*, New York: Alfred A. Knopf, 1974.

Hofstra, Warren R., "'The Extensions of His Majesties Dominions': The Virginia Backcountry and the Reconfiguration of Imperial Frontiers," *The Journal of American History*, Vol. 84, No. 4 (Mar. 1998), pp. 1281-1312.

———, *The Planting of New Virginia: Settlement and Landscape in the Shenandoah Valley*, Baltimore: The Johns Hopkins University Press, 2004.

Holley, Jennie M. (Scoville) and Homer Worthington Brainard, compilers, *Arthur Scovell and His Descendants in America, 1660-1900*, Rutland, VT: Tuttle Publishing, 1941, Reprinted by the Apple Manor Press, 2017.

Holton, Woody, "The Ohio Indians and the Coming of the American Revolution in Virginia," *The Journal of Southern History*, Vol. 60, No. 3 (Aug. 1994), pp. 453-478, https://www.jstor.org/stable/2210989.

The Homestead Act of 1862, 37th Congress Session II 1862, Chapter LXXV—An Act to secure Homesteads to actual Settlers on the Public Domain, https://digitalcommons.csumb.edu/cgi/viewcontent.cgi?article=1011&context=hornbeck_usa_2_d; https://www.nps.gov/home/learn/historyculture/abouthomesteadactlaw.htm.

Horsman, Reginald, "The Northwest Ordinance and the Shaping of an Expanding Republic," *The Wisconsin Magazine of History*, Vol. 73, No. 1 (Autumn, 1989), pp. 21-32, https://www.jstor.org/stable/4636235.

"How Colonists Acquired Land in Virginia," *Virginia Places*, 2020, http://www.virginiaplaces.org/settleland/headright.html#eight.

Hrastar, John, *Breaking the Appalachian Barrier: Maryland as the Gateway to Ohio and the West, 1750-1850*, Jefferson NC: McFarland, 2018.

Hurt, Douglas R., *The Ohio Frontier: Crucible of the Old Northwest, 1720-1830*, Bloomington: University of Indiana Press, 1996.

"Instructions to Governor Yeardley, 1618," *The Virginia Magazine of History and Biography*, Vol. 2, No. 2 (Oct. 1894), https://www.jstor.org/stable4241805.

Jameson, J. Franklin. *The American Revolution Considered as a Social Movement*, Princeton: Princeton University Press, 1926, eBook edition: Papamoa Press, 2017, https://play.google.com/books/reader?id=9RkkDwAAQBAJ&num=19&printsec=frontcover&pg=GBS.PT1.

Jefferson, Thomas, "A Summary View of the Rights of British America," *Lillian Goldman Law Library, Yale Law School, The Avalon Project*, 2020, https://avalon.law.yale.edu/18th_century/jeffsumm.asp.

Johnson, Ben, "The UK and Great Britain—What's the Difference?" *Historic UK*,

2020, https://www.historic-uk.com/HistoryUK/HistoryofBritain/The-UK-Great-Britain-Whats-the-Difference/.

"Juan Ponce de Leon, Spanish Explorer," *Encyclopædia Britannica*, 2019, https://www.britannica.com/biography/Juan-Ponce-de-Leon.

Keith, Robert G., "Hacienda and Corregimiento in Spanish America: A Structural Analysis," *The Hispanic American Historical Review*, Vol. 51, No. 3 (Aug. 1971).

Kelsey, R. W., "Exploring Diversity in Pennsylvania History: An Early Description of Pennsylvania," *The Historical Society of Pennsylvania, the Sower Letter*, 2021, https://hsp.org.

Kemper, Charles E., "The Early Westward Movement of Virginia, 1722–1734," *The Virginia Magazine of History and Biography*, Vol. 13, No. 2 (Oct. 1905).

Kingsbury, Susan M., *An Introduction to the Records of the Virginia Company of London*, Library of Congress, Washington: Government Printing Office, 1905.

———, *The Records of the Virginia Company of London, Volume I*, Washington: Government Printing Office, 1906.

Knepper, George W., *The Official Ohio Lands Book*, Columbus, OH: Publication of the Auditor of the State, 2002, www.auditor.state.oh.us.

———, *Ohio and Its People*, Bicentennial Edition, Kent, OH: The Kent State University Press, 2003.

Kulikoff, Allan, *From British Peasants to Colonial American Farmers*, Chapel Hill: The University of North Carolina Press, 2000.

Land, Aubrey C., *Colonial Maryland: A History*, Millwood, NY: kto press, A U.S. Division of Kraus-Thompson Organization Limited, 1981.

———, "A Land Speculator in the Opening of Western Maryland," *Maryland Historical Magazine*, Vol. 48, No. 3 (Sep. 1953).

———, "Provincial Maryland," Chapter One in *Maryland: A History, 1632–1974*, edited by Richard Walsh and William Lloyd Fox, Baltimore: Maryland Historical Society, 1974.

"Land Claims," *End of the Oregon Trail: Historic Oregon City*, 2021, https://historicoregoncity.org/2019/04/03/land-claims/#:~:text=Married%20couples%20were%20allowed%20to,and%20accept%20or%20reject%20them.

"Land Is Free," *Land Is Free*, 2020, https://www.landisfree.co.uk/.

Laub, C. Herbert, "British Regulation of Crown Lands in the West, the Last Phase 1773–1775," *The William and Mary Quarterly*, Vol. 10, No. 1 (Jan. 1930), pp. 52–55, http://www.jstor.com/stable/1921753.

"The Letters Patents Graunted by Her Maiestie to Sir Humfrey Gilbert (June 11, 1578)," *Encyclopedia Virginia, Virginia Humanities*, 2019, https://www.encyclopediavirginia.org/Letters_Patents_graunted_by_her_Maiestie_to_Sir_Humfrey_Gilbert_June_11_1578_The.

Lewis, Charles Albert, family genealogy provided to author by Mr. Lewis.

Leyburn, James G., *The Scotch-Irish: A Social History*, Chapel Hill: The University of North Carolina Press, 1962.

Lingelbach, W. E., *The Merchant Adventurers of England: Their Laws and Ordinances with Other Documents*, 1902, https://play.google.com/books/reader?id=KnZlzjYtmPoC&pg=GBS.PR5.

Linklater, Andro, *Owning the Earth: The Transforming History of Land Ownership*, New York: Bloomsbury, 2013.

Livermore, Shaw, *Early American Land Companies: Their Influence on Corporate Development*, New York: The Commonwealth Fund, Oxford University Press, 1939.

Locke, John, *Two Treatises of Government, Book II, Chapter V, Of Property*, London: Printed for Whitmore and Fenn, Charging Cross; and C. Brown, Duke Street, Lincoln's-Inn-Fields, 1821, https://play.google.com/books/reader?id=K5UIAAAAQAAJ&pg=GBS.PR3.w.2.0.0.

Lockhart, James, "The Evolution of the Great Estate in the Spanish Indies," *The Hispanic American Historical Review*, Vol. 49, No. 3 (Aug. 1969), https://www.jstor.org/stable/2511778.

Lockridge, Kenneth, *A New England Town, the First Hundred Years*, New York: W.W. Norton, 1970.

"Louis, XIII, King of France," *Encyclopædia Britannica*, 2020, https://www.britannica.com/biography/Louis-XIII.

Lucas, Charles Prestwood, *A Historical Geography of the British Colonies, Vol. V, Canada-Part I (New France)*, Oxford: At the Clarendon Press, 1901.

MacDonald, Norman, "English Land Tenure on the North American Continent: A Summary," *Contributions to Canadian Economics*, Vol. 7 (1934), https://www.jstor.org/stable/136552.

MacMillan, Ken, *Sovereignty and Possession in the English New World: The Legal Foundations of Empire, 1576–1640*, New York: Cambridge University Press, 2006.

Maitland, Fredric William, *Domesday Book and Beyond: Three Essays in the Early History of England*, Cambridge: At the University Press, 1897.

Malthus, Thomas, *An Essay on the Principle of Population*, London: Printed for J. Johnson, in St. Paul's Church-Yard, 1798.

Marks, Mary A. M., *Landholding in England: Considered in Relation to Poverty*, London: A.C. Fifield, 1908.

Marshall, Peter, "Sir William Johnson and the Treaty of Fort Stanwix, 1768," *Journal of American Studies*, Vol. 1, No. 2 (Oct. 1967), pp. 149–179 https://www.jstor.org/stable27552784.

Martineau, Harriet, *Society in America, Two Volumes in One*, Paris: Baudry's European Library, 1842.

"Massachusetts Bay Company," *Encyclopedia.com*, 2019, https://www.encyclopedia.com/history/united-states-and-canada/us-history/massachusetts-bay-company.

"The Massachusetts Government Act: May 20, 1774," *Avalon Project, Yale Law School, Lillian Goldman Law Library*, 2020, https://avalon.law.yale.edu/18th_century/mass_gov_act.asp.

Mathews, Lois Kimball, *The Expansion of New England: The Spread of New England Settlement and Institutions to the Mississippi River, 1620–1865*, Boston: Houghton Mifflin, 1909.

Mathieu, Jacques, "Seigneurial System," *The Canadian Encyclopedia*, 2020, https://www.thecanadianencyclopedia.ca/en/article/seigneurial-system#.

McAlister, Lyle N., *Spain and Portugal in the New World*, Minneapolis: University of Minnesota, 1984.

McBride, George McCutchen, *The Land Systems of Mexico*, New York: American Geographical Society, 1923.

McConnell, Michael N., *A Country Between: The Upper Ohio Valley and Its Peoples, 1724–1774*, Lincoln: University of Nebraska Press, 1992.

McCormac, Eugene Irving, *White Servitude in Maryland, 1634–1820*, Baltimore: Johns Hopkins Press, 1904.

"Medieval Sourcebook: Tables on Population in Medieval Europe," *Fordham University*, 2020, https://sourcebooks.fordham.edu/source/pop-in-eur.asp.

Menard, Russell R., *Economy and Society in Early Colonial Maryland*, New York: Garland Publishing, 1985.

"Mercantilism," *Encyclopædia Britannica*, 2019, https://www.britannica.com/topic/mercantilism.

"Merchant Adventurers," *Encyclopedia Britannica*, 2019, https://www.britannica.com/topic/Merchant-Adventurers.

Mereness, Newton D., *Maryland as a Proprietary Province*, New York: Macmillan, 1901.

Middleton, Richard, *Colonial America: A History, 1607–1760*, Cambridge, MA: Blackwell, 1992.

Mitchell, Jean Brown, "European Exploration: The Age of Discovery," *Encyclopædia Britannica*, 2019, https://www.britannica.com/topic/European-exploration/The-Age-of-Discovery.

Morgan, Edmond S., "The First American Boom: Virginia, 1618–1630," *The William and Mary Quarterly*, Vol. 28, No. 2 (Apr. 1971), pp. 169–198, https://www.jstor.org/stable/1917308.

Morison, Samuel Eliot, "The Plymouth Colony and Virginia." *The Virginia Magazine of History and Biography*, Vol. 62, No. 2 (Apr. 1954).

Mulkearn, Lois, "Why the Treaty of Logstown, 1752," *Virginia Magazine of History and Biography*, Vol. 59, No. 1 (Jan. 1951), pp. 3–20, http://www.jstor.com/stable4245750.

_____, compiler and editor, *George Mercer Papers: Relating to the Ohio Company of Virginia*, Pittsburgh: University of Pittsburgh Press, 1954.

"The Museum Gazette: The Homestead Act of 1862," *Jefferson National Expansion Memorial, National Park Service, U.S. Department of the Interior*, 2021, https://www.nps.gov/jeff/learn/historyculture/upload/homestead.pdf.

"Navigation Acts, United Kingdom." *Encyclopædia Britannica*, 2020. https://www.britannica.com/event/Navigation-Acts.

"NC Land Records before 1800: 1663–1775," *State Library of North Carolina*, 2020, https://statelibrary.ncdcr.libguides.com/nclandrecords1800/1663-1775.

Nead, Daniel Wunderlich, *The Pennsylvania-German in the Settlement of Maryland*, Lancaster: Pennsylvania-German Society, 1914.

Nisbet, Jack and Claire, "Hudson's Bay Company," *HistoryLink.org*, 2020, https://www.historylink.org/File/9881.

"'N.N.': On the Tenure of the Manor of East Greenwich, 6 January 1766," *National Archives-Founders Online*, 2019, https://founders.archives.gov/documents/Franklin/01-13-02-0006#-BNFN-01-13-02-0006-fn-0002.

"North Carolina Land Grant Images and Data," *North Carolina Land Grants*, 2020, http://www.nclandgrants.com/index/.

North, Douglas C., and Robert Paul Thomas, "The Rise and Fall of the Manorial System: A Theoretical Model," *The Journal of Economic History*, Vol. 31, No. 4 (Dec. 1971).

"Northwest Ordinance; July 13, 1787," *Avalon Project, Yale Law School, Lillian Goldman Law Library*, 2021, https://avalon.law.yale.edu/18th_century/nworder.asp.

Nova Britannia, "Nova Britannia: Offering Most Excellent fruites by Planting in Virginia. Exciting all such as be well affected to further the same," London: Printed for Samuel Macham, and are to be sold at his Shop in Pauls Churchyard, at the Signe of the Bul-head, 1609, http://www.virtualjamestown.org/exist/cocoon/jamestown/fha/J1051.

"Opportunity and Challenge: The Story of BLM (Chapter 1)," *National Park Service, Department of the Interior*, 2021, https://www.nps.gov/parkhistory/online_books/blm/history/chap1.htm.

Otterness, Philip, "The 1709 Palatine Migration and the Formation of German Immigrant Identity in London and New York," *Pennsylvania History: A Journal of Mid-Atlantic Studies*, Vol. 66, (1999), pp. 8–23, https://jstor.org/stable27774234.

Ousterhout, Anne M., "Pennsylvania Land Confiscations During the Revolution," *The Pennsylvania Magazine of History and Biography*, Vol. 102, No. 3 (Jul. 1978), pp. 328–343, https://www.jstor.org/stable/20091279.

Pagden, Anthony, "The Struggle for Legitimacy and the Image of Empire in the Atlantic to c. 1700," Chapter 2 from *The Origins of Empire: British Overseas Enterprise to the Close of the Seventeenth Century*, edited by Nicholas Canny, Oxford: Oxford University Press, 1998.

Page, Thomas Walker, *The End of Villeinage in England*, London: Macmillan, published for the American Economic Association, 1900.

Parkman, Francis, *La Salle and the Discovery of the Great West*, Boston: Little, Brown, 1879.

"Patent Granted by Henry VII to John Cabot and His Sons, March 1496" *Heritage: Newfoundland and Labrador*, https://www.heritage.nf.ca/articles/exploration/1496-cabot-patent.php.

Peters, Richard, ed., *Public Statutes at Large of the United States of America, Vol. III*, April 24, 1820, Chap. LI, Boston: Charles C. Little and James Brown, 1850, https://digitalcommons.csumb.edu/hornbeck_usa_2_d/.

———, *The Public Statutes at Large of the United States of America, Vol. V*, September 4, 1841, Chap. XVI, Boston: Charles C. Little and James Brown, 1846, https://digitalcommons.csumb.edu/hornbeck_usa_2_d/.

"Petition for a Charter of New England by the Northern Company of Adventurers: March 3, 1619/20," *Avalon Project, Yale Law School, Lillian Goldman Law Library*, 2019, https://avalon.law.yale.edu/17th_century/charter_002.asp.

"The Pierce Patent," *Plymouth Company Archive Project*, 2020, http://www.histarch.illinois.edu/plymouth/piercepat.html.

Pomfret, John E., "The First Purchasers of Pennsylvania, 1681–1700," *The Pennsylvania Magazine of History and Biography*, Vol. 809, No. 2 (Apr. 1956), pp. 137–163.

"Population in the Colonial and Continental Periods," *U.S. Census*, 2019, https://www.census.gov/history/pdf/colonialbostonpops.pdf.

"Population in the Colonial and Continental Periods," *U.S. Census*, 2020, https://www.census.gov/history/pdf/colonialbostonpops.pdf.

Porter, Frank W. III, "From Backcountry to County: The Delayed Settlement of Western Maryland," *Maryland Historical Magazine*, Vol. 70, No. 4 (Winter 1975).

"Proceedings of the Albany Congress, 19 June 1754–11 July 1754," *National Archives-Founders Online*, 2020, https://founders.archives.gov/documents/Franklin/01-05-02-0096.

Prowse, D. W., *History of Newfoundland from the English, Colonial, and Foreign Records*, London: Macmillan, 1805.

Puryear, Cynthia L. "The Effects of the Norman Conquest on the Anglo-Saxon Aristocracy," (1976) *Honors Thesis*. Paper 711, http://scholarship.richmond.edu/honors-theses.

"The Quartering Act; June 2, 1774," *Avalon Project, Yale Law School, Lillian Goldman Law Library*, 2020, https://avalon.law.yale.edu/18th_century/quartering_act_1774.asp.

"The Quebec Act: October 7, 1774," *Avalon Project, Yale Law School, Lillian Goldman Law Library*, 2020, https://avalon.law.yale.edu/18th_century/quebec_act_1774.asp.

Quinn, David B., "Gilbert, Sir Humphrey," *Dictionary of Canadian Biography*, 2019, http://www.biographi.ca/en/bio/gilbert_humphrey_1E.html.

Ramsey, Robert W., *Carolina Cradle: Settlement of the Northwest Carolina Frontier, 1747–1762*, Chapel Hill, North Carolina: The University of North Carolina Press, 1964.

"*Repartimiento*: Spanish-American History," *Encyclopædia Britannica*, 2019, https://www.britannica.com/topic/repartimiento.

Rhoades, Matthew L., "Blood and Backcountry: Virginia Backcountry Violence and the Origins of the Quebec Act, 1758–1775," *West Virginia History*, New Series, Vol. 3, No. 2 (Fall 2009), https://www.jstor.org/stable/43265120.

Rice, Otis, *West Virginia; A History*, Lexington: The University of Kentucky Press, 1985.

Robbins, William G., "Oregon Donation Land Law," *Oregon Encyclopedia*, 2021, https://www.oregonencyclopedia.org/articles/oregon_donation_land_act/#.YCQWWmhKiUk.

Robinson, W. Stitt, Jr., *Mother Earth, Land Grants in Virginia, 1607–1699*, Virginia 350th Anniversary Celebration Corporation, Williamsburg, Virginia, Historical Booklet, Number 12, 1957, https://babel.hathitrust.org/cgi/pt?id=ucl.b000866728&view=1up&seq=19.

Rohrbough, Malcom J., *The Land Office Business: The Settlement and Administration of American Public Lands, 1789–1837*, New York: Oxford University Press, 1968.

Ross, Frank E., "The Fur Trade of the Ohio Valley," *Indiana Magazine of History*, Vol. 34, No. 4 (Dec. 1938), pp. 417–442.

"The Royal Proclamation, 1763," *University of Toronto Libraries*, 2020, https://exhibits.library.utoronto.ca/items/show/2470.

Scisco, L. D., "The Plantation Type of Colony," *The American Historical Review*, Vol. 8, No. 2 (Jan. 1903), https://www.jstor.org/stable/1832925.

"The Second Charter of Virginia; May 23, 1609," *Avalon Project, Yale Law School, Lillian Goldman Law Library*, 2019, https://avalon.law.yale.edu/17th_century/va02.asp.

"Silk Road," *Encyclopædia Britannica*, 2019, https://www.britannica.com/topic/Silk-Road-trade-route.

"Sir Walter Raleigh's Patent to Settle Virginia," 2019, https://encyclopediavirginia.org/entries/sir-walter-raleighs-patent-to-settle-virginia-1584/.

"1629: Agreement of the Massachusetts Bay Company," *Online Library of Liberty*, 2019, https://oll.libertyfund.org/pages/1629-agreement-of-the-massachusetts-bay-company.

Skelton, R. A., "Cabot, John," *Dictionary of Canadian Biography*, 2019, http://www.biographi.ca/en/bio/cabot_john_1E.html.

Smith, Abbot Emerson, "The Indentured Servant and Land Speculation in Seventeenth Century Maryland," *The American Historical Review*, Vol. 40, No. 3 (Apr. 1935), pp. 467–472.

Smith, Stephen G. "Loyal Company." *e-WV: The West Virginia Encyclopedia*, 2013, https://www.wvencyclopedia.org/articles/1462.

"Socage, Law" *Encyclopædia Britannica*, 2019, https://www.britannica.com/topic/socage.
Sosin, Jack M., *Whitehall and the Wilderness: The Middle West in British Colonial Policy, 1760-1775*, Lincoln: University of Nebraska Press, 1961.
Steinbeck, John, *The Grapes of Wrath*, New York: The Viking Press, Inc., 1939.
Strock, Daniel, Jr., *Pictorial History of King Philip's War*, Boston: Horace Wentworth, 1851.
Sturm, Philip, "Battle of Point Pleasant," *The West Virginia Encyclopedia*, 2020, http://www.wvencyclopedia.org/articles/1889.
Sugrue, Thomas J., "The Peopling and Depeopling of Early Pennsylvania: Indians and Colonists, 1680-1720," *The Pennsylvania Magazine of History and Biography*, Vol. 116, No. 1 (Jan. 1992), pp. 3-31, https://www.jstor.org/stable/20092669.
Tawney, R. H., *The Agrarian Problem in the Sixteenth Century*, London: Longmans, Green, 1912.
Taylor, Henry Charles, *The Decline of Landowning Farmers in England*, PhD thesis, University of Wisconsin, 1901.
"Tea Act," *Encyclopædia Britannica*, 2020, https://www.britannica.com/event/Tea-Act.
Tindall, George Brown, and David Emory Shi, *America: A Narrative History*, New York: W.W. Norton, 1999.
Tran, Tu Kha, "Growth of Joint Stock Companies in the Seventeenth Century," *San Jose State University, SJSU ScholarWorks*, Master's Thesis, 2008.
"The Treaty of Lancaster, 1744," *The Virginia Magazine of History and Biography*, Vol. 13, No. 2 (Oct. 1905).
"The Treaty of Logg's Town, 1752," *The Virginia Magazine of History and Biography*, Vol. 13, No. 2 (Oct. 1905).
"Treaty of Paris 1763," *Avalon Project, Yale Law School, Lillian Goldman Law Library*, 2020, https://avalon.law.yale.edu/18th_century/paris763.asp.
Trewartha, Glenn T., "Types of Rural Settlement in Colonial America," *Geographical Review*, Vol. 36, No. 4 (Oct. 1946), pp. 568-596, https://www.jstor.org/stable/211416.
Trimble, David, B., "Christopher Gist and Settlement on the Monongahela, 1752-1754," *The Virginia Magazine of History and Biography*, Vol. 63, No. 1 (Jan. 1955), pp.15-27.
Turner, Frederick Jackson, *The Frontier in American History*, New York: Henry Holt, 1920, http://www.gutenberg.org/files/22994/22994-h/22994-h.htm#Page_1.
"Unit 1-Spain in the New World to 1600," *National Park Service*, 2019, https://www.nps.gov/fora/learn/education/unit-1-spain-in-the-new-world-to-1600.htm.
Vachon, Andre, "Jolliet, Louis," *Dictionary of Canadian Biography*, 2020, http://www.biographi.ca/en/bio/jolliet_louis_1E.html.
_____, "Talon, Jean," *Dictionary of Canadian Biography*, 2020, http://www.biographi.ca/en/bio/talon_jean_1E.html.
Vance, William Reynolds, "Quest for Tenure in the United States," *Yale Law Journal, Yale Law School Legal Scholarship Repository*, Yale Law School, 1923.
"Virginia Resolutions on Lord North's Conciliatory Proposal, 10 June 1775," *National Archives-Founders Online*, 2020, https://founders.archives.gov/documents/Jefferson/01-01-02-0106.
Virtue, George O., "British Land Policy and the American Revolution: A Belated Lecture in Economic History," *University of Nebraska Studies*, New Series, No. 11 (Sept. 1953).
Volwiler, Albert T., "George Croghan and the Westward Movement, 1741-1782, I. The Indian Trader," *The Pennsylvania Magazine of History and Biography*, Vol. 46, No. 4 (Oct. 1922).
Walbert, David, "Land Ownership and Labor in Carolina," *Anchor, North Carolina History Online Resource*, https://www.ncpedia.org/anchor/land-ownership-and-labor#:~:text=Headrights%20gave%20100%20acres%20of,per%20head%2C%20or%20per%20person.
Warren, Jason W., "King Philip's War, *Encyclopædia Britannica*, 2020, https://www.britannica.com/event/King-Philips-War.
Wertenbaker, Thomas J., *The Planters of Colonial Virginia*, Princeton: Princeton University Press, 1922.
White, Richard, *The Republic for Which It*

Stands: The United States During Reconstruction and the Gilded Age, 1865–1896, New York: Oxford University Press, 2017.

Whittle, Jane, ed., "Introduction: Tawney's Agrarian Problem Revisited," *Landlords and Tenants in Britain, 1440–1660: Tawney's Agrarian Problem Revisited*, Woodbridge, UK: Boydell and Brewer, 2013, http://www.jstor.org/stable/10.7722/j.ctt31nh5b.9.

Wien, Tom, Suzanne Gousse, "Filles du Roi," *The Canadian Encyclopedia*, 2020, https://thecanadianencyclopedia.ca/en/article/filles-du-roi.

Wokeck, Marianne S., "Part Four: German Settlements in the British North American Colonies: A Patchwork of Cultural Assimilation and Persistnce," *In Search of Peace and Prosperity: New German Settlements in Eighteenth-Century Europe and America*, edited by Hartmut Lehman, Hermann Wellenreuther, and Renate Wilson, University Park, PA: The Pennsylvania State University Press, 2000.

Wolfe, Brendan, "The Roanoke Colonies," *Encyclopedia Virginia, Virginia Humanities*, 2019, https://www.encyclopediavirginia.org/roanoke_colonies_the.

———, and Martha McCartney, "Indentured Servants in Colonial Virginia," *Encyclopedia Virginia*, October 28, 2015, https://encyclopediavirginia.org/entries/indentured-servants-in-colonial-virginia/.

Wood, Gordon S., *The Radicalism of the American Revolution*, New York: Vintage Books, 1990.

Woodard, Colin, *American Nations: A History of the Eleven Rival Regional Cultures of North America*, New York: Viking, 2011.

Index

Administration of Justice Act 208, 209
Africa 3, 24, 49, 154, 172
Albany Conference (Congress) 150, 187, 188, 190; Plan 152
American Revolution 1, 10, 11, 12, 64
Amherst, Gen. Jeffery 188, 189, 190, 191, 192
Anglo-Spanish War 48
Appalachian Mountains 7, 122, 126, 140, 144–146, 153, 155, 162, 178
Articles of Confederation 231–233, 235, 237
Asia 23, 24, 43, 49
Audiciencia 30
Aztec 27

Bacon, Francis 52
Berkeley, Sir William 86, 102, 103, 108
Black Death 17, 18, 19, 21, 222
Blue Ridge 109, 128, 144, 145, 181, 182
Boston Port Act 10, 208, 211
Boston Tea Party 10, 208
Bouquet, Col. Henry 173, 174, 190, 191, 219
Braddock, Gen. Edward 186, 187
British America 12, 45, 117, 122, 125, 194, 208, 209, 210, 220

Cabot, John 4, 24, 35, 39, 40, 41, 44, 45, 48–50, 137, 138, 156, 223
Calvert, George (Lord Baltimore) 65; Cecil 76, 78, 114, 115
Cambridge Agreement 71, 76
Canada 7, 9, 11, 43, 151, 155, 156, 158–160, 163, 164, 171, 193, 195, 196, 212, 214, 215, 219, 229, 233
Cartier, Jacques 43, 156
Catholicism 11, 12, 44, 67, 70, 77, 133, 159, 162, 195, 212, 214, 215, 218, 219
Celoron de Bienville 165–167
Central America 24, 44
Charles I (king) 27, 71, 76, 132

Charles II (king) 78, 81, 82, 83, 105, 129, 207
Charles V (king) 43
Cherokee 175, 199–205
Chesapeake (Bay, colony) 47, 57, 72, 101–103, 105, 114, 224
Christianity 27, 53
Coercive Acts 10, 208, 209, 211, 218, 220
coloni 16
Columbus, Christopher 24, 25, 39, 40
Company of One Hundred Associates 158–160
conquistadores 4, 27–30, 32, 34
Continental Congress 177, 178, 211, 216, 218, 220, 232
copyhold 18, 19, 20, 21, 39, 83
corregidores 30
corregimiento 32, 34
corregimiento de Indios 30
Cortez, Hernan 26, 28, 30, 43
Crown of Castile 27
Council for New England 66–68, 70, 71, 75, 82

Dale, Governor Thomas 63, 93, 97
de Champlain 43, 156, 157
Declaration of Independence 2, 11, 210, 211, 221, 228, 231
de Duquesne, Marquis 168, 169
Demesne land 15–19, 58, 61
DeSoto, Hernando 42
Dinwiddie, Robert 145, 168, 169
Domesday Book 14
Drake, Sir Francis 48
Dunmore, John Murray 177, 178, 205, 206
Dunmore's War 177, 206
Dutch 51, 80–82, 116, 121, 124, 157, 161

East India Company 38, 50, 51, 54–56, 208, 217, 218
Edward III (king) 36

279

Elizabeth I 23, 35, 36, 37, 39, 44–46, 48, 49, 50- 53, 56, 58, 132, 223
encomenderos 29–32, 41, 64, 118
encomienda 26, 28–33, 41, 64, 107, 118
England-Scotland borderlands 6, 7, 9, 122, 129, 131–134, 140, 152, 225
English America *see* British America
English Civil War 6, 21, 102, 116, 127, 225
English Crown 3, 8, 65, 118, 120, 222
estancia 32, 41
Europe 2–4, 8, 12, 23, 28, 29, 35, 37, 38, 41, 48, 49, 55, 59, 87, 107, 110, 118, 119, 122, 123, 140, 144, 153, 155, 157, 159, 161, 163, 170, 172, 179, 185, 187, 198, 218, 227

Far East 24, 28, 38, 50
fee-farm tenure 45
fee simple 44–46, 58, 74, 78, 81, 138
Ferdinand and Isabella 25, 40
feudalism 4, 14, 15, 16, 55, 59, 158, 223, 224
fief 4, 14, 41, 45, 67, 71, 82, 137, 138, 222, 224
Florida 9, 42
Forbes, Gen. John 184, 187–190
Forks of the Ohio 146, 147, 149, 150, 163, 168, 169, 182
Fort Duquesne 170, 172, 173, 184
Fort Pitt 172–174, 190, 192, 198, 206
Fort Stanwix 10, 175, 200–205, 219
Francis I (king) 42
freehold 20, 74, 78
French and Indian War 1, 2, 8, 145, 146, 155, 167, 169, 178, 181, 185, 186, 192, 205, 211, 221, 224
Fundamental Constitutions 83

General Court 5, 6, 72, 73, 111–113, 227
Germany 6, 79, 87, 116, 117, 122–126, 128–131, 134, 135, 139, 140–143, 148, 152, 153, 154, 162, 172, 225, 239
Gilbert, Sir Humphrey 35, 44–46, 48, 50, 56, 58
Gist, Christopher 147, 148, 169, 183
Gooch, Lt. Gov. William 128, 129, 139, 146, 147, 182
Gorges, Fernando 51, 56, 66
Grand Ohio Company 175, 204; *see also* Vandalia
Great Migration 72, 86, 109, 110
Great Valley Road 4
Greenbrier Company 145, 201, 204
Grenville, Sir Richard 47

hacendados 5, 31
hacienda 31–33, 64
Hakluyt, Richard 23, 46, 49, 50, 56, 100, 124

Hard Labor, Treaty of 10, 204, 219
headright 4, 6, 62, 72, 73, 77–79, 82, 93, 95, 97–100, 102, 103, 105–107, 111, 114, 115, 117, 119, 121, 127, 140, 144, 145, 149, 179, 224, 225, 227, 231, 240
Henry II (king) 36, 132
Henry IV (king) 37, 156
Henry VI (king) 18
Henry VII (king) 4, 20, 24, 35, 37, 39, 40, 45, 48, 138
Henry VIII (king) 35, 39, 43, 48, 67
Hispaniola 24–26
Holland 4, 6, 79, 128, 141, 160
Homestead Act 237, 239, 241
House of Burgesses 4, 5, 68, 76, 127, 204, 205, 227
Huguenots 7, 124, 159

indentured servants 4, 5, 77–79, 86, 100–104, 106–108, 114, 115, 119, 120–122
Indian 2, 4, 5, 7, 9, 10, 25, 26, 29, 31–34, 40, 41, 53, 116, 122, 125, 127–129, 136, 145–151, 155, 157, 160–171, 173–181, 183–192, 194–208, 211, 212, 215, 217–219, 221, 224–226, 234, 235, 238, 239
Indiana Company 175, 195, 201, 202, 204
Indies 31, 44, 52, 60, 86, 193
indigenous American 2, 4, 6, 86; *see also* Indian
Instructions to Governor Yeardley 97–99
Intolerable Acts 10, 208, 212, 214, 220
Ireland 39, 44, 53, 58, 79
Iroquois 146, 148, 149–151, 160, 163–165, 175, 181, 182, 188, 203, 205; *see also* Indian
Isabela 24, 25

James I (king) 51, 56–58, 67, 90, 132, 221–223
James VI (king) 57, 132
Jamestown 42, 59, 60, 61, 63, 66, 68–70, 72, 94, 97, 98, 102, 119, 133, 179
Jefferson, Thomas 11, 197, 204, 206, 208–211, 214, 218, 220, 221, 224, 226, 231, 233, 236, 237
John (king) 13
Johnson, Sir William 175, 197–199, 202, 203, 204, 205
Joint Stock Companies 34, 35, 38, 40, 55, 59, 60, 64, 90, 97, 223

Kanawha River 149, 200, 201, 203
King George's War 145, 155, 165
King Philip's War 180
King William's War 155

Index

Lake Erie 151, 164, 168
Land Ordinance 233–235
land tenure 14, 18, 21, 22, 25, 31, 33, 57–59, 64, 65, 80, 82, 210, 222
la Salle 161, 162, 165, 170
latifundia 16
leaseholds 18, 20
Lewis, Col. Andrew 145, 200, 201, 203, 204, 206
Lewis family 13, 116, 117, 141–143, 239
Locke, John 5, 7, 53, 83
Logstown 148, 167, 183, 184
London 11, 36, 37, 48, 49, 52, 55, 57, 59, 65–68, 71, 79, 84, 90, 95, 96, 99–101, 127, 132, 138, 142, 147–149, 168, 171, 175, 176, 183, 194, 197, 204
London Company *see* Virginia Company of London
Louis XIII (king) 158
Louis XIV (king) 161, 162
Louisiana 42, 144, 151, 162, 164, 193, 237
Loyal Company 146, 195, 201, 202, 204

Manorial System 15, 19, 222
Mason, Capt. John 82
Massachusetts Bay Company 5, 68, 70–73, 75, 76, 82, 86, 88, 108, 111, 112, 122, 152, 157, 208, 209, 227
Massachusetts Government Act 208
mercantilism 55
merced 31
Merchant Adventurers 37, 38
mesne 15
Mesoamerica 27, 42; *see also* Central America
Mexican Revolution 33, 34
Mexico 28, 30, 34
Middle Ages 15, 16
Mississippi River 8, 11, 42, 151, 161, 162, 171, 175, 201, 202, 212, 214, 215, 229, 232
Mongols 23
Montezuma 27
Montreal 8, 43, 156, 159, 160–162, 165, 166, 188, 189, 195, 212

New England 7, 44, 66, 67, 68, 70–77, 79, 80, 82, 86, 88, 110–113, 115, 117, 119, 120, 121, 125, 134, 149, 154, 155, 159, 180, 190, 209
New France 7, 8, 122, 125, 140, 144–147, 149, 153, 155–171, 185, 188, 194, 198, 226
New Spain 27–33, 41, 63; Spanish America 5, 25, 32, 33; Spanish Conquest 41, 64; Spanish Crown 4, 42, 64, 223
New York 65, 67, 80–84, 121, 123, 124, 128, 150, 152, 164, 181, 190, 203, 217, 219, 230, 235

Newfoundland 24, 35, 39–46, 48, 138, 156, 223
Norman conquest 13, 40, 58
North America 3, 5, 9, 22, 25, 35, 39, 40, 41, 46, 48, 53, 54, 56, 58, 60, 64, 65, 68, 70, 76, 86, 87, 100, 118, 120–122, 138, 151, 152, 155–160, 162, 165, 170–172, 174, 179, 185, 188, 191, 193, 198, 201, 205, 221–224, 237; *see also* British America
North Carolina 43, 46, 57, 65, 84, 131, 140, 142, 143, 146, 176, 177
Northwest Passage 51, 156
Northwest Territory 213, 229, 233, 235, 237
Nova Britannia 90

Ohio Company of Associates 234
Ohio Company of Virginia (Ohio Company) 8, 146, 148, 163, 167, 168, 171, 174–176, 178, 182–184, 195, 204, 218, 226, 234
Ohio Country 7, 8, 11, 146–148, 150, 151, 163, 165–168, 170, 173, 174, 182, 183, 186–191, 198, 206, 224; *see also* Ohio River; Ohio Valley
Ohio River 7, 8, 11, 146–149, 151, 161, 163, 166, 167, 169, 175–177, 183, 200–203, 206, 212, 215, 219, 229, 233, 236; *see also* Ohio Country; Ohio Valley
Ohio Valley 7, 148, 149, 161–167, 169, 171, 173, 178, 182, 186, 187, 196, 205; *see also* Ohio Country; Ohio River
One Hundred Years War 24

Parliament 1, 10, 21, 46, 56, 71, 84, 105, 116, 120, 133, 134, 208, 209, 211, 214, 215, 217, 218, 221, 232
Penn, William 4, 6, 78, 79, 80, 84, 115–117, 123, 135–138, 140, 141, 179, 180, 197, 225, 230
peones 33
Peru 28, 29
Piedmont 105, 115, 127, 128, 129, 137, 140, 144, 145
Pietists 6, 123, 154, 159
Pittsburgh 8, 146, 172, 188, 190, 236
Pizzaro 28, 29, 42
Plymouth 5, 70, 73, 82, 88, 90, 111, 157, 180, 224
Plymouth Company *see* Virginia Company of Plymouth
pobladores (settlers) 25
Polo, Marco 23
Ponce de Leon, Juan 42
Pontiac's Rebellion 10, 192, 194, 195, 205
Popham, Sir John 51, 56, 57

Index

population 6, 9, 17, 18, 21, 22, 25, 27, 29–32, 42, 43, 48, 49, 52, 53, 55, 62, 63, 65, 78–80, 86–88, 93–106, 108, 110, 111, 113–119, 121, 124, 128, 134, 140, 145, 149, 152–154, 157–164, 166, 170–173, 179, 189, 194, 210–212, 215, 216, 221, 225–227, 232, 233, 237, 240
primogeniture 74, 75, 102, 230
private plantations 93, 94–97, 99, 100, 103, 107
Proclamation of 1763 9–11, 174–176, 191, 194–200, 204–206, 212, 214, 217–219, 220, 229
proprietary colonies 65, 66, 76, 77, 84
proprietor 20, 32, 39, 58, 65, 76–79, 82–84, 104, 105, 112–115, 123, 129, 130, 136, 137, 140, 149, 174, 177, 188, 194, 230
Protestant 11, 12, 67, 128, 129, 134, 140, 159, 172, 215, 218, 219
Puritans 5, 66, 67, 70–73, 76, 77, 86, 88, 108, 110, 121, 122, 134, 140, 149, 152, 159, 218

Quakers 4, 6, 78, 79, 84, 87, 115–117, 121–123, 128, 136, 141, 142, 152, 159, 225
Quartering Act 209, 221
Quebec 8, 11, 156, 157, 159, 160, 168, 170, 188, 190, 194, 195, 208, 211, 215, 216; Quebec Act 2, 10, 11, 12, 208, 211, 212, 213, 214, 217, 218, 220, 221, 228, 229
Queen Anne's War 155
Queen Elizabeth *see* Elizabeth I
Queen Isabella 26; *see also* Ferdinand and Isabella
quitrent (quit rent) 58, 61, 74, 78, 114, 126, 130, 136, 194, 207, 224

Raleigh, Sir Walter 35, 44, 45, 48, 50, 56, 58, 83
Renaissance 23
repartimiento 26, 28, 31, 33
res nullius 45, 52, 53
Richelieu, Cardinal 158
Rolfe, John 63
Roman Empire 16
Royal Council of Virginia 57

St. Lawrence River 11, 43
Salem 70, 71, 72, 86
Scotland 6, 7, 9, 22, 39, 79, 132, 133, 137, 139, 140, 142, 172, 225
Scots-Irish 2, 7, 9, 87, 117, 122, 131, 133, 134, 136, 139–143, 145, 153, 154, 159, 162, 172, 178, 196, 225
Scovell, Arthur 75, 112
seigneuries 7

Separatists 5, 67, 68, 70
serf 4, 14, 15, 16, 21, 29, 32, 33, 37, 40, 61, 83, 107, 124, 222, 224
seven ranges 234
Seven Years War 8, 145, 155, 170, 171, 185, 212; *see also* French and Indian War
Shenandoah Valley 4, 6, 109, 128, 129, 131, 139, 140, 143–145, 147, 148, 162, 172, 181, 182, 225; Great Shenandoah Valley Road (Great Valley Road) 4, 131, 140
Silk Road 23
Six Nations *see* Iroquois
slavery 3, 15, 103, 106–108, 127, 128, 137, 152, 172, 180, 191, 220, 240
South America 24, 28, 44
South Carolina 84, 134, 240
South Sea 60, 146, 150, 161
Spotswood, Gov. Alexander 127, 128, 181, 182
squatter 5, 7, 113, 130, 136–138, 173, 174, 196, 198, 199, 205, 207, 215, 220, 225, 227, 230, 231, 233, 237, 238
Stamp Act 1, 10, 193, 199, 217
Stanwix, Fort 10, 175, 200–205, 219
Statue of Laborers 1
Stuart, Col. John 197, 199–205
Sugar Act 1, 10, 193, 199, 217
Susquehannah Company 149, 150, 187, 188, 190, 191

Talon, Jean 160, 161
Tea Act 10, 217
Thirty Years War 123
Tidewater 78, 96, 101, 103, 105, 115, 129–131, 137
tobacco 5, 62, 63, 78, 95, 100–106, 109, 110, 115, 128, 129, 157
tomahawk right 136, 139
Townshend Acts 217
trading company 4, 34, 38, 56, 86
Transylvania Company 177, 178, 195, 216
treasury right 91, 93, 94, 96, 106, 107, 127, 144
Treaty of Easton 173, 174, 188, 190
Treaty of Fort Stanwix *see* Stanwix, Fort
Treaty of Lancaster 163, 183
Treaty of Lochaber 10, 204, 219
Treaty of Paris 9, 170, 171, 179, 185, 186, 192, 194, 195, 201, 212, 229, 233
Turner, Frederick Jackson 3, 107

Ulster 6, 7, 9, 122, 131, 133, 134, 137, 139, 143, 152, 153, 225, 239; Plantation 6, 9, 131, 133, 225

Vandalia 176, 177, 195, 204, 216

Index 283

vassal 4, 14, 27, 28, 29, 30, 32, 40, 45
Verrazzano, Giovanni de 43, 44
Viceroyalty of New Spain 27, 29, 30
Villa Rica de Vera Cruz 27
villein 15–21, 29, 33, 39, 40, 107
Virginia 4, 8, 10, 35, 46, 50, 52, 54, 56–68, 70, 72, 73, 75, 76, 78, 79, 80, 82, 83, 86–110, 113–115, 117,120–122, 125–131, 133, 137–140, 143–153, 157, 162–164, 168–171, 173–178, 180–183, 187, 190, 198, 190, 198–208, 210, 211, 214, 215, 218, 220, 221, 223–227, 230–234, 235, 240; Charter 4, 5, 52, 60, 61, 62, 63, 64, 88, 89, 91, 109, 110, 138
Virginia Company of London (London Company, Virginia Company) 4, 8, 57–59, 61, 64–68, 87–90, 92, 95, 100, 104, 119, 153, 163, 223, 224, 227
Virginia Company of Plymouth (Plymouth Company) 57, 66

Wales 22, 79, 117, 121, 141
Walker, Dr. Thomas 117, 145, 146, 200, 201, 202, 203, 204
Walking Purchase 180, 187, 188
War of the Grand Alliance 123
War of the League of Augsburg 127
War of the Roses 24
War of the Spanish Succession 123, 155
Washington, George 8, 169, 175, 186, 197, 205, 206, 233
Waymouth, George 51, 56
Weiser, Conrad 150, 188
West Indies 25, 26, 52, 193
White, Thomas 47
William I (king) 13–15, 22, 40, 41, 222
Winthrop, John 71, 72
Witen (Witenagemot) 14

Yeoman 3, 19, 20, 21, 39, 74, 107, 114, 129, 231

www.ingramcontent.com/pod-product-compliance
Lightning Source LLC
Chambersburg PA
CBHW021349300426
44114CB00012B/1137